The
Historical
Jesus

The Biblical Seminar
33

The **Historical Jesus**
A Sheffield Reader

edited by
**Craig A. Evans &
Stanley E. Porter**

Sheffield
Academic Press

Copyright © 1995 Sheffield Academic Press

Published by Sheffield Academic Press Ltd
Mansion House
19 Kingfield Road
Sheffield, S11 9AS
England

Printed on acid-free paper in Great Britain
by The Cromwell Press
Melksham, Wiltshire

British Library Cataloguing in Publication Data

A catalogue record for this book is available
from the British Library

ISBN 1-85075-731-3

CONTENTS

Preface to the Series   7
Abbreviations   9

JESUS, DISCIPLESHIP, AND COVENANT

G.D. KILPATRICK
    Jesus, his Family and his Disciples   13
E.P. SANDERS
    Jesus and the Sinners   29
D.C. ALLISON, JR
    Jesus and the Covenant: A Response to E.P. Sanders   61
D.J. MOO
    Jesus and the Authority of the Mosaic Law   83

EXEGETICAL ASPECTS OF JESUS' TEACHING

D.M. COHN-SHERBOK
    An Analysis of Jesus' Arguments Concerning the Plucking
    of Grain on the Sabbath   131
A. ITO
    The Question of the Authenticity of the Ban on Swearing
    (Matthew 5.33-37)   140
B. GREEN
    Jesus' Teaching on Divorce in the Gospel of Mark   148
D.M. COHN-SHERBOK
    Jesus' Defence of the Resurrection of the Dead   157
F.G. DOWNING
    The Resurrection of the Dead: Jesus and Philo   167
J.G. JANZEN
    Resurrection and Hermeneutics: On Exodus 3.6
    in Mark 12.26   176

B. CHILTON
Jesus *ben David*: Reflections on the *Davidssohnfrage*   192

LINGUISTIC AND STYLISTIC ASPECTS OF JESUS' TEACHING

L.D. HURST
The Neglected Role of Semantics in the Search for the
Aramaic Words of Jesus   219
M. BLACK
The Aramaic Dimension in Q with Notes on Luke 17.22
and Matthew 24.26 (Luke 17.23)   237
R. BAUCKHAM
The Son of Man: 'A Man in my Position' or 'Someone'?   245
B. LINDARS
Response to Richard Bauckham: The Idiomatic Use of
Bar Enasha   256
D.C. ALLISON, JR
Matthew 23.39 = Luke 13.35b as a Conditional Prophecy   262
J. GIBSON
Jesus' Refusal to Produce a 'Sign' (Mark 8.11-13)   271

Index of Biblical References   300
Index of Authors   310

Preface to the Series

This Series, of which *The Historical Jesus* is one, collects what the Series editors believe to be the best articles on the topic published in the first 50 issues (1978–1993) of *Journal for the Study of the New Testament*. Founded in 1978, with one issue in its inaugural year, *JSNT* was produced from 1979 to 1990 in three issues a year, and then, from 1991 to the present, in four issues a year. The continuing success of the journal can be seen in several ways: by its increasing circulation, by its increased publication schedule, by its fostering of a significant supplement series, which has now reached its one-hundredth volume (JSNT Supplement Series), by its public exposure and influence within the scholarly community, and, most of all, by the quality of the essays it publishes. This volume contains a representative group of such articles on a specific area of New Testament studies.

Once it was decided that such a Series of volumes should be issued, the question became that of how the numerous important articles were going to be selected and presented. The problem was not filling the volumes but making the many difficult choices that would inevitably exclude worthy articles. In the end, the editors have used various criteria for determining which articles should be reprinted here. They have gathered together articles that, they believe, make significant contributions in several different ways. Some of the articles are truly ground-breaking, pushing their respective enquiry into new paths and introducing new critical questions into the debate. Others are assessments of the critical terrain of a particular topic, providing useful and insightful analyses that others can and have built upon. Others still are included because they are major contributions to an on-going discussion.

Even though back issues of *JSNT* are still in print and these essays are available in individual issues of the journal, it is thought that this kind of compilation could serve several purposes. One is to assist scholars who wish to keep up on developments outside their areas of specialist research or who have been away from a topic for a period of time and wish to re-enter the discussion. These volumes are designed to be representatively selective, so that scholars can gain if not a thorough grasp of all of the developments in an area at least significant insights into major topics of debate in a field of interest. Another use of these volumes is as textbooks for undergraduates, seminarians and even graduate students. For undergraduates, these volumes could serve as useful readers, possibly as supplementary texts to a critical introduction, to provide a first exposure to and a sample of critical debate. For seminary students, the same purpose as for undergraduates could apply, especially when the seminarian is beginning critical study of the New Testament. There is the added use, however, that such material could provide guidance through the argumentation and footnotes for significant research into a New Testament author or topic. For graduate students, these volumes could not only provide necessary background to a topic, allowing a student to achieve a basic level of knowledge before exploration of a particular area of interest, but also serve as good guides to the detailed critical work being done in an area. There is the further advantage that many of the articles in these volumes are models of how to make and defend a critical argument, thereby providing useful examples for those entering the lists of critical scholarly debate.

Many more articles could and probably should be reprinted in further volumes, but this one and those published along with it must for now serve as an introduction to these topics, at least as they were discussed in *JSNT*.

Craig A. Evans   Stanley E. Porter
Trinity Western University   Roehampton Institute London
Langley, B.C., Canada   England

ABBREVIATIONS

AB	Anchor Bible
ALGHJ	Arbeiten zur Literatur und Geschichte des hellenistischen Judentums
AnBib	Analecta biblica
BETL	Bibliotheca ephemeridum theologicarum lovaniensium
BHT	Beiträge zur historischen Theologie
Bib	*Biblica*
BJRL	*Bulletin of the John Rylands University Library of Manchester*
BNTC	Black's New Testament Commentaries
BR	*Biblical Research*
BT	*The Bible Translator*
BZ	*Biblische Zeitschrift*
BZNW	Beihefte zur *ZNW*
CBQ	*Catholic Biblical Quarterly*
CBQMS	*Catholic Biblical Quarterly*, Monograph Series
CGTC	Cambridge Greek Testament Commentary
CNT	Commentaire du Nouveau Testament
ConBNT	Coniectanea biblica, New Testament
CRINT	Compendia rerum iudaicarum ad Novum Testamentum
DJD	Discoveries in the Judaean Desert
EKKNT	Evangelisch-Katholischer Kommentar zum Neuen Testament
ETL	*Ephemerides theologicae lovanienses*
ETR	*Etudes théologiques et religieuses*
EvT	*Evangelische Theologie*
ExpTim	*Expository Times*
FRLANT	Forschungen zur Religion und Literatur des Alten und Neuen Testaments
HTKNT	Herders theologischer Kommentar zum Neuen Testament
HTR	*Harvard Theological Review*
HUCA	*Hebrew Union College Annual*
ICC	International Critical Commentary
Int	*Interpretation*
JAAR	*Journal of the American Academy of Religion*
JJS	*Journal of Jewish Studies*
JNES	*Journal of Near Eastern Studies*
JPOS	*Journal of the Palestine Oriental Society*
JQR	*Jewish Quarterly Review*
JSJ	*Journal for the Study of Judaism in the Persian, Hellenistic and Roman Period*

JSS	*Journal of Semitic Studies*
JTS	*Journal of Theological Studies*
LCL	Loeb Classical Library
NCB	New Century Bible
NHS	Nag Hammadi Studies
NICNT	New International Commentary on the New Testament
NIDNTT	C. Brown (ed.), *The New International Dictionary of New Testament Theology*
NIGTC	The New International Greek Testament Commentary
NovT	*Novum Testamentum*
NTD	Das Neue Testament Deutsch
NTS	*New Testament Studies*
RB	*Revue biblique*
RNT	Regensburger Neues Testament
RSR	*Recherches de science religieuse*
RTL	*Revue théologique de Louvain*
SANT	Studien zum Alten und Neuen Testament
SBLDS	SBL Dissertation Series
SBLMS	SBL Monograph Series
SBLSCS	SBL Septuagint and Cognate Studies
SBT	Studies in Biblical Theology
SE	*Studia Evangelica* I, II, III (= TU 73 [1959], 87 [1964], 88 [1964], etc.)
SNTSMS	Society for New Testament Studies Monograph Series
SPB	Studia postbiblica
ST	*Studia theologica*
Str–B	[H. Strack and] P. Billerbeck, *Kommentar zum Neuen Testament aus Talmud und Midrasch*
SUNT	Studien zur Umwelt des Neuen Testaments
TDNT	G. Kittel and G. Friedrich (eds.), *Theological Dictionary of the New Testament*
TDOT	G.J. Botterweck and H. Ringgren (eds.), *Theological Dictionary of the Old Testament*
THKNT	Theologischer Handkommentar zum Neuen Testament
TS	*Theological Studies*
TU	Texte und Untersuchungen
TWNT	G. Kittel and G. Friedrich (eds.), *Theologisches Wörterbuch zum Neuen Testament*
TZ	*Theologische Zeitschrift*
UNT	Untersuchungen zum Neuen Testament
USQR	*Union Seminary Quarterly Review*
VT	*Vetus Testamentum*
WMANT	Wissenschaftliche Monographien zum Alten und Neuen Testament
WUNT	Wissenschaftliche Untersuchungen zum Neuen Testament
ZNW	*Zeitschrift für die neutestamentliche Wissenschaft*

JESUS, DISCIPLESHIP, AND COVENANT

JSNT 15 (1982), pp. 3-19

JESUS, HIS FAMILY AND HIS DISCIPLES

G.D. Kilpatrick†

When we read the story of the paralytic in Mk 2.1-12 do we think of Jesus sitting in his own house and watching his own roof being dug through and the paralytic being let down in front of him? Yet this is what a careful reading of the story may suggest.

I was first set on the path which led to this question by an investigation of the use of the two words οἶκος and οἰκία in Mark.[1] It is a sound practical rule that where an author uses two words with apparently the same or similar general meaning, they deserve scrutiny to see if we can distinguish precisely between the two. This principle led me to examine the use of οἶκος and οἰκία in Mark. Examination showed that οἶκος and οἰκία were not interchangeable. First, οἶκος, and not οἰκία, was used for the house of God (Mk 2.26; 11.17).

Secondly, οἶκος is used only in the accusative singular with the preposition εἰς (Mk 2.1, 11, 26; 3.20; 5.19, 38; 7.17, 30; 8.3, 26; 9.28). Only in the quotation 11.17 (Isa. 16.7), where we have the nominative, is οἶκος used in another case. At 2.1 we should read εἰς οἶκον, not ἐν οἴκῳ (apart from considerations of Mark's consistency) for the reasons given by C.H. Turner.[2]

Thirdly, we either have εἰς οἶκον without article and dependent genitive (2.1; 3.20; 7.17; 9.28) or with both article and dependent genitive (2.11, 26; 5.19, 38; 7.30 and 8.26). At 8.26 we should read τον οἶκον αὐτοῦ. Only at 8.3 does εἰς οἶκον αὐτῶν have a dependent genitive without the article, but here οἶκον is generic and we may translate, e.g., 'to their homes'.

1. G.D. Kilpatrick, 'Some Notes on Marcan Usage', *BT* 7 (1956), pp. 5-6.
2. C.H. Turner, 'Marcan Usage: Notes, Critical and Exegetical, on the Second Gospel', *JTS* 26 (1925), pp. 14-20.

What is the meaning of εἰς οἶκον, without article and dependent genitive? At all four places Jesus is the central figure and the implication is that εἰς οἶκον describes his home. 2.1 makes it quite clear that this is the Capernaum and the other three passages do not conflict with this.

What is the resulting picture for Jesus' ministry? In trying to answer this question we must keep in mind three things, his relationship to his family, the emergence of the disciples and the area where the ministry took place. We shall speedily see that the first and third items are related.

In considering these two items our starting point is Mark. 1.9 of which the usual translation is 'And it came to pass in those days Jesus came from Nazareth of Galilee and was baptised'. This rendering is permissible only if we read ὁ 'Ιησοῦς with the article.

Printed texts however read 'Ιησοῦς without the article and the clue to the interpretation of this reading is given by the rules about the use of the article with 'Ιησοῦς in Mark. Normally 'Ιησοῦς has the article, but where there is an expression in apposition to 'Ιησοῦς the article is absent, for example, 'Ιησοῦς ὁ Ναζαρηνός at 10.47, cf. 16.6. This rule is widely followed in the Gospels and Acts. As article is lacking in the printed texts of Mk 1.9 we are encouraged to look for an expression in apposition and this is supplied by the phrase ἀπὸ Ναζαρὲτ τῆς Γαλιλαίας.

Are these parallels for such phrases in apposition? Mk 15.43 'Ιωσὴφ ἀπὸ 'Αριμαθαίας would be one if we omit the article ὁ before ἀπό. In any case 'Ιωσήφ is anarthrous. As G.D. Fee has shown,[3] John's practice is very much like that of Mark. From John we may quote 19.38 'Ιωσὴφ ἀπὸ 'Αριμαθαίας corresponding to Mk 15.43 and Jn 11.1 Λάζαρος ἀπὸ βηθανίας. We may notice that ἀπό rather than ἐκ is used to indicate the place of origin in such expressions.

We are now however at the end of our difficulties with this passage. Some witnesses (D M Γ Δ Θ Σ Φ f13 28 157 565 579 *al pl*) have the reading ὁ 'Ιησοῦς which will require the usual translation 'Jesus came from Nazareth of Galilee'.

To decide between the two readings and two interpretations at Mk 1.9 we must look at the organization and significance of 1.1-9 as a whole and in particular at two features which require careful linguistic exposition.

First comes the understanding and punctuation of 1.1-3. These have been frequently debated but a rule of language enables us to decide. In

3. G.D. Fee, 'The Use of the Definite Article with Personal Names in the Gospel of John', *NTS* 17 (1970–71), pp. 168-83.

the New Testament as a whole where καθώς introduces a quotation it follows its main clause, and wherever in Mark the punctuation is certain the καθώς clause follows its main clause. Accordingly we may punctuate and interpret 'The beginning of the Gospel of Jesus Christ as it is written in Isaiah the prophet', etc. 'Jesus Christ' which occurs here only in Mark identifies Mark's central figure with him who is known in the Church as Jesus Christ. The first of the series of events which constitute his Gospel is foretold in the quotation and identified with the coming of John the Baptist.

John is introduced in v. 4 which should probably read καὶ ἐγένετο Ἰωάννης ὁ βαπτίζων ἐν τῇ ἐρήμῳ κηρύσσων. Here we note Ἰωάννης without the article which encourages us to look for an expression in apposition which we can find in ὁ βαπτίζων. In Mark ὁ βαπτίζων and not ὁ βαπτιστής seems to be the designation of John (see 6.14, 24, 25, v.1; 8.28, v.1.). Q has no designation but Matthew, Luke and Josephus seem to agree independently in ὁ βαπτιστής. On the above interpretation Mk 1.4 'And John the Baptist came in the wilderness' is parallel to 1.9 καὶ ἐγένετο ἐν ἐκείναις ταῖς ἡμέραις ἦλθεν Ἰησοῦς ἀπὸ Ναζαρὲτ τῆς Γαλιλαίας and 'Jesus from Nazareth of Galilee' corresponds to 'John the Baptist'.

To this we may add one footnote. As long as Jesus was active principally in Nazareth he would not be known as Jesus from Nazareth of Galilee. Only when he had moved out from and beyond Nazareth would this designation be appropriate and intelligible. This is important when we try to define the area of Jesus' activity. The indications of the introductory verses of Mark 1 are borne out by the rest of the Gospel. Only at 6.1-6 does Nazareth appear again in Mark. There Nazareth is not mentioned by name and only designated as ἡ πατρίς 'his home town'.

We may consider here a question: how far is Jesus connected with Nazareth in the tradition? So far we have noticed Mk 1.9, if we read Ἰησοῦς without the article. We have similar references with ὁ ἀπὸ Ναζαρεθ and the like at Mt. 21.11, J. 1.45, A. 10.38. Two adjectives are associated with this place of origin: Ναζαρηνός which alone occurs in Mk 1.24; 10.47; 14.67; 16.6 and Lk. 4.34; 18.37 v.1; 24.19; and Ναζωραῖος Mt. 2.23; 26.71; Lk. 18.37 v.1, Jn 18.5, 7; 19.19, Acts 2.22; 3.6; 4.10; 6.14; 22.8; 24.5; 26.9. If Ναζωραῖος has its problems, the derivation of Ναζαρηνός from Ναζαρέτ, etc., is not difficult. In addition do we have any clear evidence to suggest that in the Gospels and Acts Ναζωραῖος was understood as connoting any other place of origin than Nazareth? In this connexion we may notice that our interpretation of Mk 1.9 where Nazareth is Jesus' place of origin favours the view that ἡ πατρίς at Mk 6. 1, 4 is Nazareth.

At Lk. 18.37 we have the following variant:

Ναζωραῖος]
      Ναζαρηνός D fl (-118²) 22 Or
           L a aur r² δ vg
      Ναζωρηνός 697
           L e i l.

We may conclude that Ναζωρηνος is the product of a confusion between Ναζωραῖος and Ναζαρηνός. We may also argue that (5b) Ναζαρηνός is an assimilation to Mk 10.47, but we notice that Luke uses elsewhere not Ναζωραῖος but Ναζωρηνός.

After the baptism and temptation Jesus came to Galilee preaching, and at 1.16-20 he is in the neighbourhood of Capernaum. For 1.21-38 he is in Capernaum, but for 1.39-45 he is preaching in Galilee and we have suggested that in 2.1 he is in his house at Capernaum and we may infer that 2.1–3.6 takes place in Capernaum or its neighbourhood. We notice a number of recurrent features: Capernaum, the synagogue, the lakeside, the boat and apparently Jesus' home.

τὸ πλοῖον occurs 16 times in Mk 1.19–8.14. Except at 4.36 it is always in the singular and has the article except at 4.1 where ℵ B* C L Θ 33 517 565 569 892 omit it. We may assume that the article is regular and reflects Semitic idiom meaning no more than 'the boat in this story'.[4] We may compare Mk 1.13 where οἱ ἄγγελοι is 'the angels in the story' and should be translated 'angels'. An interesting example is Lk. 18.2 where the editions read ἔν τινι πόλει but ἐν τῇ πόλει is read by D L X Ψ 047 063 579 *pc* Hipp(2 MSS). This seems to be right and would mean 'the city in this story'.

These features dominate the ministry into ch. 9. There are the excursions to Nazareth and Caesarea Philippi and the north, but Jesus always returns to Capernaum where his house is. Only at 10.1 does he finally leave Capernaum and Galilee; at 10.46 he is in Jericho and by 11.1-11 he has reached Jerusalem. We may conclude that from Mark 1 until Mark 10 Jesus' ministry is centred on Capernaum and that in Mark there is no evidence for an earlier period of activity at Nazareth.

---

4.   M. Black, *An Aramaic Approach to the Gospels and Acts* (Oxford: Clarendon Press, 3rd edn, 1967), pp. 93-94.

If Nazareth plays next to no part in the ministry the same appears to be true of Jesus' family. Only at Mk 3.20-35 does the family appear in the story and even there we have no reference to Nazareth. 3.20 εἰς οἶκον places the succeeding event firmly in Jesus' house at Capernaum. In 3.21 we have the reaction of Jesus' family to his ministry 'When his family heard about him they departed to take control of him; for they said that he was beside himself'. (I agree with Vincent Taylor on the interpretation of this verse.)

We are not told why they thought him deranged or what the differences were between him and them, but we may argue that the juxtaposition of 3.20-21 and 22 indicates the matter at issue. The scribes from Jerusalem explained that Jesus had Beelzebub and cast out demons through the ruler of demons. Further, we may read back into Mark 3 the evidence of Acts and Galatians where James, the brother of Jesus, appears in outlook much nearer to the Pharisees than do Peter and Paul. In Mark the Pharisees (2.16, 24; 3.6; 7.1; 8.11; 9.11; 5.1; 10.2) with the scribes from Jerusalem (3.22; 7.1) seem to be principal opponents of Jesus. None the less we have to recognize that this reconstruction does not rest on any explicit statement at Mk 3.21. We are reading not the lines of the text but between the lines.

In contrast Mk 3.31-35 is quite clear. Jesus' family comes to him at Capernaum to take control of him. Outside his house his family summons him and his reaction when he is told of this is to renounce his family. For his family he substitutes his hearers, 'those sitting in a circle about him'. We may understand this phrase as including his disciples, but we should perhaps interpret it as meaning more generally his followers. In any case Jesus rejects his family outright in favour of his followers. It may be significant that this rejection follows closely on the appointment of the twelve, Mk 3.13-19.

Mk 6.1-6 tells of Jesus' visit to Nazareth. We notice his unenthusiastic reception there. Though his family is mentioned as living in Nazareth we are not told in so many words that they were present in the synagogue on that sabbath, still less of any meeting between him and them. On the contrary Jesus said: 'A prophet is not without honour except in his native place and among his kinsmen and in his own household'. Nazareth, townsfolk and family alike, rejected him.

If Mark tells of how Jesus rejected his mother and his family in ch. 3, and how his family and townsmen cold-shouldered him in ch. 6, the Gospel also represents the disciples as his constant companions from the first calling of some of them in Mark 1 to the end. References to 'his disciples' (and similar forms) are frequent throughout the Gospel and unless the context indicates otherwise we may assume that 'his disciples' includes the twelve. Among exceptions we may note 11.1 'two of his disciples', 13.1 'one of his disciples', 14.13 'he sends two of his disciples'. Sometimes the twelve are mentioned by name as at 3.14, 4.10, 6.7, 9.35, 10.32, 11.11, 14.10, 17, 20, 43. By contrast, except for 6.1-6, his mother and his family do not appear after Mark 3.

This double rejection may have certain consequences. John represents Jesus as going up more than once to Jerusalem (Jn 2.13; 5.1; 7.10; cf. 10.22). In principle this is not improbable, but the breach with his family causes difficulties. One of the arguments against the Last Supper being a Passover is the fact that the Passover is a family meal whereas Jesus' family is conspicuous for its absence, though the Law prescribes the family's participation (cf. Exod. 12.3-4, 21). In view of this basic requirement the picture of Jesus going up to Jerusalem year by year for the Passover is improbable on Mark's evidence. This is not to suggest that Jesus never went up to Jerusalem between his baptism and his passion, but the regular annual visits to Jerusalem for the Passover as implied by John (see especially Jn 2.13) are highly questionable.

Let us see how much of Mark's picture survives in Matthew. First, we have the association of Jesus with Nazareth at Mt. 2.23, but Matthew takes over the substance of Mk 1.9 with modifications. Nazareth disappears, and Matthew's text is unambiguous that Jesus comes from Galilee to John's baptism. In Mt. 4.12-16 Jesus returns to Galilee and leaves Nazareth for Capernaum.

The explicit statement at Mt. 4.13 goes beyond Mark: καταλιπὼν τὴν Ναζαρὰ ἐλθὼν κατῴκησεν εἰς Καφαρναούμ. On the basis of this we may claim that our interpretation of Mark is as old as Matthew.

One feature of the text may encourage us to speculate even further. The reading Ναζαρα at Mt. 4.13, Lk. 4.16 seems to be right and occurs here only in the New Testament, but the context of the two occurrences is different. Mt. 4.12-17 is a development of Mk 1.14-15, but Lk. 4.16 stands at the beginning of Lk. 4.16-30, Luke's peculiar account of Jesus' visit to Nazareth. We may infer that Ναζαρά is derived from a common source, but the differing contexts do not enable us to go beyond this to argue, for example, that either Mt. 4.12-16 or Lk. 4.16-30 is derived from Q.

Jesus' migration to Capernaum is followed by a tour of Galilee and the Sermon on the Mount. At 8.5 Jesus is again at Capernaum which at 9.1 is described as τὴν ἰδίαν πόλιν. Mark 3.21 with its comment from Jesus' family is not repeated in Matthew but the rejection in Mk 3.31-35 recurs at Mt. 12.46-50 (do not omit 12.47) and the visit to Nazareth, Mk 6.1-6, is repeated with little change at Mt. 13.53-58. Jesus' family is absent from the rest of Matthew as it is from Mark.

At Mt. 28.10 Jesus says 'Tell my brethren' (τοῖς ἀδελφοῖς μου). There is nothing in the context to suggest that these are members of his family. On the other hand ἀδελφός is used of the disciples at 12.49-50 (cf. 23.8) and 25.40.

We may conclude from this survey that Matthew follows Mark. There is the clear and explicit breach with the family at 12.46-50 but the family does not appear in normal contact with Jesus after Matthew 2.

In Luke the picture is different. Already in the story of Jesus in the Temple, 2.41-52, he distances himself from his parents, v. 49. With this we may associate 2.35 καὶ σοῦ δὲ αὐτῆς τὴν ψυχὴν διελεύσεται ῥομφαία. This saying is often understood as by Creed in his commentary 'Mary's heart will be pierced by the suffering which will fall upon her son'.[5] Origen however understood this of Mary's reaction to Jesus' passion: quid putamus quod scandalizatis apostolis mater domini a scandalo fuerit immunis?[6] We may hesitate to accept Origen's interpretation with its reference to the scandal of Jesus' passion but may suspect that he is right in detecting a certain alienation in the remark.

Mt. 10.34-36/Lk. 12.51-53 may point us on the right way. Matthew's form of the saying connects closely with Lk. 2.35 'Do not think that I came to cast peace upon the earth; I came not to cast peace but a sword' (μάχαιραν). Luke seems to interpret this: 'Do you suppose that I was here to give peace in the earth? No, I tell you not peace but division'. Matthew and Luke go on to relate this to family quarrels and Matthew ends: 'A man's enemies are the members of his household'. In the light of these two passages we may understand Lk. 2.35 as an anticipation of the subsequent alienation of Jesus from his mother and his brothers and sisters.

Mk 3.20-35 is repeated at Lk. 8.4-21 with omissions and other changes. Mk 3.21, 'When his relatives heard they went out to lay hold

---

5. J.M. Creed, *The Gospel According to St Luke* (London: Macmillan, 1930), p. 42.

6. J. Reuss in P. Koetschau *et al.* (eds.), *Origenes Werke* (12 vols., Leipzig: Hinrichs, 1899–1955), IX, p. 106.

of him; for they said he was beside himself', is omitted as is Mk 3.22-30, though Luke has the substance of this in 11.14-22. Thus his relatives' explanation of Jesus' activity disappears as does the mention of the 'scribes from Jerusalem'. Mk 3.31-35 is taken over by Lk. 8.19-21 but in an abbreviated form which blunts the sharpness of Mark's account. We may notice that where Mark has 'His mother and his brothers came and standing outside sent to him calling him', Luke gives us 'His mother and his brothers came to him and could not make contact with him because of the crowd'. This makes Jesus' final remark a little less abrupt.

We may compare Lk. 8.20-21 'He was told: "Your mother and your brothers stand outside wishing to see you". He answered and said to them: "My mother and my brothers are those who hear the word of God and do it"', with Lk. 11.27-28 'It came to pass while he was saying these things a woman from the crowd lifted up her voice and said to him: "Blessed is the womb that bare you and the breasts that you did suck". But he said, "Blessed are they who hear the word of God and keep it".' The rejection is not as explicit as in Mark, but in effect Jesus' family is displaced.

The account of Jesus' visit to Nazareth differs from Mk 6.1-6. First, it comes earlier in the narrative in Luke. Lk. 8.4-21 (Mk 3.20-35) follows much later and so is not in the background to the visit to Nazareth in Luke as it is in Mark. The hostile words of Lk. 4.28-29 are provoked not by a fundamental rupture between Jesus and his family but by his sympathetic reference to the proselytes, Naaman the Syrian and the widow of Sarepta. The family disappears from the story. Only Joseph, who may have been dead by then, is mentioned.

Luke 14.26 has drastic language: 'If anyone comes to me and does not hate his father and his mother and wife and children and brothers and sisters'. This is much stronger language than that of the parallel Mt. 10.37-38. In both Gospels this rejection is a condition of discipleship. It is more easily understood if there is a rupture between Jesus and his family in the background.

Further, Luke preserves a main feature of Mark's picture. Mary and the family are conspicuous by their absence from the Gospel story as much in Luke as in Mark. Lk. 8.4-21 repeats Mark with modifications. Otherwise Jesus' family does not appear and in particular as in Mark is unmentioned in the Passion story.

On the other hand, while Luke 2 already indicates Jesus' distancing himself from his family and a painful separation from his mother, the severe rupture is played down at Luke 8. If we have Mark's story in mind, we can read Luke in terms of Mark, but if we come to Luke without Mark in mind we can form a less severe picture.

Before we turn to John we may notice one Pauline passage. 1 Cor. 15.7 mentions an appearance of Jesus to James after his resurrection. It is usually assumed without discussion that this James is the Lord's brother, but there is no evidence to support this.

We may now turn to Acts. At Acts 1.14 'Mary the mother of Jesus, and his brothers' reappear without explanation. The next appearance is at 12.17. Herod has killed James the brother of John, and Peter has just escaped from prison and says 'Tell James and the brethren these things'. Here James should be James the brother of Jesus. With this reference we may take Gal. 1.18-19. Paul went up to Jerusalem to get information from Peter. He also saw James the Lord's brother and at Gal. 2.9 James and Peter and John are the three pillars of the church at Jerusalem. By this time James had become a leading figure in the Jerusalem community. This is confirmed by the part that he plays in the discussion in Acts 15 where he seems to have the decisive word, though Peter has an important part in the council. At Acts 21.18 James is alone and seems to take the lead.

We know from other sources a little about James's subsequent history. Josephus, *Ant.* 20.200, tells how Ananus, the high priest, contrived the death of James AD c. 61, a report confirmed by Hegesippus (Eusebius, *H.E.* 2.23).

This is an intriguing picture in which one element is puzzling. Nothing prepares us for the appearance of Mary and Jesus' brothers at Acts 1.14 after his Ascension, nor does this reference lead on to any sequel. Mary does not appear again in Acts and nothing is heard of James until Acts 12.17.

If we look carefully at Acts 1.14 we see that is not a description of the Ascension day evening but of what was customary in the months following on the Ascension. We are not told precisely when Mary and Jesus' brothers rejoined the disciples. Still less are we told of any moment of reconciliation. This silence is much easier to understand when we recall how Luke blurs the rupture between Jesus and his family as we find it in Mark. We may find that Acts 1.14 causes less difficulty if we read it with Luke only and not Mark in mind. Before we leave v. 14 we may notice one other feature of the resurrection stories in Luke-Acts. In Mark by implication and in Matthew and John we have appearances of

Jesus in Galilee, but in Luke-Acts Galilee disappears and Jesus appears only in Jerusalem. This suggests that our evangelist was ready on occasion to revise the tradition for his own ends. We may have another such revision in v. 14.

Subsequent events do not relate to Acts 1.14. James the brother of the Lord does not appear during the years of persecution, Acts 3–11. Christians from the Jerusalem community fled to other centres and, though the Twelve continued in Jerusalem, they too were subject to attack. James the son of Zebedee was killed and Peter arrested for execution. At this point James the brother of the Lord first appears as a leader in the church, a position he holds in subsequent chapters.

In particular we have noticed the significant part he plays in Acts 15. It is important to determine as precisely as we can what this part was. At v. 5 we have believing Pharisees who assert that Gentile converts must be circumcised and keep the law of Moses. Acts 15.1 especially as it stands in D, implies that emissaries from Judaea (v. 2 Jerusalem D) are of the same persuasion. They urged Paul and Barnabas and others to go up to Jerusalem to have the matter decided. We may infer that they expected to find support in Jerusalem for this point of view. Peter is represented as taking a more liberal line and we might imagine that James was expected to be more exigent, but in fact he does not insist on circumcision and the Law. Nor does the narrative in Acts 15 anywhere explicitly identify him with this point of view.

It is Paul in Gal. 2.12 who makes the identification. He mentions Peter's eating with the Gentile converts before one or more persons came from James. When they came, Peter withdrew and separated himself 'fearing those of the circumcision'. According to this account James is behind emissaries at Antioch in their insistence on a more rigorous line of conduct.

There is one further piece of evidence that supports this. At Acts 21.18 Paul, on the next day after his arrival in Jerusalem, appears before James and all the elders and reports on his ministry. They suggest to him that he should undertake the support of four men in fulfilling a vow according to the Law, and, in this way, demonstrate his own fidelity to the Law. He is alleged to teach Jews not to circumcise their children and not to keep the Law, a rumour which would be discredited if he were to accept the suggestion made above, as he did. The important point here is that this proposal is made in James's presence and to all appearances with his approval. This supports the implication of Acts 15 and the explicit statement of Gal. 2.12.

There is one external piece of evidence in agreement with this. As we have seen Josephus, *Ant.* 20.200 reports the death of James and others at the hands of Ananus on the charge that they had transgressed the Law. This action offended Jews in Jerusalem who were strict in observing the Law, the implication being that James and his fellows were also observant Jews.

If we may go back to Acts 15, James's supporters are described as believing members from the sect of the Pharisees who stressed circumcision and the keeping of the Mosaic Law. Granted that we may understand οἱ ἐκ τῆς περιτομῆς accordingly, likeminded believers appear in the story of Cornelius (Acts 10.45; 11.2). Their complaint against Peter (11.2-3) is that 'he entered in to uncircumcised men and ate with them'.

With this mention of the Pharisees we may associate the other references to Pharisees where the Pharisees are not members of the Christian community. At 5.34 it is Gamaliel, a Pharisee, who advised no action against Christians. At 23.6-9 Paul succeeded in splitting the Pharisees off from the Sadducees and temporarily winning their support. With these passages we may take 15.6 mentioned above and infer that the Pharisees found themselves sympathetic to Christians of the strict observance.

The earliest references to James, the brother of the Lord, in the Jerusalem community are at Gal. 1.19 and Acts 12.17. Later comes the reference to the brothers of the Lord, 1 Cor. 9.5, where they seem to be ranked with the apostles. We may infer from this that the brothers of the Lord and James in particular enjoyed an established position in the Jerusalem church from AD c. 35-40 and that they led the more rigorously observant of the Jerusalem community.

How did the brothers of the Lord come to have this position after their alienation from Jesus during his lifetime? We have no clear answer to this question in our texts, but we may notice that during the early years the community at Jerusalem was under attack, Acts 3–12. Following on the killing of Stephen the Jerusalem community was largely dispersed. Paul was an agent of the rigorous repression until his conversion. The apostles themselves continued in Jerusalem but under Herod were exposed to attack. Josephus's account suggests that James, the brother of the Lord, enjoyed general respect in the Jewish community, and we may infer that this was true of the earlier years also. There is something to be said for the view that James and the brothers of the Lord came into prominence because they were less liable to attack from the Jewish authorities.

This may be illustrated from the story of Stephen. There is no evidence that Stephen was interested in Gentiles. He was denounced because he spoke against the Temple ('this holy place') and the Law, 'saying that Jesus of Nazareth will destroy this place and change the customs that Moses handed down to us' (Acts 6.13-14). Speaking against the Temple goes back to Mk 13.1-2, 14.58 and speaking against the Law to Mark 2–3. On the other hand Mark, like Luke, reports no mission to the Gentiles. We may infer that from Jesus' ministry until Acts 12 Jesus and his disciples were accused of overriding the Law on a number of points and of speaking against the Temple. So we need not be surprised if there fell on them the weight of the Jewish authorities' repression.

We have seen that Mk 3.20-21 does not tell us in so many words why Jesus was estranged from his family. His choosing of the twelve follows on his disputes with the Pharisees (2.1–3.6) and is followed by other disputes with them. It is only when we combine the implications of Mark with the statements of Acts that we can arrive at a coherent picture. In this way we may detect two groups throughout Mark and Acts. The first is Jesus and his disciples, not only in his lifetime, but subsequently in Acts as can be seen from the story of Stephen. The second is that of Jesus' family, quite opposed to him during his ministry and passion, insisting on a strict observance of the Law on the evidence of Acts and yet reconciled with the disciples after Jesus' Ascension. Perhaps James is significant in this connexion. In view of the way in which he established himself in the Jerusalem community we may regard him as a principal agent of reconciliation, and with this would agree his willingness to achieve a compromise over the admission of the Gentiles.

This enables us to look at a third group. Jesus, we believe, left to his church no Gentile mission. His teaching is continued by his disciples, a fact that would explain Peter's wavering at Gal. 2.11-13, as the disciples had no clear guidance from Jesus himself. As far as Peter is concerned Cornelius remains an isolated phenomenon, constituting no effective precedent. The initiative for a Gentile mission seems to have been taken at Antioch, Acts 11.19-21. The missionary journey, Acts 13–14, seems to be a development of this and the missioners are clearly represented in Acts 15.

We may contrast this complex picture with what we find in John. First, there is no breach between Jesus and his family and there is nothing in John corresponding to Mk 3.20-21, 31-35. We have the saying 'A prophet is without honour in his native place' (Jn 4.44) but there is no accompanying story about an unfriendly reception at Nazareth. His brothers are sceptical about him (Jn 7.2-5, 10), but Mary and his brothers are with him at the wedding of Cana, and at the ensuing visit to Capernaum (Jn 2.1-5, 12). He is present at the Passover in Jerusalem, a family occasion (Jn 2.12-13; 6.4 v.1; cf. 11.55 etc.), and Mary is at the cross, 19.25-27, and perhaps Jesus' brothers are mentioned at 20.17 v.1. Here not only is there no suggestion of a clash between Jesus and his family, but 19.25-27, the commitment of Mary to John, indicates a close relationship between Mary and one of the disciples. Nowhere do we have the disciples put in the place of the family as at Mk 3.35.

How are we to explain this difference between the Synoptic Gospels and John? As we have seen, evidence for a breach between Jesus and his family is not confined to Mark, but occurs independently in Luke also while Matthew repeats substantially what we have in Mark. In contrast to this John represents a harmony that anticipates the state of affairs in Acts 12–21 where in principle the family seems to have accepted Jesus in the terms of the disciples. This reconciliation has been read back into the Gospel story in John where the only hint of a breach occurs in Jn 7.2-5, 10, where v. 5 reveals a scepticism in Jesus' brothers comparable to the scepticism in most of his disciples, 6.60-71.

How do our Gospels relate to the three trends or traditions that we have noticed? Of the Synoptic Gospels only Matthew shows a sympathetic attitude to the Gentiles. In Mark and Luke everything, with a few dubious exceptions, depicts Jesus as teaching and thinking only in terms of Israel. This would mean that as far as Matthew can be distinguished from Mark in these matters it is in line with the pro-Gentile party that Acts associates so clearly with Antioch.

It is hard to find concrete evidence that would take John beyond Mark and Luke in this matter and we have nothing as forthcoming to Gentiles in John as Mt. 21.43, 28.19-20. We can pick out a few generalizations such as Jn 4.22-24 but these do not amount to an authorization of the Gentile mission. On the other hand the breach with Judaism of the Tannaim has clearly taken place and has affected the Gospel's picture. We may ask ourselves if John does not have affinities with the second line of tradition, that of Jesus' family. This would explain both the relative reserve about the Gentiles and the playing down of the rupture between Jesus and his family.

The first line of tradition is that of the disciples and this seems to be most clearly represented in Mark. Here there is no playing down of the gulf between Jesus and his family and from Mark 1 onward it is the disciples who provide the context of Jesus' ministry. They would be the preservers of Jesus' teaching *ex officio* and it is noteworthy that when Paul went up to Jerusalem, Gal. 1.18, it was to get information from Peter ἱστορῆσαι Πέτρον (or Κηφᾶν) that he went. Presumably he regarded Peter as a principal source of information about the life and teaching of Jesus. When Papias traces Mark's material back to Peter we may find difficulties in accepting his statement without reservations but we may at least infer that the disciples' tradition about Jesus' life and teaching has survived to an important degree in Mark. This view does not exempt us from careful scrutiny of Mark's material but it does seem to square in many respects with our reconstruction of the three main lines of tradition that we find in Acts.

In one aspect we may feel ourselves encouraged to modify the dominant interpretation of Mark today. Form critical analysis of Mark sometimes seems to lead us to regard Mark as being to a large extent a collection of smaller pieces brought together in a somewhat artificial way. In other words the separate bits and pieces which we detect in Mark may to a considerable extent go back to Jesus, but the order in which these items occur may be to a large degree secondary. Consequently the interpretation of the order of Mark's material plays an important part in the interpretation of Mark as, for example, in some explanations of the messianic secret.

In the interpretation of Mark's picture of the relations between Jesus and his family, we suggest, certain developments are consistently presented. After his baptism Jesus makes Capernaum his headquarters. He establishes himself in a house there, calls his disciples and breaks with his family and the Jewish leaders, including the Pharisees. Even when he finally leaves Galilee, his disciples remain the significant group and the breach with his family and the Jewish leaders is maintained. If we regard these lines which run through the Gospel as being in principle historical, we have admitted that the common view of the order of events in Mark cannot be rigorously maintained. In other words, just as we regard the content of Mark as consisting in both original and secondary features, so we may consider the order of the material in Mark to be partly historical and partly secondary.

If we take the three groups we find in Acts, the disciples principally

Peter, Jesus' brothers principally James, and the pro-Gentile party, we may be able to relate the several Gospels more or less to these groups, but what are we to say of Q? There are those who would answer 'nothing, because Q never existed'. All I will say here is that I assert the existence of Q as being the best explanation available of certain features in our Synoptic Gospels.[7]

On this evidence where would we put Q? In the surviving material there seems to be nothing which conflicts with Mark's picture of Jesus' relations with his family, his disciples and the Jewish leaders. On the other hand Dr. Polag argues for a positive attitude in some Q material, and so in Q, toward the Gentiles.[8] If this is right, then Q goes beyond Mark at this point and is nearer to the attitude of the pro-Gentile group which, on the evidence of Acts, we would associate with Antioch. This remains a possibility, but we may suspect that behind a document that may have immediate connexion with Antioch there lie the traditions of the disciples.

We may, however, notice that Q seems to conform much more nearly to the picture that the form-critics draw of the material about Jesus. It appears very much to be a collection of disconnected items which we may think of as having existed as separate pieces in oral tradition. Any thread running through this material seems difficult, if not impossible, to detect. Nor does this characteristic of Q help us to locate it in early Christianity.

We have travelled some distance from the scene in Mark 2 where Jesus sits teaching in his house surrounded by a crowd while men dig a hole in his roof through which they lower the paralytic on a pallet. Let us look at some of the consequences of our journey.

First, it assumes that if we take Mark seriously, we are asked to accept that in the order of the material, as in the several stories and sayings themselves, we have reliable elements for our reconstruction of the ministry as well as the Passion story. Beyond that, it is suggested that Mark is right in the prominence he gives to the disciples and in the rigorous absence of any participation of Mary and Jesus' brothers from the record after Mark 3.

7.   A. Polag, *Die Christologie der Logienquelle* (WMANT, 45; Neukirchen-Vluyn: Neukirchener Verlag, 1977); *idem, Fragmenta Q: Textheft zur Logienquelle* (Neukirchen-Vluyn: Neukirchener Verlag, 1978).

8.   Polag, *Christologie*, pp. 90-93.

Secondly, Mary ceases to be the significant figure in the Gospel story that she has become in many reconstructions of Jesus' life. This prominence depends on two pieces of evidence, the picture of Mary in Lk. 1.26–2.51, and the occasional references to her in John, especially Jn 19.25-27. As we have seen, in John the evidence for the alienation of Jesus from his family disappears almost entirely and the part given to Mary in Luke 1–2 conflicts with Matthew 1–2. In Matthew the central figure is not Mary but Joseph. It is interesting to speculate on an answer to the question: why is Mary so prominent in Luke 1–2?, but we must bear in mind that in Luke 3–24 the evangelist is in principle in line with Mark.

Thirdly, we perceive a remarkable continuity between Jesus' ministry and the story in Acts. The tradition of Jesus' teaching in the Synoptic Gospels and especially in Mark and Luke is faithfully maintained by the disciples in Acts. Just as Jesus' family dissents from his teaching in Mark in favour, apparently, of a more vigorous legalism, so James and those about him, though they are reconciled to the disciples' claims about Jesus, maintain a more intransigent attitude in Acts. In particular we notice the faithfulness of the disciples to Jesus' teaching in a negative aspect, the failure to provide for the Gentiles in the church, and the difficulties in which this involves them in Acts.

We may conclude that in the picture of Jesus' family and his disciples the Synoptic Gospels, Acts and Paul give us, in the main, a strikingly coherent account of their relationships.

JSNT 19 (1983), pp. 5-36

JESUS AND THE SINNERS

E.P. Sanders

The one distinctive note which we may be certain marked Jesus' teaching about the kingdom is that it would include the 'sinners'. Even if we
grant that Jesus may have held the view that the kingdom was breaking
in with his own words and deeds (Mt. 11.2-6; 12.28), we must also note
that such a view is very difficult to find in the didactic material which is
attributed to him. Thus the opening sentence: the promise of salvation to
sinners is the undeniably distinctive characteristic of Jesus' preaching.
Everyone agrees that this is at least one of the characteristic traits of
Jesus' message, but we may nevertheless ask how such happy concord
is reached. There are three considerations. (1) The material which conveys that message is large in extent. (2) It reaches us in many diverse
forms—parables, other sayings, flat declarations of purpose, reports of
Jesus' activity, and reported accusations against him. (3) A high tolerance
for sinners was not a characteristic of the early church, as far as we can
know it. The description of Jesus' group as 'sinners' would probably not
have been created by the post-Easter church, and the term probably
originated, as Jeremias and others have suggested, as an accusation.[1]
That Jesus' group was said to consist of (or at least include) sinners has
the same probability of authenticity as has the accusation that Jesus
exorcized by a demon. This is one instance in which the usual criteria for
authenticity of the sayings material really work.

Of the material which conveys the promise of salvation to sinners, I,
with others, would single out 'flat declarations of purpose' as having the
slightest claim to authenticity.[2] Jesus may have said 'I came not to call

---

1.   J. Jeremias, *New Testament Theology I: Proclamation of Jesus* (ET London:
SCM Press, 1971), pp. 109-11.

2.   See, for example, Peter Fiedler, *Jesus und die Sünder* (BET, 3; Frankfurt am
Main: Peter Lang, 1976), p. 271.

the righteous, but the sinners' (Mk 2.17) and 'I was sent only to the lost sheep of the house of Israel' (Mt. 15.24; the same restriction is laid on the disciples in 10.6), but all the 'I came' and 'I was sent' passages are under the suspicion of being creations of the later church.[3] If these statements are such, however, it would appear that the church expanded an authentic motif.

Passages about the 'sinners' show us how tenuous it is to rely on the authenticity of any individual saying. What I am proposing is this: (1) The church would not have created the description of Jesus' proclamation as being directed towards 'sinners'. (2) Nevertheless some of the summary statements (especially Mt. 9.11-13 // Mk 2.16-17 // Lk. 5.30-32, Jesus came to call sinners, not the righteous) were probably created in the early church. Here as elsewhere we can rely on general probability more than on the analysis of any individual passage.[4] It is unlikely that the church created from nothing the charge that Jesus associated with sinners; but once that charge was fixed in tradition, it would appear that further sayings could be generated. The saying in Mk 2.16-17 and parr. seems to have an apologetic thrust: the righteous are all right: they have no need of a physician. Yet Jesus' special mission was to call sinners. Luke heightens the apologia by adding 'unto repentance' (Lk. 5.32). It is also quite possible that the first statement, 'that he eats with sinners and tax collectors' (Mk 2.16a), is an addition. Matthew and Luke elsewhere have no objection to incorporating that description. Similarly Lk. 15.1-2 (as we shall see below) is almost certainly an editorial creation; and I would regard the parable of the Pharisee and the Tax Collector (Lk. 18.9-14), with its heavy accent on breast-beating and repentance, as a Lukan (or pre-Lukan) creation.[5] The story of Zacchaeus, who in public restored of all that he had unfairly gained, is also peculiar to Luke (Lk. 19.1-10).[6] One may also note as dubious Luke's conclusion to the Parable of the Lost Sheep (joy over one sinner who repents, Lk. 15.7), which is an

---

3.   H.J. Cadbury, *The Peril of Modernizing Jesus* (London and New York: Macmillan, 1937; repr. 1962), pp. 135-45; Arland J. Hultgren, *Jesus and his Adversaries: The Form and Function of the Conflict Stories in the Synoptic Tradition* (Minneapolis: Augsburg, 1979), pp. 109-11.

4.   Cf. Hultgren, *Jesus and his Adversaries*; Fiedler, *Jesus und die Sünder*, p. 271.

5.   Cf. Fiedler, *Jesus und die Sünder*, pp. 228-33, 271.

6.   Fiedler (*Jesus und die Sünder*, pp. 129-35, 271), correctly in my view, regards the story as a secondary construction.

edifying remark not present in the Matthean parallel (Mt. 18.10-14).[7] Luke concludes the Parable of the Lost Coin in the same way (Lk. 15.10).[8] We shall return to the question of repentance, noting here only that Luke was concerned to emphasize that the disreputable people with whom Jesus associated were moved to repentance and reformation. At any rate we see that the theme of Jesus' concern for the 'sinners', once it was embedded in the synoptic tradition, could be expanded, especially if a moral could be attached.

But what can we learn from the fact that Jesus was accused of associating with 'tax collectors and sinners'? The answer to this question is, I think, harder to discover than is usually thought to be the case, and we shall have to spend some time evaluating the predominant view.

The Sinners, the Wicked, the Poor and the 'Amme Ha-'arets

Jeremias presents under the heading 'the poor' the position that several terms in the Gospels are synonymous; more precisely, that they refer to the same group.[9] He proposes that the reader of the Gospels sees this group from two perspectives, that of Jesus' opponents and that of Jesus himself. The former called his followers 'tax collectors and sinners' or 'sinners', as well as other derogatory names—'the little ones' (Mk 9.42 and elsewhere) or 'the simple ones' (Mt. 11.25). About the terminology for Jesus' group as seen by his enemies (here tacitly assumed to be the Pharisees), Jeremias says this:

> Summing up, then, we can now say that Jesus' following consisted predominantly of the disreputable, the *'ammē-ha-'areṣ*, the uneducated, the ignorant, whose *religious* ignorance and *moral* behaviour stood in the way of their access to salvation, according to the convictions of the time.[10]

From Jesus' own point of view, this group was called 'the poor' (a well-known term to mean 'our group, presently out of power', the biblical background of which Jeremias concisely presents). The term occurs in

---

7. N. Perrin, *Rediscovering the Teaching of Jesus* (New York: Harper & Row, 1967), p. 99.

8. That Lk. 15.7 and 15.10 are editorial additions is generally agreed. See, for example, Perrin, *Rediscovering*, p. 101.

9. For what follows, see Jeremias, *Proclamation*, pp. 108-13.

10. *Proclamation*, p. 112.

Mt. 11.5 // Lk. 7.22; Lk. 4.18; 6.20. An alternative phrase is 'those who labour and are heavy laden' (Mt. 11.28).[11]

Jeremias's position, then, is that Jesus' opponents could call his followers *either* 'sinners' *or* '*amme ha-'arets* (or words equivalent to it) with no distinction of meaning. This position I believe to be incorrect. There are, in fact, several views about Jesus, the sinners, the '*amme ha-'arets* and the Pharisees which are widely held, but which I think can be shown to be completely wrong.[12] Principal discussion of the Pharisees as

11. *Proclamation*, pp. 112-13.

12. It would require a small dissertation to sort out the views of New Testament scholarship on the relationship of the sinners and the '*amme ha-'arets*. The older generation generally accepted the equation without discrimination. Thus, for example, W. Bousset, *Jesus* (ET ed. W.D. Morrison; London: William and Norgate; New York: Putnam, 2nd edn, 1911), p. 65: the 'sinners' were 'those who had refused in any way to fall in with the forms of the ruling Pharisaic piety'. Many more recent scholars also accept the simple equation: thus Hultgren, *Jesus and his Adversaries*, p. 111: the 'sinners' are the '*amme ha-'arets* of *m. Dem.* 2.3. On p. 98 n. 93 he gives a long bibliography. R. Pesch ('Der Anspruch Jesu', *Orientierung* 35 [1971], pp. 56, 67, 69) also seems to make a flat equation between the 'sinners' and the '*amme ha-'arets* in the Pharisaic view. Jesus accepted them, and thus overcame Jewish *Heilsegoismus, Selbstgerechtigkeit, ängstliche Religiosität*, etc. (pp. 67-68). Albert Nolan (*Jesus before Christianity: The Gospel of Liberation* [London: Darton, Longman & Todd, 1980 (1976)], p. 22), following Jeremias, also informs us that the 'poor' and those of 'low class' were considered sinners by the Pharisees.

Jeremias's view shows that he was caught in a difficult position. When he simply defined the 'sinners' in the Jewish view, he did it accurately enough: they were deliberate and unrepentant transgressors of the law, not simply those who did not follow the purity code of the *haberim* (the '*amme ha-'arets*). See, for example, his *Parables of Jesus* (rev. ET London: SCM Press; New York: Charles Scribner's Sons. 1963), p. 132. But when he came to write his theology of Jesus' preaching (*Proclamation*), he had to go against his own knowledge, and equate the '*amme ha-'arets* with the 'sinners', partly to put all those with whom Jesus was especially concerned under one heading ('the poor'), and partly—at least so it appears—to magnify the supposed opposition between Jesus and the Pharisees: if the Pharisees considered the common people (the '*amme ha-'arets*) sinners, and if Jesus favoured the inclusion of the common people in the kingdom, the enmity was obvious. Jeremias, in effect, reasoned like this: the Pharisees and the *haberim* were identical; the *haberim* would not eat with the '*amme ha-'arets*; Jesus ate with them; therefore he offended Pharisaic *purity* regulations. This is all wrong, as the succeeding discussion will, I hope, show.

Scholars could have learned decades ago that there is no connection in Jewish materials between the common people, the '*amme ha-'arets*, and those called 'sinners'. See, for example, J. Klausner, *Jesus of Nazareth* (ET London and New York:

Jesus' opponents will have to await another occasion, but we may here lay out the complex of interrelated views which dominate New Testament scholarship and begin to evaluate the evidence. The views are these: (1) That 'Pharisees', '*haberim*', and 'rabbis' are more-or-less equivalent terms. (2) That in Jesus' day the Pharisees (= the *haberim*) controlled Judaism. (3) That the term 'sinners' includes the ordinary people, those called '*amme ha-'arets* in rabbinic literature. (4) That the leaders of Judaism (believed to be the Pharisees) successfully made these people feel excluded. (5) That Jesus' uniqueness consists in part in his offering forgiveness to repentant sinners (= common people). (6) That Jesus offended the Pharisees by associating with the common people and offering them forgiveness. The association, in the form of table-fellowship, is held to have transgressed the Pharisaic purity code. (7) That Jesus' behaviour was so offensive as to account, in no small part, for his execution.

The discussion which immediately follows will focus on the first, third, fourth, fifth and sixth points, but aspects of the second and seventh will also be touched on. The discussion will be a bit involved, and I have resorted to an enumeration scheme to keep the points straight. We shall begin with terminological points (under 1) and proceed to the common people and salvation (under 2). Finally, we shall offer a new proposal about the significance of Jesus' inclusion of the 'sinners' (under 3).

1. *The Sinners*. Many scholars have recognized that the inclusion of the common people under the term 'sinners' is not correct,[13] but it still seems that the erroneous view is popular enough, and is contained in sufficiently important books, to require one more (at least!) refutation. There should be no confusion about the basic meaning of the term 'sinners' in the Gospels. The word in English versions of the Bible

Macmillan, 1925; orig. 1922), p. 276; L. Finkelstein, *The Pharisees*, II (Philadelphia: Jewish Publication Society of America, 3rd edn, 1962), pp. 754-61; I. Abrahams, *Studies in Pharisaism and the Gospels*, First Series (Cambridge and London: Cambridge University Press, 1917; repr. New York: Ktav, 1967), ch. 7, 'Publicans and Sinners'. Finally, it should be pointed out that some scholars who have in theory learned that the '*amme ha-'arets* were not 'sinners' still do not get the point, since they continue to think that those who transgressed the purity code of the *haberim* were considered 'sinners' (see below). In fact, failing to keep the priestly purity code is precisely what defines an '*am ha-'arets*—not a sinner.

13. Stephen Westerholm, *Jesus and Scribal Authority* (Lund: Gleerup, 1978), pp. 69-70. See further the discussion in Fiedler, *Jesus und die Sünder*, pp. 140-44.

translates the Greek word *hamartōloi*. Behind *hamartōloi* stands, almost beyond question, the Hebrew word *resha'im* (or the Aramaic equivalent). The Semitic languages have other words which are used in parallel with *resha'im*, but it is the dominant term. *Resha'im* is virtually a technical term. It is best translated 'the wicked', and it refers to those who sinned wilfully and heinously and who did not repent.[14] It is often said that the wicked were 'professional sinners', and Jeremias has collected lists of such from here and there in rabbinic literature.[15] Certainly the term would include professional sinners, such as usurers, who in their daily business transgressed Lev. 25.36-38:

> Take no interest from him [your brother who becomes poor] or increase, but fear your God; that your brother may live beside you. You shall not lend him your money at interest, nor give him your food for profit. I am the Lord your God, who brought you forth out of the land of Egypt to give you the land of Canaan, and to be your God.

The clear implication of the passage is that those who renounce the commandment not to charge interest also renounce the Lord God, who brought them out of the land of Egypt: they renounce the covenant. These are 'the wicked'. The rabbis understood the implication very well, and rabbinic literature spells it out, dealing with this and other similarly weighted injunctions in detail.[16] There is every reason to think that this understanding of the 'wicked' prevailed also before 70.[17] How can one read the biblical passage and not see the point? Those who fear God do not charge interest; those who charge interest do not fear God.

Jeremias, in making a basically correct point, follows the late rabbinic homiletical exaggeration in making all sorts of trades the equivalent of usury.[18] These lists and similar ones have an observable tendency to

14. E.P. Sanders, *Paul and Palestinian Judaism* (London: SCM Press; Philadelphia: Fortress Press, 1977) (hereafter *PPJ*), pp. 142-43, 203 (n. 119: the wicked do not accept the Torah), 342-45, 351-55, 357-58, 361, 399-405, 414. See also, 'Jesus from the Semitic Point of View', in *The Cambridge History of Judaism*. III. *The Roman Period* (ed. W.D. Davies and L. Finkelstein; Cambridge: Cambridge University Press, forthcoming).

15. J. Jeremias, *Jerusalem in the Time of Jesus* (ET London: SCM Press; Philadelphia: Fortress Press, 1969), ch. 14.

16. See *PPJ*, pp. 92-94.

17. See *PPJ*, pp. 243-44, 257, 272 (Dead Sea Scrolls), 351 (*1 En.* 83–90), 391, 399-406 (*Psalms of Solomon*).

18. Note 15 above.

lengthen,[19] and we should not follow Jeremias to the bottom line of the latest list; but the general point is correct.

The wicked need not be involved in a profession which requires renunciation of the God who redeemed Israel. There are other ways of renouncing the covenant. The apocryphal story about Elisha b. Abuya makes the point perfectly well. He rode his horse in front of the Temple site on the Day of Atonement when it fell on a Sabbath.[20]

Thus we know in general terms who the wicked were, and we can readily understand why 'tax collectors' and 'sinners' go together in several passages in the Gospels: they were all traitors. Tax collectors, more precisely, were quislings, collaborating with Rome. The wicked equally betrayed the God who redeemed Israel and gave them his law. There was no neat distinction between 'religious' and 'political' betrayal in first-century Judaism.

There are two principal passages in the Gospels in which Jesus is said to have been criticized for eating with the tax collectors and the wicked. One is a triple tradition passage, usually called 'The Call of Levi' (Mt. 9.9-13 // Mk 2.13-17 // Lk. 5.27-32). Jesus calls a tax collector to follow him, and he does so. They enter a house to eat and are joined by other 'tax collectors and sinners'. The Pharisees, ever on the look-out for Jesus' table companions, since they are constantly concerned with the question of with whom Jesus eats, ask the disciples why Jesus eats with tax collectors and sinners. This serves to introduce the statement which we earlier mentioned, 'I came not to call righteous, but sinners'. The story as such is obviously unrealistic. We can hardly imagine the Pharisees as policing Galilee to see whether or not an otherwise upright man ate with sinners. But the charge, I think, is authentic, and we shall eventually come back to it.

The second story is more realistic. The passage in Matthew (11.16-19) is set in a context of accusations against 'this generation'. Jesus complains that they rejected John, and now they reject him. They call him 'a glutton and a wine-bibber, a friend of tax collectors and sinners' (Mt. 11.19; cf. Lk. 7.34). This has a ring of authenticity.[21] Jesus is in something like despair: nothing works, neither John's asceticism and austerity, nor his own different tactic.

But we do not need to try to prove that the passage is a verbatim

19. See *PPJ*, p. 149.
20. *y. Ḥag.* 77b (2.1).
21. Cf. Hultgren, *Jesus and his Adversaries*, pp. 109-11.

account. As we said above, the general charge that Jesus associated with tax collectors and sinners is very likely one that was actually levelled against him, even though none of our accounts may be verbatim reports. Thus here I can happily join the consensus and agree that Jesus associated with the wicked and was criticized for it.

The wicked (more precisely, the lost) appear prominently in three consecutive parables in Luke, and these parables also seem to indicate Jesus' view of them. The parables are The Lost Sheep, The Lost Coin, and the Prodigal Son (Lk. 15.1-32). I do not wish to allegorize the parables,[22] but it is hard not to see the lost coin and the lost sheep as corresponding to the tax collectors and sinners that Jesus associated with. If we can make this equation, then we can note that they are called 'the lost' (Lk. 15.4, 6, 9, 32), and the prodigal son characterizes himself as one who has 'sinned' (Lk. 15.18). Luke's setting in 15.1-2 (tax collectors and sinners were near Jesus, and the Pharisees and scribes said that Jesus eats with sinners) is of course his own contribution, as are the concluding summaries to the first two parables ('more joy in heaven over one sinner who repents', Lk. 15.7, 10). But, again, Luke seems to have been on the right track. 'The lost' of the parables are doubtless 'the sinners' or 'the wicked' with whom Jesus was especially concerned.

Thus, to conclude this sub-section: Jesus did see his mission as being to 'the lost' and the 'sinners': that is, to the wicked. He was doubtless also concerned with the poor, the meek and the down-trodden, and in all probability he had an appreciable following among them. But the *charge* against him was not that he loved the *'amme ha-'arets*, the common people. If there was a conflict, it was about the status of the *wicked*. It is a mistake to think that the Pharisees were upset because he ministered to the underprivileged. To drive this point home, we should now turn to the relationship—or lack thereof—between the wicked and the common people.

1.1. *The wicked and the 'amme ha-'arets*. The problem with Jeremias's position is that the term 'the wicked' (in Greek, 'sinners')— which is used with complete consistency in the Gospels and in Jewish literature from Ben Sira to the close of the Mishnah, a period of 400 years—does not include the *'amme ha-'arets*. Rabbinic literature is the only source to which one may look for traces of Pharisaic attitudes towards the ordinary people. I maintain that there is absolutely no

22. See the caution in Perrin, *Rediscovering*, p. 97.

passage in the entirety of that literature—which is large enough to contain some element of virtually every known attitude and emotion—which in any way supports the assertion that the scrupulous and learned regarded the ordinary people as 'the wicked', those who flagrantly and persistently disobeyed the law. Earlier Jewish literature generally used the terms 'wicked' and the like for the powerful who oppress the 'pious'.[23] In short, I know of no passage in Jewish literature which indicates that any group which can reasonably be connected with the Pharisees considered the common people as beyond the pale.[24]

There is one passage in the New Testament which attributes to the Pharisees the view that 'this crowd, who do not know the law, are accursed' (Jn 7.49). Further, the Parable of the Pharisee and the Publican may be read as attributing to the Pharisees the view that *all* others are 'extortioners, unjust, adulterers' and the like (Lk. 18.9-14). (The note on the latter passage in the New Oxford Annotated Bible describes these faults as being ritual failures. This indicates very well how deeply committed New Testament scholarship is to the view that the Pharisees were interested only in ritual and trivia.) Neither passage can be regarded as actually indicating the views of pre-70 Pharisaism,[25] but may well reflect one side of the hostility between the learned and the unlearned which sometimes appears in rabbinic literature.[26] It is not unreasonable to think that both before and after 70 there was some hostility between the learned and the scrupulous (the *haberim*, scribes and Pharisees), on the one hand, and the common people on the other. But we must remember that feelings of hostility do not add up to a fixed view on the part of the Pharisees or the *haberim* that those less learned and scrupulous were cut off from access to salvation, as many would have it. We shall later note the significance of the fact that the hostility was mutual.

In rabbinic literature the term *'am ha-'arets* is used in two contexts: they are contrasted with the *haberim* and with the *hakamim*.

23. See the Index to *PPJ*, *s.v.* 'The wicked'.

24. I have proposed before that the view that the Pharisees considered the *'amme ha-'arets* cut off from Israel is without foundation (*PPJ*, pp. 149, 152-57). No one has challenged the proposal; but, on the other hand, it does not seem to have been accepted.

25. Jeremias (*Proclamation*, p. 119) seems to accept Jn 7.49 as evidence for the view of pre-70 Pharisaism.

26. E.g. *b. Pes.* 49b.

1.2. The *'amme ha-'arets* are contrasted with the *haberim*, the 'associates', who thought that the laity should observe the laws with regard to the handling of food which governed the priesthood. Finkelstein puts the matter with complete clarity:

> The *'am ha-arez* did not accept the Hasidean norm requiring even profane food to be kept pure so far as possible and to be consumed only in a state of purity. The Hasideans themselves admitted that these norms were not 'biblical' in the usual sense of the term; but regarding the world as a Temple they insisted that all normal life should be in a state of purity... [The person violating this view] might not be a *haber*, but neither was he a transgressor.[27]

It is noted that the *'amme ha-'arets* are those who do not keep the special purity laws of the *haberim*—those which originally governed only the priesthood.

Purity laws are strange to most of us in the West, and confusion seems to settle like a cloud around the heads of New Testament scholars who discuss Jewish purity laws. Some clarifications may be useful. There are biblical laws concerning purity which all who counted themselves at all observant would have kept. These laws, however, do not require people to avoid impurity. They regulate, rather, what must be done after contracting impurity *in order to enter the Temple*. Josephus put it very well: in several instances the law prescribes purification 'in view of the sacrifices': 'after a funeral, after childbirth, after conjugal union, and many others' (*Apion* 2.23; cf. *War* 5.227).

The most pervasive laws concerning purity are probably corpse uncleanness (Num. 19), menstruation, intercourse and childbirth (Lev. 12.1-8; 15.16-24). Care for the dead was and is considered a firm religious duty, and contracting corpse-uncleanness was therefore required in a family in which there was a death. Childbirth and intercourse are good, and menstruation is natural. The impurity which is incurred by childbirth, until it is removed, prevents a woman from touching 'any hallowed thing' (that is, something intended for use in the Temple) and from entering the Temple itself (Lev. 12.4). Luke depicts Mary and Joseph (probably good *'amme ha-'arets*) as observing the purity laws regarding childbirth (Lk. 2.22-23, 39). In such matters the rule is that people who have contracted impurity should not defile the Temple (Lev. 15.31). People in a state of impurity according to biblical

---

27. Finkelstein, *The Pharisees*, II, p. 757.

law—the law which was presumably accepted by all—were not sinners, nor had they done anything which made them inappropriate companions for 'table-fellowship'.

Handwashing is an entirely different matter. As we noted at the beginning of the sub-section, the *haberim* wanted all Israelites to conform their practice to that of the priesthood and all food to be handled as was food destined for the Temple. The rabbis eventually made this extension of the priestly code 'normative', but in Jesus' day it was far from that.

The reason for making these simple observations is that, as I said above, confusion seems to surround the subject. Thus Braun takes Mk 7.6-9 (on handwashing) to be an instance in which Jesus castigated 'specific abuses in the Jewish practice of his time'.[28] Braun disguises, or did not know, the religious motive behind the program of the *haberim* (to sanctify the daily life of all Israel), and characterizes it as 'abuse'. But the particular point here is that he regards the handwashing code as a Jewish practice, when in fact it was limited to a small group. Similarly Aulén, summarizing recent New Testament scholarship, writes that Jesus' view was that prescriptions in the law of Moses, 'for example those concerning the Sabbath and purity', must give way when they come into conflict with the love commandment.[29] But handwashing is the only purity law discussed in the synoptics, and it is not a prescription of 'the law of Moses'.

To reiterate: the purity laws which governed everybody did not affect 'table-fellowship', but only access to the Temple. Incurring impurity by the biblical code did not make a person a 'sinner'. Failure to abide by the special laws of the *haberim*, which did govern eating, only made one a non-*haber*, that is, an *'amme ha-'arets*.

Thus when scholars focus on *purity* as constituting the issue behind the criticism that Jesus *ate* with 'sinners', what they are saying, sometimes without knowing it, is that the *haberim* accused Jesus of eating with the *'amme ha-'arets*, *not* that Jesus associated with those who transgressed the biblical law.[30] Similarly, when they say that Jesus' fault

28. Herbert Braun, *Jesus of Nazareth: The Man and his Time* (ET Philadelphia: Fortress Press, 1979), p. 53.

29. G. Aulén, *Jesus in Contemporary Historical Research* (ET London: SCM Press; Philadelphia: Fortress Press, 1976), p. 49.

30. Westerholm, who clearly perceives that the wicked are not the *'amme ha-'arets*, nevertheless writes that 'In taking his message to the most notorious sinners,

was that he associated with the *'amme ha-'arets*, they are saying that he was faulted by the *haberim* only for not being a *haber*. As long as *purity* and *food* are interconnected, the dispute cannot be about Jesus' attitude towards those who were, by the biblical standard, 'wicked', but must be reduced to being a dispute between the *haberim* and the *'amme ha-'arets*; and we have already seen that there is no ground for saying that the latter were considered 'sinners' in the sense of those who reject the God of Israel and his commandments.

1.2.1. *Haberim and Pharisees*. Before 70, the *haberim* were almost certainly a very small group, and it is dubious that *haberim* and Pharisees were identical.[31] The case for identity can be made if one assumes a direct equation between the Pharisees and the rabbis; for the rabbis certainly thought that the laity should eat food in a state of priestly purity. But the equation of 'Pharisees' and 'rabbis' is itself precarious. And, once we turn to rabbinic literature, we find further complications. One rabbi proposed that no *haber* should touch a corpse (the *haber* should become in this way too like a priest).[32] If all rabbis were *haberim*, and if the opinion that *haberim* should not touch a corpse were to carry the day (it did not), then who would tend the dead? Neither the rabbis, nor their wives, nor anyone who followed their rules. Thus it is doubtful that even all the rabbis were *haberim*. Before 70, there may have been an overlap between Pharisees and *haberim*; and after 70 the rabbis accepted the two main points of the *haberim* (strict tithing as well as priestly purity for the laity). But these connections do not amount to an equation.

Jesus indicated that the matter of ritual purity was at best a very subordinate consideration' (*Jesus and Scribal Authority*, p. 71).

31. Jacob Neusner (*From Politics to Piety* [Englewood Cliffs, NJ: Prentice-Hall, 1973], esp. pp. 80, 83) has moved a long way towards reasserting the old view that the Pharisees were *haberim* and the *haberim* were Pharisees. He argues that the Pharisees, after Hillel, were essentially *haberim*—a small, pacifist party concerned with purity. I am not persuaded, largely because of Josephus's description (on which, see below). But in any case the argument which will be presented here will stand. If the Pharisees were a small, relatively uninfluential party, dominated by a concern for applying the priestly purity code to the laity, they would not have been able—even if they wanted—to exclude others from the practice of religion in their own way; and the more exclusivist they were, the fewer would have been their followers. Thus, the closer one puts the Pharisees to the *haberim*, the less significance attaches to any possible conflict between Jesus and the Pharisees.

32. *m. Dem.* 2.3; R. Judah.

People who have learned who the Pharisees were by reading Jeremias, supposedly a reliable authority, will find these terminological distinctions puzzling. That is because Jeremias, obviously thinking that all Pharisees were *haberim* and all *haberim* Pharisees, simply wrote the word 'Pharisees' when he was discussing a text which contains the word *haberim*. Thus, for example, he wrote that ' "A Pharisee does not dwell with them [the *'amme ha-'arets*] as a guest" ' as his translation of *m. Dem.* 2.3,[33] but 'Pharisee' does not appear in the text: it reads *haberim*. When one adds the assumption (which was long held, and which Jeremias shared with many) that the rabbis perfectly represented the Pharisees, the use of 'Pharisee' for *'haber'* in translating rabbinic texts resulted in the simple equation of *haber*, Pharisee and rabbi which we noted above, and naturally gave the impression—in fact seemed to prove conclusively—that Pharisaism in the period before 70 was defined by insistence that the laity observe the priestly laws governing handling and eating food. But that is just what we do not know. All that we hear about Pharisaism from people who were actually Pharisees before 70 is that the party was defined by its zeal for the knowledge of the law, belief in the resurrection, and acceptance of the tradition of the elders.[34] Did the tradition of the elders insist that lay people act like priests? Not that we know of. It is noteworthy that Josephus makes a point of the fact that the Essenes would not eat other people's food (*War* 2.143-44), but says nothing about the Pharisees observing special food laws which set them off from other Jews.

1.3. *The 'amme ha-'arets and the hakamim*. In rabbinic literature the *'amme ha-'arets* are also contrasted with the *hakamim*, the learned.[35] In this context the meaning is 'uneducated', that is, by the rabbinic standard.

33. Jeremias, *Proclamation*, p. 118.

34. Paul: Gal. 1.14; Phil. 3.6; cf. Acts 23.6; Josephus: *BJ* 2.162. Ellis Rivkin has strongly insisted on this definition of the Pharisees and denies their equation with the *haberim*. See 'Defining the Pharisees: The Tannaitic Sources', *HUCA* 40–41 (1969–71), pp. 234-38; *A Hidden Revolution* (Nashville: Abingdon Press, 1978).

The new edition of Schürer continues the flat equation of *Pharisees* and *haberim*, quoting the *rabbinic* passages on the *haberim* and the *'amme ha-'arets*. Rivkin's articles appear in the bibliography, but his detailed argument that the Tannaitic sources—much less Josephus—do not equate the Pharisees and the *haberim* is not discussed. See Emil Schürer, *The History of the Jewish People in the Age of Jesus Christ*, II (ed. G. Vermes, F. Millar, and M. Black; Edinburgh: T. & T. Clark, 1979), p. 398. See also Neusner's view, n. 31 above.

35. *m. Hor.* 3.8.

2. *The 'amme ha-'arets and salvation.* Now we come to the important
point, which justifies the terminological discussion. Jeremias wrote that
the *'amme ha-'arets* (hereafter, now that the terminological clarification
is complete, the common people) were, in the accepted view of their
day, excluded from salvation.[36] That this is incorrect might be seen
simply from the preceding terminological discussion: since the term
'wicked' did not include the common people, and since the latter are to
be characterized simply as neither *haberim* nor *hakamim*, it should
follow that no one thought that the common people were excluded from
salvation. Here, however, we must not only clear out some terminological underbrush, but fell a large tree; for we are up against a dearly
cherished view: the Pharisees, who dominated Judaism, excluded everyone but themselves from salvation, and Jesus let the common people in.
Gustaf Aulén, who in theory knew that 'the sinners' were not the same
as the 'common people',[37] nevertheless accepted the view which is
expressed by Jeremias:

> Table fellowship with 'sinners' was not a simple breach of etiquette on the
> part of the individual, it was a clear defiance of both the regulations con-
> cerning purity and the ordinances which prescribed the penance required
> of such violators of the law for restoration into the religious and social
> community.[38]

In this passage Aulén, having said that 'the sinners' were not the
common people, describes 'the sinners' as not obeying the 'regulations
concerning purity' which govern 'table-fellowship'—that is, whether he
knew it or not, as being common people. Further, he writes that those
who transgressed the purity code as well as those associated with them
had to do penance to be restored to the community—precisely agreeing
with Jeremias's view that the common people were considered cut off
from salvation.

Since I am about to attack this position, I should explain why I have
quoted a distinguished bishop and theologian who, in his nineties, wrote
a remarkably good book about recent research on the life of Jesus. It is
precisely because he was not a professional New Testament scholar and
certainly not one who claimed expertise in pre-70 Judaism. On such
a point as this he could do nothing other than repeat the opinion

---

36. Above, n. 10.
37. Aulén, *Jesus in Contemporary Historical Research*, p. 59.
38. Aulén, *Jesus in Contemporary Historical Research*, p. 60.

prevailing among supposed experts. It is not difficult to compile a very long list of New Testament scholars who hold or who have held the view just quoted from Aulén's book. But the fact that Aulén wrote that sentence shows more clearly than any such list how common the opinion is that the purity laws which 'sinners' had transgressed were those of the ḥaberim which governed food and eating, that *Judaism* required such people to make atonement, and that the common people were considered cut off unless they atoned. This is all incorrect.

2.1. *The uneducated and salvation.* I shall take first the question of the uneducated. Did the sages (before or after 70, though we have opinions only from rabbinic literature) consider the uneducated to be necessarily condemned sinners? It has been often said that the unlearned *must* have been considered sinners, since they could not understand, much less do the law.[39] Thus Nolan speaks of the 'laws and customs' as being 'so complicated that the uneducated were quite incapable of understanding what was expected of them'.[40]

We may ask, first, if that was the rabbinic view. It was not. The rabbis had a strong sense of diminished responsibility. The common people were not expected by the learned to know and do everything which they (the learned) did. The light sins of the learned count as the heavy sins of the unlearned; and the heavy sins of the unlearned as the light sins of the learned.[41]

We might also try the application of common sense. It will help us get rid of nonsense. Jewish law, as I have written elsewhere, looks hard to modern Christians, not to ancient Jews.[42] And, besides, we can look around. Is it true that the uneducated cannot observe the law? Is there a high correlation between the uneducated and those who break the traffic code (a very detailed bit of law)? or those who are tax frauds (the modern equivalent in complexity to the laws of purity, except that the latter, in comparison, are quite simple)?

It may help us, in evaluating the claim that the Pharisees viewed the uneducated as excluded from Israel, and thus from salvation, to put the matter in human terms; and to do so we may take the case of Jo in Dickens's *Bleak House*. Jo is not only completely illiterate, he also has

---

39. Jeremias, *Proclamation*, p. 112: the ignorance of the *'amme ha-'arets* 'stood in the way of their access to salvation'.

40. Nolan, *Jesus before Christianity*, p. 22.

41. *b. B. Meṣ.* 33b (R. Judah b. Ilai).

42. *PPJ*, pp. 110-11.

what we might now call a very low IQ. But he knows enough to attend an inquest and be prepared to answer questions (though the coroner disdains to put them). He knows that he must 'move on' when told by the constable to do so. He even knows that it is appropriate (though not required by law) to tend a lonely and derelict graveyard. He perseveres through a short life without committing a crime. Ah, someone will say, Jo only avoided transgressing the negative commandments; he could not have *known*, let alone obey, the positive commandments. Which ones? He had no mother or father to honour, but he was completely loyal to the few people who were even passingly kind to him. He very likely observed 'the Sabbath' (that is, in Victorian England, Sunday) by necessity.[43] His 'job', sweeping a corner, would not have paid on Sunday. Had income tax forms been invented, he would not have had to fill them out. In rabbinic terms, he would not have been a *haber* and would not have needed to know their purity code. Where are those Pharisees who would look at a first-century equivalent of Dickens's Jo and say, 'You are an accursed sinner; and those who associate with you are outside the religious and social community'? Had belonging to such a religion as Judaism, which inculcates unremitting severity, deprived the Pharisees of all semblance of humanity? Will those who earnestly believe that to have been the case please produce one scrap of evidence?

2.2. *The non-haberim and salvation in rabbinic literature*. Nor can it be said that those who did not observe the priestly purity laws were considered beyond the reach of God's mercy. After 70 the rabbis certainly did not think that. Rabbinic statements on the *'amme ha-'arets* explicitly include them among those who have a share in the world to come.[44]

2.3. *Non-haberim, sin and atonement in rabbinic literature*. There is a simple test to determine whether or not the post-70 rabbis considered the *'amme ha-'arets* condemned as sinners: Did they appoint means of atonement for them? They did not. Reading the Mishnah makes it clear that the rabbis did not think that failing to observe the purity code of the *haberim* was a sin. Thus (despite Aulén's statement above)[45] there is no *penance* for the kind of impurity which separates *haber* from *'am ha-'arets*.

43. On the bleakness of a nineteenth century Sunday—and consequently its unremunerativeness—see Dickens, *Little Dorrit*, ch. 3.

44. *b. B. Meṣ.* 33b; see further *PPJ*, pp. 152-57.

45. Above, n. 38.

2.3.1. *Social exclusion in rabbinic literature.* By quoting such a passage as *m. Dem.* 2.3 (a *ḥaber* may not be the guest of an *'am ha-'arets*, nor receive him as a guest in his own raiment) the impression of a rigid exclusivism is given. In Aulén's words, the ritually impure are outside the 'religious and social community'. Certainly social and business intercourse was restricted by the *ḥaberim*. But the exclusion was not complete: note the exception to the rule in the Mishnah just quoted: A *ḥaber* may serve as host to an *'am ha-'arets* if he changes his garment. In *m. Dem.* 2.2 R. Judah offered the opinion that one who is trustworthy in tithes may be the guest of an *'am ha-'arets*. Other aspects of the Mishnah's tithing and purity laws envisage various forms of contact. *M. Dem.* 4.2, for example, has further rules for eating with an *'am ha-'arets*, and *Makš.* 6.3 allows certain purchases of food from an *'am ha-'arets*. Certainly there were restrictions, but the usual depiction of complete avoidance is exaggerated.[46]

2.4. *Exclusion from the social and religious community before 70.* Before 70 we have no literary evidence for the attitude of the *ḥaberim* towards other Jews, but for the present point we do not need any. The *ḥaberim* were not running Jewish society. Saying that lay people who transgressed the purity code were considered outside 'the religious and social community' is nonsense, just as is saying that it was 'the conviction of the time' that the *'amme ha-'arets* did not have access to salvation. Were they waiting for the *ḥaberim* to allow them in? Lounging at the door to the kingdom for someone to open it against the wedge put under it by the super-scrupulous? The notion that the *ḥaberim* or Pharisees could, in Jesus' day, effectively exclude others from the religious community seems to rest on a retrojection of the kind of dominance which rabbis in orthodox communities eventually came to possess. We should further recall that in the rabbinic passages which express hostility between the learned and the common people the hostility is mutual.[47] The common people thought that they were *right*, and there is no reason to think that, when they were in the vast majority, they felt excluded and were therefore awaiting a prophet to admit them to the kingdom. If they had considered themselves cut off from salvation for not washing their hands before eating, they could have started washing them. We should remember that, before 70, the *'amme ha-'arets* were

46. As by Jeremias, *Proclamation*, p. 117.
47. Above, n. 26.

primary members of 'normative Judaism', along with the priesthood.[48] They doubtless thought that, as long as they participated in the worship of the Temple, repented on the Day of Atonement, and did other things prescribed in the Bible for the correction of sin and the removal of impurity, they were fully members of the social and religious community.

To return to our illustration from *Bleak House* above: The coroner who refuses to hear Jo testify may reasonably be said to have held him to be a non-citizen, one unworthy to take his place in civilized society, despite his desire to do so. Let us say that there were, in pre-70 Judaism, some *haberim* who held this attitude towards the common people. Did they occupy places in Jewish society analogous to that of the coroner in Dickens's novel? Could *haberim* have effectively excluded the common people from the religious and social life of Judaism? It appears not.

This leads us to the group who actually ran the 'religious community' (that is, the national religion): the priesthood.[49] If a man had transgressed a law which required a sacrifice, and brought that sacrifice, would the priest ask him if he, though a lay person, observed the priestly purity code? And would the priest refuse the sacrifice if this were not the case? And, when the sacrifice was accepted (as it would be, if accompanied with a prayer of repentance), would the person who brought it feel outside the religious community just because some petty and legalistic group of *haberim*, crouched in their conventicle, having table-fellowship with one another, would not eat with him? Why would he want them to? The mind boggles. We might as well ask whether or not an eighteenth-century Anglican, in communion with the church, felt excluded from the religious community because the Methodists thought that, instead of using sugar in his tea, he should give the money to the poor.

48. 'The normative religion of the country is that compromise of which the three principal elements are the Pentateuch, the Temple, and the *'amme ha-'areṣ*, the ordinary Jews who were not members of any sect' (Morton Smith, 'The Dead Sea Sect in Relation to Ancient Judaism', *NTS* 7 [1960–61], p. 356).

49. On the dominance of the priests, see Josephus, *Apion* 2.184-98, esp. 187: 'the appointed duties of the priests included general supervision, the trial of cases of litigation, the punishment of condemned persons'. Cf. further M. Stern, 'Aspects of Jewish Society: The Priesthood and Other Classes', in *The Jewish People in the First Century*, II (ed. S. Safrai and M. Stern; CRINT 1.1; Assen: Van Gorcum; Philadelphia: Fortress Press, 1974), pp. 561-630, esp. 580-96, 600-12; Schürer, *The History of the Jewish People*, II, pp. 196-236.

And with regard to 'the social community': no one group ran it, certainly not the *haberim*. With regard to the social, as with regard to the religious community, we should drop the rhetoric with which Judaism and Christianity are misdescribed and think realistically.

Even if a maximum case is pursued—all Pharisees were *haberim*, and the Pharisees were a large and influential party—our argument still holds good. Could even an important party[50] of 6,000[51] (and Josephus is not noted for underestimating numbers) in any way exclude *all other Jews* (all were *'amme ha-'arets* who were not *haberim*) from the social and religious life of Judaism? They could not, and did not try to, keep them from the Temple.[52] And there is no report of their trying to keep them out of the synagogues.

It is frequently said that at the time of Jesus there were two foci of Jewish religious life, the Temple and the synagogue. There was, however, a third: the home. Even if *'amme ha-'arets* were slighted in synagogue worship (which is very doubtful),[53] there were the other two outlets for normal piety. Just as Temple worship was not under Pharisaic control, neither could be Passover, Succoth, and the other festivals kept at home.

2.5. *Conclusion: the common people*. Many scholars, not just Jeremias, observing that in the Gospels there are passages which have the word 'poor' in them and others which contain the word 'sinners', slide them together. They can then employ the fact that the *wicked* truly were considered 'cut off' by anyone who cared to think about it—

50. Josephus calls the Pharisees the leading party in *War* 2.162. They are given an even more dominant role in *Ant.* 13.298. As Morton Smith has pointed out, the more favourable description in *Antiquities* shows the success of the rabbinic movement after 70 and Josephus's desire to enhance the prestige of the surviving party: 'Palestinian Judaism in the First Century', in M. Davis (ed.), *Israel: Its Role in Civilization* (New York: Jewish Theological Seminary of America, 1956), pp. 67-81.

51. Josephus, *Ant.* 17.42.

52. The recorded debates between the Pharisees and the Sadducees about the Temple have to do with such things as whether or not the incense which was taken into the Holy of Holies on the Day of Atonement was to be lit before or after entry. See *b. Yom.* 19b; cf. also *m. Par.* 3.7. Whether or not the *'amme ha-'arets* could offer sacrifices is not an issue.

53. Smith ('Palestinian Judaism in the First Century') has proposed the Galilean synagogues were not dominated by the Pharisees. 'There is strong evidence that there were practically no Pharisees in Galilee during Jesus' lifetime' (*Jesus the Magician* [New York: Harper & Row, 1978], p. 157).

not just the Pharisees—to make it appear that the powers of the Jewish hierarchy (incorrectly believed to be the Pharisees) considered the *common people* to be cut off. Jesus then comes to the rescue of plain folk against an intolerant bunch of exclusivists. This view not only debases Judaism, it helps to prevent exploration of what it would have meant to offer the kingdom to the wicked—the positive point, which we have yet to address.

There is one last point to be made in this effort to eliminate from scholarship the view that Jesus was criticized for association with the common people. Those who propose the view that the learned and the scrupulous in first-century Judaism considered as sinners beyond redemption those who were not so learned and scrupulous as they are not offering a serious historical explanation of a first-century conflict. Doubtless without knowing it, they are carrying on theological polemic: we have love, mercy, repentance and forgiveness (more of which just below) on our side, and that is why our religion is superior to its parent. This, however, is not historical thinking: it focuses on religious abstractions and it floats into the realms of unreality. Scholars who have written, write, and will write in that way lack historical imagination. They cannot imagine the crowded streets of Jerusalem, the villages of Galilee, the farms in the plain of Esdraelon. If they did, they would know that no small group of super-pious, super-educated bigots (in case there were actually such a group) could in any way effectively exclude from religious and social life those did not meet their standards; much less would such a group have any reason for taking umbrage at a wandering Galilean healer and preacher who associated with the common people, nor would they be able to coax or coerce the Roman government into killing him.

3. *Jesus and the sinners.* But, if the significance of Jesus' proclamation to the wicked is not that he promised membership in the kingdom of God to the common people, who were excluded by the iniquitous Pharisees, what is the point? Why do the 'sinners' loom so large in the Gospels? I think that absolute clarity is not possible, although we can narrow the options. It will be helpful here to turn to Norman Perrin as representing consensus scholarship.

Perrin, unlike his teacher Jeremias, did not confuse the ordinary Jews who sinned with 'the sinners'.[54] His own proposals, however, about

54. Perrin, *Rediscovering*, pp. 91-94.

how to understand Jesus' inclusion of the sinners are at least equally off target. Thus he states that the Jews longed for ultimate, end-time forgiveness, not being able to receive it within the daily framework of Judaism. The Day of Atonement, other rituals, and works of supererogation, he assures us, 'were of limited effectiveness'. 'So, God himself must ultimately forgive sin... '[55] It is noteworthy that Perrin leaves repentance, which is crucial to the Jewish conception of atonement, out of his list. Besides, one may ask, who, in the normal Jewish view, forgives sins on the Day of Atonement? There is no justification for Perrin's separation of the Day of Atonement and other sacrificial occasions from what 'God himself' does. Put in the terms used earlier, I doubt very much that ordinary Jews, who brought sacrifices for occasional sins and prayed and fasted on the Day of Atonement, felt the need of some further, eschatological forgiveness. But this is a relatively minor point. The thrust of Perrin's case is this: the real 'sinners' were equivalent to Gentiles.[56] 'Such Jews were widely regarded as beyond hope of penitence or forgiveness...'[57] Jesus offered forgiveness to them, and thus 'confronted' Judaism with 'a crisis'.[58]

> Here was a situation in which the reality of God and his love was [sic] being revealed in a new and decisive way, and in which, therefore, the joys of the salvation time were suddenly available to those who had longed for them for so long and so earnestly.[59]

Jesus' promise of forgiveness to such people gave 'very grave offence... to his contemporaries'.[60] His disputes about the law were not especially offensive, and the cleansing of the Temple will not explain his execution.[61] He was killed, rather, because he offered sinners forgiveness.

---

55. Perrin, *Rediscovering*, p. 91.

56. Perrin, *Rediscovering*, pp. 93-96. The equation of 'sinners' and 'Gentiles' is not quite correct, although it is true that most Gentiles were regarded by most Jews as 'sinners' (see e.g. Gal. 2.15). But an apostate Jew, no matter how heinous his sin and how unrepentant his attitude, was still a Jew. See on this Lawrence Schiffmann, in E.P. Sanders *et al.* (eds.), *Jewish and Christian Self-Definition. II. Aspects of Judaism in the Graeco-Roman Period* (London: SCM Press; Philadelphia: Fortress Press, 1981), pp. 115-56.

57. Perrin, *Rediscovering*, p. 94.

58. Perrin, *Rediscovering*, p. 97.

59. Perrin, *Rediscovering*, p. 97.

60. Perrin, *Rediscovering*, p. 102.

61. Perrin, *Rediscovering*, p. 102.

> To have become such an outcast [as were the tax collectors] himself would
> have been much less of an outrage than to welcome those people back into
> the community in the name of the ultimate hope of that community.
> Intense conviction, indeed, is necessary to explain such an act on the part
> of Jesus, and such an act on the part of Jesus is necessary, we would claim,
> to make sense of the fact of the cross.[62]

Perrin's statement of the case that Jesus offended his contemporaries
by offering forgiveness to sinners is extreme, but I have presented it at
such length because it is a clear statement of a widely-held view. It was
grace that offended the Pharisees, who were committed to merit and
unremitting punishment for transgression. Riches's view is equally clear-
cut. He tries to answer the question 'why Jesus believed so strongly in
the mercy and forgiveness of God when many contemporaries held such
widely differing views'.[63] The view which I have illustrated by citing
Perrin and Riches reveals the deep-rooted Christian desire to have Jesus
die for the truth of the gospel. The position is basically this: *We* (the
Christians) believe in grace and forgiveness. Those religious qualities
characterize Christianity, and thus could not have been present in the
religion from which Christianity came. Otherwise, why the split? But the
Jews did not believe in repentance and forgiveness. They not only would
not extend forgiveness to their own errant sheep, they would kill anyone
who proposed to do so.

The position is so incredible that I wish it were necessary only to state
it in order to demonstrate its ridiculousness. But thousands believe it,
and I shall try to show what is wrong with it.

3.1. *Repentance and forgiveness*. Let us focus first on the question of
forgiveness and its corollary repentance. The tax collectors and sinners,
Perrin assures us, 'responded in glad acceptance' to Jesus' saying that
they would be forgiven.[64] But was this news? Did they not know that, if
they renounced those aspects of their lives which were an affront to
God's law, they would have been accepted with open arms? Is it a
serious proposal that tax collectors and the wicked longed for forgiveness, but could not find it within ordinary Judaism? That they thought
only in the messianic age could they find forgiveness, and thus

62. Perrin, *Rediscovering*, p. 103.
63. John Riches, *Jesus and the Transformation of Judaism* (London: Darton,
Longman & Todd, 1980), p. 99.
64. Perrin, *Rediscovering*, p. 97.

responded to Jesus 'in glad acceptance'?[65] Perrin, citing no pertinent evidence, asserts that the 'sinners' 'were widely regarded as beyond hope of penitence or forgiveness',[66] and thus he denies one of the things about Judaism which everyone should know: there was a universal view that forgiveness is *always* available to those who return to the way of the Lord.[67]

Further, he presents an extraordinary picture of the tax collectors and sinners: they *wanted* forgiveness but did now know how to obtain it. I think that a quick chat with any religious leader—that is, a priest—would have clarified the issue: God always accepts repentant sinners who turn to his way.

Finally, it is inaccurate to say that Jesus welcomed people 'back into the community' (Perrin, at n. 62 above). Did Jesus control access to the Temple? We must continue to try to think realistically. It is quite possible (in fact, as will soon appear, quite likely) that Jesus admitted the wicked into *his* community without making the normal demand of restitution and commitment to the law. That might give his followers *a* sense of community; but it is not accurate to say that 'he welcomed those people [the sinners] *back* into *the* community'. They all would have known perfectly well what to do if they wished to be considered members of the covenant in good standing.

A consideration of the story of Zacchaeus (Lk. 19.1-9) will bring home the curiosity of the reported charge that Jesus ate with tax collectors and sinners and promised them a place in the kingdom. This story was, it appears to me, created by Luke (or possibly a pre-Lukan writer) to emphasize repentance and *reform*.[68] It emphasizes these qualities so

65. N. Perrin, *The Kingdom of God in the Teaching of Jesus* (London: SCM; Philadelphia: Fortress, 1963), p. 75.

66. Perrin's 'evidence' is *m. Toh.* 7.6, which says that a tax collector defiles a house into which he enters (Perrin, *Rediscovering*, p. 94). I cannot understand why he thought this meant that the tax collector could not repent.

67. In rabbinic literature the classic statement on repentance is attributed to R. Simeon (probably b. Yohai): even the completely wicked person who repents at the end will be saved (*t. Qid.* 1.15-16). One passage does not prove a view to be universal, and I cite it to illustrate a view which can be shown to be universal—at least as being virtually universal in all the surviving Jewish literature of the period 200 BCE to 200 CE. There are minor exceptions to the rule in 1QS. One may see the various sections on 'atonement' in each of the first three chapters of *Paul and Palestinian Judaism*.

68. Cf. R. Bultmann, *The History of the Synoptic Tradition* (ET Oxford: Basil

effectively that their scarcity elsewhere becomes striking. If Jesus, by eating with tax collectors, led them to repent, repay those whom they had robbed, and leave off practising their profession, he would have been a national hero.

Who would have been offended if he converted quislings? The case with 'sinners' is similar. Let us take the case of a professional sinner, a usurer. If such a person were led by Jesus to repay the interest which he had accepted, and to turn to a life in accord with the law, who would have objected? Those who needed to borrow money, for example farmers who borrowed each year against the next harvest, would be inconvenienced if their accustomed usurer quit his profession. But presumably there would be someone from whom to borrow, and the defection of one usurer from the money market would not seriously affect the economy. Those who were zealous for the law, such as the Pharisees, would rejoice. The notion that the *conversion* of sinners was offensive to the Pharisees is, when thought about concretely, ridiculous.

3.2. *The offence.* Thus it seems to me impossible that Jesus caused offence by converting sinners. Yet it does seem to have been an accusation, not just a random comment, that he was 'a friend of tax collectors and sinners'. Could it be that he offered them inclusion in the kingdom *while they were still sinners* and *without* requiring repentance as normally understood—renouncing a sinful way of life and turning to obedience to the law? We have seen above that the emphasis on *repentance* is largely Lukan (Lk. 5.32; 15.7, 10; 19.1-10). Perhaps Jesus' offence was that he, while claiming to be a spokesman for God, said that sinners would be admitted to the coming kingdom *anyway*. I realize that this will be an unpopular proposal. Surely he desired their conversion. But if that was all he sought, what was controversial about him?

The controversy has been held to be simply that Jesus offered forgiveness (inclusion in the kingdom) *before* requiring reformation, and for this reason he could be accused of being a friend of tax collectors and sinners. Had they already reformed, they would not have been sinners. That is the way Jeremias stated the case: Judaism offers forgiveness only

Blackwell; New York: Harper & Row, 1963), p. 34: the passage is 'manifestly imaginary, an extended version of Mark 2.14 which, combined with vv. 15-17, gave rise to this story'. Fiedler (*Jesus und die Sünder*, p. 135) argues that the story is so strongly marked by Lukan language and theology that one need not look for a prior story which has been reworked. Jeremias (*Proclamation*, p. 156) treats all the details of the story as factual.

to those who are righteous. They had first to become righteous to be forgiven.[69] Jesus' offer in advance is sometimes called *unconditional* forgiveness.[70] But what precisely does this mean? The intended contrast is, of course, with Judaism, where conditional forgiveness was offered. Quite apart from the fact that Jeremias has caricatured Judaism by dividing up chronologically reformation of life and forgiveness, we must still press the question: are we dealing with a significant contrast? We should, once more, think concretely. If the result of Jesus' eating with a tax collector was that the tax collector, like Zacchaeus, made restitution and changed his way of life (we recall that Jeremias accepts the story), Jesus' proclamation of forgiveness was not unconditional. The condition of its effectiveness was obviously the conversion. I submit that the distinction proposed is too small to create much of a dispute. For clarity, I shall repeat the proposed distinction. It is this: Jesus said, God forgives you, and now you should repent and mend your ways; everyone else said, God forgives you if you will repent and mend your ways.

Modern theologians find here a significant difference, and perhaps rightly so. The courage required to say to someone who, by his very way of life, offended the law of God, 'you will enter the kingdom before the righteous' (see Mt. 21.31), must have been considerable. And it may well have been effective as a missionary tactic. But just how large would it have loomed in the first century? Were tax collectors and usurers walking around Galilee in such a state of anxiety about forgiveness that the distinction between 'if you repent' and 'assuming that you subsequently repent' was a burning issue? And would Jesus' formulation (assuming that we have correctly identified it) have offended anybody? I can well imagine that saying to a tax collector that he would enter the kingdom ahead of the righteous would have been irritating to the latter; but I cannot see that, *assuming that Jesus' aim was in fact reformation*, the righteous—those who said, 'if you repent'—would have conceived a deadly enmity for Jesus, who said, 'assuming, of course, that you subsequently repent'.

But perhaps we have not yet put our finger on the right distinction.

Let us review a few facts about repentance: John, but not Jesus, was known to have issued a call for national repentance. This is clear not only in the early parts of the synoptics, where the preaching of John is

69. Jeremias, *Proclamation*, p. 119.

70. Jeremias, *Proclamation*, p. 177. See recently W.R. Farmer, *Jesus and the Gospel* (Philadelphia: Fortress Press, 1982), p. 41.

described, but also in such a passage as Mt. 21.32: 'John came to you in the way of righteousness, and you did not believe him, but the tax collectors and the harlots believed him; and even when you saw it, you did not afterward repent and believe him'. John's was a preaching of repentance in view of the eschaton, and here we seem to have a real difference from Jesus. John came 'in the way of righteousness'. Jesus did not, at least not in John's way. The same contrast in Mt. 11.18-19, which we cited earlier: John was an ascetic (as would be expected of a prophet of repentance), while Jesus was a friend of tax collectors and sinners. Repentance does not in fact loom large in the material attributed to Jesus, apart from that in Luke. A wide call to repentance is evident in The Woes on the Cities of Galilee (Mt. 11.20-24 // Lk. 10.13-15), in the saying about the Ninevites (Mt. 12.41-42 // Lk. 11.32), and in Luke's passage about the Galileans (13.1-5); but the dominant impression of Jesus is that which we have just observed in Mt. 21.32 and 11.18, where he is contrasted to John. John was the spokesman for repentance and for righteousness ordinarily understood; Jesus, equally convinced that the end was at hand, proclaimed the inclusion of the wicked.

Could it be that Jesus saw himself as doing what John had *not* done, rather than as repeating it with slightly different tactics? John had been an ascetic who called for repentance; Jesus consorted with the outcasts and promised them that God would save them too—without the normally expected conversion. This is admittedly speculative. We are up against a fact for which there is no clear-cut explanation. The distinctive aspect of Jesus' message about the kingdom is the message of the inclusion of the wicked. This has not been problematic to scholars as long as they think that the offer of *forgiveness to repentant sinners* was unique and would have been offensive to the leaders of Judaism. Jesus proclaimed that the wicked who repented would share the kingdom, and the Pharisees were led thereby to a fatal enmity. But once we see (1) that everybody (except the Romans) would have favoured the conversion of tax collectors and other traitors to the God of Israel and (2) that Jesus' message in any case was not primarily orientated around a call to repentance, the significance of the charge that Jesus was a friend of tax collectors and the wicked becomes difficult to determine. I shall offer my proposal once more. Jesus offered companionship to the wicked of Israel as a sign that God would save them; he did not make his association dependent on their conversion to obedience to the law. He may very well have thought that they had no time to create new lives for themselves, but that if they followed him they would be saved.

It is an interesting and somewhat curious fact that scholars who write about repentance and forgiveness in the Gospels do not say just what they have in mind. Jeremias's view seems clear: he accepts the story of Zacchaeus. But Perrin, for example, wrote page after page on repentance and forgiveness without ever saying whether or not repentance, in Jesus' view, required restitution.[71] Westerholm has an interesting paragraph: Jesus' view was that all were on the same footing; all needed to repent. Some

> ... seized gratefully the chance to enter in. For others, however, the undiscriminating nature of the message proved offensive... Clinging to their claim to be righteous, they refused to enter a kingdom... where 'sinners and 'righteous' sat together at a table spread by God.[72]

But if the sinners had repented, presumably they were no longer sinners. At any rate let me say precisely what I mean in proposing that Jesus did not require his followers to repent: By normal Jewish standards offences against fellow humans required restitution as well as repentance (see e.g. Lev. 6.1-5 [Heb. 5.20-26]; Num. 5.5-7; cf. *b. B. Qam.* 9.6 and *b. B. Meṣ.* 4.8 for the rabbinic interpretation). Other offences were atoned for by repentance alone. While the Temple stood, repentance would be demonstrated by a sacrifice (see the same passage in Leviticus).[73] It may have been just these requirements that Jesus did not make of his followers.

There are three passages which seem to point in this direction: the Call of Levi // Matthew (Mt. 9.9-13 // Mk 2.13-17 // Lk.5.27-32); the Question about Fasting (Mt. 9.14-17 // Mk 2.18-22 // Lk. 5.33-39); and the story of the would-be follower who wished to bury his father (Mt. 8.21ff. // Lk. 9.59-60). The last passage will be discussed more fully on another occasion, and here I shall only indicate that it puts following Jesus above obeying the fifth commandment. The authenticity of the other two passages is less certain, but each seems to rest on a reliable kernel. Jesus probably did have a tax collector among his followers— even though later his name was not securely remembered—and it is

---

71. Perrin, *Rediscovering*, pp. 90-108.

72. Westerholm, *Jesus and Scribal Authority*, p. 132.

73. For the rabbinic rule, see *Sifra Aḥare Mot*, pereq 8.1-2. Further passages in *PPJ*, p. 179 and notes. Transgression of the Sabbath, for example, ordinarily required a Sin-offering (*m. Sanh.* 7.8; *m. Šab.* 7.1).

probably this fact which gave immediate substance to the charge that he ate with tax collectors. The Gospel tradition subsequently expanded this point ('many tax collectors and sinners', Mk 2.15 and parr.), but we can safely assume that there was at least one.[74] It is noteworthy that this one is not said to have repented, repaid those whom he robbed, and assumed a life conformable to the law. What he did was 'follow' Jesus. As I have observed before, it was left to Luke to assure his readers that the wicked with whom Jesus associated converted.

The Question about Fasting makes basically the same point: some of the traditional practices of Judaism may be foregone by those who follow Jesus.[75]

Thus I propose that the novelty of Jesus' message was that he promised inclusion in the coming kingdom to those who followed him, even if they did not make restitution and follow the normal procedures for gaining atonement.

Speculative as this proposal is, I consider it much more likely than the popular one: Jesus called sinners to repentance; and therefore mainline Judaism, being opposed to repentance and forgiveness, sought to kill him.

But before we can conclude our discussion of Jesus and those who would be included in the kingdom, there is one last topic to be considered.

Table-Fellowship
'Table-fellowship' has loomed large in recent discussion of Jesus. His eating with tax collectors and sinners has, probably correctly, been seen as a proleptic indication that they would be included in the kingdom: the meal looks forward to the 'messianic banquet', when many would come from east and west and dine with the patriarchs (Mt. 8.11).[76] Several parables tell us that the kingdom is like a banquet, to which many are called. And, most tellingly, before his death Jesus looked forward to drinking the fruit of the vine in the kingdom of God (Mk 14.25 // Mt. 26.29 // Lk. 22.19).

74. I agree with Bultmann (*History*, pp. 28, 56-57) that the passages depicting the call of the disciples are 'ideal scenes': they condense 'into one symbolic moment what was in actuality a process' (p. 57). But I still think it is likely that at least one tax collector was among Jesus' followers.

75. This interpretation takes the saying of Mark 2.19 to be an original saying, although the setting for it has been invented. See again Bultmann, *History*, pp. 18-19.

76. Jeremias, *Proclamation*, pp. 115-17; Perrin, *Rediscovering*, pp. 107-108.

Thus it would appear that Jesus' eating with 'tax collectors and sinners' promised, as clearly as words, that they would inherit the kingdom; and thus it is likely that Jesus saw his eating with tax collectors and sinners as being determinative of the coming kingdom. But did it work out that way? Did Jesus' table-fellowship with sinners help prepare the way for the church which, instead of the kingdom, followed his ministry? There is an obvious drawback to this proposal. Those who had table-fellowship with Jesus did not, with the exception of Peter and John, become major figures in the Church. One need mention only James, Paul and Barnabas to make the point clear. It would be nice to think that Jesus bound his companions to him in such a way that they could do no other than carry on his work after his death.[77] But in fact at least three of the principal leaders of the early Christian movement were not disciples—and many of the disciples drop from view. It would appear that the force which welded together the early Christian movement was not Jesus' table-fellowship with tax collectors and sinners.

Conclusion

Most of the things which we know about Jesus with virtually complete certainty fit him rather neatly into the category of a prophet of Jewish restoration. The case cannot be argued here, but we may briefly note some principal points: 1. Jesus probably began his career as a follower of John the Baptist, who called on all Israel to repent in preparation for the coming end. 2. His call of twelve disciples probably prefigures the restoration of the twelve tribes. 3. His expectation that the Temple would be destroyed and rebuilt corresponds to a known, if not universal, expectation about the hoped-for restoration of Israel. 4. After his death and resurrection the disciples worked within a framework of Jewish restoration expectation. Peter, James and John obviously thought that it was time for the Gentiles to be brought into the people of God,[78] though they may have had reservations about Paul's method (see Gal. 2.1-10).

If Jesus, in continuation of John's message, had urged the wicked among Israel to repent and make restitution to those whom they had wronged, his stance towards the sinners would also fall neatly within the framework of Jewish restoration theology. Even within the Dead Sea Scrolls, which represent an extremely exclusivist sect, there is the hope

77. So Perrin, *Rediscovering*, p. 107.
78. Gentiles would join restored Israel: Isa. 2.1-5; 56.6-8; 60.3; and often.

that 'wicked' Israelites, those outside the sect, will join in the last days (1QSa 1.1-3).

Here, however, we seem to be able to discern a departure from the common view. Jesus taught and acted out the message that those who followed him, even though they were still 'wicked' when judged by the biblical standard, would be included in the coming kingdom. This attitude, which must have made him appear to be arrogantly impious, sets him apart from his contemporaries.

There is here another puzzle, though it cannot be pursued. Did Jesus think that only those who followed him would be included in the kingdom? What about those normally counted 'righteous'? Are we to see Jesus as intending to create his own sect to the exclusion of the rest of Israel?[79] If so, what are we to make of the hope for all Israel implied by the call of the twelve?

It may be that we can reconcile a hope for all Israel with the promise to the wicked if we focus on Jesus' relationship to John. It may well be that, in his own view, Jesus did not have to do it *all*. Although we all know that we should not follow the Gospels and relegate John to the status of an intentional forerunner of Jesus, we often fail to explore the possibilities inherent in Jesus' positive relationship to John. Jesus may well have seen himself as supplementing and thus completing John's work. John had called on Israel to repent, but too few had responded. Jesus then set out to promise inclusion to the most obvious outsiders. This view is supported by the Parable of the Banquet (Mt. 22.1-10; Lk. 14.15-24): those first called did not come in, and so others were invited.

Our answer to this puzzle is obviously speculative, but it seems to be required by facts which are virtually certain: 1. Jesus followed John and saw his own work in relation to John's. 2. In general Jesus stood firmly in the tradition of Jewish restoration eschatology. 3. After his death Jesus' followers worked within the framework of that eschatology. 4. Jesus himself, however, did not stress one of the aspects of restoration eschatology: the need for all Israel to repent. 5. His special mission was

---

79. That this is a real problem may be seen from the ambiguity of Jeremias's position. He holds that Jesus intended to include only his followers, the 'poor', in the kingdom, to the exclusion of the scribes and Pharisees. This, he says, shows that Jesus did not intend to found an exclusivist sect, but to call all Israel. See *Proclamation*, pp. 116-17, 177.

to promise inclusion in the coming kingdom to the outsiders, the wicked, if they heeded his call.

If these five statements are true, it seems reasonable to suppose that Jesus thought of someone else, John, as having called all Israel to repent.

It is with pathos that one observes that the distinctive characteristic of Jesus' message, the inclusion of sinners, was not continued in the early Christian movement. Paul's struggle to have Gentile sinners (Gal. 2.15) admitted to the eschatological people of God without requiring them to observe the law is well known. We must assume that the church in Jerusalem, apparently dominated by James and influenced by people whom Paul calls 'false brethren' (Gal. 2.4), was no more enthusiastic about counting among its membership the wicked of Israel than it was about admitting Gentiles while they were still 'sinners', that is, non-observers of the law. It appears that what survived after Jesus' death and resurrection was a movement which followed more-or-less traditional expectations about the end. The end was at hand, or in the process of being realized, and it was time to turn to the Lord and his law.

I have several times remarked on Luke's special concern to show that the wicked who followed Jesus *reformed* and became morally upright. The same concern, though differently presented, appears in Matthew:

> Unless your righteousness exceeds that of the scribes and Pharisees, you will never enter the kingdom of heaven (Mt. 5.20)

> The scribes and the Pharisees sit on Moses' seat; so practice and observe whatever they tell you, but not what they do; for they preach, but do not practice (Mt. 23.3)

> If your brother sins against you, go and tell him his fault... If he refuses to listen even to the church, let him be to you as a Gentile and a tax collector (Mt. 18.15-17).

These verses show clearly that in at least one part of the church righteousness according to the law was insisted upon,[80] and the dispute which surfaces in Galatians makes it evident that this concern was present during the earliest stages of the church in Jerusalem. Important

---

80. The stratum of material in Matthew which presents Jesus as a super-Pharisee presents an interesting problem, but one which cannot be explored here. If we focus on 'Gentiles' and 'tax collectors', we see three layers: Jesus, in favour of tax collectors; an intermediate layer of material, in opposition to the inclusion of Gentiles and tax collectors (in addition to Mt. 18.15-17, just quoted, see Mt. 5.46-47 and 6.7); the final redactor, who favoured the Gentile mission (28.19).

segments of the early Christian movement were prepared to admit Gentiles and tax collectors if they were no longer Gentiles and tax collectors: if they converted and accepted the law.

We can hardly say that Jesus thought out the question of the law in the way that Paul did, but it does seem to be the case that he wished to promise inclusion in the kingdom to those who followed him, but who did not or could not attain righteousness by the law.

JSNT 29 (1987), pp. 57-78

JESUS AND THE COVENANT: A RESPONSE TO E.P. SANDERS

Dale C. Allison, Jr

1977 marked a turning point in the modern discussion of the apostle Paul. It was that year which gave us E.P. Sanders's highly acclaimed *Paul and Palestinian Judaism*.[1] Now, eight years later, we have in our hands a lengthy book by Sanders on Paul's Lord: *Jesus and Judaism*.[2] Whether this fresh and provocative work will prove to be the watershed in Gospel studies that the former has proven to be in Pauline studies remains to be seen. But it will without question provoke fruitful discussion for a long time and force many of us to reconsider cherished opinions about Jesus of Nazareth.

In his work on Paul, Sanders set out to accomplish at least two major goals. He desired first of all to describe—primarily in order to rebut the misunderstandings of Christian scholars—the fundamental 'pattern of religion' characteristic of Palestinian Judaism between 200 BC and AD 200. Secondly, he wished to compare this 'pattern of religion' with the thought of Paul. Concerning his first goal, Sanders is roundly conceded to have achieved his aim. His central conclusion, namely that 'covenantal nomism'[3] was the rule in Palestinian texts around the turn of our era, would be hard to dispute. By way of contrast, Sanders's conclusions about Paul have not been quite as enthusiastically received: many have

---

1. E.P. Sanders, *Paul and Palestinian Judaism: A Comparison of Patterns of Religion* (Philadelphia: Fortress Press, 1977).

2. E.P. Sanders, *Jesus and Judaism* (Philadelphia: Fortress Press, 1985). The page numbers in the text of the present essay refer to this book.

3. This is, in Sanders's words, 'the view that one's place in God's plan is established on the basis of the covenant and that the covenant requires as the proper response of man his obedience to its commandments, while providing means of atonement for transgression' (*Paul*, p. 75).

been moved to dissent from some of his major assertions.[4] There is, however, one point upon which scholars should, I think, concur: while there are in Paul's theology elements of 'covenantal nomism', these are not the key to his thought.[5] That is, Paul does not really exhibit in any conventional sense the fundamental 'pattern of religion' common to the Palestinian Judaism of his time. Now according to Sanders, this makes Paul a loner, for in *Paul and Palestinian Judaism* it is affirmed that of all the Jewish documents therein examined, only one—*4 Ezra*—fails to uphold 'covenantal nomism'. Moreover, in the new work, Jesus himself is said to have accepted the 'covenantal nomism' of his day. Paul appears to be more isolated than ever.

Sanders's remarks about Jesus and 'covenantal nomism' are saved until the end of *Jesus and Judaism*. Indeed, the words 'covenantal nomism' do not appear until p. 335 (the text runs to 340 pages). This is in part because Sanders does not make the idea serve as a foundation upon which to build his reconstruction of Jesus. The book's major theses seemingly stand on their own without independent consideration of what Jesus made of God's covenant with Israel. Another reason is that 'covenantal nomism' is not straightforwardly addressed in the extant sayings attributed to Jesus. As Sanders writes, 'Since he [Jesus] did not spend his time discussing the covenant *historically* (why God chose Israel, why he brought them out of Egypt, and the like), nor discussing the fine points of obedience, but rather preparing his followers and hearers for the coming redemption, I have managed to write virtually an entire book without the phrase "covenantal nomism"' (p. 337). With the statements about Jesus in this sentence I see no reason to disagree. Yet I believe it incumbent to offer for them an explanation Sanders fails to consider, this being the proposition that 'covenantal nomism' is not taught in the Gospels not because Jesus assumed its truth but precisely because he rejected it (or at least the common understanding of it). It is, in any event, the purpose of this essay so to argue. I trust that the importance of the issue for one's understanding of the history of early Christianity will become manifest as the argument proceeds.

---

4.   The most convenient way of entering into the debate of Sanders's view of Paul is through his work, *Paul, the Law, and the Jewish People* (Philadelphia: Fortress Press, 1983). This is in great measure a response to his critics.

5.   See Sanders, *Paul and Palestinian Judaism*, pp. 511-15.

1. *The Words of John the Baptist*

In Sanders's judgment, and as already observed, 'covenantal nomism' is the rule in ancient Palestinian texts composed around the time of Jesus. If there is an exception to the rule, it is *4 Ezra*. Whether or not this estimation of the apocalypse is sound I need not consider here. (Much depends upon whether one can follow Sanders in taking *4 Ezra* 14 to be a later addition.) But apart from one's evaluation of *4 Ezra*, there is, it would seem, an even clearer example of the breaking with 'covenantal nomism' within ancient Palestinian Judaism. I refer to the traditions about John the Baptist. It is, of course, very difficult to say much about John. Aside from a few lines in Josephus our only real sources for him are the canonical Gospels, and these cannot be considered unbiased. Nonetheless, most scholars would presumably agree that the sayings attributed to the Baptist in Matthew 3 and Luke 3 and typically assigned to Q have good claim to go back to the one baptized Jesus.[6] Certainly there were in early Christianity converts from the Baptist sect who could have transmitted their master's words and introduced them into the Jesus tradition (cf. Jn 1.35-42; Acts 19.1-7).

With this in mind, then, I should like to draw attention to the following saying: 'Do not presume[7] to say to yourselves, "We have Abraham as our father"; for I tell you, God is able to raise up from these stones children to Abraham' (Mt. 3.9 = Lk. 3.8). What does this mean?[8] ἀνίστημι σπέρμα is a Semitism whose sense is 'to cause to be born', 'to cause to bring forth progeny' (Deut. 18.15, 18; 2 Sam. 7.12; *Lam. Rab.* on 5.3). It equals the ἐγείρειν ἐκ τινός of Mt. 22.24. The figure then is of God giving to rocks the power to bring forth people.[9] The background for this picture is Isa. 51.1-2 (so already Chrysostom, *Hom. on Mt.* 11.3): 'Look to the rock from whence you were hewn and to the quarry whence you were digged. Look to Abraham your father and to Sarah

---

6. Distinctive Christian elements are absent. The eschatological thrust and strong note of repentance are consistent with what must have been John's orientation (cf. Mt. 11.7-18). And the attack against reliance upon baptism without authentic inward repentance has its parallel in 1QS 5.13-14.

7. Luke has 'begin', which is the only difference between Mt. 3.9 and Lk. 3.8b.

8. With what follows cf. J. Jeremias, *TDNT*, IV, pp. 270-71.

9. Cf. A. Schlatter, *Der Evangelist Matthäus* (Stuttgart: Calwer, 5th edn, 1959), p. 47.

who bore you. For when he was but one I called him and blessed him and I caused him to increase' (cf. Gen. 12.1-3 and note the reworking of Isa. 51.1-2 in *LAB* 23.4). From Abraham, a lifeless rock (cf. Gen. 17.17; 18.10-14; 21.8; Rom. 4.17), God had miraculously caused to be born Isaac and descendants as numerous as the stars of heaven. This, the Baptist declares, God can do again. The implication is patent. If Mt. 3.9 = Lk. 3.8 is not to be dismissed as rhetorical exaggeration or hortatory hyperbole, it would appear to be aimed precisely at undermining the theology Sanders has dubbed 'covenantal nomism', or at undermining the prevalent interpretation of that theology.

Indeed, one could scarcely hope to find a more straightforward rejection of the notion that to be born a Jew is to be born into the covenant community. As D. Daube has remarked, John the Baptist's words mean this: 'you must acquire him (Abraham) just like strangers'.[10] Daube, to be sure, assumes that John's water rite was a transmutation of Jewish proselyte baptism. This may or may not be so. Recent discussion causes one to be unsure as to whether the practice was established in pre-Christian Judaism.[11] Yet even if we are to look elsewhere for an explanation of John's baptism, Daube's reading stands. It is not enough to be a Jew. One must, according to the saying of the Baptist, be 'born again'. As W.G. Kümmel has put it, in Mt. 3.8 = Lk. 3.9, 'the relationship of man to God in principle is defined solely by his being human, and no longer by his belonging to the Jewish people or to any other human group'.[12] So despite the plurals ('stones', 'children'), all focus is on the individual, whose deliverance is guaranteed only by a radical turning around, by a repentance which produces good fruit. (It is important to realize that, by associating Abraham with the new children the Lord can bring forth, John shows that God will faithfully fulfil the promises in Genesis. Thus the Baptist is not overturning the fundamental idea of

10. D. Daube, *Ancient Jewish Law* (Leiden: Brill, 1981), p. 10.

11. For recent discussion, see L.H. Schiffman, 'At the Crossroads: Tannaitic Perspectives on the Jewish-Christian Schism', in *Jewish and Christian Self-Definition*, II (ed. E.P. Sanders; Philadelphia: Fortress Press, 1981), pp. 127-31; D. Smith, 'Jewish Proselyte Baptism and the Baptism of John', *RestQ* 25 (1982), pp. 13-32; and K. Pusey, 'Jewish Proselyte Baptism', *ExpTim* 95 (1984), pp. 141-45.

12. W.G. Kümmel, *The Theology of the New Testament, according to its Major Witnesses: James—Paul—John* (trans. J.E. Steely; Nashville: Abingdon Press, 1973), p. 28.

covenant but rather repudiating the popular understanding of what the Abrahamic covenant entailed. We might put it this way: John does away not with covenant but with popular 'covenantal nomism'.)

Once one rightly grasps the implications of John's saying about God raising up children to Abraham, sense can be made of his thunderings about judgment. 'Even now the axe is laid to the root of the trees; every tree therefore that does not bear good fruit is cut down and thrown into the fire' (Mt. 3.10 = Lk. 3.9). 'His (= the coming one who will baptize with fire) winnowing fork is in his hand, and he will clear his threshing floor and gather his wheat into the granary, but the chaff he will burn with unquenchable fire' (Mt. 3.12 = Lk. 3.17, with insignificant differences).[13] If the Baptist, like many rabbis, believed that, save for heretics who had put themselves outside the covenant, 'all Israelites have a share of the world to come' (*m. Sanh.* 10.1), what was he talking about? Why the sweeping, earnest warnings about damnation? If John shares his contemporaries' understanding of the covenant, what moved him to put on the prophetic mantle and trouble his hearers with threats about fire? It is natural, in my view, to suppose that John the Baptist preached a radical, one-time repentance and delivered fulminating judgments upon those who came out to him because he placed a large question mark over the 'covenantal nomism' of his day and avowed that those born of Abraham were not by that fact alone worthy members of the people of God.

13. According to F.W. Beare, *The Gospel according to Matthew* (New York: Harper & Row, 1981), p. 97, in reality the chaff or stubble would simply blow away, so the burning of it is odd. If this were indeed so, then all the more emphasis would fall upon the conclusion, the fire of judgment. But BAGD, *s.v.*, cites Ostraka 2.1168 for the burning of ἄχυρον; and ἄχυρον is the near equivalent of *qaš*, for the burning of which see Exod. 15.7; Isa. 5.24; 47.14; Obad. 18; Mal. 3.19 (4.1); *m. Šab.* 3.1; *m. Par.* 4.3. On the other side, ἄχυρον never translates *qaš* in the LXX; and if, as G. Schwarz ('τὸ δὲ ἄχυρον κατακαύσει', *ZNW* 72 [1981], pp. 247-54) has proposed, 'in unquenchable fire', which turns a true-to-life parable into something more, is a secondary addition, one could further conjecture (as does Schwarz) that κατακαίω has replaced an original verb which means 'blow away'. This is made more plausible—although far from proven—by the constant connection between 'chaff' and words like 'wind' and 'blow' in the Old Testament (Job 21.18; Pss. 1.4; 35.5; Jer. 17.13; 29.5; 41.15-16; Dan. 2.35; Hos. 13.3; Hab. 3.14; Zeph. 2.2). Interestingly enough, the third-century *Mart. Pionius* 4.14 refers to Mt. 3.12 but has the chaff simply carried off by the wind: fire is not mentioned.

If we assume, in the light of the foregoing, that John the Baptist's preaching has as one of its foundation stones the dismissal of traditional 'covenantal nomism', it is possible to rethink the question of Paul's isolation from 'mainstream' Judaism. Was Paul the first believer in Jesus to put 'covenantal nomism' to the side? Or was he in this simply following his predecessors, Christians who had in turn been influenced, ultimately, by John the Baptizer? For reasons outlined below, I believe the evidence favours the second option, and I should like to urge this reconstruction: Jesus, who came out of the Baptist movement, shared John's rejection of what Sanders takes to have been the common idea; and Jesus was the connecting link between John the Baptist on the one hand and Paul on the other in the matter at issue.

2. *Restoration Eschatology*

Why does Sanders affirm that Jesus himself accepted 'covenantal nomism'? As far as I can determine, there are two reasons. The first is this: Jesus' 'mission was to Israel in the name of the God of Israel. He thus evidently accepted his people's special status, that is, the election and the covenant' (p. 336). According to Sanders, one of the keys to understanding Jesus is Jewish restoration eschatology. The main themes of this were the future redemption and restoration of Israel, a new or renewed temple, national repentance, eschatological judgment, and the admission of Gentiles—all of which Jesus probably accepted (although Sanders remains noncommittal about the last). But one must pose a question here. Surely John the Baptist was, like Jesus, a proponent of Jewish restoration eschatology. At the same time, and as I have already argued, John does not appear to have held his contemporaries' interpretation of God's covenant with Israel. In other words, John, if I have understood his words aright, illustrates the possibility of carrying on a mission to Israel in the name of the God of Israel while at the same time rejecting the conventional understanding of 'covenantal nomism'. There is, therefore, a possible flaw at this point in Sanders's logic.

The apostle Paul can also be cited to similar effect. He was, admittedly, first of all the apostle to the Gentiles (Gal. 2.1-10). Even so, Paul did believe in the God of Israel, and he did believe in the eschatological restoration of the Jewish people. As Romans 11 leaves in no doubt, he was confident that the end-time would witness the salvation of his people:

Lest you be wise in your own conceits, I want you to understand this mystery, brethren: a hardening has come upon part of Israel, until the full number of the Gentiles come in, and so all Israel will be saved; as it is written, 'The Deliverer will come from Zion, he will banish ungodliness from Jacob'; 'and this will be my covenant with them when I take away their sins' (Rom. 11.25-27).[14]

Yet despite this assurance about the ultimate fate of Israel, the fundamental pattern of Pauline theology was *not*, by Sanders's own admission, 'covenantal nomism'. Once again, therefore, we see that adherence to Jewish restoration eschatology was not always bound up with a traditional version of 'covenantal nomism'.

What of Paul's fellow believers? Many of them carried on a mission to Israel (Gal. 2.1-10), and no doubt many of them, like Paul, hoped for the redemption of God's people Israel. But were they, any more than Paul, 'covenantal nomists' in any usual Jewish sense? It is truly difficult to think so. If our sources (e.g. Acts 3.19-20)[15] are to be trusted, they called upon the Jewish people to repent and embrace Jesus as their saviour and Messiah. Their 'soteriology', accordingly, included faith in Jesus (cf. Mk 1.15; Acts 9.42; 11.17; Gal. 2.16; Phil. 1.29; Col. 2.5). Hence they must have denied that it was sufficient to be born into the covenant and keep the law. So to make the point for a third time: restoration eschatology did not require the acceptance of the popular understanding of God's covenant with Israel.

Perhaps one should also, in this connection, ask about the Essenes. Although they, in Sanders's opinion, were 'covenantal nomists', what they believed in was a 'new' covenant. CD 6.19; 8.21; 20.12; 1QpHab. 2.3-4. Or, as CD 15.5-11 has it, the Qumran sectarians believed they were the only ones to understand God's covenant with Moses, and thus only they were true members of the covenant community:

And when the children of all those who have entered the Covenant, granted to all for ever, reach the age of enrolment, they shall swear with an oath of the Covenant. And thus shall it be during all the age of wickedness for every man who repents of his corrupted way. On the day that he speaks to

14. On the background of this text in Jewish eschatological speculation, see my article, 'Romans 11.11-15: A Suggestion', *PerspRelStud* 12 (1985), pp. 23-30.

15. On this see esp. F. Hahn, 'Das Problem alter christologischer Überlieferungen in der Apostelgeschichte unter besonderer Berücksichtigung von Act 3.19-21', in *Les Actes des Apôtres: Tradition, rédaction, théologie* (ed. J. Kremer; BETL, 48; Gembloux/Leuven: J. Duculot/Leuven University Press, 1979), pp. 129-54.

the Guardian of the Congregation, they shall enrol him with the oath of the
Covenant which Moses made with Israel, the Covenant to return to the Law
of Moses with a whole heart and soul, to whatever is found should be done
at that time.[16]

Yet while the Essenes did not see eye to eye with their contemporaries
concerning God's covenant with Israel, they still looked forward to
Israel's ultimate salvation. 1QSa 1.1-2 opens with this: 'This is the Rule
for the congregation of Israel in the last days, when they shall join [the
Community to wa]lk according to the laws of the sons of Zadok the
Priests and of the men of the Covenant... ' (Vermes). Why will Israel be
saved? It cannot be because her people now are members of the true
covenantal community. The Essenes knew themselves to be a minority.[17]
One suspects that the postulation of eschatological redemption was simply
taken over from Scripture (e.g. Ezek. 37.5-6, 12-14; Hos. 2.23). But
whatever the reason, the Essenes maintained a restoration eschatology
while simultaneously holding the majority of Jews to be (for the present
anyway) outside the covenant. What follows for our purposes? Although
Jesus certainly carried on a mission to Israel in the name of the God of
Israel and was a proponent of restoration eschatology, this by itself will
not enable us to understand what he made of the covenant or whether
he was in fact a 'covenantal nomist'.

3. *Jesus and the Law*

Sanders's second cause for classifying Jesus as a 'covenantal nomist' is
this: 'he accepted obedience to the law as the norm' (p. 336). The discussion that leads to this conclusion is on pp. 245-69 ('The Law'). Here
Sanders argues, and I think rightly, that in the synoptic tradition one
finds no firm evidence that would allow us to speak of Jesus opposing
or rejecting the Torah (cf. p. 269). No texts typically cited to this effect
are authentic or will bear the (mis)interpretations put upon them. The
few truly dominical sayings that might at first glance be taken to indicate
otherwise—the saying on divorce, the prediction of the temple's
destruction, and the call to let the dead bury the dead—show something
else, namely Jesus' 'view that the current dispensation is not final'
(p. 252). That is to say, they imply that Jesus, with his eschatological

16. Trans. of G. Vermes, *The Dead Sea Scrolls in English* (New York: Penguin,
2nd edn, 1975), p. 108.

17. Discussion in Sanders, *Paul and Palestinian Judaism*, pp. 240-57.

outlook, held the Mosaic dispensation to be near its end. While the law could not be freely transgressed, and while it remained authoritative, the new age was at hand, and this led to a certain ambiguity in Jesus' attitude towards Moses. (Sanders does not discuss whether Jesus believed in a new or messianic Torah, and perhaps this silence on the matter is wisdom. Our texts simply do not address the issue. It should be observed, however, that W.D. Davies once concluded, 'there were elements inchoate in the Messianic hope of Judaism, which could make it possible for some to regard the Messianic Age as marked by a New Torah, new indeed... not in the sense that it contravened the old, but yet not merely in the sense that it affirmed the old on a new level, but in such a way as to justify the adjective חדש that was applied to it'.[18] This conclusion may now find unexpected confirmation in 11QTemple. The nature of this peculiar document is, obviously, open to discussion; but Ben Zion Wacholder has made an intriguing case for its having been some sort of replacement for the Mosaic Torah.[19] Whether or not he will prove to be correct in this, the way in which the author of 11QTemple alters—sometimes considerably—the text of the Pentateuch, should move one to serious reflection. Perhaps Jesus' conviction that the Mosaic dispensation was not final has a sort of parallel in the attitude of the author of 11QTemple.)

Sanders's conclusion about Jesus and the law contributes to what may be a growing tendency in Gospel studies. More than one recent investigator has found reason to believe that Jesus' attitude towards the Torah may not have been as far removed from Mt. 5.17-18 as most have heretofore claimed.[20] Sanders may even, in fact, have underestimated Jesus' legal conservatism. Although maintaining that Jesus himself did not break the law, Sanders does assert, on the basis of Mt. 8.22 = Lk. 9.60 and texts about the 'sinners', that Jesus may have acted on the premise that those who followed him were not bound to fulfil the Torah

18. W.D. Davies, *The Setting of the Sermon on the Mount* (Cambridge: Cambridge University Press), p. 184.

19. B. Zion Wacholder, *The Dawn of Qumran: The Sectarian Torah and the Teacher of Righteousness* (Cincinnati: Hebrew Union College Press, 1983).

20. Noteworthy are A.E. Harvey, *Jesus and the Constraints of History* (Philadelphia: Westminster Press, 1982), pp. 36-65; G. Vermes, *Jesus and the World of Judaism* (Philadelphia: Fortress Press, 1983), pp. 44-47; and D.J. Moo, 'Jesus and the Authority of the Mosaic Law', *JSNT* 20 (1984), pp. 3-49.

in every detail. But Mt. 8.22 = Lk. 9.60 cannot prove this much,[21] and I am rather unsure about Sanders's view of the ministry to the 'sinners' (see below). Thus in my judgment, Jesus, despite his convictions about the non-finality of the Mosaic dispensation, did not break the Torah, nor did he encourage others to break it. Having, however, concluded this much, does Jesus' law-abiding attitude make him, as Sanders suggests, a 'covenantal nomist'? One may well doubt it. Law and covenant go together. To accept the one is to accept the other, and to reject the one is to reject the other. What, then, if, as apparently was the case with Jesus, the enduring nature of the Torah be called into question? How would this affect one's view of the covenant? The answer to this puzzle cannot be returned in the abstract: only the synoptic texts will give us the answer (if it can be recovered at all). Nevertheless, the idea that Moses would be surpassed might naturally have been joined with the idea that the old covenant too would be surpassed. This is all the more true because if Jewish tradition is ambiguous about the new Torah, it is not ambiguous about the new covenant. Jer. 31.31-34 is explicit:

> Behold, the days are coming, says the Lord, when I will make a new covenant with the house of Israel and the house of Judah, not like the covenant which I made with their fathers when I took them by the hand to bring them out of the land of Egypt, my covenant which they broke, though I was their husband, says the Lord. But this is the covenant which I will make with the house of Israel after those days, says the Lord: I will put my law within them, and I will write it upon their hearts; and I will be

21. Vermes, *World*, p. 167 n. 57, regards Jesus' saying about the dead burying the dead as 'rhetorical exaggeration'. He writes: 'to see in this logion a head-on clash between Jesus and the law and pious custom is, I believe, a complete misunderstanding of the gospel message'. On his reading, Mt. 8.22 = Lk. 9.60 was no more intended to overthrow the Law than Jesus' injunction to 'hate' father and mother (Lk. 14.26; cf. Mt. 10.37) was intended to do away with one of the ten commandments. In favour of Vermes's interpretation is a fact Sanders does not consider. One can detect in the synoptic tradition a tendency to tone down sayings that might be seen as undermining the authority of the Torah. Thus Luke or the editor of Q found Lk. 16.16 ('The Law and the prophets were until John; since then... ') potentially problematic and therefore added to it Lk. 16.17: 'But it is easier for heaven and earth to pass away than for one dot of the Law to become void'. And Matthew (assuming the truth of the two-document hypothesis) was moved to drop Mk 7.19c ('He declared all foods clean'). Yet neither Matthew nor Luke was sufficiently troubled by Mt. 8.22 = Lk. 9.60 so as to leave it out or to modify it in any significant way. They apparently were not disturbed by it. This is especially significant for Matthew, given his stated estimation of the Mosaic Torah (5.17-19).

their God, and they shall be my people. And no longer shall each man teach his neighbor and each his brother, saying, 'Know the Lord', for they shall all know me, from the least of them to the greatest, says the Lord; for I will forgive their iniquity, and I will remember their sin no more.[22]

Given Jesus' eschatological perspective and his conviction about the temporal status of the Mosaic law, how could we be surprised if the New Testament indicated that he spoke of a new covenant?

4. A New Covenant?

If Mk 2.21-22 does, as the vast majority of scholars have supposed, reproduce a dominical word,[23] Jesus was conscious of a changing in the times: something new had arrived:

No one sews a piece of unshrunk cloth on an old garment; if he does, the patch tears away from it, the new from the old, and a worse tear is made. And no one puts new wine into old wineskins; if he does, the wine will burst the skins, and the wine is lost, and so are the skins; but new wine is for fresh skins.

Did Jesus' awareness of a new historical situation ever express itself in terms of a new covenant? Mk 14.24 = Mt. 26.28 and Lk. 22.20 = 1 Cor. 11.25 purport that he did. There are, admittedly, notorious disagreements in wording between the four earliest accounts of Jesus' words at the last supper; but Matthew, Mark, Luke and Paul all have Jesus speak of the διαθήκη, the latter two adding what is implicit in the former, καινή ('new covenant', cf. Jer. 31.31-34). A reference to Exod. 24.7-8[24] seems manifest, as does the meaning: God is initiating a new covenantal relationship through the blood of sacrifice. The only real question concerns authenticity. Do we really know what Jesus said to his disciples as he ate with them for the last time? The arguments pro and con are well known and will not be rehearsed here.[25] For what it is

22. Discussion in Davies, *Setting*, pp. 122-30.

23. See F. Hahn, 'Die Bildworte vom neuen Flicken und vom jungen Wein', *EvT* 31 (1971), pp. 357-75.

24. 'Then he took the book of the covenant, and read it in the hearing of the people; and they said, "All that the Lord has spoken we will do, and we will be obedient". And Moses took the blood and threw it upon the people, and said, "Behold the blood of the covenant which the Lord has made with you in accordance with all these words".'

25. For recent discussion, see R. Pesch, *Das Abendmahl und Jesu Todesverständnis* (QD, 80; Freiburg: Herder, 1978), pp. 69-89; F. Hahn, 'Das Abendmahl

worth, I for one am inclined to believe that Jesus himself first uttered Mk 14.24. Yet even if another opinion be held, it remains certain that Mk 14.24 par. was formulated at a very early time. It is already tradition for Paul (1 Cor. 11.25). So at least someone within the primitive Christian community believed in a new covenant and believed that Jesus did also. This puts the idea of a new covenant very near the birth of Christianity. Can we go farther? Perhaps not. Nevertheless three facts stare us in the face. (1) Jesus was baptized by one who apparently denied the salvific significance of the Abrahamic covenant (see above). (2) The first Christians believed in a new covenant and handed down a saying in which Jesus himself gave expression to the idea. (3) Jesus had an eschatological outlook and implied that the Mosaic dispensation was coming to its conclusion. Given all this, one has to reckon seriously with the proposal that Jesus envisioned the establishment of a new, eschatological covenant between God and his people.

But even if one concedes the force of the points just made, the issue of 'covenantal nomism' would not thereby be settled. Jesus was evidently convinced of the impermanence of the Mosaic dispensation. Yet he did not set aside the authority of Moses. Similarly, he could have believed that God would soon inaugurate a new covenant while holding that this did not change the validity of 'covenantal nomism' for the present. Was this, however, indeed the case? 'Covenantal nomism' is not taught in the Gospels. This is because, as I shall presently try to show, its place has been taken by something else.

5. *Christology and Salvation*

Mk 14.24 par., if it is authentic, implies that Jesus interpreted his impending death in sacrificial terms. No doubt many modern scholars would, rightly or wrongly, shy away from this conclusion. Fortunately, therefore, Mk 14.24 is only one of several texts pointing in the same direction, namely, towards the association of salvation with the person of Jesus. The most important such text is Lk. 12.8-9 = Mt. 10.32-33 (cf. Mk 8.38). The original probably ran:

und Jesu Todesverständnis', *TheolRev* 76 (1984), pp. 265-72; H. Schürmann, *Jesu ureigener Tod: Exegetische Besinnungen und Ausblick* (Freiburg: Herder, 1975), pp. 68-96; A. Vögtle, 'Todesankündigungen und Todesverständnis Jesu', in *Der Tod Jesu: Deutungen im Neuen Testament* (ed. K. Kertelge; QD, 74: Freiburg: Herder, 1976), pp. 51-113.

> Truly I say to you, he who acknowledges me before men, the Son of man
> will acknowledge before the angels of God; but he who denies me before
> men, the Son of man will deny him before the angels of God.[26]

Whatever meaning one conjectures for 'Son of man', the saying just
quoted makes the fate of human beings at the eschatological judgment
hinge upon their response to the man Jesus. The thought is remarkable.
When first uttered it must have seemed, to say the least, presumptuous.
But it is precisely the thought of a connection between salvation and
Jesus which makes the ministry of Jesus intelligible. Without that
thought, one has great difficulty making sense of the Gospels (or in
accounting for the rise of the church). With that thought, all falls into
place. By way of illustration, consider the fact, generally acknowledged,
that Jesus chose twelve disciples.[27] What did he intend by this act?
Almost certainly he wanted to create a symbol for the eschatological
restoration of the twelve tribes (cf. Sanders, pp. 98-106). The important
point for us is this: Jesus himself stood outside the symbolic group. He
was not one of the twelve. He was instead the one who chose the
twelve. He was their leader. Who then did Jesus think himself to be? It is
hard to avoid the inference that he conceived of himself as some sort of
king, the leader-to-be of the restored people of God. What follows? A
man who took himself to be the destined king of Israel might also have
redefined salvation vis-à-vis himself and his work. This is especially so
granted Jesus' admiration for John the Baptist, who declared that 'God
is able to raise up from these stones children to Abraham'. It would not
make sense for those who did not acknowledge their king to share in his
kingdom. How could one reject God's viceroy and not risk damnation?
If Jesus did indeed think himself king or, which amounts to the same
thing, 'Messiah', the audacious and egocentric Lk. 12.8-9 = Mt. 10.32-
33 would be intelligible.

26. For this reconstruction, see R. Pesch, 'Über die Autorität Jesu: Eine
Rückfrage anhand des Bekenner- und Verleugnerspruchs Lk 12.8f. par.', in *Die
Kirche des Anfangs: Für Heinz Schürmann* (ed. R. Schnackenburg, J. Ernst, and
J. Wanke; Freiburg: Herder, 1978), pp. 25-55. For interpretation, see D.C. Allison,
*The End of the Ages Has Come: An Early Interpretation of the Passion and
Resurrection of Jesus* (Philadelphia: Fortress Press, 1985), pp. 128-37.

27. See esp. R.P. Meye, *Jesus and the Twelve: Discipleship and Revelation
in Mark's Gospel* (Grand Rapids: Eerdmans, 1968), pp. 192-209 and C.K. Barrett,
The Signs of an Apostle (Philadelphia: Fortress Press, 1972), pp. 23-34.

Let us look at another dominical text, the three beatitudes in Lk. 6.20b, 21a, and b (cf. Mt. 5.3, 6).

> Blessed are you poor,
>> for yours is the kingdom of God.
> Blessed are you who mourn,
>> for you will be comforted.
> Blessed are you who hunger,
>> for you will be filled.[28]

Jesus must have formulated these words with Isa. 61.1-3 in mind.[29] The implicit christology cannot be avoided. Isa. 61.1-2 reads:

> The Spirit of the Lord is upon me, because the Lord has anointed me to bring good tidings to the poor; he has sent me to bind up the broken-hearted, to proclaim liberty to the captives, and the opening of the prison to whose who are bound; to proclaim the year of the Lord's favor, and the day of vengeance of our God; to comfort all who mourn.

The comforting of mourners and the bringing of good tidings to the poor are themselves, according to this Old Testament passage, eschatological

---

28. See W. Grimm, 'Die Hoffnung der Armen: Zu den Seligpreisungen Jesu', *TheolBeitr* 11 (1980), pp. 100-13.

29. So Grimm, 'Die Hoffnung', and H. Schürmann, *Das Lukasevangelium: Erster Teil: Kommentar zu Kap. 1.1–9.50* (HTKNT, 3/1; Freiburg: Herder, 1969), pp. 326-27; against R. Guelich, 'The Matthean Beatitudes: "Entrance Requirements" or Eschatological Beatitudes?', *JBL* 95 (1976), pp. 427-31, and H. Frankemölle, 'Die Makarismen (Mt. 5.1-12; Lk. 6.20-23): Motive und Umfang der redaktionellen Kompositionen', *BZ* 15 (1971), pp. 60-61. The most persuasive allusions to Isa. 61 occur in Mt. 5.3, 4 and 5, and in these three verses (from Q or Q^{mt}) the links with Isa. 61 do not appear in the redactional contributions of Matthew. Moreover, since the allusion to Isa. 61.1 in Mt. 5.5 (from Q^{mt}) is weaker than the allusions in 5.3 and 4, the strongest links with Isa. 61 are to be assigned not to Q^{mt} but to an earlier stage of Q. So the farther back we go, the closer the impact of Isa. 61 seems to be. Conversely, Matthew has not done much if anything to accentuate the connections between Isa. 61 and Mt. 5.3-12. Two further observations: 1. Matthew cannot be said to have drawn upon Isa. 61 independently of his tradition. Apart from the beatitudes and Mt. 11.5 (both from Q), there are no allusions to the chapter in his book. Which is to say: the first evangelist shows no special interest in Isa. 61.2. Mt. 11.5 = Lk. 7.22 ends by clearly borrowing from Isa. 61.1 ('and good news is preached to the poor'), and this is immediately followed by a beatitude: 'And blessed is he who is not offended at me'. Can this second association of Isa. 61.1 with a beatitude be treated as the fruit of coincidence? Probably not. Mt. 11.5-6 = Lk. 7.22-23 probably shows us that Jesus associated the macarism form with the Old Testament text about good news for the poor.

events. Moreover, they are the work of the figure who in the Old Testament speaks in the first person. Thus, if Jesus did utter the beatitudes, he must have done so conscious of being the eschatological herald who had been anointed by God and given the Spirit. And those who heard him would not have missed this. When it is added to this that Jesus apparently declared that blasphemy against the Spirit was unforgivable (Mk 3.28-30 par.), what would he have said about people who rejected his Spirit-inspired ministry? He might readily have come to doubt their place in the coming kingdom. And this is exactly what Lk. 12.8-9 par. seems to imply.

What I have sought to argue in the previous paragraphs is that christology is intimately related to soteriology. If Jesus thought of himself in highly exalted and important terms, then, as the Gospels have it, he might have come to speak of salvation in connection with his own person and ministry. Furthermore, if he did in fact do this, would not consistency have demanded the dismissal of traditional ideas of salvation, including conventional 'covenantal nomism'?

6. Jesus and the 'Sinners'

One of the more intriguing and important chapters in Sanders's book on Jesus is ch. 6, 'The Sinners' (pp. 174-211). Taking up suggestions made in an earlier article,[30] Sanders urges these points:

a. The 'sinners' of the Gospel tradition should not be identified with the common people or the *'amme ha-'ares*. Rather should they be identified with 'the wicked' (*resha'im*), with tax collectors and with others who had renounced the covenant.

b. The *'amme ha-'ares* were not irreligious, and they were not thought of as deprived of salvation. They were part and parcel of the religious life of Judaism.

c. 'If Jesus, by eating with tax collectors, led them to repent, repay those whom they had robbed, and leave off practising their profession, he would have become a national hero' (p. 203). No one would have been troubled if Jesus had really converted quislings.

30. E.P. Sanders, 'Jesus and the Sinners', *JSNT* 19 (1983), pp. 5-36 [reprinted in this volume].

d.   Jesus probably offended people because he offered 'sinners'
     inclusion in the Kingdom without requiring repentance as nor-
     mally understood. That is, he promised them salvation even
     though they failed to make restitution, offer sacrifice, and
     submit to the Law.

Concerning the first two points, I see no reason to demur. On the contrary, Sanders appears to have rendered a laudable service by clarifying
for New Testament scholars in a definitive manner the status of the
'amme ha-'areṣ on the one hand and of the 'wicked' on the other. This
is an important contribution which is to be heartily welcomed.[31]

Matters are different with regard to points c. and d. But before raising
questions, two more of Sanders's suggestions need to be mentioned:

e.   Unlike John the Baptist, Jesus did not make national repentance
     central to his proclamation. This is because he thought of John
     as having fulfilled the necessary task of calling the nation to
     repentance.

f.   Jesus' novel contribution was to include the 'wicked' in the
     Kingdom. This does not mean he thought all others con-
     demned. So far from this being the case Jesus seems to have
     believed that 'all Israel would be saved'.

The congruence of these two points (e. and f.) with points c. and d.
needs little comment. If Jesus did not require repentance as normally
understood (e.) and if he promised the 'sinners' a share in the kingdom
(f.), consternation would no doubt have followed (c., d.).

Let us proceed to examine each of Sanders's points separately.
Concerning c., we may think of Paul's 'conversion'. Was it the occasion
for rejoicing on the part of all Christians? Acts—and here the narrative
seems credible—tells us it was not (see 9.26). The reason? Enemies do
not become fast friends overnight. Suspicions linger. People do not
easily embrace those they have long despised. Now if Jesus had in fact
converted a tax collector or two, that is, a couple of people who were
treated with contempt by their fellow Jews and indeed regarded as
traitors, do we really know that everybody would have sounded forth a

31. See also the article by W.D. Davies and E.P. Sanders, 'Jesus from the
Semitic Point of View', in *The Cambridge History of Judaism*. III. *The Roman
Period* (ed. W.D. Davies and L. Finkelstein; Cambridge: Cambridge University
Press, forthcoming).

loud Hallelujah? If there were people who, on other grounds, were not particularly fond of Jesus, might they not have been moved to say bad things about Jesus and the tax collectors—even if these last had tried to make restoration? The answer is not obvious. If we go behind the theological issue and consider the likelihood of personal conflict between individuals, Sanders's assertion is by no means self-evident. Furthermore, texts do not always mirror life. Sanders uses the rabbinic texts to tell us how first-century Jews would have responded to Jesus' activities as these last are reconstructed by Sanders. Yet let us think concretely. The contradictions between Christianity's foundation documents and Christian history are notoriously infinite, and who would argue from the Bible that Christians in a particular situation must have acted in a particular manner? Are the Jewish sources really so different in this regard?

Concerning point d., the key to resolution may lie in a qualifying phrase added by Sanders: repentance 'as normally understood'. Perhaps Jesus did not demand of the 'wicked' what others demanded—on the basis of oral tradition which Jesus himself did not regard as authoritative. That, however, does not entail that Jesus thereby thought of himself or his followers as transgressing the Mosaic Law. Beyond this, one is a little uncomfortable with Sanders's treatment of the synoptic evidence about restitution. To begin with, while the synoptics give us several reasons why Jesus' contemporaries took offence at him, the issue of restitution is not one of these. In addition, Lk. 19.1-9 (the story of Zacchaeus) has to be dismissed as the invention of Luke or a pre-Lukan writer, and Mk 1.40-45 must also be set aside as unhistorical. Now perhaps these two synoptic stories are indeed the creations of the church. But this does not resolve the dispute. How often do the Gospel narratives really give opportunity for the notice that Jesus demanded restitution be made by 'sinners'? I count only two: the pericope of the tax collector in Mk 2.13-17 par. and the account of Zacchaeus. Of these, one does refer to restitution and the other simply passes over it in order to address more pressing topics. Thus the alleged absence of evidence on the issue at hand may be due to the nature of our sources, not the nature of Jesus' ministry.

What of point e.? This is a truly crucial issue. On the basis of such seemingly dominical materials as Mt. 11.20-25 = Lk. 10.13-15, Mt. 12.38-42 = Lk. 11.29-32, and Lk. 13.1-5, New Testament scholars have always assumed that Jesus was in large measure a preacher of repentance. The questioning of this consensus is a daring deed. Not that

Sanders goes so far as to claim that Jesus rejected the need for national repentance: it is just that Jesus left the task to his forerunner and, besides this, did not require 'sinners' to make restitution. I have already commented on the problem of restitution. What then of the claim that Jesus left the preaching of repentance more or less to John? It may land one in a paradox. Either John's ministry was successful or it was not. If it was not, we could expect Jesus to take up where John left off. But if Jesus believed John successful, how does one explain the pessimism about Israel which runs throughout the synoptics? Particularly telling is Mt. 11.16-19 = Lk. 7.31-35:

> But to what shall I compare this generation? It is like children sitting in the market places and calling to their playmates, 'We piped to you, and you did not dance; we wailed; and you did not mourn'. For John came neither eating nor drinking, and they say, 'He has a demon'; the Son of man came eating and drinking, and they say, 'Behold, a glutton and a drunkard, a friend of tax collectors and sinners!' Yet wisdom is justified by her deeds.

These lines have, as Sanders states, 'the ring of authenticity', and they speak for themselves.

There is another way of approaching the subject of repentance in the teachings of Jesus. In his book on *Paul and Palestinian Judaism*, Sanders quoted with approval G.F. Moore's definition of 'repentance': 'the reparation of injuries done to a fellow man in his person, property, or good name, the confession of sin, prayer for forgiveness, and the genuine resolve and endeavour not to fall into sin again'.[32] Four things are involved here—restitution, confession, prayer for forgiveness, and the resolve to avoid future sins. Can these four things be found in the synoptics? The need for restitution appears in Mark (1.40-45), in L (Lk. 19.1-10), and in M (Mt. 5.23-26). That the confession of sins and prayer for forgiveness were important to Jesus can be gathered from the Lord's Prayer, which presumably tells us what Jesus thought prayer should be all about: 'Forgive us our debts, as we forgive our debtors'. Finally, the resolve not to sin is implicit throughout the Gospels. All of Jesus' moral demands presuppose the avoidance of sin and the resolution to tread the narrow way (cf. Mt. 7.13-14 = Lk. 13.24). Compare Mk 9.43-47: 'If your hand causes you to sin, cut it off...' All this does

---

32. G.F. Moore, *Judaism in the First Centuries of the Christian Era: The Age of the Tannaim*, I (Cambridge, MA: Harvard University Press, 1927), p. 117; quoted by Sanders, *Paul and Palestinian Judaism*, p. 175.

not, to be sure, prove that Jesus issued a summons for Israel's corporate repentance. It does, however, demonstrate that at least the themes associated with the repentance of individuals found a place in Jesus' preaching. When to this one adds (1) Jesus' disappointment in Israel's response to God's messengers (see above), and (2) the fact that, according to Paul, Acts, and the Gospels, the early church called Israel to repent and embrace the Messiah, it is not easy to envision a Jesus little concerned with the repentance of God's people Israel.

In view of the evidence and general considerations, the widespread agreement that Jesus called Israel to repentance stands. The evidence may not be as extensive as Sanders thinks it should be, but it is extensive enough. Moreover, there is a good explanation for the apparent paucity of material. According to both Mark (6.7-13) and Q (Lk. 10.1-16; cf. Mt. 9.37-38; 10.7-16), Jesus sent out his disciples on a preaching mission. There is no good reason to doubt this.[33] The only question is: What did the disciples preach? Mark says they preached repentance (Mk 6.12). Nothing could be more plausible. With John the Baptist in prison or already dead, it would make perfect sense for Jesus to instruct his disciples to continue John's renewal movement. In this connection, Lk. 13.6-9 is possibly instructive:

> And he told this parable: 'A man had a fig tree planted in his vineyard; and he came seeking fruit on it and found none. And he said to the vinedresser, "Lo, these three years I have come seeking fruit on this fig tree, and I find none. Cut it down; why should it use up the ground?" And he answered him, "Let it alone, sir, this year also till I dig about it and put on manure. And if it bears fruit this next year, well and good; but if not, you may cut it down."'

John the Baptist preached repentance and told how the axe was already laid at the root of the tree (Mt. 3.10 = Lk. 3.9). Sometime later Jesus announced the presence of an unexpected period of grace: the axe had not yet struck the tree, a short respite had come. It is natural to identify this respite with the period of Jesus and his disciples, as the time of Israel's second chance, her last opportunity to repent and bear fruit. And such an interpretation enables us to comprehend why the Gospels are not from one end to the other filled with words about repentance. The task started by John was primarily carried on by Jesus' disciples, and

---

33. Cf. F. Hahn, *Mission in the New Testament* (trans. F. Clarke; STB, 47: London: SCM Press, 1965), pp. 41-46 and M. Hengel, *The Charismatic Leader and his Followers* (trans. J. Greig; New York: Crossroad, 1981), pp. 73-80.

what we have in the synoptics is not page after page of what they—and John the Baptist—said over and over again but rather page after page of what Jesus purportedly said (and mostly to his disciples, not to outsiders).

Coming finally to point f., Sanders suggests that Jesus scandalized his fellow Jews because he included the 'sinners' in the kingdom without instructing them to make restitution as traditionally understood. What offended people was Jesus' *inclusivity*. I am inclined to think this turns everything upside down. What offended was Jesus' *exclusivity*. Jesus did not assume the salvation of pious Israelites and then go on to add the 'wicked' to the redemption rolls. Starting instead with a Christocentric view of things, from the assumption that he himself was the destined king of Israel, Jesus redefined salvation with reference to his own person. And what he required of all Israelites, including the 'sinners', was acceptance of God's eschatological representative. So, as in the parable of the banquet (Mt. 22.1-10 = Lk. 14.15-24), an invitation went out to all. The scandal of Jesus was therefore two-fold. First, in the new eschatological situation the 'sinners' and all other Israelites were put on an equal footing: both were in need of recognizing their king and his cause. Secondly, although Jesus' way of salvation did not overturn the Law, it displaced Law and covenant from the scheme of salvation. Salvation was no longer viewed as faithfulness to God's covenant and obedience to the Torah. Salvation was rather acceptance of and faithfulness to Jesus' way. 'He who acknowledges me before man…'

It should be stressed that my position is not so far from Sanders as it may at first appear. In Sanders's judgment, Jesus permitted the 'wicked' to enter the kingdom of God if they followed their appointed king. With this important verdict I concur, with the caveat that following Jesus never meant relativizing Moses. Sanders, however, is almost certainly wrong in asserting that what Jesus asked of the 'sinners' he asked of no one else. This is the crux of the matter, and the point at which Sanders is the most liable to criticism. One simply cannot come away from the Gospels or even from a very critical sifting of them with the impression that good Israelites are saved just because they are in the covenant. The question of who is 'in' is completely open, for a decision is required of everybody. In line with this, one of the notes most frequently sounded in the synoptic tradition is that of judgment. Jesus declares again and again that a harsh divine judgment is coming and that it will fall upon the people in Israel (Mt. 7.13-14, 15-20, 21-23, 24-27; 10.15, 32-33; 11.20-23; etc.). If in this respect the Gospels are not reliable, then as sources for the teaching of Jesus they must be utterly unyielding land. But if they are accurate in this matter, Jesus could not but have believed that all Israel would be winnowed and indeed that many would suffer damnation (cf. Mt. 13.24-30, 47-50). The proclamation of judgment did not take salvation for granted but presupposed that people were in peril. Descent from Abraham and obedience to the Law were not by themselves going to get anyone through the gates. Why not? Because the one thing needful was recognition of God's eschatological viceroy.

One final remark. If Jesus did not adopt the soteriological position I have attributed to him, that is, if he, as Sanders has it, took for granted, on the basis of 'covenantal nomism', the eschatological salvation of 'all Israel', there would appear to be a yawning chasm between Jesus and his post-Easter followers. For despite a few recent assertions to the contrary,[34] the New Testament nowhere holds that salvation is to be found apart from Jesus, the Messiah and Son of God. Although this may ride

34. See esp. L. Gaston, 'Paul and the Torah', in *Anti-Semitism and the Foundations of Christianity* (ed. A. Davies; New York: Paulist Press, 1979), pp. 48-71 and J.G. Gager, *The Origins of Anti-Semitism: Attitudes toward Judaism in Pagan and Christian Antiquity* (New York: Oxford University Press, 1983), pp. 193-264. According to both of these scholars, Paul believed in the salvation of Israel apart from Jesus Christ. Cf. K. Stendahl, *Paul among Jews and Gentiles and Other Essays* (Philadelphia: Fortress Press, 1976), p. 4. He observes that 'Paul does not say that when the time of God's kingdom, the consummation, comes Israel will accept the Messiah. He says only that the time will come when "all Israel will be saved" ([Rom.] 11.26).' The inference left for the reader is obvious, but is it correct? 1. Rom. 11.25-27 is not introduced as tradition but as a mystery apparently unknown to the recipients of Paul's letter: 'For I do not want you to be ignorant, brethren...' (cf. Rom. 1.13; 1 Cor. 12.1; 1 Thess. 4.13). This shows that the salvation of Israel was hardly taken for granted by the early church and was moreover not manifest from anything that had come before in Romans. 2. Rom. 11.13-14 reads: 'Inasmuch then as I am an apostle to the Gentiles, I magnify my ministry in order to stir my fellow Jews to emulation and thus save some of them'. Surely the implication of this sentence is that even for the Jew salvation is and will be in Jesus Christ. 3. The 'Deliverer [who] will come from Zion' (Rom. 11.26) is probably to be identified with Jesus Christ (cf. 1 Thess. 1.10), so the Jews will be saved by the Messiah. 4. When Paul speaks of the general resurrection, it is always and only those 'in Christ' who are the participants (cf. 1 Cor. 15.20-23; 1 Thess. 4.13-18). For further discussion of whether there are two ways of salvation in Paul, see E.P. Sanders, 'Paul's Attitude Toward the Jewish People', *USQR* 33 (1978), pp. 175-87; *idem, Paul, the Law, and the Jewish People*, pp. 192-98; and W.D. Davies, 'Paul and the Jewish People', in *Jewish and Pauline Studies* (Philadelphia: Fortress Press, 1984), pp. 139-43.

roughshod over our modern sensibilities, it remains no less true. The New Testament does not know two ways of salvation—one in Jesus, one apart from him. Therefore, if Jesus did bind salvation to his own person, the unity of the New Testament on this matter is comprehensible and satisfying. If, on the other hand, Jesus held the view Sanders imputes to him—the 'sinners' have salvation through Jesus, other Jews have salvation through the covenant—we have a troublesome hiatus between the church and its foundation figure. For it is historically improbable that, after Easter, Jesus' disciples carried on a mission to 'the lost sheep of the house of Israel' (Mt. 10.6; 15.24) if Jesus himself never thought Israel was lost.

JSNT 20 (1984), pp. 3-49

JESUS AND THE AUTHORITY OF THE MOSAIC LAW

Douglas J. Moo

The question of the relevance of the Mosaic law for Christian ethics, a perennial theological issue, has assumed new importance with the popularity of relativistic ethics, the 'new morality'. Proponents of this approach generally reject any appeal to moral 'rules', including especially those found in the Old Testament.[1] On the other hand, sometimes in response to this approach, others stress the eternal and absolute validity of at least the Old Testament 'moral' law.[2] The debate has focused attention on the teaching and example of Jesus, to which both sides appeal for support. And an initial glance at Jesus' teaching would seem to provide support for both alternatives.[3] This article surveys some relevant aspects of Jesus' life and teaching in the hope of discovering his fundamental approach to the issue of the authority of the Mosaic law for his followers.

The breadth and complexity of the topic may make this project appear to be overly ambitious. While acknowledging the problem, the study is, I think, manageable, granted the following limitations. First, the discussion will be confined to the Synoptic Gospels. This should not be taken to imply an *a priori* rejection of the historical value of material

1. Cf. e.g. J. Fletcher, *Situation Ethics: The New Morality* (Philadelphia: Westminster Press, 1966), pp. 69-81; N. Pittenger, *Loving Says it All* (New York/Philadelphia: Pilgrim, 1978), pp. 43-44.

2. Cf. e.g. C.F.H. Henry, *Christian Personal Ethics* (Grand Rapids: Zondervan, 1957), pp. 328-53; and the more extreme position espoused by G.L. Bahnsen, *Theonomy in Christian Ethics* (Nutley, NJ: Craig, 1977), pp. 141-84.

3. W. Rordorf, *Sunday: The History of the Day of Rest and Worship in the Earliest Centuries of the Christian Church* (Philadelphia: Westminster Press, 1968), p. 78.

within the Fourth Gospel, but is simply to recognize that study of the synoptic and Johannine traditions demands different methodologies. Secondly, while some necessary reference to the history of the traditions studied will be made, the focus of the study will be on the final, canonical shape of the Jesus tradition. The validity and importance of such a focus is being increasingly recognized.[4] It is only by careful exegetical examination of the extant material in its context that the degree of coherence within the tradition, so important in making *traditionsgeschichtlich* decisions, can be assessed. The discovery of many inconsistencies and contradictions lends credence to the search for distinct traditions responsible for the various perspectives; a high degree of coherence, on the other hand, suggests either that the final redactors have molded the material into a harmonious outlook, or that we are confronted with a reflection of Jesus' own stance which has stamped its influence on all the various traditions. Certainty on this matter is impossible; but should a unanimity of viewpoint among the final redactors (the evangelists) be found, preference should be accorded to the second alternative. This indicates the need to take into consideration the perspective each evangelist brings to bear on the material. Again, however, the study is not primarily devoted to a delineation of the evangelists' theologies. A final limitation relates to the focus of the discussion. 'Jesus and the law' is a many-faceted topic involving, potentially, Jesus' attitude toward the oral law and the various forms of Jewish piety. Our investigation will be confined to the single question: to what extent and in what manner did Jesus conceive the Mosaic law to be binding on people who had entered the Kingdom of God?

Before proceeding to an analysis of the relevant passages, it will be helpful to outline briefly some representative positions on the question of Jesus' relationship to the law. While a bewildering variety of views, with varying differences in detail, has been espoused, the following list adequately summarizes the main tendencies:[5]

---

4.   See the helpful survey of this issue in B.W. Anderson, 'Tradition and Scripture in the Community of Faith', *JBL* 100 (1981), pp. 5-21. He pleads for a recognition of the validity of 'tradition which still makes its theological witness in scripture, and scripture which theologically incorporates and crystallizes biblical tradition' (p. 21).

5.   For similar outlines, though differing in the demarcation of positions, see K. Berger, *Die Gesetzesauslegung Jesu: Ihr historischer Hintergrund im Judentum und im Alten Testament* (WMANT, 40.1; Neukirchen-Vluyn: Neukirchener Verlag,

1. Jesus summarily abrogated the law. While requiring mention, this view is almost universally rejected by serious scholars.[6]

2. Jesus' teaching is a new law, the Messianic law, which replaces the Mosaic law.[7]

3. Jesus is the last and greatest expositor of the law of God. He entirely upholds the moral law, showing complete obedience to its demands in his own life, and demonstrating in his teaching the original intent of the law's demands.[8]

4. Jesus 'radicalized' the law, intensifying the demands of the law beyond what they originally included. This 'Toraverscharfung', carried out on the basis of Jesus' immediate awareness of the will of God[9] and/or the paramount demand of love,[10] results in the abrogation of some commands.[11]

1972), pp. 4-9; R. Banks, *Jesus and the Law in the Synoptic Tradition* (SNTSMS, 28; Cambridge: Cambridge University Press, 1975), pp. 2-9.

6.   The impossibility of understanding the position and debates of the early church if Jesus has simply abrogated it is usually cited as a determinative factor. Cf. A. Harnack, 'Hat Jesus das alttestamentliche Gesetz abgeschafft?', in *Aus Wissenschaft und Leben* (Giessen: Töpelmann, 1911), II, p. 228; R. Bultmann, *Theology of the New Testament* (New York: Charles Scribner's Sons, 1951), I, p. 16; W.D. Davies, *The Setting of the Sermon on the Mount* (Cambridge: Cambridge University Press, 1964), p. 428.

7.   This position is usually identified in Matthew's Gospel. Cf. B.W. Bacon, 'Jesus and the Law: A Study of the First "Book" of Matthew (Mt. 3–7)', *JBL* 47 (1928), pp. 203-31. Davies finds fewer Mosaic traits and is more cautious in speaking of a new law, but finds a 'Messianic torah' in Matthew (*Setting*, pp. 94-107).

8.   This was the position held by most of the reformers (cf. H.K. McArthur, *Understanding the Sermon on the Mount* [London: Epworth Press, 1960], p. 36). Among modern scholars: Henry, *Ethics*, p. 316; Bahnsen, *Theonomy*, pp. 141-83; H. Ridderbos, *The Coming of the Kingdom* (Philadelphia: Presbyterian and Reformed, 1962), p. 314; N.B. Stonehouse, *The Witness of the Synoptic Gospels to Christ* (combining *The Witness of Matthew and Mark to Christ* and *The Witness of Luke to Christ*) (Grand Rapids: Baker, 1979 [1944]), pp. 197-211. Hans Windisch (*The Meaning of the Sermon on the Mount* [Philadelphia: Westminster Press, 1951], pp. 132-50) argues that Jesus stayed essentially within the framework of Judaism in his attitude to the law.

9.   Cf. W.G. Kümmel, 'Jesus und der jüdische Traditionsgedanke', *ZNW* 33 (1934), pp. 121-27.

10.   Cf. W. Gutbrod, 'νόμος', *TDNT*, IV, p. 1063.

11.   Late in the nineteenth and early in the twentieth centuries, scholars especially stressed the 'prophetic' character of Jesus' approach to the law (Harnack, 'Gesetz', pp. 230-34; B.H. Branscomb, *Jesus and the Law of Moses* [New York: Richard A.

5. Jesus intensified the requirements of the law and brought new demands of his own, without however clearly abrogating any moral commands.[12]

6. Jesus' teaching *fulfills* the law, in the sense that the law pointed forward to his teaching. His demands move in a different sphere, above and apart from the law, whose continuing validity exists only in and through him.[13]

This general survey enables us to isolate several key questions which are crucial for our purposes. First, what does Jesus' own behavior imply about his view of the law? Secondly, did Jesus establish a critical principle(s) by which the validity and meaning of the Mosaic commands could be evaluated? Thirdly, what was the place of the Old Testament in Jesus' ethical teaching? Fourthly, did Jesus, in fact, implicitly or explicitly teach the abrogation of any commandment? Fifthly, what did Jesus claim would be the effect on the law of his coming? These questions furnish the outline for the study.

Smith, 1930], pp. 262-66; C.G. Montefiore, *Some Elements of the Religious Teaching of Jesus according to the Synoptic Gospels* [New York: Arno, 1973], p. 44). More recently, Jesus' approach to the law has been compared with that of the Qumran sectarians (H. Braun, *Spätjüdische-häretischer und frühchristlicher Radikalismus: Jesus von Nazareth und die essenische Qumransekte* [2 vols.; BHT, 24.2; Tübingen: Mohr, 2nd edn, 1959]). Probably the majority of modern scholars hold something like this general view.

12. This seems to have been the dominant view in the Patristic period (cf. McArthur, *Sermon*, pp. 26-32). E. Percy (*Die Botschaft Jesu: Eine traditions-kritische und exegetische Untersuchung* [Lunds Universitets Årsskrift, n.s. 49; Lund: Gleerup, 1953], pp. 122-23) concluded: '...dass Jesus im Gesetz die Offenbarung des Willens Gottes gesehen zu haben scheint, aber eine Offenbarung, die in gewissen Fällen die tatsächliche Beschaffenheit der Menschen berücksichtigt und deshalb in solchen Fällen überboten werden muss, wenn Gottes Willen in Bezug auf die Menschen völlig verwirklicht werden soll'. Cf. also P.G. Verweijs, *Evangelium und neues Gesetz in der ältesten Christenheit bis auf Marcion* (Domplein/Utrecht: Kemink en Zoon, 1960), pp. 350-51.

13. Banks argues for this position in his important monograph, *Jesus and the Law in the Synoptic Tradition*. His basic position is accepted by J.P. Meier (*Law and History in Matthew's Gospel* [AnBib, 71; Rome: Biblical Institute Press, 1976], pp. 87-88).

Jesus' Personal Observance of the Law

Robert Banks, in the most important modern treatment of Jesus and the law, correctly stresses the need to distinguish among the written law, the oral and customs in assessing Jesus' relationship to the Judaism of his day.[14] With respect to the written law, it cannot be demonstrated that Jesus personally violated any of its commands.[15] He is seen in attendance at the great festivals in Jerusalem, pays the half-shekel temple tax (Mt. 17.24-27), wears the prescribed tassel on his robe (Mt. 9.20; cf. Num. 15.38-41) and, whatever may be said about his teaching on the subject of commands relating to the Sabbath and ritual purity, he does not transgress them.[16]

While it has been argued that Jesus displays an equal fidelity to the oral law,[17] it seems, on the contrary, that a clearer distinction can be made. His association with various 'impure' elements of society and his non-emergency Sabbath healings are rather clear infringements of the accepted *halaka*.[18] However, the verdict that there is no evidence Jesus kept *any* of the oral law cannot be sustained;[19] his regular attendance at synagogue services and his habits at meals and in prayer suggest behavior in conformity with, if not in obedience to, the oral law.[20] With

14. *Jesus and the Law*, pp. 90-91. Branscomb (*Jesus and the Law*, pp. 126-28) contests the validity of separating the oral from the written law, but against this it must be maintained that as long as a significant Jewish group (the Sadducees) rejected the validity of the oral law, such a distinction is not only possible but necessary.

15. Gutbrod, 'νόμος', *TDNT*, IV, p. 1062. R. MacKintosh (*Christ and the Jewish Law* [London: Hodder & Stoughton, 1886], pp. 59-62) who argues this notes that Jesus was not accused of law-breaking at his trial.

16. Jesus' contact with ritually unclean people in the course of his healing ministry cannot be viewed as a transgression of the law, since this kind of activity is hardly covered in the law (Banks, *Jesus and the Law*, p. 105).

17. Branscomb, *Jesus and the Law*, pp. 170-74. G. Barth argues that, at least in Matthew, the oral law is not rejected as such ('Matthew's Understanding of the Law', in *Tradition and Interpretation in Matthew*, by G. Bornkamm, G. Barth and H.J. Held [Philadelphia: Westminster Press, 1963], pp. 86-89).

18. The deliberateness and frequency with which Jesus performs miracles on the Sabbath suggests that more than 'isolated incidents' are involved (as argued by M. Hubaut, 'Jésus et la loi de Moïse', *RTL* 7 [1976], p. 406).

19 Contra Banks, *Jesus and the Law*, pp. 237-38.

20. Branscomb, *Jesus and the Law*, pp. 126-28. Banks argues that Jesus attended the synagogue solely to minister (regarding κατὰ τὸ εἰωθός in Lk. 4.16 as a reference to habits of ministering [cf. Acts 17.2]) (*Jesus and the Law*, p. 91). But

respect to both the oral law and the customs of his day, Jesus' behavior seems to have been dictated more by the needs of the ministry than by a sense of subservience.[21]

That the synoptic tradition portrays a Jesus fundamentally subservient in his behavior to the written law is clear, but it is impossible to infer from this that Jesus wished his followers to observe it equally faithfully.[22] Apart from an obvious problem inherent in this argument (there is no evidence that Jesus was less faithful to the stipulations of the 'ceremonial' law than to the 'moral'), it suffers from a basic failure to recognize the place of Jesus' ministry in the history of revelation. While Jesus' coming undoubtedly inaugurated a decisively new era in the *Heilsgeschichte*, the period of time before the culminative redemptive events of the Cross and Resurrection remains one of transition in which elements of the previous dispensation persist. Jesus' adherence to the written law *could* simply reflect an aspect of the old age which was destined to pass away in the new age.[23] Thus, the evidence from Jesus' personal observance of the law is, *taken by itself*, of almost no value for our purposes and, again, the need to determine Jesus' view of the role of the law in the new age is indicated.

Critical Principles for the Evaluation of Commands

It is frequently asserted that Jesus established love for others, or humanitarian considerations, as a principle on the basis of which the meaning and applicability of Old Testament commands could be evaluated. The passage which most clearly suggests such an interpretation is the 'Great Commandment' pericope (Mt. 22.34-40; Mk 12.28-34; cf. Lk. 10.25-28[24]). In response to the question of an inquirer, 'Which is the greatest

it is more likely that such ministry grew out of regular attendance for worship (R. Nixon, 'Fulfilling the Law: The Gospels and Acts', in *Law, Morality and the Bible* [ed. B. Kaye and G. Wenham; Downers Grove, IL: InterVarsity Press, 1978], p. 60).

21. Banks, *Jesus and the Law*, pp. 99, 237-38.

22. *Pace* MacKintosh, *Christ and the Law*, pp. 59-62.

23. Cf. the position adopted by W.D. Davies ('Mt. 5.17, 18', in *Christian Origins and Judaism* [Philadelphia: Westminster Press, 1962], pp. 50-58).

24. The narrative in Lk. 10.25-28, in which a lawyer in response to Jesus' question about his understanding of the law enunciates the two love commandments, is probably the description of a separate incident from that in Matthew/Mark. (As T.W. Manson says [*The Sayings of Jesus* (Grand Rapids: Eerdmans, 1979 [1957]), pp. 259-60], '...the chief connecting link, the conjunction of the great

commandment in the law?',[25] Jesus cites two texts from the Pentateuch, which respectively command love for God (Deut. 6.5) and love for one's neighbor (Lev. 19.18).[26] The conjunction of the commands clearly suggests that, for Jesus, love for God and love for others are inseparable and *together* constitute the 'greatest' commandment (note particularly Matthew's 'the second is like it').[27]

commandments, is precisely the sort of thing that would appear over and over again'. Cf. also C.E.B. Cranfield, *The Gospel according to Saint Mark* [CGTC; Cambridge: Cambridge University Press, 1966], p. 376; I.H. Marshall, *The Gospel of Luke* [NIGTC; Grand Rapids: Eerdmans, 1978], pp. 440-41; Banks, *Jesus and the Law*, p. 164. For an alternative view, cf. V.P. Furnish, *The Love Command in the New Testament* [Nashville/New York: Abingdon Press, 1972], pp. 36-38).

25. μεγάλη is almost certainly an example of the Hellenistic tendency to use the positive with a superlative meaning (BDF, §245 [2]; M. Zerwick, *Biblical Greek* [Scripta Pontificii Instituti Biblici, 114; Rome: Pontifical Biblical Institute, 1963], pp. 48-49).

26. In Mark, the command to love is prefaced with the *Shema* (Deut. 6.4), which some have taken as an indication of a Hellenistic missionary provenance for Mark's tradition (G. Bornkamm, 'Das Doppelgebot der Liebe', in *Neutestamentliche Studien für Rudolf Bultmann* [BZNW, 21; Berlin: Töpelmann, 1954], pp. 87-88). That Mark has Gentile readers in mind is not improbable, but it is unnecessary to suppose that he has added the *Shema*; for it comes immediately before the command to love God in Deuteronomy and was, of course, a prominent element in the Jewish liturgy. As such, it is more likely that Matthew has *omitted* it with Jewish readers in mind (J. Moffatt, *Love in the New Testament* [London: Hodder & Stoughton, 1929], p. 120).

27. Furnish, *Love Command*, pp. 26-27; D. Hill, *The Gospel of Matthew* (NCB; London: Oliphants, 1972), p. 307. Some of the ethical implications of this combination are explored by R. Schnackenburg in 'Mitmenschlichkeit im Horizont des Neuen Testaments' (*Die Zeit Jesu* [Festschrift H. Schlier; ed. G. Bornkamm and K. Rahner; Freiburg/Basel/Vienna: Herder, 1970], pp. 70-92.

The combination of these two virtues as summarizing morality has parallels in Jewish literature; cf. especially *T. Iss.* 5.2; 7.6; *T. Dan* 5.3; Philo, *Abr.* 208; *Spec. Leg.* 2.63. Because these summaries stem from Hellenistic Judaism, it has been argued that the double love command of the Gospels must have a Hellenistic provenance (Berger, *Gesetzesauslegung*, pp. 136-89; C. Burchard, 'Das doppelte Liebesgebot in der frühen christlichen Überlieferung', in *Der Ruf Jesu und die Antwort der Gemeinde* [Festschrift J. Jeremias; ed. E. Lohse; Göttingen: Vandenhoeck & Ruprecht, 1970], pp. 53-57). But the explicit reference to scriptural commands is unique to the Gospel tradition and fundamentally distinct from the Stoic-tinged expressions in Philo and the *Testaments* (R.H. Fuller, 'The Double Commandment of Love: A Test Case for the Criteria of Authenticity', in *Essays on the Love Command* [Philadelphia: Fortress Press, 1978], pp. 48-51).

What is involved in establishing the double love commandment as the 'greatest' is explicated more fully in Jesus' concluding assertion (according to Matthew): 'on these two commandments depend [κρέμαται] all the law and the prophets'. The phrase 'law and prophets' is found only rarely in Jewish literature as a denotation of the Old Testament Scriptures but is used with this meaning in the New Testament.[28] However, Matthew's use of the term here and in 5.17 and 7.12, clearly gives a particular nuance to the phrase, so that the 'commanding' or ethical aspect of the Scriptures is highlighted.[29] Crucial for the understanding of the relationship between the 'law and the prophets' and the love commandment is the meaning of the word κρεμάννυμι. The term is often compared with the Hebrew תלוי, which is used by the rabbis in formulations similar to that in the Gospels.[30] But the purpose of the rabbis is to isolate a command or principle from which the rest of the law could be derived,[31] and this essentially scholastic exercise is foreign to the context in the Gospels.[32] A second alternative is to view the love command as constituting *the* fundamental hermeneutical principle, which can serve to discriminate among the different Old Testament laws.[33] Thirdly, the role of the love

28. 2 Macc. 15.9; *4 Macc.* 18.10; *Midr. Ps.* 90 §4; Mt. 5.17; 7.12; Lk. 16.16; 24.44; Jn 1.45; Acts 13.15; 24.14; 23.23; Rom. 3.21. Str-B (I, p. 240) note that the phrase is rare in Jewish literature; it may be that it reflects a Christian emphasis on prophecy (E. Lohmeyer, *Das Evangelium des Matthäus* [ed. W. Schmauch; MeyerK; Göttingen: Vandenhoeck & Ruprecht, 2nd edn, 1958], pp. 105-106). Berger (*Gesetzesauslegung*, p. 224) argues that the phrase denotes the canon of the Old Testament only when an explicit reference to the Scriptures is present.

29. W. Trilling, *Das wahre Israel: Studien zur Theologie des Matthäus-Evangeliums* (SANT, 10; Munich: Kösel, 1964), pp. 173-74; G. Strecker, *Der Weg der Gerechtigkeit: Untersuchungen zur Theologie des Matthäus* (FRLANT, 82: Göttingen: Vandenhoeck & Ruprecht, 1962), p. 144; A. Feuillet, 'Morale ancienne et morale chrétiene d'après Mt. V. 17-20: Comparison avec la doctrine de L'Épître aux Romains', *NTS* 17 (1970–71), p. 124.

30. E.g., *b. Ber.* 63a; Str-B I, pp. 907-908. Cf. also Berger, *Gesetzesauslegung*, p. 230; R. Schnackenburg, *The Moral Teaching of the New Testament* (New York: Seabury, 1965), p. 93.

31. Str-B I, pp. 907-908. Despite discussions as to the relative value of commandments, the rabbis maintained their theoretical equality (cf. *m. Ab.* 2.13; *b. Šab.* 31a; and E.E. Urbach, *The Sages: Their Concepts and Beliefs* [2 vols.; Jerusalem: Magnes, 1975], p. 349).

32. Furnish, *Love Command*, pp. 32-34.

33. Furnish, *Love Command*, p. 74; Branscomb, *Jesus and the Law*, p. 263. Barth

commandment as denoted by κρεμάννυμι has been compared to the hinges of a door or the nail from which objects are suspended.[34] According to this analogy, the love commandment is set apart from all others as the most basic demand of the law, but does not displace any other commandments.[35] On the basis of evidence from within the pericope, it is almost impossible to determine which of these last two alternatives should be accepted. Hence, it is necessary to postpone a decision until other relevant passages have been considered.

It is appropriate to begin with the dialogue between Jesus and the scribe immediately following Jesus' enunciation of the love commandment. This interchange, recounted only by Mark, may provide an important indication as to how he, at least, viewed the great commandment. In keeping with a prevalent Markan motif, the scribe, after expressing agreement with Jesus' formulation, goes on to assert the superiority of love over sacrifices. To this Jesus responds by declaring that the scribe is 'not far from the Kingdom of God'. Inasmuch as the sentiment here expressed has exact parallels in the prophets (e.g., Hos. 6.6) and in the rabbinic literature,[36] it is hardly legitimate to find a rejection of the sacrificial system in deference to love (and could the one 'replace' the other?).[37] In itself, this pericope indicates no more than that love for God and others is a demand of God more fundamental than the offering of sacrifices.

Mark's Gospel is alone in containing a pronouncement of Jesus which is related to the present issue: 'the Sabbath was made for man, not man for the Sabbath' (Mk 2.27). Despite the complex traditions-history, and frequent assertions to the contrary, there is insufficient justification for

('Matthew's Understanding', pp. 78-85) views love as the basis upon which Matthew re-interpreted and thereby retained the law. J.L. Houlden (*Ethics and the New Testament* [New York: Oxford University Press, 1973], p. 107) sees the love commandment as interpreting the law in Matthew, but in Mark and Luke, he claims, the law is 'rivalled and supplanted'.

34. For the former, cf. BAGD, p. 451; and C. Spicq, *Agape in the New Testament. I. Agape in the Synoptic Gospels* (St Louis/London: B. Herder, 1963), p. 30; for the latter, Bertram, 'κρεμάννυμι', *TDNT*, III, p. 920.

35. Banks, *Jesus and the Law*, p. 169.

36. Cf. *b. Suk.* 49b; *Ber.* 55a.

37. V. Taylor, *The Gospel according to St Mark* (London: Macmillan, 2nd edn, 1966), p. 489; H. Anderson, *The Gospel of Mark* (NCB; London: Oliphants, 1976), p. 282; Banks, *Jesus and the Law*, p. 168.

denying the authenticity of this verse.[38] The statement is remarkably similar to the dictum attributed to R. Simeon b. Menasya (c. AD 180): 'The Sabbath is delivered over for your sake, but you are not delivered over to the Sabbath'.[39] But Simeon is seeking only to justify technical breaches of the Sabbath *halaka* which are necessary to prevent death;[40] clearly, Jesus' application of the saying covers more than this. But how much more? To answer this, it will be necessary to study the scriptural example adduced by Jesus immediately before this saying.

All three synoptists record Jesus' appeal to 1 Sam. 21.1-6, where it is told how David and his followers ate the bread of the presence, 'which is not lawful for any but the priests to eat' (Mk 2.25-26; Mt. 12.3-4; Lk. 6.3-4). Jesus' intention in adducing this example is not clear. Often it is alleged that Jesus is seeking to excuse his disciples' behavior by asserting the priority of human needs over requirements of the ceremonial law.[41] But there is no indication whatever in Mark and Luke, and

---

38.   Verses 27-28 are frequently understood as a separate complex which has been added to vv. 23-26 (Taylor, *Mark*, p. 218; R. Pesch, *Das Markusevangelium* [HTKNT; 2 vols.; Freiburg: Herder, 1977], I, pp. 178-79); some regarding only v. 28 as an authentic *logion Jesu* (F. Fils, '"Le Sabbat a été fait pour homme et non l'homme pour le Sabbat" [Mc II.27]', *RB* 69 [1962], pp. 516-23); others only v. 27 (E. Lohse, 'Jesu Worte über den Sabbat', in *Judentum, Urchristentum und Kirche* [ed. W. Eltester; BZNW, 26; Berlin; Töpelmann, 1964], pp. 84-85; A.J. Hultgren, 'The Formation of the Sabbath Pericope in Mark 2.23-28', *JBL* 91 [1972], p. 40; Taylor, *Mark*, p. 220); others neither (F.W. Beare, '"The Sabbath was Made for Man"', *JBL* 79 [1960], pp. 131-35). A thorough discussion of the verse, with extensive bibliography, is provided by F. Neirynck, 'Jesus and the Sabbath: Some Observations on Mark II.27', in *Jésus aux origines de la christologie* (ed. J. Dupont; BETL, 46; Leuven: Leuven University Press/Gembloux: Duculot, 1975), pp. 227-70.

The difficulties in accepting the authenticity of v. 27 are the presence of a parallel in Jewish literature, its omission in Matthew and Luke and the redactional καὶ ἔλεγεν αὐτοῖς which introduces it. But the last point may indicate nothing more than a break in Mark's narrative, because of the omission of material (W.L. Lane, *The Gospel according to Mark* [NICNT; Grand Rapids: Eerdmans, 1974], pp. 118-19) and Matthew and Luke may feel (as have many scholars!) that the verse interfered with the christological conclusion (Banks, *Jesus and the Law*, p. 120). The Jewish saying has a very different thrust from Jesus' application of the verse and the uniqueness of the sentiment is a strong indication of authenticity (cf. Pesch, *Markusevangelium*, I, p. 186; Marshall, *Luke*, pp. 229-30).

39.   *Mek.* Exod. 31.13.

40.   Lohse, 'Jesu Worte', p. 85.

41.   Verweijs, *Evangelium*, p. 23; Anderson, *Mark*, p. 110.

little in Matthew ('they were hungry'), that the disciples were in any need.[42] The contrast with the rabbinic approach to the passage is instructive: they sought to justify David's action by suggesting that he was in danger of starving to death.[43] Other scholars assert that Jesus is simply correcting the current interpretation of the Sabbath law by pointing out that the Scripture itself allows greater leniency than do the Pharisees.[44] This approach has the merit of noting that the action of the disciples is a breach of the oral law only, but is unable to do justice to the fact that Jesus explicitly characterizes David's action as illegal.[45] A more satisfactory view can be attained when the emphases in the text itself are noted: (1) all three narratives strongly highlight, with awkward insertions, the relation of David and his followers;[46] (2) all three narratives conclude with a claim of christological authority over the Sabbath; and (3) Matthew adds immediately after the reference to 1 Samuel 21 an explicitly typological appeal to the Old Testament. Taken together, these factors suggest that the point of the allusion is to set up a typological relationship between David and Jesus: if David, along with his followers, has the right to break the law, David's 'greater Son' and his followers have an even greater right.[47] The comparison is even more appropriate, if, as seems probable, David's action occurred on the Sabbath, although this is not brought out by Jesus.[48] To be sure, the typological relationship is not clearly enunciated here,[49] but this

42. Cf. H. Schürmann, *Das Lukasevangelium* (HTKNT; Freiburg: Herder, 1969), I, pp. 303-304; Beare correctly notes that the reference to David's action does *not* justify what the disciples did ('The Sabbath', pp. 133-34).

43. Str-B, I, pp. 618-19.

44. Cranfield, *Mark*, p. 115; Lane, *Mark*, pp. 116-17.

45. Marshall, *Luke*, p. 232.

46. 'And those who were with him' is found twice in all three narratives. Cf. on this especially Lane, *Mark*, pp. 116-17.

47. Pesch, *Markusevangelium*, I, pp. 181-82; Schürmann, *Lukasevangelium*, I, pp. 303-304; R.T. France, *Jesus and the Old Testament* (London: Tyndale, 1971), pp. 46-47; cf. Marshall, *Luke*, p. 232; L. Goppelt, 'πεινάω', *TDNT*, VI, p. 19.

48. The fact that the bread of the presence was set out suggests that it was a Sabbath; the rabbis explicitly bring this out (Str-B, I, pp. 618-19; H.J. Schoeps, 'Jesus und das jüdische Gesetz', in *Aus frühchristlicher Zeit: Religionsgeschichtliche Untersuchungen* [Tübingen: Mohr, 1950], p. 217).

49. Banks contests the typological interpretation, claiming that '... nowhere else in the gospels does Jesus portray himself as David's successor' (*Jesus and the Law*, p. 115). But, against this, cf. especially S.E. Johnson, 'The Davidic-Royal Motif in the Gospels', *JBL* 87 (1968), pp. 136-50.

interpretation suffers from fewer difficulties than the others.

The interpretation of vv. 25-26 in a typical-christological rather than in an ethical-hermeneutical sense renders the connection between these verses and Mk 2.27 difficult to explain, unless 'man' is to be understood as a mistranslation of an Aramaic *bar nasha*, 'Son of Man'.[50] This suggestion, however, is most improbable.[51] It seems best not to establish any close connection between vv. 25-26 and v. 27, a conclusion which Mark's introductory formula, καὶ ἔλεγεν αὐτοῖς, suggests in any case.[52] If, on the other hand, v. 27 should not be joined with v. 28 (as will be argued below), Jesus' saying must be seen as an isolated logion. That the saying asserts the priority of human need over obedience to the Sabbath law is widely held,[53] but the scope of the intended application must be carefully delineated. If the rabbis could enunciate this principle without overturning the Sabbath law, there is no *a priori* reason to think Jesus must have overturned it. On the contrary, it would appear proper to confine the applicability of the dictum to the immediate point at issue, which is the validity of the scribal tradition. We conclude therefore that Jesus, in asserting that 'the Sabbath was made for man', is criticizing the tendency of the oral law to define appropriate Sabbath observance apart from the (partially) humanitarian thrust of the original legislation. He is not establishing the primacy of 'human needs' over the Sabbath law.

A statement very similar to Mk 2.27 is made by Jesus in response to the hostility with which his intention to heal a man on the Sabbath is met: 'Is it lawful on the Sabbath to do good or to do harm, to save life or to destroy it?' (Mk 3.4; Lk. 6.9; Matthew gives a simple statement— 12.12). Interpretations of this assertion have fallen into three types. According to the first, 'doing good' and 'doing evil', further defined in Mark and Luke by the alternative 'saving life' or 'destroying life', refer to the attitudes of the protagonists in the conflict: while Jesus is intent on healing, his antagonists are plotting Jesus' death.[54] However, this

50. Beare, 'The Sabbath', p. 131.

51. Cranfield, *Mark*, pp. 117-18.

52. Lane, *Mark*, pp. 117-18.

53. Branscomb, *Jesus and the Law*, pp. 145-46; E. Lohse, 'Σάββατον', *TDNT*, VII, p. 22; Anderson, *Mark*, pp. 110-11; O.S. Barr, *The Christian New Morality: A Biblical Study of Situation Ethics* (New York: Oxford University Press, 1969), pp. 24-25; Rordorf, *Sunday*, p. 62.

54. H.B. Swete, *Commentary on Mark* (Grand Rapids: Kregel, 1977 [1913]), p. 52; Taylor, *Mark*, p. 222; Pesch, *Markusevangelium*, I, pp. 192-93.

approach appears to be over-subtle, and it is impossible to explain Matthew's narrative on this basis.[55] Secondly, it is asserted that 'doing good' is set forth as one of God's fundamental demands, in the pursuit of which occasional breaches, or the outright overthrow of the Sabbath can be tolerated.[56] But it is probable that the third view, according to which Jesus is interpreted as seeking to define what the Sabbath law itself allows, is to be accepted.[57] Favoring this approach are the explicit assertions in the saying itself that Jesus is speaking in terms of 'what is lawful';[58] the conjunction in Matthew and in Lk. 14.1-6 (where a similar statement occurs) of the principle with the reference to what the scribal law allows when an animal is in need on the Sabbath; and the fact that, again, the Sabbath law in question is from the *oral*, not the written law. While, then, it is undeniable that love for the neighbor (= 'doing good') is here set forth as a consideration which must be taken into account when determining what is 'lawful' on the Sabbath, there is no warrant for regarding the principle as one that can effect the abrogation of commandments.[59]

In turning now to evidence for the application of the love command and similar ideas found only in Matthew's Gospel, an important phase of the investigation is reached, for it is particularly Matthew who is said to have given fundamental importance to this principle. Twice in Matthew, Jesus quotes Hos. 6.6, 'I desire mercy and not sacrifice', in order to justify the behavior of himself or his disciples: in 9.13, in response to Jewish criticism at his association with 'sinners' and in 12.7, with reference to the transgression of the Sabbath *halaka*. Some commentators have

55. D.E. Nineham, *The Gospel of St Mark* (The Pelican New Testament Commentaries; Harmondsworth: Penguin, 1963), p. 109 (on the former point).

56. Branscomb, *Jesus and the Law*, p. 148; Nineham, *Mark*, pp. 109-10; C. Carlston, 'The Things that Defile (Mark VII.14) and the Law in Matthew and Mark', *NTS* 15 (1968-69), p. 87; Braun, *Radikalismus*, II, pp. 69-70; Barth, 'Matthew's Understanding', p. 79; Rordorf, *Sunday*, p. 70; Anderson, *Mark*, p. 113.

57. MacKintosh, *Christ and the Law*, p. 65; Schürmann, *Lukasevangelium*, I, pp. 308-309; Marshall, *Luke*, p. 235. Nineham (*Mark*, pp. 109-10) argues that the Sabbath can be broken because Jesus' miracles are 'emergency' healings relating to the coming of the Kingdom. But the statement appears to be much broader than that.

58. ἔξεστιν, in light of the question put to Jesus, almost certainly relates to the law itself.

59. Marshall says: '... Jesus relates the institution of the Sabbath to the good purpose of God for men which lay behind it and hence to the principle of love for each other which ought to characterize their use of it' (*Luke*, p. 235).

understood in the contrast between 'mercy' and 'sacrifices' a reference to the moral and ceremonial laws respectively.[60] But this is not really the issue in either context. The generally accepted interpretation of the function of this quotation understands 'mercy' as the quality of human compassion which is more important than a rigid adherence to the law or to traditions.[61] Yet while this explanation suffices in 9.13, it can be applied to the situation in Matthew 12 only with great difficulty, for it is improbable that Jesus castigates the Jews for failing to have compassion on the hungry disciples.[62] Some have felt this difficulty and have interpreted the quotation as a statement about the mission of Jesus which is exhibiting the 'mercy' of God.[63] But this approach cannot adequately explain the contrasting element, 'sacrifice'. A more fruitful approach is to note that the prophet Hosea probably intended to present a contrast not between compassion on others and sacrifice, but between heart-felt loyalty to God (חסד) and the offering of sacrifices which was bereft of that inner faith.[64] There is no reason to think that Jesus did not interpret the verse in this way, since it makes excellent sense in both Matthean contexts: the Jews' failure to discern in Jesus the gracious will of God to 'call sinners' and to recognize him as 'one greater than the Temple' stems from a pettifogging preoccupation with the development and the application of God's law severed from a heart-felt loyalty to the living God.[65]

The saying which is most similar to the love commandment in Matthew's Gospel is the so-called 'Golden Rule' (Mt. 7.12). Often considered a decisive summary of Jesus' demands in the Sermon on the

60. W.C. Allen, *A Critical and Exegetical Commentary on the Gospel according to St Matthew* (ICC; Edinburgh: T. & T. Clark, 1907), p. 90.

61. A. Plummer, *An Exegetical Commentary on the Gospel according to St Matthew* (London: Robert Scott, 1915), p. 173.

62. *Pace* H.-H. Esser, 'Mercy', in *The New International Dictionary of New Testament Theology* (ed. C. Brown; 3 vols.; Grand Rapids: Zondervan, 1975–78), II, p. 596.

63. Barth, 'Matthew's Understanding', p. 83; D. Hill, 'On the Use and Meaning of Hosea VI.6 in Matthew's Gospel', *NTS* 24 (1977–78), pp. 109-18.

64. Cf. J.L. Mays, *Hosea: A Commentary* (Philadelphia: Westminster Press, 1969), p. 98; H.W. Wolff, *Hosea* (Hermeneia; Philadelphia: Fortress Press, 1974), p. 120; Hill, 'Hosea VI.6', pp. 109-10.

65. That the quotation of Hos. 6.6 in Mt. 12.7 is intended to refer primarily to v. 6 is suggested by the repetition of ἀναιτίους after the quotation.

Mount,[66] the saying, like the Great Commandment, gives a decisive word about the Old Testament: it '*is* the law and the prophets'. But as with the love commandment, it is difficult to determine the nature of the relationship so established with the Old Testament. Besides which, it is questionable whether the saying can be interpreted as a summary of Jesus' teaching in the Sermon, for there is much in it which can in no way be subsumed under that principle.[67]

Our survey of passages which appear to bear some relationship with the kind of axiom enunciated in the great commandment concludes with a saying common to Matthew and Luke. As part of Jesus' denunciation of the scribes and Pharisees, both Matthew and Luke record the criticism that while scrupulously tithing the smallest vegetables, they are neglecting more basic principles (Mt. 23.23; Lk. 11.42). Typically, Matthew relates the denunciation more closely to the law by characterizing these principles as 'the weightier matters of the law' and describing them with language reminiscent of Mic. 6.8.[68] Obviously, a hierarchy is established here, priority in the law's demands being accorded to the cardinal virtues of justice, covenant-loyalty and faithfulness (Matthew; Luke: justice and love of God). But it is made explicit that Jesus does not demand adherence to the 'weightier matters' as a *replacement* of attention to the *minutiae*: 'these you ought to have done, *without neglecting the others*'.[69] Here, as elsewhere, Jesus' criticism of the scribes and Pharisees is not that their attention to the details of the law is in itself wrong, but that, as a result of such attention, more fundamental demands of God are often neglected. And far from representing a radical new principle for the evaluation of the law, such an emphasis is entirely in keeping with large segments of the prophetic tradition.[70]

---

66. Barth, 'Matthew's Understanding', p. 80; Strecker, *Der Weg*, p. 137.

67. Especially difficult to fit under the rubric of Mt. 7.12 is the teaching in ch. 6, which concentrates on man's relationship with *God* (Meier, *Law and History*, p. 42).

68. Probably Matthew's κρίσις represents משפט, ἔλεος חסד and πίστις 'walking humbly with God'.

69. The final clause, commending the tithing (which was apparently a scribal tradition developed on the basis of Deut. 14.22-23 and Lev. 27.30 [Str-B, I, pp. 932-33]) has been attributed to a conservative Jewish-Christian community (Branscomb, *Jesus and the Law*, pp. 207-13; Berger, *Gesetzesauslegung*, p. 50) but there is no reason to think that Jesus took an unrelentingly critical stance toward the oral law (Davies, 'Matthew 5.17, 18', pp. 47-48).

70. W.C. Kaiser, Jr, 'The Weightier and Lighter Matters of the Law: Moses, Jesus and Paul', in *Current Issues in Biblical and Patristic Interpretation* (ed.

It is now possible to return to the love commandment. The preceding survey was undertaken in order to garner evidence which might allow a decision as to whether the double commandment of love represented a principle by which the validity and applicability of other commandments could be assessed or whether it established a basic demand of God which, while given precedence over others, could not displace them. It should be clear that the evidence points decisively to the latter interpretation as being correct. In no instance was love or humanitarian concerns shown to effect the abrogation of a commandment; with respect to the Sabbath, concern for the fellow man was recognized as an important factor in the original promulgation of the commandment itself. For Jesus, it is not a question of the 'priority of love over law'[71] but of the priority of love *within* the law. Love is the greatest commandment, but it is not the *only* one; and the validity and applicability of other commandments cannot be decided by appeal to its paramount demand.

The Place of the Old Testament in Jesus' Ethical Demands

Of perhaps the most direct relevance for the topic under consideration is the way in which Jesus employed the Old Testament in his own ethical teaching. The nature of his application of the Old Testament, while not necessarily normative, is nevertheless of great significance. However, the investigator who hopes to draw determinative conclusions from a study of this material is doomed to disappointment, for perhaps the most significant aspect of this topic is the paucity of references to the Old Testament. Before discussing the significance of this fact it is necessary to examine the relevant texts.

A number of examples have already been introduced in the previous section. The fundamental demand of love is expressed by means of two Old Testament commands, although the significance of this is mitigated by the fact that the question which led to these quotations was framed in terms of the Old Testament.[72] We have also seen that Jesus appealed on

G.F. Hawthorne; Grand Rapids: Eerdmans, 1975), p. 185; Ridderbos, *Kingdom*, pp. 302-303; A.H. M'Neile, *The Gospel according to St Matthew* (London: Macmillan, 1928), p. 335.

71. Carlston, 'Things that Defile', p. 87.

72. Banks downplays the role of love in Jesus' ethics, claiming that the love command is a decisive demand only within the law (*Jesus and the Law*, pp. 243-44). But passages such as Mt. 5.43ff. suggest that love plays a prominent part in the

three occasions to the prophetic tradition in order to highlight the need for inner obedience in addition to outward conformity to the law's demands (Hos. 6.6. in Mt. 9.13 and 12.7; Mic. 6.8 in Mt. 23.23). However, in view of the polemical contexts, it cannot be certainly concluded that Jesus is doing anything more than pointing out that his Jewish detractors' behavior is inconsistent with their own principles.

In the discussion about divorce common to Mark and Matthew (Mk 10.2-12; Mt. 19.3-12), Jesus appeals to Gen. 1.27 and 2.24 in order to correct the commonly accepted interpretation of Deut. 24.1-4. This procedure is sometimes compared with the rabbinic practice of seeking to construe harmoniously two apparently conflicting statements in the law.[73] Yet this view does not take sufficient cognizance of the emphases in the text. While little should be made of the fact that the Deuteronomy quotation is attributed to *Moses* and the Genesis statement to *God*,[74] it is important to note that Jesus characterizes the legislation in Deuteronomy as having been given because of 'hardness of heart'.[75] Rather than harmonizing the passages, Jesus rather clearly suggests that the need for the Mosaic legislation arose from a new factor—human sinfulness. Further, it has been claimed that Jesus utilizes the Genesis account not as Old Testament revelation *per se*, but as an indication of God's original purposes.[76] However, this is a distinction which is illegitimate and it is necessary to see in this incident an appeal to the will of God revealed in the Old Testament as indicative of what is forever appropriate in the marriage relationship.

An undoubted example of an appeal to a Mosaic commandment in ethical debate is encountered in the narrative of the conflict over ritual defilement (Mk 7.1-23; Mt. 15.1-20). Jesus, in responding to the criticism that his disciples 'eat with unwashed hands', broadens the issue by

demands of the Kingdom also (Strecker, *Der Weg*, pp. 136-37).

73. J.D.M. Derrett, *Law in the New Testament* (London: Darton, Longman & Todd, 1970), p. 377; Davies, *Setting*, pp. 104-105; Stonehouse, *Witness*, pp. 204-205; Anderson, *Mark*, pp. 241-42.

74. Banks, *Jesus and the Law*, p. 149; contra Schoeps, 'Jesus und das jüdische Gesetz', pp. 215-16; Trilling, *Israel*, pp. 205-206; V. Hasler, 'Die Herzstuck der Bergpredigt: Zum Verständnis der Antitheser in Matth. 5.21-48', *TZ* 15 (1959), p. 96.

75. K.J. Thomas correctly notes the differences between the rabbinic technique and Jesus' approach. As he says, '... one citation is used to interpret the other by placing it in a new context' ('Torah Citations in the Synoptics', *NTS* 24 [1977–78], p. 88; cf. also Banks, *Jesus and the Law*, pp. 147-50).

76. Trilling, *Israel*, pp. 205-206.

launching an attack on the 'tradition of the elders'. The implications of
this attack for Jesus' view of both the oral and written law will be considered in due course, but our interest here is in the fact that the tradition is criticized primarily because it has the effect of 'making void the
word of God'.[77] The portion of God's word at issue, the fifth commandment, is clearly held up as a norm applicable to the Jews, who are
criticized for their failure to take it into consideration in the development
of their tradition. Once again, all that can be definitely proved from this
is that Jesus expected the Jews of his day to observe the commandments
under which they lived.

Another incident in which the commandments of the decalogue play a
role is the encounter between Jesus and a rich enquirer, who asks about
the means of attaining eternal life (Mt. 19.16-22; Mk 10.17-22; Lk. 18.18-
23). Jesus responds by quoting five of the ten commandments (Mark adds
'do not defraud', Matthew 'you shall love your neighbor as yourself').
When the young man asserts that he has observed these, Jesus goes on to
demand that he also sell all that he has and follow him. Although it is
argued that these further demands are simply attempts to bring out the
real meaning of the commandments in the case of this particular
individual,[78] this interpretation must be rejected: while the command to
'sell all' might conceivably be construed as implied in the commandments, it is impossible to interpret the demand of discipleship ('follow me')
in the same way. Clearly this climactic demand is something that goes well
beyond any requirement of the Old Testament.[79] Moreover, it may be
that Jesus' citation of the commandments was simply a 'set-up', intended
to expose the man's shallowness in terms of his own religious framework
and to pave the way for the enunciation of the really applicable demands.[80]
This understanding of the citation is possible, but it is not certain that it
should be accepted: it is perhaps better to view the decalogue commands

77. It is wholly unjustified to find in Mk 7 a criticism of the tradition because it
did not put 'human needs and interests' first (contra Anderson, *Mark*, p. 186). The
emphasis throughout the narrative is on the word of God which is ignored because of
the tradition.

78. Henry, *Ethics*, p. 375; Ridderbos, *Kingdom*, p. 293; Cranfield, *Mark*,
p. 330; Lane, *Mark*, p. 367; Thomas, 'Torah Citations', p. 89.

79. C.F.D. Moule, 'Prolegomena: The New Testament and Moral Decision',
ExpTim 74 (1962–63), p. 370; Bacon, 'Jesus and the Law', p. 214; Taylor, *Mark*,
pp. 427-28; Banks, *Jesus and the Law*, pp. 162-63; Meier, *Law and History*, p. 88.

80. Banks, *Jesus and the Law*, p. 164.

as genuine, though incomplete, demands of discipleship.[81]

These references exhaust the evidence for Jesus' direct use of the Old Testament in his ethical teaching (the 'antitheses' of Matthew 5 will be considered below).[82] It is clear that they provide little support for the view that Jesus simply took over and applied the moral demands of the Old Testament for the new age. Not only are Jesus' demands made, for the most part, independently of the Old Testament, but those occasions on which the law is cited are exclusively polemical in character. However, it is illegitimate to conclude from this that Jesus saw no place for the Old Testament in the ethics of the Kingdom, for it could be argued that Jesus simply *assumes* the relevance and acceptance of the Old Testament demands in the Jewish context of his ministry. The independent authority on the basis of which Jesus formulated his ethical demands *is* obvious, however, and the next stage of our inquiry will illuminate that further.

Abrogation of Old Testament Commands?

In attempting to assess the applicability of Old Testament commandments to Christian believers, it is important to determine whether Jesus abrogated any commandments. By 'abrogation' is meant the declaring invalid of the natural meaning of a commandment for the Christian dispensation. Put in this way, virtually all Christians at all times have accepted the abrogation of *some* Old Testament commandments—those relating to the sacrificial system, for example. A more crucial question is whether the abrogation of commandments with a distinctly ethical thrust occurs.

Two matters in the dispute over ritual defilement require comment. We have seen that Jesus came to the defense of his disciples' transgression of the *halaka* concerning the washing of hands by criticizing the oral law as a whole for its effectual negation of scriptural commands. As an example of this, Jesus cites the prevalent scribal interpretation according to which something declared *Corban*, dedicated to God, could not be used by anyone but its possessor. By insisting on the inviolability of the vow, the scribes were creating a situation in which parents could be legally denied the use of their children's possessions, a state of affairs

81. Gutbrod, 'νόμος', *TDNT*, IV, p. 1063; Taylor, *Mark*, pp. 427-28.

82. Luke 11.28, in which the blessedness of 'those who hear and keep the word of God' is pronounced, has reference to Jesus' teaching, not the Old Testament (Marshall, *Luke*, p. 480).

which Jesus viewed as a transgression of the fifth commandment.[83]
Some scholars have argued that the real issue in this passage is the
conflict between two *written* laws, the fifth commandment and the
demand to fulfill a vow.[84] But in both accounts the emphasis is repeatedly placed on the 'tradition of the elders'. It seems clear that Jesus perceives the real problem to lie with the *Corban* procedure, which opened
the door for such a conflict.[85]

The *Corban* example is not directly relevant to the original point of
dispute, but this issue is taken up at the end of the narrative, when Jesus
solemnly announces to the crowd: 'there is nothing outside a man which
by going into him can defile him; but the things which come out of a
man are what defile him' (Mk 7.15; Mt. 15.11 is briefer, but makes the
same point). Immediately afterward, Jesus reiterates the point privately
to his disciples, in the course of which Mark parenthetically notes 'thus
he declared all foods clean' (7.19b). This remark interprets Jesus as
having effectively annulled the Levitical food laws, and this interpretation appears to be a legitimate conclusion from the principle enunciated

---

83. Montefiore questions the historicity of this criticism, noting that the Mishnah
tractate *Nedarim* in fact solves the issue of a conflict between the inviolability of vows
and the provision for parents in much the same way as does Jesus (*The Synoptic
Gospels* [New York: Ktav, 1968 (1927)], I, pp. 164-65). This criticism is well
answered by M'Neile: 'It is precarious to argue that, because of the majority of
Michnic [sic] Rabbis had agreed to adopt a certain view, that must have been the
prevailing one in the time of Jesus' (*Matthew*, p. 225).

84. Branscomb, *Jesus and the Law*, pp. 168-69; Kümmel, 'Jüdische Traditionsgedanke', pp. 123-24; Anderson, *Mark*, p. 182.

85. Thomas, 'Torah Citations', p. 90; Banks, *Jesus and the Law*, p. 136.

Mt. 23.2-3, in which Jesus tells the people to do 'all things' that the scribes
and Pharisees teach, is often brought up as evidence that Jesus upheld the scribal
tradition. Many therefore relegate the verses to a conservative Jewish group in the
early church (Branscomb, *Jesus and the Law*, pp. 231-33; Kümmel, 'Jüdische
Traditionsgedanke', p. 127). Against this, however, M'Neile rightly comments: '... it
is so Jewish that it could hardly have originated in later tradition even in Jewish-
Christian circles' (*Matthew*, pp. 329-30). Others qualify 'all things' as 'all things that
are in agreement with the written law' (Stonehouse, *Witness*, pp. 196-97; A.N. Wilder,
Eschatology and Ethics in the Teaching of Jesus [Westport, CT: Greenwood Press,
rev. edn, 1978 (1950)], p. 130; Plummer, *Matthew*, p. 314), but it is best to see in the
statement hyperbole, and perhaps irony, the stress falling on the condemnation of the
scribes for not *doing* what they teach (J. Jeremias, *New Testament Theology: The
Proclamation of Jesus* [New York: Charles Scribner's Sons, 1971], p. 210; Banks,
Jesus and the Law, pp. 175-76).

in v. 15: 'Was er aber hier sagt muss die alten Reinheitsgesetze sprengen'.[86] The authenticity of the saying is sometimes questioned because of the difficulty in explaining the controversies over food laws in the early church if Jesus had declared his mind on the matter.[87] But Jesus' almost parabolic pronouncement is not so clear as to settle all questions on this issue; Mark's interpretation is undoubtedly an insight gained only after long, and perhaps continuing, debate.[88]

The different elements in the pericope we have just been considering raise an important question: how can Jesus first appeal to the written law to castigate the scribal tradition (Mk 7.7-13), and then, if only implicitly, overturn part of that written law (v. 15)?[89] Many would respond by advocating the need to observe a distinction between the moral and the ceremonial law.[90] It is claimed that such a distinction was unknown in Judaism and that it is thereby illegitimate to introduce this principle into Jesus' teaching on the law.[91] While it is true that a theoretical distinction of this sort was not made, there emerges, for instance in Philo and at Qumran, a *practical* differentiation of this nature. Jesus' appropriation of the prophetic emphasis on the need for *inner* obedience, his comment about 'the weightier matters', the elevation of the love command and his transformation of the Passover meal all suggest that he may have operated with a similar distinction.[92] Thus, while the evidence does not allow us to assume that Jesus and his hearers presupposed a clear and conscious demarcation between the moral and ceremonial law, it is not illegitimate to find the seeds of this kind of a distinction in passages such

86. Verweijs, *Evangelium*, p. 22; S. Schulz, *Die Stunde der Botschaft: Einführung in die Theologie der vier Evangelisten* [Hamburg: Furche, 1967], p. 174; Kümmel, 'Jüdische Traditionsgedanke', pp. 124-25; Pesch, *Markusevangelium*, I, p. 384; Davies, 'Matthew 5.17, 18', pp. 40-41. Contra Barth, 'Matthew's Understanding', pp. 89-90.

87. Q. Quesnell, *The Mind of Mark: Interpretation and Method through the Exegesis of Mark 6.52* (AnBib, 38; Rome: Pontifical Biblical Institute, 1969), p. 98; Carlston, 'The Things that Defile', p. 95; Percy, *Botschaft*, p. 118.

88. Davies, 'Matthew 5.17, 18', p. 41; Taylor, *Mark*, pp. 341-43; Lane, *Mark*, p. 254. Lambrecht, after a detailed *traditionsgeschichtlich* investigation, concludes for the authenticity of Mk 7.15 ('Jesus and the Law: An Investigation of Mk 7.1-23', *ETL* 53 [1977], p. 75).

89. Cf. Quesnell, *Mark*, pp. 93-94.

90. Bahnsen, *Theonomy*, p. 214.

91. Cf. Banks, *Jesus and the Law*, pp. 242-43.

92. Kaiser, 'Weightier and Lighter Matters', pp. 181-85; D. Wenham, 'Jesus and the Law: An Exegesis of Matthew 5.17-20', *Themelios* 4 (April, 1979), p. 95.

as Mk 7.1-23. Ultimately, the basis for the acceptance or abrogation of laws lies elsewhere. As Cranfield, commenting on Mark 7, says, 'the key is rather that Jesus spoke as the one who is, and knew himself to be τέλος νόμου (Rom. 10.4)'.[93]

The synoptic evangelists recount four conflicts between Jesus and various Jewish authorities over the observance of the Sabbath. Jesus' attitude toward the Sabbath and his justification of his own and his disciples' conduct is frequently cited as constituting an abrogation of the Sabbath command.[94] Basic to the decalogue Sabbath commandment is the prohibition of work. What precisely is meant by 'work' is not clearly defined in the Old Testament, although there are indications that all types of normal activity were included.[95] As the Sabbath became increasingly important in post-exilic Judaism, the need was felt to define more clearly the kinds of activity prohibited, and this led to the development of the oral Sabbath law.[96] It appears that it was only this scribal tradition, not the written law, which Jesus and the disciples violated.[97] The case for finding an abrogation of the written Sabbath law rests on the justifications given by Jesus for this activity. These justifications can be grouped into two types according to whether humanitarian or christological concerns predominate.

The humanitarian arguments have already been dealt with in a previous section. The principles that 'the Sabbath was made for man' and that 'it is lawful to do good (or heal) on the Sabbath' were seen to function as indicators of the kind of activity which the Old Testament law

93. *Mark*, p. 244.

94. E. Käsemann, 'The Problem of the Historical Jesus', in *Essays on New Testament Themes* (SBT, 42; London: SCM Press, 1964), p. 40; Rordorf, *Sunday*, pp. 65-71; Kümmel, 'Jüdische Traditionsgedanke', pp. 121-22.

95. Activities specifically prohibited are: regular plowing and harvesting (Exod. 34.21); kindling a fire (Exod. 35.3); carrying burdens (Jer. 17.21-27); trade (Neh. 10.32); treading the winepress, loading beasts, and holding markets (Neh. 13.15-22); long journeys and the pursuing of business (Isa. 56.2). Cf. Lohse, 'Σάββατον', *TDNT*, VII, p. 5.

96. The Mishnah tractates '*Erubin* and *Šabbat* are devoted to this task. Cf. Str-B, I, pp. 616-18.

97. D.A. Carson, 'Jesus and the Sabbath in the Four Gospels', in *From Sabbath to Lord's Day: A Biblical, Historical and Theological Investigation* (ed. D.A. Carson; Grand Rapids: Zondervan, 1982), p. 61. Cf. also, for Matthew's narrative, Hill, *Matthew*, pp. 211-12, and Davies, *Setting*, pp. 103-104; and for Luke's, J. Jervell, 'The Law in Luke–Acts', *HTR* 64 (1971), p. 29.

was intended to allow.[98] In neither case does Jesus suggest that the Sabbath law is to be wholly rejected or even that occasional breaches are allowed in the interests of human need. His intent is not to replace the Sabbath law but to define what that law in fact allows. Nevertheless, it must be asked whether Jesus' definition of what is allowed is somewhat broader than what the Old Testament seems to indicate. Particularly significant is the fact that all the healings which Jesus performed on the Sabbath were non-emergency cases; indeed the duration of the illness is often stressed.[99] The synagogue ruler in Lk. 13.14 objects to Jesus' performance of Sabbath healing. Jesus' reply is interesting in that he asserts that it was necessary ($\delta\epsilon\hat{\imath}$) for the miracle to fall on the Sabbath (Lk. 13.16).[100] This indicates that Jesus regarded the Sabbath as a particularly appropriate time for his ministry of healing and may represent a slight shift from the trend of the Old Testament Sabbath tradition. Nevertheless, Jesus' working of miracles stands in a unique category and too much cannot be made of this.[101]

In the second line of the argument Jesus highlights his own status as a means of justifying his disciples' Sabbath behavior. As we have argued, this is the point of the allusion to 1 Sam. 21.1-6 found in Mk 2.25-26 and parallels. A similar typological appeal to the Old Testament is recorded by Matthew immediately after this (Mt. 12.5-6): if the priests who serve in the Temple on the Sabbath are innocent of wrong-doing (according to the rabbinic dictum that the 'Temple service takes precedence over the Sabbath'[102]), how much more innocent are the disciples, who are 'serving' Jesus, 'one greater than the Temple'?[103] Both of these allusions to

---

98. As Jesus points out (Mt. 12.12; Lk. 14.5), even the rabbis allowed men to help animals on the Sabbath (cf. *m. Šab*. 5.1-4; *b. Šab*, 128b). Apparently the Qumran sectarians (CD 11.13-17) and some rabbis (cf. *b. Šab*. 128b) forbade even this.

99. Rordorf, *Sunday*, pp. 65-66. The rabbis allowed medical attention that was necessary to prevent death on the Sabbath (Str-B, I, pp. 622-29).

100. Since the woman is described as having been 'bound by Satan', the work of healing is obviously not only physical.

101. Nineham (*Mark*, pp. 109-10) stresses the *messianic*, eschatological aspect of Jesus' Sabbath healings. But as suggested above, some of the sayings suggest a broader application.

102. *b. Šab*. 132b.

103. The aptness of the parallel between the priests, innocent because they serve the Temple, and the disciples, innocent because they follow Jesus, is too clear to overlook (cf. B. Gerhardsson, 'Sacrificial Service and Atonement in the Gospel of Matthew', in

the Old Testament focus attention on the person of Christ, in whose service disobedience to the letter of the law can sometimes be justified. The third christological argument is the climax of this approach: 'the Son of Man is Lord of the Sabbath' (Mt. 12.8; Mk 2.28; Lk. 6.5). It is possible that the saying has been placed here by the early church as a conclusion stemming from the claims made in the narrative,[104] but it is more likely that the claim is Jesus' own.[105] It is impossible to understand this other than as an assertion of superiority over the Sabbath and, hence, of the authority to abrogate or transform the Sabbath law.[106] The significance of this claim must not be missed: as I.H. Marshall says, 'Jesus claims an authority tantamount to that of God with respect to the interpretation of the law'.[107] But while Jesus undoubtedly claimed this right, there is no evidence that he exercised it; the most that can be said is that his Sabbath healings 'stretch' the written Sabbath law. Whether the New Testament church acted on the authority inherent in Jesus' claim is a question that is not of legitimate concern here.[108]

The single most important passage in determining the relationship between Jesus and the law is undoubtedly Mt. 5.17-48. Inasmuch as Jesus' direct statements about the Old Testament in vv. 17-19 are difficult to interpret and can be properly understood only in relation to

Reconciliation and Hope: New Testament Essays on Atonement and Eschatology presented to L.L. Morris on his 60th Birthday [ed. R. Banks; Grand Rapids: Eerdmans, 1974], p. 28).

104. Lane, *Mark*, p. 120. Mk 2.28 is variously understood as an attempt to 'tone down' the radical claim of Mk 2.27 (Käsemann, 'Historical Jesus', pp. 38-39) or to make more radical the claim of v. 27 (Schürmann, *Lukasevangelium*, I, p. 305; C. Colpe, 'ὁ υἱὸς τοῦ ἀνθρώπου', *TDNT*, VIII, p. 452). Others argue for the authenticity of v. 28, but understand the original statement to have had 'man' as the subject (M'Neile, *Matthew*, p. 170; Pesch, *Markusevangelium*, I, pp. 185-86).

105. Besides the difficulties felt by some over a 'Son of Man' saying so early in the Gospel (against which, see M. Hooker, *The Son of Man in Mark* [London: SPCK, 1967], pp. 99-102), the difficulty of the transition between v. 27 and v. 28 is cited as a major problem. But the ὥστε introducing v. 28 can be regarded as a conclusion stemming from the christological arguments throughout the incident rather than an inference drawn from v. 27.

106. F. Godet, *A Commentary on the Gospel of St Luke* (2 vols.; Edinburgh: T. & T. Clark, 5th edn, n.d.), I, p. 290; R. de Vaux, *Ancient Israel* (2 vols.; New York/Toronto: McGraw-Hill, 1961), II, p. 483.

107. *Luke*, p. 233.

108. On this, cf. further especially Rordorf, *Sunday*, and D.A. Carson (ed.), *From Sabbath to Lord's Day*.

vv. 21-48, it will be advantageous to consider the latter passage first.

Scholars are deeply divided over the nature of the relationship which is exhibited between the Old Testament quotations and Jesus' demands.[109] It is proper that the antitheses be considered at this point in our discussion because most scholars hold that Jesus clearly abrogated commandments of the Old Testament, but there is no agreement on which of the antitheses fall into this category.[110] It will be necessary to examine each of them in turn, but first some comments should be made about the introductory formula which all six have in common.[111]

109. Exposition of the law (Henry, *Ethics*, pp. 300-307; Ridderbos, *Kingdom*, p. 299; Bahnsen, *Theonomy*, p. 90; J. Murray, *Principles of Conduct: Aspects of Biblical Ethics* [Grand Rapids: Eerdmans, 1957], p. 158); deepening, radicalizing or intensifying the law (M. Dibelius, *The Sermon on the Mount* [New York: Charles Scribner's Sons, 1940], pp. 69-71; J. Dupont, *Les Béatitudes*. I. *Le problème littéraire—Les deux versions du Sermon sur la Montagne et des Béatitudes* [Bruges: Abbaye de Saint-André, 3rd edn, 1958], pp. 146-58; Davies, *Setting*, pp. 101-102); the promulgation of a new law (Spicq, *Agape*, I, pp. 5-6); the setting forth of a new teaching which does not abrogate the law (Percy, *Botschaft*, pp. 163-64).

110. Various divisions of the antitheses along these lines are popular: (1) That the third, fifth and sixth antitheses abrogate the law, while the first, second and fourth deepen it (R. Bultmann, *The History of the Synoptic Tradition* [New York: Harper & Row, rev. edn, 1963], pp. 135-36; Schulz, *Botschaft*, p. 186; E. Lohse, '"Ich aber sage euch"', in *Der Ruf Jesu*, pp. 189-90; A. Sand, *Das Gesetz und die Propheten: Untersuchungen zur Theologie des Evangeliums nach Matthäus* [BU, 11; Regensburg: Pustet, 1974], pp. 52-53; E. Schweizer, *The Good News according to Matthew* [London: SPCK, 1975], pp. 110-11; Carlston, 'Things that Defile', pp. 80-81; Davies, 'Matthew 5.17, 18', p. 44; R.A. Guelich, *The Sermon on the Mount: A Foundation for Understanding* [Waco, TX: Word, 1982], p. 268); (2) That the third, fourth and fifth abrogate the law, while the first, second and sixth deepen it (Jeremias, *Theology*, p. 252; Meier, *Law and History*, p. 135); (3) That the third and fifth abrogate the law, while the others deepen it (G. Sloyan, *Is Christ the End of the Law?* [Philadelphia: Westminster Press, 1978], pp. 50-51); (4) That the third, fourth, fifth and sixth abrogate the law, while the others deepen it (A. Descamps, *Les Justes et la justice dans les évangiles et le christianisme primitif hormis la doctrine proprement paulinienne* [Louvain: University of Louvain/Gembloux: Duculot, 1950], p. 122; Schnackenburg, *Moral Teaching*, p. 75; R.G. Hamerton-Kelly, 'Attitudes to the Law in Matthew's Gospel: A Discussion of Matthew 5.18', *BR* 17 [1972], p. 22); (5) That the fourth, fifth and sixth abrogate the law, while the others deepen it (Braun, *Radikalismus*, II, p. 13).

111. Some remarks on the tradition-history of the antitheses are in order here. Bultmann, noting that the *content* of the third, fifth, and sixth appears elsewhere (Luke) without the antithetical framework, regarded them as secondary (*Tradition*,

Although the introductory formulas are not identical in every case, it is almost certain that they are all variations of a single basic formula, represented most fully in v. 21 and v. 33: ἠκούσατε ὅτι ἐρρέθη τοῖς ἀρχαίοις... ἐγὼ δὲ λέγω ὑμῖν.[112] There has been some question about the meaning of the dative with ἀρχαίοις, but it seems certain that it should be given a purely dative ('to the ancients') rather than an ablatival ('by the ancients') sense.[113] With this meaning, it is difficult to exclude some reference to the generation who received the law at Sinai,[114] although it should not be too quickly concluded that the *written* law only must thereby be involved; it was the Jewish belief that the *oral* law, too, was given at Sinai (cf. *Ab.* 1.1-2).[115] Similarly, it is most natural to interpret 'you have heard' as a reference to the reading of the Scriptures in the synagogue,[116] but it should not be forgotten that the

pp. 134-36); M.J. Suggs has argued that all six antithetical forms are Matthew's work ('The Antitheses as Redactional Products', in *Essays on the Love Commandment*, pp. 95-101). But it is equally possible that Luke, in accordance with an *observable* tendency, has omitted the Old Testament quotations (Percy, *Botschaft*, pp. 148-50; cf. Meier, *Law and History*, p. 127). The uniquely authoritative stance suggested by the formula (ἐγώ, is a strong pointer to the authenticity of the basic framework (cf. Stauffer, 'ἐγώ', *TDNT*, I, p. 348; B.F. Meyer, *The Aims of Jesus* [London: SCM Press, 1979], p. 291). Descamps presents a strong case for tracing the *contents* of the antitheses back to Jesus ('Essai d'interprétation de Mt. 5.17-48: "Formgeschichte" ou "Redaktionsgeschichte"?', *SE*, I [ed. K. Aland *et al.*; TU, 73; Berlin: Akademie, 1959], pp. 171-72).

112. Meier, *Law and History*, p. 131. Every antithesis has Jesus' ἐγὼ δὲ λέγω ὑμῖν, but τοῖς ἀρχαίοις is omitted in the second, fifth and sixth, while the third has only ἐρρέθη δέ.

113. There is, apparently, only one instance of the dative of agency in the New Testament—Lk. 23.15 (BDF, §191; cf. also P. Fairbairn, *The Revelation of Law in Scripture* [Grand Rapids: Zondervan, 1957 (1869)], pp. 228-29; Percy, *Botschaft*, pp. 123-24; contra Ridderbos, *Kingdom*, pp. 297-98; W. Hendriksen, *New Testament Commentary: Exposition of the Gospel according to Matthew* [Grand Rapids: Baker, 1973], pp. 295-96.

114. Cf. the rabbinic זורות חראשונים (Barth, 'Matthew's Understanding', p. 93; Verweijs, *Evangelium*, p. 18). Included also is probably the 'chain' of teachers who transmitted the law (Str-B, I, p. 253; Meier, *Law and History*, p. 132).

115. Percy, *Botschaft*, p. 124.

116. M.-J. Lagrange, *Evangile selon Saint Matthieu* (EBib; Paris: Gabalda, 5th edn, 1941), p. 97; Manson, *Sayings*, p. 155; Guelich, *Sermon*, p. 182. Since Matthew consistently uses the passive form of λέγω to introduce quotations of Scripture, it is likely that some reference to the Old Testament is included when ἐρρέθη is found in the formula (G. Kittel, 'λέγω', *TDNT*, IV, pp. 111-12; Schweizer, *Matthew*, p. 117;

Scripture was usually read in interpreted ('targumized') form.[117] An important alternative to the view that the formula refers to the reading of the law in the synagogue is the possibility that Jesus is utilizing a standard rabbinic formula which was employed to contrast the teaching of one sage with another.[118] But this alternative probably must be discarded; the attestation for the formula is rather late, the Sermon presents anything but the academic milieu in which the rabbinic formula appears, and the christological ἐγώ introduces a strongly distinctive element into the formula in Matthew 5.[119] Therefore it can be concluded that the formula used by Jesus suggests he is quoting the Old Testament as it is usually heard by his audience. Whether that 'hearing' involved interpretative elements not properly a part of the text can be determined only by carefully studying the actual quotations and Jesus' response to them.[120] One final point should be made: while it has become standard to label the six citations with Jesus' responses as 'antitheses', this term itself might represent an illegitimate assumption. The grammar allows at least three different nuances of translation: 'you have heard, but I (*in contrast*

Meier, *Law and History*, p. 131; contra Str-B, I, p. 253; Barth, 'Matthew's Understanding', p. 93).

117. Cf. G. Dalman, *Jesus-Jeshua: Studies in the Gospels* (New York: Macmillan, 1929), p. 58. ἠκούσατε may well suggest the fact of 'traditionally interpreted' quotation (Str-B, I, p. 253; M. Black, *An Aramaic Approach to the Gospels and Acts* [Oxford: Clarendon Press, 3rd edn, 1967], p. 300; Trilling, *Israel*, pp. 268-69; Percy, *Botschaft*, p. 124).

118. See especially D. Daube (*The New Testament and Rabbinic Judaism* [New York: Arno, 1973 (1956)], pp. 55-60) who suggests the paraphrase 'you have understood the meaning of the law to have been' for the first, second and fourth antitheses, 'you have understood literally' for the others. Cf. also I. Abrahams, *Studies in Pharisaism and the Gospels*, first series (New York: Ktav, 1967 [1924]), p. 16; Lohse, 'Ich aber', pp. 193-96; Davies, *Setting*, p. 101; Hill, *Matthew*, p. 120. M. Smith has suggested that τοῖς ἀρχαίοις is parallel to the rabbinic בראשונה, which would yield a meaning for the antithetical formula something like 'at first they used to say ... they came around to saying' (*Tannaitic Parallels to the Gospels* [JBLMS, 6; Philadelphia: SBL, 1951], p. 28).

119. Meier, *Law and History*, p. 133; Guelich, *Sermon*, p. 182. Percy points out that the rabbinic formula is always used in the context of a refutation of one opinion *by means of appeal to Scripture*; a process completely unlike that in the antitheses (*Botschaft*, pp. 124-25; cf. also Lohmeyer–Schmauch, *Matthäus*, p. 117).

120. Meier properly notes the diversity in the antitheses and cautions about '...making general statements that are meant to apply to all six equally' (*Law and History*, pp. 128-29).

to that) say to you'; 'you have heard, and I (*in addition to that*) say to you'; 'you have heard, and I (*in agreement with that*) say to you'.[121]

It is generally agreed that no abrogation of the law occurs in the first two antitheses, but it is more difficult to determine whether Jesus is simply drawing out the actual meaning of the commands or whether he is *extending* their application. The numerous parallels to Jesus' teaching on anger and adultery in the Old Testament and Jewish literature are frequently cited to prove that Jesus' demands would not be unfamiliar to his hearers.[122] But it is not clear that these sentiments were widely taught or accepted in Jesus' day[123] nor do any of the parallels give evidence that such sentiments were derived from the sixth and seventh commandments. It is the *conjunction* of inner motive with the decalogue commandments that is distinctive to Jesus' demands.

But that Jesus understood this conjunction to be implied in the Old Testament law, at least with respect to the sixth commandment, is shown, it is argued, by the clause quoted after the commandment. 'Whoever kills shall be liable to judgment' is often interpreted as a reference to a scribal tradition which prescribed punishment only for the outward deed and ignored the inner motive. Against this, Jesus associates anger with murder by prescribing the same punishment for each.[124] But this clause is more likely to be a representation of the Old Testament laws pertaining to the punishment of the murderer.[125] The same point can be made if this is so, however: the error would then lie in the juxtaposing of the penalty for 'case law' with the general ethical principle,

121. P. Bonnard, *L'Evangile selon Saint Matthieu* (CNT; Neuchâtel: Delachaux & Niestlé, 1963), p. 64.

122. G. Friedlander, *The Jewish Sources of the Sermon on the Mount* (New York: Ktav, 1969), pp. 40-53; C.G. Montefiore, *Rabbinic Literature and Gospel Teachings* (New York: Ktav, 1970 [1930]), pp. 38-56; Str-B, I, pp. 276-82, 298-301.

123. Windisch, *Sermon*, p. 132.

124. Plummer, *Matthew*, p. 78; M'Neile, *Matthew*, p. 61.

125. Banks, *Jesus and the Law*, pp. 188-89. Cf. especially Gen. 9.6; Exod. 21.12; Lev. 24.17. κρίσις probably connotes the punishment of God rather than a 'court of law' (BAGD, p. 454) and is probably chosen so as to provide a clear connection between the penalties for murder and for anger. The second and third descriptions of punishment in v. 22 are probably not intended to represent a *gradation* in punishment, but to expand and explain the first (G. Bertram, 'μωρός', *TDNT*, IV, pp. 841-42; J. Jeremias, 'ῥακά', *TDNT*, VI, pp. 975-76). For another explanation, see C.F.D. Moule, 'Uncomfortable Words: I. The Angry Word: Matthew 5.21f.', *ExpTim* 81 (1969–70), pp. 10-13.

thereby suggesting an illegitimate restriction on the latter.[126]

Certainty on this question is almost impossible, but the apparent lack of evidence for the subsuming of anger and lust under the prohibitions of the decalogue might suggest that Jesus' interpretation does go beyond the legitimate intent of the law. Should we therefore speak, as do many, of the 'radicalization' or 'deepening' of the law in these first two antitheses? The difficulty with these descriptions is that they suppose Jesus is 'doing something to' the law, whereas this is not obvious. Rather it would appear that Jesus, with the emphatic 'but *I* say to you', enunciates principles neither derived from, nor intended to extend, the meaning of the laws which are quoted.[127]

In contrast to the first two antitheses, it is commonly asserted that in the third antithesis Jesus revokes the Old Testament law concerning divorce.[128] In order to determine the validity of this assertion, it will be necessary to deal with several difficult questions and to take into consideration Jesus' teaching elsewhere on the question.

First, it is important to note that in none of the passages recording Jesus' teaching on divorce does he present the right of divorce as a Mosaic *command*. In Mt. 5.31, the quotation from Deut. 24.1 presents the giving of the certificate of divorce as the command, and Mk 10.2-11 // Mt. 19.3-12 is in agreement with this.[129] Inasmuch as divorce is not *commanded* in Deut. 24.1-4,[130] nor, indeed, anywhere in the Old Testament, it is incorrect to speak of an abrogation of the divorce command.

---

126. On the distinction between the decalogue as 'principial' law and the developed system as 'case' law, see G. Wenham, 'Law and the Legal System in the Old Testament', in *Law, Morality and the Bible*, p. 28.

127. Banks, *Jesus and the Law*, pp. 189, 191; Guelich, *Sermon*, pp. 238, 258.

128. Although some would view vv. 31-32 as a continuation of the second antithesis (G. Schmahl, 'Die Antitheses der Bergpredigt: Inhalt und Eigenart ihrer Forderungen', *TTZ* 83 [1974], p. 290), it is probably a separate unit (Meier, *Law and History*, p. 129; Guelich, *Sermon*, p. 197).

129. Cf. Mt. 19.7 and Mk 10.5, in which 'this commandment' probably refers not to *divorce*, but to the need to give the bill of divorce, *when* divorce occurs (contra Banks, *Jesus and the Law*, p. 149).

130. It is probable that the apodosis of Deut. 24.1-4 does not come until v. 4 (cf. RSV), in which case the only *command* is that a divorced woman, whose second husband has died, cannot remarry her first spouse (C.F. Keil and F. Delitzsch, *Commmentary on the Old Testament*. I. *The Pentateuch* [Grand Rapids: Eerdmans, n.d.], pp. 416-17).

Secondly, it is necessary to ask whether Jesus withdraws the *permission* of divorce granted by Moses. In Mark 10 and Lk. 16.18, this would seem to be the case, for the prohibition of divorce appears to be absolute. According to Mk 10.5 (see also Mt. 19.8), Jesus views the Mosaic toleration of divorce as a concession to the people's stubborn insensibility to the divine will (= 'hardness of the heart').[131] In contrast to this (δέ, v. 6) stands the original creation intention of God which, it would appear, Jesus seeks to restore and uphold (οὖν, v. 9).[132] This view can be defended in Mark, but it fails to explain the Matthean parallel. For the effect of the 'exception clause' (Mt. 19.9; cf. also Mt. 5.32) is to bring Jesus' teaching on the legitimacy of divorce into rather close agreement with that of the Deuteronomic legislation.[133] Indeed, this is often denied, it being argued on grammatical grounds that no exception exists in Matthew or that πορνεία, the basis for the exception, is significantly narrower in meaning than the equivalent concept in Deut. 24.1. Lending weight to these arguments is the fact that Jesus' line of argument in Matthew, as in Mark, appears to point toward a teaching which is stricter than Moses' and in harmony with the creation will of God. Despite the plausibility of this approach, it does not appear that either the grammatical or the lexical argument cited above can be sustained.[134]

131. The term in question is σκληροκαρδία, used only in this context in the New Testament. In the LXX this word, and its adjectival form (σκληροκάρδιος), are found four times, in each case with the sense 'spiritual obduracy'. Important also is the verbal form σκληρύνω which J. Behm defines as '... the persistent unreceptivity of a man to the declaration of God's saving will...' (*TDNT*, III, p. 614).

132. Thus, essentially, Lane, *Mark*, p. 355.

133. ערות דבר, the phrase which appears to establish legitimate grounds for divorce, refers to a serious sexual sin (S.R. Driver, *A Critical and Exegetical Commentary on Deuteronomy* [ICC; Edinburgh: T. & T. Clark, 3rd edn, 1895], pp. 270-71). The school of Shammai advocated this translation, stressing the word ערות. Jesus' position in Mt. 5.32 and 19.9 would seem to be rather close to Shammai's (and λόγος πορνείας *may* be a rough translation of the phrase from Deuteronomy, since the word order דבר ערות *does* occur [*m. Git.* 9.10; cf. Str-B, I, p. 313]).

134. The grammatical case rests on understanding εἰ μή in Mt. 19.9 and παρεκτός in 5.32 in a 'preteritive' sense, in which case πορνεία is simply excluded from consideration (cf. Banks, *Jesus and the Law*, pp. 153-59). But, as Fitzmyer says, this and other less likely grammatical re-interpretations are 'subterfuges to avoid the obvious' ('The Matthean Divorce Texts and Some New Palestinian Evidence', *TS* 37 [1976], p. 207).

More popular, and more defensible, have been attempts to give πορνεία a meaning other than the usual: anything forbidden by Old Testament law (B. Malina,

Of course, another alternative is to deny the authenticity of the exceptive clauses in Matthew, but real difficulties exist for this possibility also.[135] Thus it must be concluded that both the Matthean pericopae give teaching on divorce closely similar to the Mosaic provisions.[136] This being the case, the 'hardness of heart' to which Jesus attributes the Mosaic teaching is not done away with in the new age of the Kingdom; indeed the case of 'serious sexual sin' (πορνεία) which justifies divorce is a prominent example of just that. As under the Mosaic law, the fact of human sin is recognized and provision made for it.

To return to Mt. 5.31-32, it is now important to determine what effect Jesus' teaching has on the actual commandment quoted— viz., to give a bill of divorce. The pronouncement of Jesus juxtaposed with this quotation suggests that the root problem which Jesus attacks is a liberal divorce procedure based on the Deuteronomy passage. As such, the bill of divorce command is never really addressed, though it might be inferred that Jesus envisages a context in which such a provision would be inappropriate.[137]

Thus, it is not clear that Jesus abrogates any Mosaic commandments respecting divorce and remarriage. On the other hand, Jesus *does go beyond* the Old Testament in forthrightly labelling remarriage after an improper divorce 'adultery'.[138] Once again, then, more than straightforward 'exposition' of the Old Testament is involved in the third antithesis. Nor does Jesus 'deepen' or 'intensify' the commandment

'Does *Porneia* mean Fornication?', *NovT* 14 [1972], pp. 10-17); premarital sex (A. Isaakson, *Marriage and Ministry in the New Temple* [Lund: Gleerup, 1965], pp. 127-41); marriage within prohibited degrees of kinship (J. Bonsirven, *Le divorce dans le Nouveau Testament* [Paris: Desclée, 1948], pp. 50-60; Fitzmyer, 'Divorce Texts', pp. 213-23; Meier, *Law and History*, pp. 148-50; and especially H. Baltensweiler, *Die Ehe im Neuen Testament* [Zurich: Zwingli, 1967], pp. 87-102; Guelich, *Sermon*, pp. 204-10). It is clear that πορνεία can have such a restricted meaning (particularly in the latter sense) when the context so indicates, but there are insufficient contextual factors to justify such a restriction in the Matthean texts.

135. As Hill points out, Jewish law required divorce in cases of adultery, and it is quite possible that Matthew simply makes this explicit (*Matthew*, pp. 124-25, 280-81). Moreover, the tendency in Matthew is uniformly to make the demands of the law stricter, not to provide 'loopholes'.

136. Perhaps Mark and Luke are to be regarded as presupposing the exception (Hill, *Matthew*, pp. 124-25, 280-81). But the omission is certainly a problem.

137. Ridderbos, *Kingdom*, p. 299.

138. Branscomb, *Jesus and the Law*, p. 152.

which is quoted or any part of the Mosaic divorce legislation.[139] Jesus'
purpose is to emphasize in a new way the seriousness of initiating an
illegitimate divorce ('causes her to commit adultery') and to place blame
on the one who marries an improperly divorced person. His agreement
with Deut. 24.1-4 as far as the basis for a legitimate divorce is concerned
is, as it were, incidental to his central intention.

The fourth 'thesis' cited by Jesus as a springboard for his own teaching is an accurate summary of a number of Old Testament passages
commanding the faithful performance of oaths and vows.[140] T.W.
Manson argues that v. 33b, pertaining to vows (e.g., between man and
God), is an intrusion and that the original teaching had to do only with
speaking the truth with men.[141] But the distinction implied by this is too
rigid: the Old Testament does not always clearly distinguish between
oaths and vows, both ἐπιορκέω and ὅρκος can refer to either, and
'both are solemn affirmations of a truth, both having some connection
with God'.[142] The rabbis accepted with reluctance the need for oaths,
but they never prohibited them, although the Essenes may have.[143]
Jesus' prohibition appears, however, to be absolute: 'do not swear at
all'—in which case a clear difference with respect to the Old Testament
is found.[144] On the other hand, the examples cited in vv. 34-36 strongly
suggest that Jesus had in mind the casuistic development regarding oaths

139. Contra, e.g., Hill, *Matthew*, p. 124.

140. Cf. especially Lev. 19.12; Num. 30.3; Deut. 23.21; Ps. 56.14. It is improbable
that a reference to the third commandment is included (J. Schneider, 'ὀμνύω',
TDNT, V, p. 178; Banks, *Jesus and the Law*, pp. 193-94).

141. *Sayings*, p. 158; cf. also P.S. Minear, 'Yes or No: The Demand for Honesty
in the Early Church', *NovT* 13 (1971), pp. 2-3; Davies, *Setting*, p. 24.

142. Meier, *Law and History*, pp. 151-52.

143. For the former, see Str-B, I, pp. 321-28; Friedlander, *Jewish Sources*, pp. 60-
65; Montefiore, *Rabbinic Literature*, pp. 48-50. Josephus claims that the Essenes
forbade swearing (*War* 2.8.6) but also mentions a solemn entry oath (*War* 2.8.7).
The evidence from the Scrolls is inconclusive, but it is probable that an entrance oath
alone was allowed (Davies, *Setting*, pp. 240-41).

144. E. Kutsch, '"Eure Rede aber sei ja ja, nein nein"', *EvT* (1960), pp. 208-209;
Schneider, 'ὀμνύω', *TDNT*, V, p. 178; Montefiore, *Synoptic Gospels*, II, p. 68;
Friedlander, *Jewish Sources*, p. 60; Banks, *Jesus and the Law*, pp. 194-95; Meier,
Law and History, pp. 153-55. To view the phrases introduced by μήτε... μήτε as a
list of oaths prohibited by Jesus is incorrect; μήτε is equivalent to μηδέ here and
introduces examples of the kind of thing Jesus is combatting (Str-B, I, p. 328).
Neither is it legitimate to view v. 37a as a new oath introduced by Jesus (Schneider,
'ὀμνύω', *TDNT*, V, pp. 180-81).

in the scribal tradition.[145] This feature, combined with undoubted examples of hyperbole in the Sermon and the conclusion in v. 37a, may serve to indicate that Jesus' main point is the need for absolute truthfulness and that he intends to prohibit only those oaths whose purpose is to avoid that truthfulness.[146] In this case, Jesus' teaching would be almost indistinguishable from the Old Testament position. Nevertheless, it is difficult to uphold any restriction on Jesus' prohibition: the final words of v. 37, 'anything more than this comes from the evil one', repeat the categorical abolition of oaths. Furthermore, James, who *may* preserve an independent witness to Jesus' words, also gives an absolute prohibition (5.12).[147] However, the forbidding of all *voluntary* oaths cannot be legitimately styled an abrogation of an Old Testament command because there is no Old Testament text which *commands* oaths; the custom is presumed and regulations are given for its practice.[148] Again, Jesus does not exposit or deepen the commandment, but effectively cancels legislation which is no longer needed since the practice it regulated is prohibited in the coming Age.[149]

John P. Meier claims that Jesus' teaching with regard to the *lex talionis* is 'perhaps the clearest and least disputable case of annulment in the antitheses'.[150] While it is precarious to contest so strong a statement, it does not seem that this judgment can be sustained. The law requiring equivalent compensation, found at three places in the Pentateuch, had the purpose not to justify, but to restrain private retribution, by establishing a judicial procedure to which all could appeal.[151] Jesus does not question the legitimacy of this policy (nor does he uphold it), but

145. For examples, cf. Str-B, I, pp. 328-36.

146. Hasler, 'Herzstück', pp. 98-99; Stonehouse, *Witness*, pp. 206-207; Murray, *Principles*, p. 171.

147. μὴ ὀμνύετε... μήτε ἄλλον τινὰ ὅρκον.

148. Meier (*Law and History*, p. 152) claims that oaths are commanded in the Old Testament, but there is only one text of which this can be said (Exod. 22.10-13) and this is limited to a specific situation in the courts. Deut. 6.13 and 10.20, which Meier cites, should be regarded not as commands that vows be made, but that any vows made by God's people should be made to the Lord.

It would not appear that Jesus' words have relevance to the taking of an oath in a law court; he prohibits *all* oaths *voluntarily undertaken*.

149. Dupont, *Béatitudes*, I, p. 158.

150. *Laws and History*, p. 157; cf. also Barth, 'Matthew's Understanding', p. 94.

151. Cf. M. Noth, *Exodus: A Commentary* (Philadelphia: Westminster Press, 1962), p. 132.

prohibits his disciples from using the principle in personal relations. Inasmuch as application of the *lex* to private parties is not envisaged in the Old Testament, it is likely that Jesus is opposing a misuse of the law among his contemporaries.[152] Thus, nothing is done to the Old Testament law as such.[153]

The final statement quoted by Jesus in Matthew 5 is unique among the antitheses as including a clause which is not drawn from, nor representative of, the Old Testament. This is sometimes contested, it being urged that the restriction of the love command in Lev. 19.12 to the fellow-Israelite (רֵעַ[154]) and the frequent expressions of hostility to Israel's enemies in the Old Testament render 'you shall hate your enemy', 'die logische und praktische Konsequenz'.[155] But even within Leviticus 19, the command of love is widened to embrace the 'resident alien' (v. 34) and, when the entire thrust of the Old Testament is considered, a command to hate can hardly be considered a fair extrapolation.[156] The source from which the sentiment is taken cannot be certainly identified, although perhaps most likely is the demand that the members of the Qumran sect hate the 'sons of darkness'.[157] In contrast to this, Jesus demands that his followers love even their enemies, which in the context particularly includes their persecutors.[158] Once again, the demand of

152. Hasler, 'Herzstück', pp. 101-102; Stonehouse, *Witness*, p. 209; Murray, *Principles*, pp. 174-75.

153. A number of scholars find in this antithesis the introduction of a new demand: whereas the law had *restrained* vengeance, Jesus *prohibits* it (Gutbrod, 'νόμος', *TDNT*, IV, p. 1064; M'Neile, *Matthew*, p. 69; Dupont, *Béatitudes*, I, p. 158; Marshall, *Luke*, p. 116).

154. Cf. J. Fichtner, 'πλησίον', *TDNT*, VI, p. 314.

155. Schulz, *Botschaft*, p. 186 (quoting Klostermann). Cf. also Banks, *Jesus and the Law*, p. 199. Spicq (*Agape*, I, pp. 9-10) and O.J.F. Seitz ('Love your Enemies', *NTS* [1969–70], pp. 42-43) allow that 'hate your enemy' is a not unnatural extrapolation from the Old Testament teaching.

156. O. Linton, 'St Matthew 5.43', *ST* 18 (1964), p. 66.

157. 1QS 1.3, 9-10; 2.4-9. Cf. H. Bietenhard, 'Enemy', in *NIDNTT*, I, p. 554; Furnish, *Love Command*, pp. 42-47; Davies, *Setting*, p. 245 (possibly). Otherwise, it is possible that a popular maxim is involved (Str-B, I, p. 353; Seitz, 'Love', p. 51; O. Michel, 'μισέω', *TDNT*, IV, p. 690). M. Smith suggests that the phrase may have been a gloss in a targum ('Mt. 5.43: "Hate thine Enemy"', *HTR* 45 [1952], pp. 71-72).

Montefiore, in a thorough survey of the rabbinic evidence, concludes that the sages did teach, in theory, a universal love; many teachings, in practice, failed to express it (*Rabbinic Literature*, pp. 59-104).

158. W. Foerster, 'ἐχθρός', *TDNT*, II, p. 814; Furnish, *Love Command*, pp. 46-47.

Jesus does not abrogate any Old Testament commandment, but neither can it be regarded as a natural extrapolation from Old Testament teaching.[159]

Having examined each of the antitheses, it can be concluded that none of the usual characterizations of Jesus' handling of the Old Testament is sufficient to embrace all of the evidence. 'Exposition' can in no manner account for the situation in the final four antitheses, although it cannot be ruled out as a description of the first two. Besides the inadequacy of the term to do justice to the evidence, it is highly questionable whether the antithetical formula would have been chosen had simple exegesis been Jesus' goal. Likewise, the process observed in the first two antitheses *might* be best described by the terms 'deepening' or 'radicalization', but the latter four cannot be understood in this way.What is the dominant note, hinted at in the emphatic 'I say to you', testified to by the crowds at the conclusion of the Sermon and observed in all the antitheses, is the independent, authoritative teaching of Jesus, which is neither derived from nor explicitly related to the Old Testament.

As a summary of the evidence relating to Jesus' abrogation of the Old Testament, it should be noted that only one commandment, that a bill of divorce be given, was seen to be implicitly revoked, and it is important to note that Jesus explicitly characterizes it as a less-than-adequate statement of God's perfect will. One practice (swearing) allowed in the Mosaic law was forbidden by Jesus to his disciples and in two other instances (Sabbath observance and food laws), Jesus enunciated principles which would allow for the abrogation of laws.

Direct Statements about the Old Testament

We have argued that, to determine the manner in which the Christian believer can use the Old Testament as a guide for behavior, it is necessary to understand the impact of Jesus' coming on the older revelation. In this final section, it is our task to examine the text which most directly treats that question: Mt. 5.17-19 and the partial Lukan parallel, 16.16-17.

In Lk. 16.16, Jesus clearly announces a fundamental shift in Salvation-history: 'The law and the prophets were until John; since then the good news of the Kingdom of God is preached, and every one enters it violently'. Especially in light of v. 17, it is impossible that Jesus intends

---

159. Contra Henry, *Ethics*, p. 226.

to announce the *termination* of the relevance of the Old Testament;[160] rather, the period during which men were related to God under its terms has ceased with John.[161] Matthew's parallel (11.13a) presents some interesting differences: 'all the prophets and the law prophesied until John'. Unique and particularly striking is the notion of the law 'prophesying', but it is difficult to know what to make of it. Banks sees in it an indication of a Matthean theological theme which regards the law as well as the prophets as pointing forward to Christ.[162] This understanding will have to be pursued further in discussing Mt. 5.17, but the present verse need only indicate that the entire Old Testament is being viewed as the first member in a 'prophecy-fulfillment' understanding of history.[163]

Study of Mt. 5.17-19 is complicated by the complex and debated tradition history of the verses. According to some, each of the three verses has to be assigned to a different stratum of the early community as they present differing views of the law.[164] The validity of the various suggestions concerning the history of these verses can be assessed only after their meaning has been determined. But as a working procedure, we will seek to determine the meaning of each verse within its present context, since it is certainly legitimate to suppose that the final redactor, at least, intended them to be understood in relation to one another.

The meaning given to the phrase 'the law and the prophets' has an important bearing on the exegesis of v. 17. We have already noted that the phrase appears to connote the Old Testament Scriptures in the New

160. R. Banks, 'Matthew's Understanding of the Law: Authenticity and Interpretation in Matthew 5.17-20', *JBL* 93 [1974], p. 235. *Pace* Schulz (*Botschaft*, p. 189) and Barth ('Matthew's Understanding', pp. 63-64), it is not legitimate to find in Matthew's version a greater emphasis on the permanency of the law.

161. It is probable that Luke intends to include John *within* the period of the Kingdom (cf. Lk. 3.18 and Acts 1.22—W.G. Kümmel, '"Das Gesetz und die Propheten gehen bis Johannes"—Lukas 16.16 im Zusammenhang der heilsgeschichtlichen Theologie der Lukasschriften', in *Verborum Veritas* [Festschrift Gustav Stählin; ed. O. Böcher and K. Haacker; Wuppertal: Brockhaus, 1970], pp. 94-98; Marshall, *Luke*, p. 628; contra H. Conzelmann, *The Theology of Saint Luke* [New York: Harper, 1961], pp. 25-26 *et passim*).

162. *Jesus and the Law*, p. 210; Meier, *Law and History*, pp. 71-73; Descamps, *Justes*, pp. 161-62.

163. W. Grundmann, *Das Evangelium nach Matthäus* (THKNT; Berlin: Evangelische Verlag, 1968), p. 310.

164. Hamerton-Kelly, 'Attitudes', pp. 19-32, provides a convenient discussion.

Testament generally, but that Matthew gives the phrase a particular nuance, stressing the normative or imperatival aspect of the Old Testament. The fact that νόμος is used alone in v. 18 and that v. 19 speaks of 'commandments' strongly suggests that this connotation is present in 5.17 as well.[165] But it is not legitimate to press this distinction to the extent that the phrase is taken to imply simply 'the will of God';[166] reference to the written Scriptures cannot be eliminated.[167]

It is not to 'abolish' the demands of the Old Testament Scriptures that Jesus has come, but to *fulfill* them. The determination of the meaning of 'fulfill' in this context is a notorious *crux*, for while the sense of the term as applied to prophecies appears easy to establish, its significance with respect to commands is much less obvious. Any acceptable interpretation will have to do justice to the following factors:

1. When Septuagintal usage is considered, it is almost certain that πληρόω is more closely related to קלא than to קוס.[168]
2. The term with which πληρόω is contrasted, καταλύω, means 'abolish', 'annul'.[169]
3. The focus in Matthew 5 is clearly on the relationship between the Old Testament and Jesus' *teaching*, not his actions.

A number of suggested interpretations can be immediately eliminated when these factors are given sufficient consideration.[170] The remaining

---

165. T. Zahn, *Das Evangelium des Matthäus* (Leipzig: Deichert, 4th edn, 1922), pp. 209-10, 215; Trilling, *Israel*, pp. 173-74; Strecker, *Der Weg*, p. 144. (The use of ἤ rather than καί in 5.17 is probably due to the negative form of the sentence [Bonnard, *Matthieu*, p. 61].)

166. As do Sand, *Gesetz*, p. 186; Berger, *Gesetzesauslegung*, p. 224.

167. Bahnsen, *Theonomy*, pp. 50-51.

168. B.S. Childs, 'Prophecy and Fulfillment: A Study of Contemporary Hermeneutics', *Int* 12 (1958), p. 204; Banks, *Jesus and the Law*, pp. 208-209. The LXX never uses πληρόω to translate קוס (on the LXX usage of πληρόω, cf. Descamps, *Justes*, pp. 124-25) and the interchange of מלא and קוס in the targums (Meier, *Law and History*, p. 74) is insufficient basis to overturn this factor.

169. The closest parallel to Mt. 5.17 in the use of καταλύω is 2 Macc. 2.22, where it is used with reference to the law and must mean 'abolish' or 'annul' (Grundmann, *Matthäus*, p. 145; Banks, *Jesus and the Law*, p. 207; contra H. Ljungman, *Das Gesetz Erfüllen: Matth. 5.17ff. und 3.15 untersucht* [Lunds Universitets Årsskrift, n.s. 50; Lund: Gleerup, 1954], pp. 60-61).

170. (1) Supposing קוס to lie behind πληρόω, the word has been translated 'confirm' or 'sustain' (Dalman, *Jesus-Jeshua*, pp. 56-58; Branscomb, *Jesus and the Law*, pp. 226-28; Daube, *New Testament*, pp. 60-61); (2) πληρόω has been

possibilities posit a relationship between Jesus' teaching and the Old Testament according to which the former (1) 'fills up' the law by expressing its full intended meaning;[171] (2) 'fills up' or 'completes' the law by extending its demands;[172] or (3) 'fulfills' the law by bringing that to which it pointed forward.[173] Two further considerations are crucial in deciding which of these positions is correct: the usage of πληρόω in Matthew and the implications of the use of the Old Testament in the antitheses.

The most obvious and distinctive use of πληρόω in Matthew comes in the introductions to the so-called 'formula quotations', which declare the 'fulfillment' of an Old Testament prophecy or historical event in the life of Jesus. It is this aspect of Matthew's employment of πληρόω

identified with קום and καταλύω with בטל to give the contrast between 'doing' and 'neglecting' the law (cf. *m. Ab* 4.9; Str-B, I, p. 341; A. Schlatter, *Der Evangelist Matthäus* [Stuttgart: Calwer, 1957], pp. 153-54; J. Jocz, *The Jewish People and Jesus Christ: The Relationship between Church and Synagogue* [Grand Rapids: Baker, 3rd edn, 1979], p. 26); (3) On the analogy of prophetic fulfillment, πληρόω has been interpreted to mean 'obey' (Zahn, *Matthäus*, pp. 212-13; T.W. Manson, *Ethics and the Gospel* [London: SCM Press, 1960], pp. 53-54); (4) with reference to a supposed parallel to Mt. 5.17 in *b. Šab.* 116b, it has been suggested that πληρόω means 'add to' (Jeremias, *Theology*, pp. 83-84); (5) 'to observe completely' is the sense suggested by Descamps (*Justes*, pp. 127-31); (6) Ljungman, with reference to Mt. 3.15, argues for the meaning 'accomplish as a unity in Jesus' work' (*Gesetz*, pp. 58-61); (7) Jesus' coming has been viewed as the basis for enabling himself and others to carry out God's demands (J. Schniewind, *Das Evangelium nach Matthäus* [NTD; Göttingen: Vandenhoeck & Ruprecht, 7th edn, 1954], p. 54).

171. R.C.H. Lenski, *The Interpretation of St Matthew's Gospel* (Minneapolis: Augsburg, 1943), pp. 206-207; Henry, *Ethics*, p. 318; Ridderbos, *Kingdom*, p. 294; Bahnsen, *Theonomy*, pp. 61-72; Nixon, 'Fulfilling', pp. 56-57.

172. Although the following authors disagree on the exact nuance, they are united in giving πληρόω the sense 'give the complete or perfect meaning': Kümmel, 'Jüdische Traditionsgedanke', pp. 128-29; Lagrange, *Matthieu*, pp. 93-94; Dupont, *Béatitudes*, I, pp. 138-44; Lohmeyer–Schmauch, *Matthäus*, pp. 107-108; Wilder, *Eschatology*, p. 130; Schnackenburg, *Moral Teaching*, pp. 57-58; Davies, 'Matthew 5.17, 18', pp. 33-45; F.V. Filson, *A Commentary on the Gospel according to St Matthew* (BNTC; London: A. & C. Black, 1960), p. 83; Feuillet, 'Morale', p. 124; Grundmann, *Matthäus*, pp. 145-46; Schweizer, *Matthew*, p. 107; Schulz, *Botschaft*, p. 182; Trilling, *Israel*, pp. 174-79; C. Burchard, 'The Theme of the Sermon on the Mount', in *Essays on the Love Command*, p. 73.

173. Banks, *Jesus and the Law*, pp. 207-10; Meier, *Law and History*, pp. 75-85. Meyer (*Aims of Jesus*, p. 153) says: 'His [Jesus'] crowning revelation "fulfilled" the Torah by bringing it to its appointed eschatological completion'.

which is stressed by Banks, who argues that 'precisely the same meaning should be given to the term πληρόω when it is used of the Law as that which it has when it is used of the prophets'.[174] The fact that the Law itself is said to 'prophesy' according to Matthew (11.13) demonstrates that the law as well as the prophets can be regarded as possessing a 'prophetic' function. Thus, it is suggested, as Jesus fulfilled the Old Testament prophecies in his activity so he 'fulfilled' the Old Testament law in his teaching.[175]

Against this view, however, it can be argued that the closest parallel to the use of πληρόω in Mt. 5.17 is found not in the formula quotations, which all have the passive form, but in Mt. 3.15, which, like 5.17, has the active infinitive. And 'to fulfill all righteousness' in 3.15, it is argued, must mean something like 'to obey (e.g., "complete") every righteous demand of God'.[176] Furthermore, Matthew uses πληρόω elsewhere, albeit in non-theological senses, to mean 'fill up' or 'complete' (13.48; 23.32).

It is difficult to determine which of these lines of evidence should be taken as most significant in determining the meaning of πληρόω in Mt. 5.17. On the one hand, the difference between the passive formulation in the formula citations and the active in Mt. 5.17 may preclude their association, but, on the other hand, the meaning of Mt. 3.15 is not clear and not much may be gained by comparing Mt. 5.17 with it.[177] On the whole, there would appear to be a slight balance of evidence in favor of Banks's interpretation. The reference to the law 'prophesying' (11.13), taken in conjunction with the dominant use of πληρόω in the formula quotations, is very suggestive. Moreover, the idea of fulfillment of the law is in accord with the broad scope of fulfillment in Matthew, including, as it does, historical events with no clearly predictive element (cf. 2.15).

More decisive support is given this interpretation of πληρόω if the

174. *Jesus and the Law*, p. 210.

175. Banks, *Jesus and the Law*, p. 210. Guelich similarly stresses the redemptive-historical focus of v. 17 and views the verse as a pronouncement of Jesus' bringing in the eschatological 'Zion-torah' (*Sermon*, pp. 137-38, 163). And see also Meyer, *Aims of Jesus*, pp. 143-51.

176. Cf. G. Schrenk, 'δικαιοσύνη', *TDNT*, II, p. 198.

177. Meier (*Law and History*, pp. 76-81) deals with both these points. He argues that there is no significant difference between the passive use of πληρόω in the quotations and the active in 5.17. But it may be that he minimizes the difference: never in the New Testament is πληρόω in the passive followed by Jesus as the agent, which would be the parallel to 5.17. As to 3.15, he suggests that πληρόω there may tie in with the use of the term in the fulfillment quotations.

understanding of the antitheses developed above is correct. Most scholars recognize the need to interpret the basic 'theory' enunciated in vv. 17-19 in light of the specific practical examples of vv. 21-48. Hence, those who regard 'fulfill' as connoting the bringing out of the true intention of the law find exposition of the Old Testament in the antitheses; while 'deepening', 'radicalizing', or 'intensifying' the law is found by supporters of the view that 'fulfill' implies an extension of the law's demands. Yet if Jesus in the antitheses is doing neither, but is rather bringing new demands only indirectly related to the Old Testament commands which are cited, then the law can perhaps be best viewed as an *anticipation* of Jesus' teaching. Jesus fulfills the law by proclaiming those demands to which it looked forward.[178]

Can this interpretation be reconciled with vv. 18-19? At first sight, no stronger endorsement of the eternal validity of even the most insignificant item in the law could be found than appears in these verses.[179] But such an interpretation poses insuperable problems for anyone who is concerned to discover a consistent position within Matthew. Many scholars simply deny that this is possible and find in vv. 18-19 a tradition stemming from the conservative Jewish community in the early church, a tradition which Matthew has for some reason inserted in its present context.[180] While it is possible that one could be forced to this view, it must be said that it seems a very difficult one; is it likely that the final redactor would have deliberately inserted sayings which appear, when compared with vv. 21ff., to present Jesus as 'the least in the Kingdom of Heaven'? Surely it is incumbent on us to seek out other alternatives before this position is accepted.

Attempts to avoid the conclusion that there is in these verses an absolute endorsement of every demand in the law focus on three things: the scope of the ἕως clauses in v. 18, the meaning of νόμος in v. 18 and the antecedent of τούτων in v. 19.

The first ἕως clause in v. 18, 'until heaven and earth pass away', must be compared with Lk. 16.17: 'it is easier for heaven and earth to pass

178. Exponents of the view that Jesus 'intensified' the law in the antitheses are forced to argue that this intensification does not act directly on the commands which are cited. The view advocated is able to retain the direct contact.

179. Cf. the parallels in Jewish literature (Str-B, I, pp. 244-45).

180. E.g. Kümmel, 'Jüdische Traditionsgedanke', p. 127; H.-T. Wrege, *Die Überlieferungsgeschichte der Bergpredigt* (WUNT, 9; Tübingen: Mohr, 1968), p. 40.

away, than for one dot of the law to become void'. It is probable that the Lukan verse must be understood as an assertion of the continuing validity of the law, in order to guard against the drawing of antinomian conclusions from v. 16.[181] Almost certainly, the Matthean ἕως clause must be given the same meaning: 'until heaven and earth pass away' is simply another way of saying, 'until the end of the present world order'.[182]

The second ἕως clause in v. 18 is less easy to interpret, since πάντα, 'all things', has no clear antecedent and the precise meaning of γένηται is uncertain.[183] One approach understands πάντα to refer to the demands of the law which are to be 'done' or 'obeyed'.[184] But, when Matthean usage is considered, γένηται must almost certainly be translated 'happen', 'come to pass', so this approach must be excluded.[185] A second interpretation takes πάντα as a reference to *events* which are to come to pass, and inasmuch as this interpretation gives a natural sense to both γένηται and πάντα, it should probably be accepted. The events denoted by πάντα have been variously identified: the death or resurrection of Christ;[186] those things prophesied of his first coming or of his entire career;[187] or the end of the Age.[188]

---

181. Marshall, *Luke*, p. 630.

182. Inasmuch as Jesus, in both Matthew (24.35) and Luke (21.33) clearly predicts the 'passing away of heaven and earth', it is incorrect to view this saying as equivalent to saying 'never' (H. Traub, 'οὐρανός', *TDNT*, V, p. 515; Meier, *Law and History*, p. 61).

183. It seems clear, however, that the ἕως clause is temporal (contra E. Schweizer ["Noch einmal Mt. 5.17-20', in *Das Wort und die Wörter* (Festschrift G. Friedrich; ed. H. Balz and S. Schultz; Stuttgart: Kohlhammer, 1973), p. 71], who wants to give the clause a *final* meaning and A.M. Honeyman ['Matthew V. 18 and the Validity of the Law', *NTS* 1 (1954–55), pp. 141-42], who finds a Semitic construction which yields an inclusive and modal sense).

184. Wrege, *Bergpredigt*, p. 39; Sand, *Gesetz*, p. 38; Grundmann, *Matthäus*, p. 148; Schulz, *Botschaft*, p. 183; Hill, *Matthew*, p. 118. Schweizer has argued that the love command in particular is the subject ('Matth. 5.17-20: Anmerkungen zum Gesetzesverständnis des Matthäus', in *Neotestamentica: Deutsche und Englische Aufsätze 1951–1963* [Zürich/Stuttgart: Zwingli, 1963], pp. 400-405).

185. Cf. especially Meier, *Law and History*, pp. 53-54, 61-62.

186. Jesus' death: Davies, 'Matthew 5.17, 18', pp. 44-63; the Resurrection: Hamerton-Kelly, 'Attitudes', p. 30.

187. Meier (*Law and History*, pp. 62-64; cf. Guelich, *Sermon*, pp. 145-48) argues for the former; for the latter, cf. Lenski, *Matthew*, p. 204.

188. M'Neile, *Matthew*, p. 59.

A consideration of Mt. 24.34-35, which presents several striking linguistic parallels to v. 18, can aid in making a decision. In that context, 'until all these things come to pass' is probably to be interpreted as a reference to the signs enumerated by Jesus earlier in the chapter.[189] πάντα ταῦτα, then, indicates *predicted events*. πάντα in 5.18, without the ταῦτα, leaving it unspecified, is likely to mean much the same thing: all predicted events, the 'whole divine purpose'.[190] While it is claimed that this interpretation makes the second ἕως clause tautologous to the first and hence superfluous, this is not really the case: the second introduces the idea, absent from the first, of God's redemptive purposes. If these interpretations of the ἕως clauses are correct, then they provide no help in delimiting the statements of vv. 18-19.

νόμος in v. 18 probably means, basically, the Old Testament Scriptures,[191] although it is probable also that the imperatival aspect of the Scriptures is still particularly in view. Another kind of delimitation is suggested by those who suppose that νόμος here is a reference to the *moral* law only.[192] But such a meaning is unlikely in view of the lack of attestation for any clear distinction in Judaism among moral, ceremonial and civil law and the stress on detailed parts of the Scriptures in 5.18.[193] A better suggestion is that the continuing validity of the law is to be understood in the light of its 'fulfillment' (v. 17).[194] In all its details, the Scripture remains authoritative, but the manner in which men are to relate to and understand its provisions is now determined by the one who has fulfilled it. While this view cannot be demonstrated exegetically, the position of v. 18 between v. 17 and the antitheses surely suggests that it can be understood only in conjunction with the new approach to the law. It is precisely the same with Lk. 16.17, placed between v. 16 and the saying about divorce in v. 18.

This statement about the permanent validity of the law leads to the

189. Banks, *Jesus and the Law,* p. 216. And for more evidence for this view of this difficult logion, see especially Cranfield, *Mark*, pp. 407-408.

190. Plummer, *Matthew*, p. 76.

191. BAGD, p. 545; contra Gutbrod ('νόμος', *TNDT*, IV, p. 1059), Banks (*Jesus and the Law,* pp. 214-15) and Meier (*Law and History*, p. 52) who restrict the reference to the Pentateuch.

192. Fairbairn, *Law*, pp. 226-27; MacKintosh, *Christ and the Law*, p. 23.

193. Bahnsen, *Theonomy*, p. 48.

194. Lagrange, *Matthieu*, p. 94; Bonnard, *Matthieu*, p. 62; Trilling, *Israel*, p. 179; G. Schrenk, 'ἐντολή', *TDNT*, II, pp. 548-49; Sloyan, *End of the Law*, pp. 49-51; Wenham, 'Jesus and the Law', p. 95.

practical conclusion (οὖν) of v. 19:[195] even 'the least of these commandments' must be practiced and taught; not to do so is to risk exclusion from the Kingdom.[196] But what are *these* commandments? Attempts to restrict the reference to the decalogue, Jesus' commands, or the antitheses cannot be justified.[197] Most likely, the antecedent of τούτων is to be located in νόμος, the whole (v. 18) being broken down into its parts (v. 19). In the same way then as νόμος in v. 18 must be understood in light of its fulfillment, so 'these commandments' should be understood as referring to the commandments as fulfilled (and thereby, perhaps re-interpreted) in Jesus.[198]

The function of vv. 18-19 is rather clearly to guard against a possible antinomian interpretation of v. 17 and, perhaps, of the following antitheses.[199] While it is generally held that it was Matthew's concern about antinomian tendencies in his church that led him to insert these Jewish-Christian sentiments here, it must be asked whether Jesus, too, would not have been concerned about the possibility of his listeners drawing such a conclusion. Could not he have appropriated a perhaps popular Jewish saying about the eternal validity and applicability of the law and applied it to the 'fulfilled law' in order to demonstrate his essential

195. Most scholars hold that v. 19 comes from Matthew's special tradition (Hamerton-Kelly, 'Attitudes', pp. 21-27), although some suppose that it was joined to v. 18 in 'Q' (H. Schürmann, ' "Wer daher eines dieser geringsten Gebote auflöst..." ', *BZ* 4 [1960], pp. 240-49; Meier, *Law and History*, pp. 101-103).

196. Although Meier (*Law and History*, pp. 92-95) argues that gradations in rank, not exclusion from the Kingdom, is meant.

197. For the first, see Schrenk, 'ἐντολή', *TDNT*, II, p. 548; for the second, Banks, *Jesus and the Law*, pp. 221-23; for the third, Carlston, 'Things that Defile', p. 79. Against the last-named view, it does not appear that Matthew ever uses οὗτος prospectively.

198. A.T. Lincoln, 'From Sabbath to Lord's Day: A Biblical and Theological Perspective', in *From Sabbath to Lord's Day*, p. 374. J.D.G. Dunn (*Unity and Diversity in the New Testament: An Inquiry into the Character of Earliest Christianity* [Philadelphia: Westminster Press, 1977], p. 246) sees Matthew to be advocating 'continuing *loyalty* to the law, that is, for him, *the law as interpreted by Jesus*'. Guelich (*Sermon*, pp. 153-55) finds v. 19 to be restricted by v. 20, which introduces the idea of the eschatological 'Zion-torah' (the term is Hartmut Gese's).

199. Barth ('Matthew's Understanding', pp. 94-95) is a good representative of those who believe that the seemingly divergent views of the law in Matthew are due to the fact that he was fighting on 'two fronts'—against a rabbinic-like stress on the law on the one hand and against antinomians on the other.

continuity with it? It would appear that such an evaluation is at least as probable as supposing that Matthew has done the same.[200]

Conclusion

In his direct statements about the law Jesus upholds the continuing validity of the entire Old Testament Scriptures, but also asserts that this validity must be understood in light of its fulfillment. It can be readily seen that the evidence gleaned from other lines of investigation in the course of the study is compatible with this position. No sensation-causing revolutionary, Jesus adhered to the law in his own life, but used it remarkably little in his teaching about the righteousness expected of members of the Kingdom. Jesus evidenced in the antitheses and claimed in his statement about the Sabbath an authority over the law, such as only God possesses. On the basis of this authority, Jesus denied to his disciples at least one practice tolerated in the old dispensation (vows), and set forth a principle destined to abrogate large segments of Pentateuchal laws (cf. Mk 7.15). But none of this occurs as a deliberate attack on the law; rather the validity or abrogation of laws appears to be decided entirely by their relationship to Jesus' teaching and to the new situation which his coming inaugurates.[201]

This general perspective is found in all three synoptic Gospels with differences in emphasis, but without significant contradictions. Each evangelist combines statements upholding the validity of the law with pronouncements of Jesus regarding his authority over the law. Little use of the law is made in any Gospel in the formulation of kingdom ethics and dietary regulations receive criticism in all three also. These conclusions depend for their cogency on the exegetical decisions reached in the course of the study; and particularly Mt. 5.18-19, and the general approach to the law in the first Gospel, are likely to be raised as fundamental objections to this unified outlook.[202] Yet for all Matthew's

200. Banks ('Matthew 5.17-20', pp. 236-40) defends the substantial authenticity of vv. 17-20. Although his interpretation differs slightly from mine, his arguments are nonetheless relevant here.

201. Cf. especially Banks, *Jesus and the Law*, pp. 242-45; and also Verweijs, *Evangelium*, p. 351.

202. Matthew's viewpoint is often characterized as 'Jewish-Christian' and seen to take a far more positive stance toward the written and oral law than, e.g., Mark or Luke (see, for instance, the presentation of Dunn, *Unity and Diversity*, pp. 246-51).

concern with Judaism and his apparent reluctance to sever relationships with the synagogue, he transmits some of Jesus' most far-reaching claims with respect to the law (5.17, 21-48; 12.8) and it seems preferable to understand more conservative statements within this 'fulfillment' motif rather than speak of contradictions in his material. The unanimity in outlook found in the synoptics on this matter, when contrasted with first-century Jewish beliefs and even some circles in the early church, suggests that we are in touch here with the *ipsissima vox Jesu*.

What may we then conclude from this about the authority of the Mosaic law in the new age of fulfillment? Any conclusions drawn from Jesus' teaching must, of course, be tentative and subject to the correction and expansion of the more explicit treatment of some of these questions in the epistles. The most that can be done here is to suggest some directions in which the evidence would seem to lead.

First, and most basically, every Mosaic law must be, as Ridderbos puts it, 'placed under the condition of its fulfillment'.[203] On the basis of Jesus' teaching, it does not seem that any Mosaic commandment can be assumed to be directly applicable to the believer. Jesus' authority as the law's fulfiller stands even over the decalogue, as his claim of lordship over the Sabbath shows; and most believers have utilized that authority in refusing to 'honor the *seventh* day'.[204] Nor do statements about the discontinuity/continuity of the law presume the tripartite division of the law, so popular in much of Christian history. The *whole* law came to culmination in Christ. As the sole ultimate authority of the Messianic community, he takes up the law into himself and enunciates what is enduring in its contents. In doing so, it may be inaccurate to speak of a 'new law',[205] but it cannot be denied that Jesus' commandments include both general principles and some detailed demands—much more than the bare requirement of love is involved.[206] The change in redemptive

203. *Kingdom*, p. 308.

204. The letter of the fourth commandment clearly specifies the *seventh* day, not simply a 'one-in-seven' principle.

205. Davies has suggested that the early Christians, taking up some inchoate indications in this direction in contemporary Judaism, may have come to view Jesus' teaching as a new *torah (Torah in the Messianic Age and/or the Age to Come* [JBLMS, 7; Philadelphia: SBL, 1952]; *Setting*, pp. 122-88). But this is contested by P. Schäfer, 'Die Torah der messianischen Zeit', *ZNW* 65 (1974), pp. 27-42; and R. Banks, 'The Eschatological Role of Law in Pre- and Post-Christian Jewish Thought', in *Reconciliation and Hope*, pp. 175-85.

206. Meyer, *Aims of Jesus*, p. 143.

'eras' brings with it a change in the locus of authority for the people of God,[207] but it does not bring a liberation from authority as such.

Thus, secondly, the teaching of Jesus gives little support to those who would want to apply the criterion of love to discriminate among the applicability of Mosaic commandments. It was not on the basis of 'the demands of love', but on the basis of his unique intuitive knowledge of God's will that Jesus interpreted and applied the law.

Finally, Jesus by no means countenances the abandonment of the Mosaic law; indeed (if Mt. 5.18-19 be accepted as authentic), he explicitly commands that it be taught. However, this teaching must always be done with due attention to the fulfillment of the law (v. 17) and the way in which this fulfillment affects the meaning and applicability of its provisions.

207. Bahnsen's treatment (*Theonomy*) is flawed by a consistent failure to give adequate attention to such salvation-historical considerations. Similarly, approaches which emphasize the difference in *interpretation* of the law evidenced by Jesus and the Pharisees (cf. S. Westerholm, *Jesus and Scribal Authority* [ConBNT, 10; Lund: Gleerup, 1978]) often fail to come to grips with the radical shift in perspective brought by the coming of the Kingdom.

EXEGETICAL ASPECTS OF JESUS' TEACHING

JSNT 2 (1979), pp. 31-41

AN ANALYSIS OF JESUS' ARGUMENTS CONCERNING
THE PLUCKING OF GRAIN ON THE SABBATH

Rabbi D.M. Cohn-Sherbok

Introduction

Recently there has been some debate as to the nature of the arguments put forward by Jesus in Mt. 12.1-8, Mk 2.23-28, and Lk. 6.1-5 to defend his disciples for having plucked ears of grain on the Sabbath. D.E. Nineham, for example, in *St Mark* writes, 'his reply took the form of an argument deduced from the Old Testament very much in the manner of the rabbis themselves... The dispute up to this point might have occurred between any two rabbis, and no doubt many of the more liberal rabbis of the time would very largely have agreed with Jesus'.[1] In a similar vein B.H. Branscomb in *The Gospel of St Mark* asserts that Jesus 'was familiar with the rabbinic teaching in this respect, and possibly even with their use of this particular passage from the Scriptures. He drew from it a far wider deduction—ritual laws were subordinate to human needs. His view was in line with rabbinic teaching, but went much further—so much further, indeed, as to become quite a new and independent teaching'.[2] Again, W. Rordorf in *Sunday* argues that in this Sabbath conflict story 'it cannot be denied that there is a formal similarity to rabbinical disputes, and this similarity is especially evident in the manner of adducing Scriptural proof'.[3]

This identification of Jesus' argument with rabbinic disputation has led a number of scholars to specify the type of rabbinic argument used. In the *Journal of Biblical Literature* S. Cohon points out that when Jesus

1. D.E. Nineham, *St Mark* (Middlesex: Penguin, 1969), pp. 105-106.
2. B.H. Branscomb, *The Gospel of Mark* (London: Hodder & Stoughton, 1964), p. 57.
3. W. Rordorf, *Sunday* (London: SCM Press, 1968), p. 72.

called for a departure from the Pharisaic conception of the law, he based himself on a Scriptural verse, or some analogy or principle laid down in another law or practice, in a manner reminiscent of some of the exegetical rules of Hillel. Thus,

> with regard to the Sabbath, Jesus resorts to Pharisaic arguments to counteract Pharisaic rules. He justifies his disciples in plucking ears of corn on the Sabbath by an analogy (*gezera shava*) from David, who under compulsion ate the shewbread, which was contrary to the Law. Matthew adds another analogy: "Have you not read in the Law that the priests in the Temple are not guilty when they desecrate the Sabbath?" and concludes with a *kal vechomer*: I tell you one is here who is greater than the Temple... The Son of Man is Lord of the Sabbath.[4]

This same analysis is presented by J.W. Doeve in *Jewish Hermeneutics in the Synoptic Gospels and Acts* where he writes,

> That which was permitted to David, who had received the Kingdom, viz. an infringement of the Halakah, is also permitted to the Son of Man... That the nature of the infringement is not quite the same in both cases does not affect the matter. David and Jesus are in the same case; with both it is a matter of food unlawful for them. It was permitted to David, so it is also permissible for Jesus. We have here a *gezerah shavah*. Verses 5 and 6 contain a particular *kal wahomer*. The Temple and its service set aside the law of the Sabbath; for the Tamid, the daily offering, is brought upon the Sabbath. Jesus is more than a Temple. So he has certainly the right to set aside the Law of the Sabbath.[5]

An alternative view was put forward by D. Daube in *The New Testament and Rabbinic Judaism* where he states that the argument from David's conduct was not conclusive from a scholarly, legal point of view. This was so because the argument was essentially haggadic in character; such an argument might serve to inculcate moral lessons, general religious truths and wisdom, and they might also serve to illustrate and corroborate a halakah. But it could not be used to justify the abrogation of a law. Thus in the context of rabbinic hermeneutics the argument concerning David is not valid. However, the argument concerning the Temple service on a Sabbath in Matthew (though not in Mark and Luke) is completely acceptable because

---

4. S. Cohon, 'The Place of Jesus in the Religion of his Day', *JBL* 48 (1929), pp. 82-108, esp. p. 97.
5. J.W. Doeve, *Jewish Hermeneutics in the Synoptic Gospels and Acts* (Assen: Van Gorcum, 1954), p. 71.

it rests on a definite precept. The scholarly, strict rabbinic character of this argument is underlined by the employment of a hermeneutic norm... the inference *a fortiori*, the qal wahomer. Scripture—thus the argument of Matthew runs—ordains that the observance of the Sabbath must yield to the Temple service; *a fortiori* it must yield to the Temple case where something greater than the Temple demands consideration.[6]

Commenting on Daube's analysis, W.D. Davies emphasizes that, 'Matthew adds to the Markan account of the Plucking of the Corn on the Sabbath (Mk 2.23-28) another verse (Mt. 12.5). As Daube has made brilliantly clear, this seems to provide a precedent for the action of the disciples in the Law itself (Num. 28.9-10)... Its force is to place Jesus securely within the law'.[7]

The purpose of this paper is to look more closely at the arguments Jesus used to defend his disciples. On the basis of an analysis of the analogy of *gezera shava* and the inference of *kal vechomer*, it can be seen that though Jesus seems to have been familiar with rabbinic hermeneutics, the arguments he employs are invalid from a rabbinic point of view. This should not surprise us since it bears out the truth of the Gospels' claim that Jesus was a carpenter by trade, teaching on his own authority in the synagogue, far removed from the technical casuistry of the Scribes, Sadducees and Pharisees.

Did Jesus Use the Analogy of Gezera Shava ?

The analogy of *gezera shava* denotes analogy of expressions, that is, an analogy based on identical words occurring in two different passages of Scripture. On the basis of an analogy of *gezera shava*, it can be shown that when identical words occur in these passages the legal provisions made in one case must apply also to the other case even though they were not explicitly mentioned. Hillel who first delineated this rule of interpretation applied it in the following case concerning the question whether it should be permitted to sacrifice the Paschal Lamb on the Sabbath. In the law concerning the daily offering it is said (Num. 28.2) that it is to be brought במועדו (in its due season), and in the law regarding the Paschal lamb (Num. 9.2) we read: 'The children of Israel shall keep

---

6. D. Daube, *The New Testament and Rabbinic Judaism* (London: The Athlone Press, 1956), p. 71.

7. W.D. Davies, *The Setting of the Sermon on the Mount* (Cambridge: Cambridge University Press, 1966), pp. 103-104.

the Passover במועדו (in its due season)'. Concerning the daily offering, Scripture also states (Num. 28.10) that it is to be brought on the Sabbath day. Thus, the expression במועדו means that the offering must take place at the appointed time under *all* circumstances, even on the Sabbath; therefore the same expression במועדו when referring to the Paschal offering likewise enjoins that the offering take place at the time appointed, even on a Sabbath day.

Turning to the Gospels, we can see that although Jesus used an analogy between David and himself to defend his disciples, this argument is not a *gezera shava*, as Cohon and Doeve suggest. Though David and his entourage violated the law out of hunger as did the disciples of Jesus, there is no identical word or expression in Mt. 12.1-8, Mk 2.23-28, and Lk. 6.1-5 and in Sam. 21.1-6 which could serve as a link between passages. Rather than a *gezera shava* this argument resembles another kind of analogy, somewhat similar to a *gezera shava*, a היקש of דומיא where a comparison is made which infers from the similarity of two cases that what has been decided in one applies also to the other. Thus, Jesus was not pointing to an identical work or expression in 1 Sam. 21.1-6 to justify the action of his disciples; the examples of David served simply as an analogous case.

It is obvious, however, that this comparison fails because the resemblance between the two cases is merely superficial. In the case of David, the breach of law was justified by reference to the actual danger to his life,[8] a justification in full accord with the general rabbinic principle that when a human life is in danger the Sabbath laws are to be set aside.[9] However, in the case of Jesus' disciples, they were not in mortal danger, nor were they bringing help to others in urgent need. Thus, since the disciples were not famished, there was no obvious necessity which would justify this breach of the Sabbath. As Rordorf points out, 'the disciples would have to be reproached for not having prepared their meals on the previous day as everyone else did; and even if they omitted to do this not out of carelessness, but because of the turmoil of their

---

8.   This breach of Law had been the subject of considerable rabbinic discussion, David's action being justified by reference to the actual danger to his life which hunger had brought about. See R. Banks, *Jesus and the Law in the Synoptic Tradition* (SNTSMS, 28; Cambridge: Cambridge University Press, 1975), p. 114. See also *b. Men.* 95a: 'even that which has been sanctified this day in the vessel you may give him to eat for he is in danger of his life'.

9.   G.F. Moore, *Judaism*, II (repr. New York: Schocken Books, 1971), p. 30.

missionary activity, they could have fasted for the whole day'.[10]

Thus, the clear points of difference between David and his followers and the disciples of Jesus vitiate the analogy Jesus used. Similar fallacious uses of analogy are found throughout rabbinic literature. For example, in *b. Giṭ.* 33a two fourth-century rabbis, R. Nahman and R. Shesheth, differ as to how many judges are needed to cancel a bill of divorce. R. Shesheth contends that three are needed since the Mishnah stipulates that they must compose a Bet Din. R. Nahman argues that only two are necessary because the law stipulates that either the judges or two witnesses need to sign the decree, implying that since two witnesses suffice, so only two judges are necessary. R. Shesheth, however, points out that this inference is not valid because judges and witnesses are not analogous: 'Judges and witnesses each follow their own rule'. Therefore, despite the fact that only two men are needed if they act as witnesses, three judges are needed because in that capacity they would function as members of a Bet Din. Thus, here, as in the case of Jesus and his disciples and David and his followers, the cases are so dissimilar that the inference drawn from an analogy between them is invalid.

Another fundamental problem connected with this analogy is that it could not be conclusive from the scholarly, legal point of view for two reasons. First, in the case of David, the violation of the law did not take place on the Sabbath; thus this text does not prove that one might in a similar circumstance break the Sabbath. Secondly, and more importantly, the Scriptural passage Jesus utilized concerns the conduct of an historical personage rather than a law. He quoted a narrative saying that David had acted in a particular way, without referring to a particular legal precept, and it is of the essence of the rabbinic system that any detailed rule must rest on an actual precept promulgated in Scripture. Historical narrative belongs to the province of *haggadah*; it might serve to edify, teach religious truths, or illustrate and corroborate a *halakah*, but it could not form its primary source.[11] Thus, the use of this analogy as a basis for violating the Sabbath law is invalid; even if the analogy between Jesus and his disciples and David and his entourage had been appropriate, the argument could not technically have been conclusive because it does not rest on a Scriptural precept.

10. Rordorf, *Sunday*, pp. 61-62.
11. Daube, *New Testament and Rabbinic Judaism*, pp. 68-69.

Did Jesus Use the Inference of Kal Vechomer?

The inference of *kal vechomer* occupies the first place in the hermeneutical system of Hillel (first century BC) as well as in that of R. Ishmael
(second century AD) whose thirteen hermeneutical rules have been
adopted as the authoritative rules of rabbinical interpretation. The word
kal ('light' in weight) designates that which, from a legal point of view,
is regarded as being less important, less significant; *chomer* ('heaviness'),
on the other hand, specifies what is comparatively of great weight and
importance. By the term *kal vechomer* therefore is meant an inference
from the less to the more important, and vice versa, from the more to
the less important.

The principle underlying the inference of *kal vechomer* is that if a certain restrictive law applies to a matter of minor importance, we may
infer that the same restriction is applicable to a matter of major importance; conversely, if a certain allowance applies to a thing of major
importance, we may infer that the same allowance is applicable to that
which is of comparatively minor importance. Thus, for example, since
the Sabbath is more important than a common holiday, if a certain kind
of work is forbidden on a common holiday, we can infer that it must be
forbidden on the Sabbath; conversely, if a certain kind of work is permitted on the Sabbath, it can be inferred that such work is permissible
on a common holiday.

Logically every *kal vechomer* has three propositions, of which two are
the premises, and one the conclusion. The first premise states that two
things A and B stand to each other in the relation of major and minor
importance. The second premise states that with one of these two things,
A, a certain restrictive or permissive law is connected. The conclusion is
that the same law is applicable to the other thing, B.

The inference from minor to major is illustrated by an example from
the book of Exodus. In Exod. 22.14, the law is laid down that if a man
borrows from his neighbor an animal or a thing, and the animal dies or
the thing is destroyed, the borrower must restore the loss. However, it is
not explicitly mentioned whether the borrower is also responsible in
cases when the borrowed animal or thing is stolen. We do read, though,
in Exod. 22.10-12 that a paid caretaker is not bound to make restitution
when the animal entrusted to his care dies or becomes hurt, but is
responsible if the entrusted object is stolen. Taken together these two
passages provide the basis for an inference of *kal vechomer*. The first

premise of the inference is that the case of the paid caretaker who is not bound to make restitution if what is entrusted to him dies or becomes hurt is of minor significance compared to the case of a borrower who must make restitution. The second premise is that the paid caretaker must make restitution if what is entrusted to him is stolen. The conclusion is that this restrictive law regarding the restitution of stolen things which applies to the paid caretaker (the minor case) applies to the borrower (the major case) as well. The Talmud (*b. B. Meṣ.* 95a) expresses this inference as follows: 'If the caretaker, though free from responsibility for damage and death, is still bound to restore the thing stolen from him, ought not the borrower, who is responsible for damage and death, to be the more bound to restore the thing stolen from him?'

Turning to Jesus' arguments concerning the plucked ears of grain, an inference of *kal vechomer* has been detected by Doeve and Daube in vv. 5-6. Here a comparison is drawn between the Temple and Jesus, and the inference runs as follows: The first premise asserts that the Temple and Jesus stand in relation to one another as of minor and major importance. The second premise states that with regard to the Temple a permissive law is attached, namely the neglect of the Sabbath observance. The conclusion is that this same law is applicable to the disciples of Jesus. As Daube points out, the application of the inference of *kal vechomer* in this context rests on a definite precept, that offerings should be brought to the Temple even on a Sabbath (Num. 28.9). Yet, the fact that this inference is based on a definite precept, and that it corresponds formally to a *kal vechomer* does not demonstrate that it is valid. As M. Mielziner points out in his classic study of rabbinic hermeneutics, not all are correct and valid, and that in the Talmud 'we sometimes find there very problematic and even sophistical inferences set forth...'[12]

Unlike the example cited from Exodus, Jesus' argument contains only one biblical passage; the second case concerns a person, Jesus, who is alleged to be greater than the Temple. Jesus intended to point out that just as priests were free to profane the Sabbath because they were occupied with Temple observances, so his disciples were justified in satisfying their hunger by plucking corn (an action expressly forbidden according to rabbinic law),[13] because Jesus is greater than the Temple. However, if this inference were valid, the first premise would have to be:

12. M. Mielziner, *Introduction to the Talmud* (New York: Bloch, 1968), p. 136.
13. According to *m. Šab.* 7.2, the third kind of the 39 activities forbidden on the Sabbath was reaping.

If A (Temple Observance), which is of minor importance, is subject to a certain permissiveness of the law, then B (service to Jesus), which is of major importance, must be subject to the same permissiveness. What is clear, however, is that, unlike the priests, Jesus' disciples were not engaged in any form of religious observance, nor were they serving Jesus by plucking ears of grain. They were simply concerned to satisfy their own hunger. Thus, since B has nothing to do with service to Jesus, Temple observances and the disciples plucking grain on the Sabbath cannot legitimately be compared in the first premise of a *kal vechomer*, and this renders Jesus' inference invalid.

Such a defective inference resembles that used by the Sadducees against the Pharisees in *m. Yad.* 4.7:

> The Sadducees said, we have a strong argument against you Pharisees. You teach that one is responsible for a damage caused by his ox or ass, but not responsible for a damage caused by his slave or bondsman; is this not contrary to a simple rational inference?: 'If I am responsible for my animals regarding which I have no religious obligation, how much more must I then be responsible for the damage caused by my servants regarding whom I have a religious obligation?'

The objection raised by the Pharisees against this argument is that, though one does have religious obligations for slaves, unlike animals, they have free will and deliberation; therefore one is not responsible for damage caused by them. In other words, the Pharisees point out that animals and slaves are dissimilar in a fundamental way and cannot be compared in the manner the Sadducees suggest. Similarly, in the case of Jesus, priestly obligations in the Temple and the actions of his disciples are radically dissimilar, and cannot legitimately be compared. Thus, we can see that although Jesus seems to have used a *kal vechomer* in reply to the Pharisees, his argument, like that of the Sadducees, was fallacious because the comparison he drew was inappropriate.

Conclusion

Assuming that Matthew, Mark and Luke accurately record Jesus' defence of his disciples for having plucked ears of corn on the Sabbath, it appears that Jesus was familiar with rabbinic hermeneutics. Yet, the arguments he utilized are not valid from a rabbinic point of view: the first, concerning David and his entourage, because it is based on a false analogy and also because it is not grounded on a definite precept; the second, concerning the priests eating shewbread on the Sabbath, because their action and the action of Jesus' disciples are fundamentally dissimilar and cannot be drawn together in a *kal vechomer*. This misuse of rabbinic reasoning should not surprise us since it bears out the truth of the Gospel in asserting that Jesus was not a skilled casuist in the style of the Pharisees and Sadducees, and helps explain why, when he argued with them, he provoked their indignation and hostility.

JSNT 43 (1991), pp. 5-13

THE QUESTION OF THE AUTHENTICITY OF THE BAN ON SWEARING (MATTHEW 5.33-37)

Akio Ito

This study represents a critical reply to G. Dautzenberg's article 'Ist das Schwurverbot Mt. 5.33-37; Jak 5.12 ein Beispiel für die Torakritik Jesu?'[1] His essay aims mainly at repudiating the authenticity of Jesus' prohibition of swearing which is usually accepted. The question of authenticity certainly involves various slippery arguments that will become apparent in the course of our discussion of Dautzenberg's reasoning.

Since there is no essay which responds to Dautzenberg extensively,[2] I feel justified in writing this response to his article although it was published some time ago. Here I shall first look at Dautzenberg's arguments against the authenticity of the prohibition of swearing and then critically assess them.

Dautzenberg's main arguments against the authenticity of the prohibition of swearing can be summarized as follows:

> 1. Negative attitudes towards oaths—some more negative than the others—were predominant and widespread among the Jews of the day on the basis of Exod. 20.7 and Lev. 19.12. So we cannot exclude the possibility that the prohibition entered into Jesus tradition from traditional Jewish material ('Ist das Schwurverbot', pp. 53-56).

1. *BZ* 25 (1981), pp. 47-66.
2. G. Strecker (*Die Bergpredigt* [Göttingen: Vandenhoeck & Ruprecht, 1984], p. 82 n. 37) and U. Luz (*Das Evangelium nach Matthäus. Mt. 1–7* [EKK, 1.1; Zürich/Neukirchen–Vluyn: Benziger Verlag/Neukirchener Verlag, 1985], p. 282 n. 16) refer to Dautzenberg's article only in passing.

2.   There is a tension (or almost contradiction) between the prohibition of swearing and the use of asseverations and amen-sayings in the Synoptic tradition ('Ist das Schwurverbot', pp. 57-60).

3.   James[3] seems to be ignorant of the dominical origin of the prohibition of swearing, while his exhortation not to swear seems to represent a more original tradition than the Matthaean version which represents it as a Jesus saying ('Ist das Schwurverbot', pp. 61-63).

4.   In view of his frequent use of oath formulae Paul was probably ignorant of the dominical prohibition of swearing. This is the case despite the possible counter-argument based on 2 Cor. 1.17-20, because this passage testifies only to his possible knowledge of the 'Yes, yes', 'No, no' saying, but not to his possible familiarity with the prohibition of swearing ('Ist das Schwurverbot', pp. 63-65).

Although Dautzenberg's cumulative arguments against the authenticity of the prohibition of swearing appear to be impressive at first sight, none of his arguments in fact turns out to be convincing. Due to the limitation of space here I have to omit detailed analysis of Jewish material and the New Testament passages which are relevant to my evaluation of Dautzenberg's main four points.

While Dautzenberg's first point is basically a correct observation, there is a fine distinction between Jewish criticism of swearing and Jesus' prohibition of swearing:[4] Jewish criticism of swearing was concerned with the upholding of the biblical regulations about swearing such as Exod. 20.7 and Lev. 19.12, and the protecting of the institution of oath-taking and the name of God from abuses, whereas Jesus' prohibition appears to be more radical. Dautzenberg fails to see that the main concern and basic intention of the Jewish criticism of swearing was to protect the institution of oath-taking and the divine names by excluding any possible misuse and abuse of swearing and of the divine names.[5]

---

3.   Jas 5.12 reads: 'But above all, my brethren, do not swear, either by heaven or by earth or with any other oath, but let your yes be yes and your no be no, that you may not fall under condemnation'.

4.   Although he observes this fine distinction ('Ist das Schwurverbot', p. 52), he seems to consider it an insignificant one.

5.   What I refer to as Jewish criticism of swearing is found in the Dead Sea Scrolls, Philo, Josephus, the Old Testament Apocrypha and Pseudepigrapha and the

Furthermore, Dautzenberg understands Jesus' prohibition of swearing as concerning only the non-judicial use of swearing, whereas the language of the prohibition seems to be more comprehensive. It is uncertain whether or not this fine distinction is enough to claim that Jesus' prohibition is supported by the criterion of dissimilarity.[6] In any case we would be unwise to rely purely on this sort of argument for authenticity in the light of recent criticisms of the criterion of dissimilarity.[7] But at least we can say that there exists a fine distinction which may be clearer than Dautzenberg is willing to admit between Jewish criticism of swearing and the prohibition of swearing in Mt. 5.33-37/Jas 5.12.[8]

---

rabbinic writings. For example, Ben Sirach 23.9-11 reads: 'Do not accustom your mouth to oaths, and do not habitually utter the name of the Holy One…A man who swears many oaths will be filled with iniquity…; if he has sworn needlessly, he will not be justified…' *CD* 15.1-2 reads: 'swear, nor by *Aleph* and *Lamedh* [i.e. El, Elohim], nor by *Aleph* and *Daleth* [i.e. Adhonai], but with an oath of agreement by the curses of the covenant. Even the Law of Moses let him not mention, for…' (C. Rabin, *The Zadokite Documents* [Oxford: Oxford University Press, 1954], pp. 70-72).

6.   The criterion of dissimilarity is that 'material which can be accounted for neither as traditional Jewish material nor as later church material can be safely attributed to Jesus' (E.P. Sanders, *Jesus and Judaism* [London: SCM Press, 1985], p. 16).

7.   E.g. R.H. Stein, 'The "Criteria" for Authenticity', in *Gospel Perspectives*, I (ed. R.T. France and D. Wenham; Sheffield: JSOT Press, 1980), pp. 242-44. Since the validity of the criterion of dissimilarity has been questioned, Dautzenberg's first point is certainly weak.

8.   Luz writes: 'Da das kategorische Schwurverbot im Judentum singulär ist, stammt es wohl von Jesus' (*Matthäus*, I, p. 282). Against Dautzenberg, Luz writes (*Matthäus*, I, p. 282 n. 16) as follows: 'Ist ein—nicht jesuanisches, aber auch nicht jüdisches—Schwurverbot als eigener Beitrag einer judenchristlichen Gemeinde zur jüdischen Eiddikussion wirklich denkbar? M.E. liegt hier ein klassischer Fall für das Unähnlichkeitskriterium vor.' Similarly G. Strecker, 'Die Antithesen der Bergpredigt', *ZNW* 69 (1978), p. 60.

Although *2 En.* 49.1-2 presents a negative view on swearing which is as absolute as Mt. 5.33-34a (*2 En.* 49.1-2 (J) reads: 'For I am swearing to you, my children—But look! I am not swearing by any oath at all, neither by heaven nor by earth nor by any other creature which the Lord created. For the Lord said, "There is no oath in me, nor any unrighteousness, but only truth". So, if there is no truth in human beings, then let them make an oath by means of the words "Yes, Yes!" or, if it should be the other way around, "No, No!" And I make an oath to you—"Yes, Yes!"' [*The Old Testament Pseudepigrapha*, I (ed. J.H. Charlesworth; London: Darton, Longman & Todd, 1983), p. 176]), it is dubious whether it can be regarded as the Jewish background to Mt. 5.34 since *2 En.* 49.1-2 seems to be a Christian interpolation (as

The second and fourth points of Dautzenberg's arguments against the authenticity of the prohibition of swearing depend on two suppositions: (1) that Jesus could not make contradictory statements, and (2) that his followers could not contradict his teachings. However, if we accept that Jesus employed asseverations and frequently pronounced amen-sayings, does it follow that he could not prohibit swearing? Against this it is arguable, first, that alleged oath formulae on the lips of Jesus in the Gospels are not oath formulae in a strict sense.[9] Secondly, 'amen' fits in quite well with the prohibition of swearing if the 'Yes, yes', 'No, no' saying forms part of an original prohibition:[10] 'amen' and ναί ('Yes') correspond to each other in meaning. Hence it is likely that 'amen' is not included in the prohibition, provided that the 'Yes, yes', 'No, no' saying was part of an original saying.[11]

But even if Dautzenberg's argument that the very existence of Jesus' prohibition of swearing creates a contradiction within the Synoptic tradition is correct,[12] this does not prove the inauthenticity of the saying, since it is perfectly possible for one to make (at least, apparently) contradictory statements, still more statements containing significant tensions.[13] The same points apply to the argument about Paul's supposed use of oaths: Jesus' followers could contradict his teachings. Paul may

Dautzenberg also thinks ['Ist das Schwurverbot', p. 56]). If *2 En.* 49.1-2 is not a Christian interpolation, I must concede that this is a real exception. If so, this exception weakens my case. But we cannot deny the authenticity of the prohibition of swearing altogether simply because it does not pass the test of dissimilarity.

Apoc. Mos. 18.1–20.2 is an interesting passage in relation to Jewish criticism of swearing. The passage can be understood as a retelling of Gen. 3 which incorporates criticism of oaths: the serpent employs an oath as an effective weapon to entice Eve. It is difficult to assess its precise attitude to swearing.

9. The passages which I have in mind are: Mk 8.12; 14.25; Mt. 26.63-64; etc.

10. Doubts have been cast on the authenticity of the non-responsive use of 'amen', but I assume its authenticity for the sake of the present argument because Dautzenberg assumes its authenticity in his argument ('Ist das Schwurverbot', p. 57).

11. I understand the double 'yes' and 'no' of the Matthaean version as being a simple emphatic form of 'yes' and 'no' (cf. R. Guelich, *The Sermon on the Mount* [Waco, TX: Word Books, 1982], pp. 216-18 and Luz, *Matthäus*, I, pp. 285-86) against Strecker ('Die Antithesen', pp. 62-63 and *Die Bergpredigt*, p. 84) who regards it as an asseveration formula (*Beteuerungsformel*) used as a surrogate oath formula in the Matthaean church.

12. Hence exclusion of the prohibition of swearing can remove the contradiction among Jesus' sayings material.

13. Stein, 'The "Criterion"', p. 250.

not have known Jesus' prohibition, or he may have transgressed it even with his knowledge of it.

Furthermore, what appears to be contradictory to us may not have been contradictory to Jesus and his contemporaries.[14] Again this is dependent on our interpretation of the respective passages and our understanding and knowledge of the contemporary world.

For instance, Dautzenberg's observation concerning Paul's use of oath formulae is basically correct, but he misses two important points: (1) the peculiar function and use of oath formulae in the Pauline Epistles, and (2) the possible context of the 'Yes, yes', 'No, no' saying. On the first point I must draw attention to the fact that Paul employs oath formulae only in order to testify to the divine origin of certain matters like his apostleship, his mission plan and his gospel.[15] In other words he appeals to God to testify that what he believes to be of divine origin is genuinely of divine origin. If we remember that God is usually appealed to in an oath for the purpose of testifying to the truth of secular matters, we may appreciate that the Pauline use of oaths is distinct from ordinary uses. It may be regarded as a use of oaths not covered by the prohibition of swearing; or at least Paul could well have considered it an exception to the prohibition if he knew it.

On the second point, the fact that both Matthew and James put the 'Yes, yes', 'No, no' saying in the context of the prohibition of swearing points to the possibility that the 'Yes, yes', 'No, no' saying was originally, or at least at an early stage, attached to the prohibition of swearing.[16] If it was, Paul's knowledge of the 'Yes, yes', 'No, no' saying may well testify to his knowledge of Jesus' prohibition of swearing.

Further, although Dautzenberg is hesitant about narrowing the meaning of the prohibition in order to harmonize Jesus' use of an oath formula and his frequent use of asseverations and amen-sayings with the prohibition of swearing, the question of whether or not all these fit in well with each other depends on how we understand the main thrust of the prohibition of swearing. Generally the question of the authenticity of Jesus' sayings involves slippery arguments, and whether one answers

14. Stein, 'The "Criterion"', p. 250.

15. See Rom. 1.9; 9.1-3; 1 Cor. 15.31; 2 Cor. 1.18, 23; 2.17; 4.2; 11.10-11, 31; 12.19; Gal. 1.20; Phil. 1.8; 1 Thess. 2.5, 10. Cf. O. Bauernfeind, 'Der Eid in der Sicht des Neuen Testamentes', in *Eid, Gewissen, Treuepflicht* (ed. H. Bethke; Frankfurt am Main: Stimme, 1965), pp. 102-103.

16. Cf. Guelich, *Sermon*, pp. 216-18.

the question in the affirmative or in the negative very much depends on one's interpretation of the respective sayings.

With regard to the latter part of Dautzenberg's third argument that James represents a more original tradition we must wait for another paper which reconstructs an underlying tradition behind Mt. 5.33-37/Jas 5.12.[17]

The first part of Dautzenberg's third argument is James' apparent ignorance of the dominical origin of the prohibition: James presents the prohibition of swearing as his own exhortation whereas Matthew attributes it to Jesus. Dautzenberg particularly draws our attention to the fact that James gives no hint of its dominical origin, by contrast with the Pauline awareness of the distinction between his own opinion and the 'command of the Lord', in, for example, 1 Cor. 7.25. However, against this we may note that Paul himself does not always seem to make explicit his dependence on the dominical tradition (authority) for his instruction to churches.[18] In other words even when the dominical origin or dependence of certain exhortations is not acknowledged, it does not necessarily follow that the author is ignorant of the dominical origin, or denying it. On the contrary it may be the case that its dominical origin is taken for granted so that the author does not consider it necessary to acknowledge it.

It seems easier to explain the passage in question in this way, that is, that James took it for granted that the prohibition of swearing was dominical tradition, and did not feel it necessary to articulate it. Responding to the objections that '(i) James does not quote the saying as a dominical saying; (ii) it occurs in the Gospels only in Matthew, and it is precisely in Matthew that legal prescriptions of a Jewish origin

17. Suffice it to say here that I shall argue that the Matthaean version is closer to the original tradition than James'.

18. D. Wenham writes: 'Any suggestion that Paul was unfamiliar with or uninterested in the Jesus tradition must be considered improbable in view of the evidence accumulated for Paul's use of the pre-synoptic eschatological traditions. It appears on the contrary that Paul's teaching is very heavily dependent on the teaching of Jesus, even though he does not often explicitly acknowledge this dependence' (*The Rediscovery of Jesus' Eschatological Discourse* [Sheffield: JSOT Press, 1984], p. 372). Cf. Wenham, *Rediscovery*, pp. 54-55, 89-91, 110-17, 282-84, 295-96, 304-306, 351-52, 366-67, 372; *idem*, 'Paul's Use of the Jesus Tradition: Three Samples', in *Gospel Perspectives*, V (ed. D. Wenham; Sheffield: JSOT Press, 1984), pp. 7-37. More cautiously, P. Richardson and P. Gooch, 'Logia of Jesus in 1 Corinthians', in *Gospel Perspectives*, V, pp. 39-62.

occasionally appear as dominical sayings; (iii) there are Jewish parallels to this saying',[19] Dibelius writes:

> these arguments are only apparently valid. Because of their very nature, the last two naturally prove nothing. Regarding the first argument, the absence of a quotation formula in James does not qualify as evidence that the saying about swearing was not regarded as a dominical saying in the time of James. Other sayings of Jesus whose provenance is more assured are also used in paraenetic texts without special introductory identification.[20] This is not surprising, for all paraenesis which is delivered by teachers who are considered bearers of the Spirit stems ultimately from the Lord, and, therefore, it possesses an even higher authenticity than a quotation formula can provide.[21]

Although Dibelius pushes his argument too far,[22] his last point seems to me to be an important one. Because of their nature as hortatory material, the admonitions in James are woven together to call for right behaviour, so quotation formulae could be considered inappropriate, and the dominical origin of the prohibition of swearing might be presupposed by both James and the reader.

Another factor seems to strengthen this point. Although 5.12, the prohibition of swearing, is a singular instance which has such striking similarities in wording to the dominical saying in the Gospels that we can term it an indirect citation, the Epistle of James is full of allusions to dominical sayings.[23] We would need a detailed study to analyse the way

19. M. Dibelius and H. Greeven, *James* (Hermeneia; Philadelphia: Fortress Press, 1975), p. 251.

20. Here his footnote reads: 'Rom. 12.14, or the Christian interpolation in the "Two Ways" section in Did. 1.3ff.; see Dibelius, *From Tradition to Gospel*, 240f.'

21. Dibelius and Greeven, *James*, p. 251.

22. That 'all paraenesis which is delivered by teachers who are considered bearers of the Spirit stems ultimately from the Lord, and, therefore, it possesses an even higher authenticity than a quotation formula can provide' seems to be an over-statement of his case. Cf. J.D.G. Dunn, 'Prophetic "I"-Sayings and the Jesus Tradition: The Importance of Testing Prophetic Utterances within Early Christianity', *NTS* 24 (1977–78), pp. 175-98.

23. P.H. Davids, 'James and Jesus', in *Gospel Perspectives*, V, pp. 63-84; *idem*, *The Epistle of James* (NIGTC; Exeter: Paternoster Press, 1982), pp. 47ff. He counts 47, including obvious allusions, possible allusions and indirect citations (5.12). He attempts to understand 'the twin phenomena in the epistle of James of its closeness to the Jesus tradition on the one hand and its lack of formal citations of the tradition on the other' in terms of his hypothesis that 'the Jesus tradition...forms the underlying rule of life for the early community' ('James and Jesus', p. 76).

James makes use of the Jesus tradition in his Epistle to substantiate this point clearly, but we can at least say that James employs the Jesus tradition in his instruction to churches in his Epistle without acknowledging it. In short, 5.12 is not the only instance where James makes use of the Jesus tradition implicitly in his Epistle.

Since we can think of all sorts of reasons for James' use of the dominical saying without making reference to its origin, it seems untenable to conclude from the fact that James does not attribute the prohibition of swearing to Jesus that it is Matthew who attributed a saying of James to Jesus. Therefore, it can be concluded that it is more likely that James made use of the Jesus tradition in his exhortation of 5.12 than that Matthew attributed James' exhortation to Jesus.

To sum up, the present arguments are far from conclusive, and it is very difficult to present any definitive answer to the question of the authenticity of the prohibition of swearing, but I have demonstrated that Dautzenberg's arguments against the authenticity of the prohibition of swearing may not be sufficient to disprove its authenticity.

JSNT 38 (1990), pp. 67-75

Jesus' Teaching on Divorce in the Gospel of Mark

Barbara Green, O.P.

The question posed to Jesus in Mk 10.2 continues to be asked, though perhaps not always in the particular form in which the Pharisees phrase it there: '"Is it lawful for a man to divorce his wife?"' The question of dissolution of the marriage bond is always serious in any tradition that values the family, as does the Judeo-Christian. The Christian churches have needed to do further interpretation of the New Testament divorce sayings in order to provide positive law and practical norms for believers, though the various churches (and individual denominations throughout their own histories) have not always agreed; nor do the members always agree with the prescriptions of their church. To complicate the issue further: the sayings in the New Testament and even the sayings of Jesus do not agree exactly about question and answer. And sometimes interpreters understand the words of Jesus very literally (e.g. the divorce sayings), sometimes as ideals (e.g. 8.34-37), and sometimes as figures of speech (e.g. 9.43-47), with clear distinguishing criteria not evidenced.

So recognizing the urgency and relevance of the question and the complexity of the sources, we can look at the scene Mark offers us in 10.1-12 and explore its meaning and our access to that meaning.

Towards an Hypothesis

Several observations about patterns in Mark's Gospel can point us toward a working methodology and an hypothesis.

1. Mark's Jesus speaks enigmatically at least as often as he speaks with unambiguous clarity—or anything near that.
2. Mark seems fond of using chiastic structure in order to point out relationships and significance which might not otherwise be apparent.

3. Mark has an interest in timing which provides useful clues to meaning.
4. He also uses space significantly in the Gospel.
5. The evangelist employs a particular 'in the house privately' motif, in which Jesus, having given some teaching outside with which his hearers had difficulty, explains it more clearly in the house later.
6. Mark uses with consistency a controversy setting or genre, giving Jesus a particular modus operandi which guides us usefully once we allow it to do so.

All of these factors are relevant to the information Mark gives us in 10.1-12.

So an hypothesis: To understand the teaching of the Markan Jesus on divorce, one must approach carefully, utilizing the various patterns, clues and contexts which affect meaning; to extract the teaching from its contexts without first recognizing their contribution to meaning is dubious. Any larger investigation of biblical teaching on divorce needs to approach all the other texts as carefully before exploring their interrelationships and asking questions leading toward pastoral use.

And a method: Reference to section 2.1–3.6 of the Gospel (with one foray into ch. 4) will ground our approach to the late material we wish to examine.

Exposition of the Patterns

The first Markan pattern to consider involves Jesus' speech. He speaks sometimes with unambiguous clarity: ' "Stretch out your hand" '(3.5); but more often he speaks enigmatically, in figures, in Old Testament allusions, in riddles: of the bridegroom (2.19), with reference to the example of David (2.25-26), by the suggestion of alternatives (2.9). In ch. 10 Jesus is enigmatic: he answers a question with a question, interprets the mind of Moses and the mind of God, quotes an Old Testament narrative, speaking more clearly and less ambiguously only at the end of the passage.

Secondly, Mark's use of chiastic structure (if correctly discerned by scholars) illumines an emphasis not otherwise, perhaps, perceived. There is some agreement that 2.1–3.6, falling by content into five controversies, unfolds also into a chiastic shape (see Figure 1) where the bridegroom saying is at the heart of the structure, suggesting that it is

Mark's central focus for us.[1] The controversies, one can then see, are most essentially about Jesus' identity. Who is Jesus? How does he share his bridegroom identity with the 'other' bridegroom, God? Jesus' teaching and the resistance to it in 2.1–3.6 concern that central issue of just who Jesus is, is claimed to be, is claiming to be.

The divorce teaching is found in section five of Mark's Gospel, commonly called 'The Way', stretching from 8.22 to 10.52. It, too, has been seen chiastically (see Figure 1) with in fact a double chiasm: 8.27–9.13 and 9.14–10.45, bounded by pericopae raising again the issue of the identity and authority of Jesus (8.22-26; 10.46-52). The central focus in the first structure is 8.34–9.1, a teaching whose importance in Mark's Gospel can scarcely be over-emphasized; and the central focus in the second chiasm is the teaching on divorce: 10.1-12. Assuming that the central element in a chiastic structure has singular importance, let us move on to the question of how these two centers might be related, assuming, again, that we are meant to ask the question and to seek a relationship.

The teaching of Jesus in 8.34–9.1 is surely a discipleship teaching, but it is an 'outside' teaching, inviting everyone to listen to it. Itself carefully structured, it offers a key insight into life and death, the one self and the many, God's existence and our own. Jesus is neither the first great teacher not the last to recognize that clinging to a separate self is futile and that humanity is at its best when willing to merge with larger purposes beyond its own single vision and wish. The teaching is crucial to Mark's portrait of Jesus, who is the first to take up the cross, to lose his life and regain it, to resist saving himself from the cross, so that he can in losing his own life save others. The widow with the pennies (12.42) and the woman with the perfume flask costing the year's wages (14.3-9) both embody for us the gesture described in 8.34–9.1 and offer Jesus models for what he must do as the time for doing it comes close and he dreads the cost. The saying itself is a paradox, an ideal to be striven for, and in fact an energy of selfless love to be surrendered to and carried by. Such love is not an acquisition of our own.

The 'matching piece' on divorce may perhaps be seen also as a paradox, an ideal, an invitation that needs a response but a response that will

---

1.   J. Dewey, 'The Literary Structure of the Controversy Stories in Mark 2.1–3.6', *JBL* 92 (1973), pp. 394-401 and R. Lafontaine, S.J. and P.M. Beernaert, S.J., 'Essai sur la structure de Marc 8.27–9.13', *RSR* 57 (1969), pp. 543-61 provide basic work in the structures elaborated in this article.

be responded to by God's grace. To love another so deeply that we see the other(s) as a part of our very self is the essence of the teaching of each chiastic center. If that is so, then to take one figuratively and the other literally misses the point twice. Both are tremendous challenges—the same tremendous challenge—to be responded to by those who wish to be one with Jesus and God.

Mark's use of time and space (patterns three and four) provides throughout the Gospel significant clues to meaning. The controversies in 2.1–3.6 occur in the early itinerant days of the ministry, in Galilee, as part of the teachings of the circuit preacher. But looking more deeply at the time we see that the behavior of the disciples (followers of Jesus) depends on their recognition of the time: it is the time when the bridegroom is present in a particular way, a mode that will not last long. The time of the bridegroom gives meaning to other time, rearranges custom now to a new calendar of events and reality.

The second section under consideration here takes place or is placed on the journey to Jerusalem, the journey south and up to the holy city where prophets die. The teachings on the road are urgent, since once the journey to Jerusalem has begun, the time of the bridegroom's presence is running out. And the teaching itself pushes time back oddly, as Jesus (in a perspective which seems unusual for a Jew of his time) makes Mosaic law a matter of concession to behavior.[2] Moses, Jesus seems to say to his questioners, catered to your weakness and set up a procedure to regularize human deficiency. The standard or ideal is quite other, coming from the beginning of creation when the man and woman and all else that existed—God, the garden, its flora and fauna—lived in harmony and collaboration, none seeking to exalt self at the expense of other. (The decision to eat the fruit would commence the era of choosing self over others and in the process losing much.) So again, recognition of what time it is determines human behavior. To love one's spouse as oneself and to commit oneself to doing so involves—requires—recognizing what time it is and where one wishes to head, whom one is choosing to follow, where one is being drawn.

---

2.   C.S. Mann (*Mark: A New Translation with Introduction and Commentary* [AB, 27; Garden City, NY: Doubleday, 1986], p. 391), referring to an article of D. Daube ('Concessions to Sinfulness in Jewish Law', *JJS* 10 [1959], pp. 1-13), points out the notion that the Mosaic law limits the consequences of human sinfulness but does not condone them. It is the historical angle on the Mosaic law that seems surprising.

In order to look at the fifth pattern, the 'later in the house' motif (which does not exist in the second section of the Gospel quite as it does in subsequent material), we move ahead to ch. 4, Mark's first cluster of parables. In ch. 4 Jesus teaches the crowds about the kingdom of God, using agricultural images to do so. Later in the house (4.10ff.) the disciples ask for clarification, which is given but only after the enigmatic and disquieting reference (italicized here) to the prophet Isaiah: ' "To you has been given the secret of the kingdom of God, but for those outside everything is in parables; *so that they may indeed see but not perceive, and may indeed hear but not understand; lest they should turn again, and be forgiven*" '. A digression into all the issues involved in the sower parable, the particular use of the 'hardening' quotation, and the sower allegory is not possible here. Suffice it to say that the parable is more richly ambivalent (and unclear), the allegory delivered in the house flatter (and clearer), and the 'hardening' quotation from Isaiah functions to call our attention to the difference between the two sower similitudes. Not everyone is able to hear the larger challenge, and peculiarly though quite consistently in Mark, the disciples in the house are less able than some other characters who usually emerge, unnamed, from the outside and connect well with what Jesus offers (e.g. the women with coins and perfume mentioned previously).

In the divorce pericope, Jesus delivers a teaching that is apparently (and understandably) not sufficiently clear to the disciples, who ask for further information in the house. Jesus then clarifies the teaching, perhaps flattening it out in the process. He explicates that divorce followed by remarriage constitutes adultery against the original spouse, and that the situation is not different for men and women. Clearer, yes. And with a wholly different feeling than the 'outside' teaching, with its reference to God, Adam and Eve.[3]

---

3.   The redactional issue, involving argumentation about whether anyone after Jesus might have presumed to 'make up' the divorce teachings or whether the teachings were in fact devised as a concession to Gentile churches, is outside the scope of this article. For a sensible discussion, see J.A. Fitzmyer, 'The Matthean Divorce Texts and Some New Palestinian Evidence', *TS* 37 (1976), pp. 197-227, specifically pp. 204-205 and 222. Fitzmyer also offers useful information about divorce teachings in first-century Palestine, pointing out that prohibition of divorce would not have been unheard of at that time. R. Banks (*Jesus and the Law in the Synoptic Tradition* [SNTSMS, 28; Cambridge: Cambridge University Press, 1975], p. 147) notes that rabbinic interpretation of and commentary on Deuteronomy indicates that divorce was permissible only for Jews, not for Gentiles.

Finally, and perhaps most compellingly, the factor of the controversy genre (sixth pattern) can be examined for its proffered insight into Mk 10.1-12. Mark's controversy pattern is consistent in the Gospel, in 2.1–3.6, 7.1-23, in 10, in 12, and in the Sanhedrin trial of 14. Whether Mark clearly tags the initiating question as deceitful or not, Jesus always recognizes a trap and refuses to be drawn into it. Typically, he sidesteps the particular question asked and poses another one larger but related, and then makes a statement far more offensive to the questioner than the trap itself would have required. For example, in 2.23-28, when asked why he condoned a particular action of his disciples which appeared to be a sabbath violation, Jesus does not engage the question of whether plucking equals harvesting. Ignoring the issues of the quality of their action and his response to it, he alleges relevance of an action of King David (itself dubious in the extreme, when examined in the context of the David stories), implies that he is perhaps on a par with David, and then claims authority over the sabbath—far exceeding any charge implied in the question of 2.24 but hitting squarely the question of his own unique identity.

So in ch. 10 can we discern a controversy setting. Jesus is approached by Pharisees who have, Mark identifies clearly, the intention of laying a trap, not of asking a sincere question or inviting a real exchange: '"Is it lawful for a man to divorce his wife?"' Nor does Jesus fail to perceive their intent. He does not answer but directs the question back to them: '"What did Moses command you?"' Given their answer, Jesus transcends, no doubt, their fondest hopes, as the quibblings of the schools of Shammai and Hillel seem minor compared to what Jesus says. Seeming to dismiss the Mosaic law as irrelevant (if in one case, what of others?) he refers to Genesis for a narrative rather than a legal answer. Minimizing the rationale of the Mosaic law, he holds up instead the higher ideal and the more generous goal. His response is far more damning than his opponents could have wished or accepted.

To summarize: We have prepared ourselves for mysterious speech from Jesus, speech demanding at several levels sophisticated interpretation. Jesus tends to talk that way in Mark, one supposes, because it challenges his hearers either to dig deeply or to give up; it discourages easy satisfaction with facile conclusion. When pressed for precision, Jesus gives it, but Mark indicates clearly that the gain in precision has lost some of the nuance of the more subtle teaching. And particularly when he senses a trap topic, Jesus avoids clarity on the point at issue, speaking, as it were, somewhat over the heads, or beyond the range, of his opponents. And then when he does pronounce on some aspect of the trap, his communication is not so much clear as bold. Using figures, he implies more than he defines.

Mark himself has helped us prepare to appreciate the backdrops of significant time and space, and by his careful literary arrangements has encouraged us to expect significant interrelationships among sections of the material.

Exposition of the Passage on Divorce

Let us now, with the various contexts appreciated, look again at the episode of 10.1-12. While on the journey which will culminate in his own giving of his life for the salvation of all, Jesus teaches the crowd. Approached by Jewish leaders whose purpose is to discredit him by getting him to offend in his teaching, Jesus refuses to be baited. When asked a question about the legal justification for a man's divorcing his wife, he first refuses to answer directly, turning the specific question back on its authors. The datum they hand him to deal with involves reference to the Mosaic law, specifically Deut. 24.1 and (slightly less clearly) 22.22. Moses says that divorce is permitted if a man finds his wife 'in the nakedness of the thing'. (The exact meaning of the offense is unclear, and since it is not relevant to Jesus' teaching, we will not digress over it. But since Moses adds that adultery is punishable by death, presumably the offense is not adultery.)

At the time of Jesus, Pharisaic understanding of the passages varied, with the school of Shammai holding that divorce pertained in cases of the woman's sexual misconduct (including adultery), and the school of Hillel allowing divorce for anything shameful. The Pharisees' question to Jesus presumably intends to align him with one rather than another of these schools, again presumably alienating the other.

But, ignoring that trap, Jesus moves also beyond the question of what is licit, of what law does to regulate behavior, beyond the question of paperwork to record the procedures. He goes to the heart of the matter— specifically to hard hearts, a serious moral condition in Scripture and in Mark's Gospel, and then beyond hard hearts to responsive hearts. The teaching he gives, then, is not about how to divorce another but how to love another, and the answer is: to the full, as another self, to the end. The teaching is not precise and legal, for such precision does not suit the topic Jesus has raised for his hearers: how to love. The language is somewhat metaphorical, drawing on the images in Genesis 2 of God as potter shaping the human being from clay, and later in that same chapter, of God as surgeon differentiating male and female. The saying is also paradoxical, in that it invites those previously one and now two to consider themselves as one in a new way, and more one than any of us is one with those who engendered us. And the saying is challenging, calling us to an ideal—ideal in the sense that it is not capable of perfect accomplishment, as though we could say that we have loved our neighbor perfectly, have finished loving another as a second self, and thus have completed the task.

When, in the house, the disciples push for precision, Jesus supplies it, but the precision is not so easily matched with the teaching he gave outside. It is a matter of hearts: hard ones cannot hear the call to greater love. And it is a matter of timing, a matter of sight—or insight. The disciples in the house have not yet experienced what they must learn from watching Jesus love to the full, see beyond the saving of his own life, demonstrate his sense of unity with the other.

Conclusions

So what are we to make of the teaching? Does our study mitigate the saying? The question is a false one. The point is not how little we can do (even the in-the-house teaching is fairly demanding) but how much we are invited, taught and helped to do. To love the other as oneself, to lose one's individual life if it helps the other, then to see one's own gain as the other is oneself is no mitigation for a follower of Jesus. Can divorce be legitimate? Jesus does not answer that without having first offered a fuller option. Mark shows: John the Baptist giving all he has over a similar question of marriage custom; the poor widow putting in all she has to live on and being praised by Jesus; and the woman who anoints him just before his death, investing a year's salary in a beautiful pot of precious ointment, breaking the pot, pouring all out. And of course we see Jesus, giving his own life for all of us, resisting up to the moment of his death the temptation to love self more than others, to cling rather than to give. Maybe that action mitigates the teaching.

Figure 1: Chiastic Structures

2.1.9 forgiveness and cure of paralytic
   2.10-12 Son of Man saying
      2.13-17 call of Levi and banquet question
         2.18-22 fasting question, bridegroom saying
      2.23-26 plucking of grain and question
   2.27-28 Son of Man saying
3.1-6 cure of man with withered hand

8.27-28 question: identity: Jesus and Elijah and others
   8.29-30 you are the Christ: secret saying
      8.31-33 passion prediction; role for Peter
         8.34–9.1 central teaching
      9.2-6 transfiguration; role for Peter
   9.7-10 this is my son: privileged saying
9.11-13 question: identity: Jesus, Elijah and others

9.14-29 disciples and performance; ability/inability
   9.30-32 passion prediction
      9.33-41 misunderstanding; children
         9.42-50 hindrance; priorities
            10.1-12 divorce
         10.13-16 hindrance; priorities
      10.17-31 misunderstanding; childhood
   10.32-34 passion prediction
10.35-45 disciples and performance; ability/inability

JSNT 11 (1981), pp. 64-73

JESUS' DEFENCE OF THE RESURRECTION OF THE DEAD

Rabbi D.M. Cohn-Sherbok

Introduction

For some time a number of scholars have asserted that Jesus' answer to the Sadducees concerning the resurrection of the dead in Mt. 22.31-32, Mk 12.26-27, and Lk. 20.37-38 is typically rabbinic.[1] Yet Jesus' defence of this doctrine does not strictly follow the hermeneutical rules laid down by Tannaitic exegetes,[2] and in contrast with arguments in rabbinic

---

1. See, for example, J.C. Fenton, *Saint Matthew* (Middlesex: Penguin, 1963), p. 335: 'The method of arguing here is typically rabbinic'; V. Taylor, *The Gospel according to Saint Mark* (New York: St Martins Press, 2nd edn, 1966), p. 484: 'The argument that Ἐγὼ ὁ Θεὸς Ἀβραὰμ καὶ ὁ Θεὸς Ἰσαὰκ καὶ ὁ Θεὸς Ἰακώβ means that God is the God of the living illustrates contemporary methods of exegesis'; G.B. Caird, *The Gospel of Saint Luke* (Middlesex: Penguin, 1968), p. 224: 'In form the argument is typically rabbinic, relying as it does on the precise wording of the sacred text'; J.W. Doeve, *Jewish Hermeneutics in the Synoptic Gospels and Acts* (Assen: Van Gorcum, 1954), pp. 105-106: 'An exposition of Jesus which is immediately noticeable as being completely in the style of rabbinic exegesis, is to be found in Mt. xxii, 32'.

2. In *Jewish Hermeneutics in the Synoptic Gospels and Acts*, Professor Doeve notes that in trying to determine how far Jewish exegesis can be important for the examination of problems in the New Testament, it is desirable to confine oneself to the data from the time of Hillel to the time of Akiba and Ishmael (p. 63). He also writes in this connection, 'with Hillel the exegesis of Scripture in rabbinic Judaism comes clearly within our view. His seven middoth do not mean that the method of exegesis was now formulated once and for all. R. Jishmael one of the younger of the second generation of the Tannaites (floruit 110–130 AD) formulated thirteen middoth. In the years between 130 and 160 R. Eliezer ben R. Jose the Galilean supplemented and extended these thirteen to thirty-two. But Jishmael and Eliezer b. Jose the Galilean did no more than continue to build upon the foundation laid by Hillel' (p. 61).

literature concerning the resurrection which do follow these rules, it seems strikingly inadequate from a rabbinic point of view. The fact that Jesus could use such an argument should not surprise us, since it bears out the truth of the Gospel tradition in suggesting that Jesus was not a skilled casuist in the style of the Pharisees and Sadducees.

Mt. 22.31-32

31 But as touching the resurrection of the dead, have ye not read that which was spoken unto you by God saying,

32 I am the God of Abraham, and the God of Isaac, and the God of Jacob? God is not the God of the dead but of the living.

Mk 12.26-27

26 And as touching the dead, that they rise: have ye not read in the book of Moses, how in the bush God spoke unto him, saying, I am the God of Abraham, and the God of Isaac, and the God of Jacob.

27 He is not the God of the dead, but the God of the living: ye therefore do greatly err.

Lk. 20.37-38

37 Now that the dead are raised, even Moses shewed at the bush, when he calleth the Lord the God of Abraham, and the God of Isaac and the God of Jacob.

38 For he is not a God of the dead, but of the living: for all live unto him.

An Analysis of Jesus' Response

It may be that Jesus responded to the Sadducees concerning resurrection in the way he did because he was familiar with the Amidah which juxtaposes the phrase אלהי אברהם אלהי יצחק ואלהי יצקב in the first prayer[3] with the resurrection of the dead (מחי המתים) in the second prayer.[4] Yet, it is not clear, as Professor Doeve points out, whether Jesus' statement that 'God is not the God of the dead, but of the living'

3.   See *m. Roš Haš.* 4.5.

4.   According to I. Abrahams the second prayer goes back to the time of the reign of John Hyrcanus (135-104 BCE) (I. Abrahams, *Companion to the Authorised Daily Prayer Book of the United Hebrew Congregations of the British Empire* [London: Eyre and Spottiswoode, 1932], p. lix) and is referred to in *m. Roš Haš.* 4.5.

is an auxiliary premise or the conclusion.[5] If this statement is an auxiliary premise, then Jesus' train of thought would run as follows: I am the God of Abraham, Isaac and Jacob. God is not the God of the dead, therefore Abraham, Isaac, and Jacob cannot be dead. Thus Abraham, Isaac and Jacob must be alive now, and this proves that they must have been resurrected. However, if the statement 'God is not the God of the dead but of the living' is not an auxiliary premise, but the conclusion, then the argument runs as follows: The tense of Exod. 3.6 where no copula is used must be the present—it does not say that God *was* the God of Abraham, Isaac and Jacob. This present tense also applies to the present time. Thus, at the moment Jesus is speaking (as when Moses was speaking), God is the God of Abraham, Isaac and Jacob. In other words, Abraham, Isaac and Jacob are necessarily in being at that moment, and this proves that they must have been resurrected. On this basis Jesus concluded that 'God is not the God of the dead but of the living'.

Regardless whether Jesus' second statement is an auxiliary premise or the conclusion, Jesus' argument does not follow the rules of the Tannaitic exegetes whose activity preceded and overlapped with his ministry. Jesus' argument, for example, is not a קל וחומר, the first of Hillel's seven מידות. The principle underlying the inference of קל וחומר is that if a certain restrictive law applies to a matter of minor importance, we may infer that the same restriction is applicable to a matter of major importance; conversely, if a certain allowance applies to a thing of major importance, we may infer that the same allowance is applicable to that which is of comparatively minor importance. Logically, every קל וחומר has three propositions of which two are the premises and one the conclusion. The first premise states that two things, A and B, stand to each other in the relation of major and minor importance. The second premise states that with one of these two things, A, a certain restrictive or permissive law is connected. The conclusion is that the same law is applicable to the other thing, B.

Assuming that Jesus' second statement 'God is not the God of the dead but of the living' is an auxiliary premise, it is clear that Jesus' argument is not a קל וחומר, since the statement 'I am the God of Abraham, Isaac and Jacob' does not show that two things, A and B, stand in relation to one another as of minor and major importance, nor does the second statement 'God is not the God of the dead but of the

5. Doeve, *Jewish Hermeneutics*, p. 106.

living' state that with regard to one of these two things, A, another thing is connected.

It is possible, however, to construe the conjunction of Jesus' two statements, 'I am the God of Abraham, and the God of Isaac, and the God of Jacob' and 'God is not the God of the dead, but of the living', in a different way. Taken together, these two statements could point to a comparison between God being the father of Abraham, Isaac and Jacob (A), and God being the God of the living rather than the dead (B). Even so, there is nothing in what Jesus says to suggest whether A is more important than B, nor anything which shows that what applies to A must apply to B, or vice versa.

If, on the other hand, the statement 'God is not the God of the dead, but of the living' is the conclusion rather than an auxiliary premise, it is obvious that no other comparison is being drawn in the premise 'I am the God of Abraham, and the God of Isaac, and the God of Jacob', and it is difficult indeed to see how Jesus drew the inference from this premise that God is the God of the living rather than the dead. Thus we can see that when the statement 'God is not the God of the dead, but of the living' is interpreted as an auxiliary premise or a conclusion, Jesus' argument is not an example of a קל וחומר.

Similarly, Jesus' argument is not an example of a גזירה שוה the second of Hillel's מידות. The term גזירה שוה means literally either a similar section (part) or a similar decision (decree) and denotes an analogy of expressions; that is, an analogy based on identical or similar words occurring in two different passages of Scripture. In the case of Jesus' response to the Sadducees, no identical or similar words appear, other than the name of God (אלהי in Exod. 3.6 and Θεός in the Gospels). Thus this argument lacks the basis for a גזירה שוה.

Again, Hillel's third rule בנין אב מכתוב אחד—the generalization of one special provision—has no application here. The formula for a בנין אב מכתוב אחד is: As A (normally a case mentioned in the law) being particularized by a certain peculiarity is subject to a certain provision, so any case similar to it by having the same peculiarity is subject to the same provision. In Jesus' response, however, the scriptural statement 'I am the God of Abraham, and the God of Isaac and the God of Jacob' is not particularized by a certain peculiarity, nor subject to a certain provision. Thus, this statement does not provide a basis for generalizing a specific law so as to make it applicable to other cases, which is the main characteristic of a בנין אב מכתוב אחד.

It might be objected, however, that the statement 'I am the God of Abraham, and the God of Isaac and the God of Jacob' refers to the present tense; in other words, the tense in Exod. 3.6 applies to the present. Therefore Abraham, Isaac and Jacob are still alive. This is the provision of the verse, and one can generalize the principle that all those who have died (like Abraham, Isaac and Jacob) are still alive. Though it is possible to construe Jesus' response in this way, such an argument, if admitted, would prove too much; it would prove, besides the intended conclusion, others which are manifestly inadmissible.[6] This is so because the peculiarity of this verse is that it lacks a copula. Generalizing this peculiarity, we would be entitled to say that wherever the copula is absent in a scriptural verse, the verse is in the present tense. This, however, is patently false, for we can point to a host of counter-examples where the copula is missing and the scriptural verse is intended to be understood in tenses other than the present.[7]

As in the case of Hillel's third מידה, the fourth rule בנין אב משני כתובים is not applicable either. Like the third rule, a בנין אב משני כתובים generalizes a special law, but from a combination of two special provisions (found either in one and the same passage or in two different passages of Scripture) rather than one. Yet, as in the previous case, it is not possible to point to any common peculiarity shared by the statements 'I am the God of Abraham, and the God of Isaac and the God of Jacob' and 'God is not the God of the dead, but of the living'.

Hillel's fifth rule governing general (כלל) and specific (פרט) terms stipulates that where particular terms are followed by a general term it is assumed that the law refers to anything included in the general—the particulars being regarded merely as illustrative examples. Using this rule it could be argued that taken together these verses illustrate that all those who have died (like Abraham, Isaac and Jacob) are now alive. The flaw here, however, is that the general term refers to the living, whereas the particulars refer to those who have died. Abraham, Isaac and Jacob can only be regarded as resurrected if one employs a further argument to prove that Exod. 3.6 should be understood as referring to the present tense, and such arguments have already been criticized above.

---

6. The faultiness of this argument, if it were interpreted as a בנין אב מכתוב אחד is highlighted by the fact that a similar mode of refutation to the one used here is very frequently applied in Talmudic discussions. See, for example, *b. Ber.* 13a, *Pes.* 7b, *Beṣ.* 8b.

7. See, for example, Exod. 11.3; 1 Kgs 2.45; 2 Kgs 4.8.

Regarding the subdivisions of this rule in R. Ishmael's hermeneutical system,[8] it is self-evident that Jesus' response is not an example of a case when a general term is followed by an enumeration of particulars (Ishmael's Rule 4), nor the case of one general preceding and another following a particular (Ishmael's Rule 6). Similarly, Ishmael's modifications of Hillel's Rule 5[9] are not applicable since Jesus' response is not an example of a general case that requires the particular, and a particular that requires the general (Ishmael's Rule 7), nor of the situation when a general case, though already included in a general law, is expressly mentioned so that the provision connected with it applies to all other cases included in that general law (Ishmael's Rule 8). Further, it is not an example where a single case, though already included in a general law, is expressly mentioned with a provision similar to the general so that a case is mentioned for the purpose of alleviating, but not of aggravating (Ishmael's Rule 9), nor where a single case, though included in a general law, is separately mentioned with a provision differing from that contained in the general so that a case is mentioned for the purpose of alleviating as well as of aggravating (Ishmael's Rule 10). Nor, finally, is Jesus' response an example where a single case, though included in a general law, is excepted from it by an entirely new provision so that such a case is not to be brought again under the general law, unless this be expressly indicated in Scripture (Ishmael's Rule 11).

Hillel's sixth Rule[10] כיוצא בר ממקום אחד—the analogy made from another passage—is intended to solve different cases by means of a comparison with another passage in Scripture. It is clear, however, that Exod. 3.6 to which Jesus appeals does not serve this function since the phrase, 'The God of Abraham, and the God of Isaac and the God of Jacob', simply points to God's identity.

Hillel's seventh and final rule דבר הלמד מעניינו—the explanation derived from the context—specifies that the true meaning of a law or clause in a law is to be interpreted by considering the whole context in which it stands. Yet, the context of Exod. 3.6, God's appearance to Moses at the burning bush, sheds no light on the resurrection of the dead; nor for that

8. Rules 4-6 in R. Ishmael's system. Rules 1-2 in Ishmael's system are identical with Hillel's Rules 1-2. Rule 3 in Ishmael's system is a contraction of Hillel's Rules 3-4, and Rule 4 in Ishmael's system is identical with Hillel's 5th Rule.

9. Rules 7-11 in Ishmael's system.

10. Unlike the גזירה שוה no common word or phrase is required; instead a common trait is sought to establish an analogy.

matter, using Ishmael's addition to this rule, דבר הלמד מסופו—a word is to be explained from what follows—does the specification of God's name and God's promise of deliverance from Egypt later in this chapter add any further information about the resurrection of the dead. Thus, neither of these rules is applicable here.

Lastly, Ishmael's thirteenth rule, שני זה את זה המכחישים כתובים when two passages contradict each other, they may be reconciled by a third, is also not relevant. It is possible to regard the claim that God is the God of the living and the claim that God is the God of Abraham, Isaac and Jacob as contradictory. Yet though the doctrine or resurrection could be viewed as a means of reconciling these claims, Jesus' argument is clearly not an example of Ishmael's thirteenth rule since Jesus does not use a third scriptural verse to harmonize these seemingly contradictory statements.

Hillel's seven and Ishmael's thirteen rules which we have covered complete the formal Tannaitic exegetical systems from the period we are examining. There were, however, other rules applied in rabbinic exegesis to which we must now turn. Though not included in either Hillel's or Ishmael's list of rules, an argument from analogy (הקיש) was used, for example, by Hillel.[11] The principle of this type of argument is that from the similarity of two cases, one can infer that what has been decided in the one applies to the other. But in Jesus' response, there is no apparent similarity between God's being the God of the living rather than the dead, and of God being the God of Abraham, Isaac and Jacob which would warrant such an inference.

Similarly, in rabbinic writings we come across the hermeneutical method termed ומעיוט רבוי which was developed by Nahum of Gimzo, a contemporary of Johanan ben Zakkai. According to this method certain particles, such as מן, רק, כל, אך, את, גם, are employed to indicate the extension or limitation of the provisions of a law. In Exod. 3.6, however, none of the particles is used; thus there is no indication that Jesus was appealing to this sort of exegetical method.

Further, it should be noted, as Professor Doeve remarks,[12] that one can find examples of methods in the haggadah of this period which were not brought into formulae until the thirty-two מידות of Eliezer ben Jose the Galilean. Yet, a thorough examination of these מידות reveals that none could have been used by Jesus. 1-4, for example, are simply Nahum of Gimzo's ומעיוט רבוי with modifications, and 5, 6, 7, 8, 15 and 25 are

11. *b. Pes.* 66a.
12. Doeve, *Jewish Hermeneutics*, p. 64.

simply rules, with modifications, from Hillel's and Ishmael's systems. With regard to the other rules of this system, close inspection shows that they as well are not instantiated in Jesus' argument.[13]

From this examination we can see that the argument put forward by Jesus to defend the doctrine of the resurrection of the dead does not follow the hermeneutical מידות of the Tannaitic exegetes. This suggests that Jesus' response would not have stood up to the rigorous standards of hermeneutics established by the rabbis. As Professor Doeve remarks, rabbinic exegesis 'is a really systematic exegesis, and certainly not an ingenious play upon the text... To the rabbis the expounding of Scripture is not a game, but a sacred and serious matter.'

Rabbinic Proofs of the Resurrection of the Dead

In rabbinic literature we find a number of arguments, like that of Jesus, which derive the doctrine of the resurrection of the dead from a scriptural verse. These arguments, however, are in strict conformity with Tannaitic exegetical rules. In *b. Pes.* 68a, for example, R. Samuel b. Nahmani said in Reb Johnathan's name, the righteous are destined to resurrect the dead. He proves this by a גזירה שוה (Hillel's second rule): Elisha says, 'Lay my staff upon the face of the child' (2 Kgs 4.29). In Zechariah we find the verse, 'There shall yet old men and old women sit in the broad places in Jerusalem, every man with his staff in his hand for very age' (Zech. 8.4). Thus, it is argued that because Elisha used his staff to resurrect the dead child, similarly the staff in the men's hands in the Zechariah prophecy is used to resurrect the dead.

Again, in *b. Ber.* 12b, the sages cite Deut. 16.3, 'The day when thou camest out of the land of Egypt all the days of Thy life'. Following Nahum of Gimzo's method of רבוי ומעיוט they point out that if the text simply said 'days of Thy life', this would refer to this world. The text, however, uses the particle כל so as to include the Hereafter (ימות המשיח), and this illustrates the resurrection of the dead is to take place.

In *b. Sanh.* 90b, the question is asked, 'How is resurrection derived from the Torah?' Following Hillel's seventh principle, דבר הלמד מעניינו— the explanation is derived from the context—an appeal is made to Num. 18.28; 'And ye shall give there of the Lord's heave offering to Aaron the priest'. But since Aaron did not enter Palestine, the heave

---

13. See H. Strack, *Introduction to the Talmud and Midrash* (New York: Harper & Row, 1965), pp. 95-98 for a list of these rules.

offering could not have been given to him since it was only given in Palestine. Therefore Aaron must have been resurrected there to receive it. Similarly Rabbi Gamaliel in *b. Sanh.* 90b said that resurrection is to be derived from Deut. 11.9, 'And the land which the lord swore unto your fathers to give to them'. This verse specifically states that the land is to be given personally to the Patriarchs, but they were not alive to receive it. Thus they must have been resurrected.[14]

Using this same מידה R. Meir said, 'Whence do we know resurrection from the Torah?' From the verse, 'Then shall Moses and the children of Israel sing this song unto the Lord' (Exod. 15.1). Not 'sang' but 'shall sing' is written here. Since they did not sing a second time in this life, this verse must mean that they will sing after resurrection.

Following Hillel's sixth rule, כיוצא בו ממקום אחר—the analogy made from another passage—in *b. Pes.* 68a the statement 'I will kill, and I make alive' (Deut. 32.39) is compared with another phrase in the same verse, 'I have wounded and I heal'. Just as wounding and healing obviously refer to the same person, so death and life refer to the same person. This, they contend, refutes those who claim that resurrection is not to be found in the Torah.

In addition to the proofs of resurrection derived from the Bible, there are examples in rabbinic literature of discussions where rabbis employ hermeneutical principles in defending the doctrine of the resurrection of the dead. In *b. Sanh.* 90b, for example, in a discussion allegedly between Queen Cleopatra and R. Meir, the question is posed whether the dead will be resurrected nude or in their garments. Using Hillel's first principle, קל וחומר—the inference from minor and major—R. Meir argues that if a 'bare' grain of wheat which is planted in the ground comes out covered with leaves, how much more obvious is it that the righteous, who are buried in their shrouds, will come up clothed.

14. Some scholars (such as E. Schweizer, *The Good News according to Mark* [London: SPCK, 1971], p. 248; D.E. Nineham, *St Mark* [London: Penguin, 1963], p. 321) have noted that there is a parallel between Gamaliel's and Jesus' argument since both appeal to the resurrection of the Patriarchs. However, Gamaliel's exegesis of Scripture, unlike Jesus', is based on the rabbinic principle of דבר הלמד מעניינו. In this passage God states that he had promised to give the land of Canaan to Abraham, Isaac and Jacob. But it was not until centuries later that the land was given to Israel. Therefore God must have raised the Patriarchs back to life since this would be the only way that God could keep his pledge.

Conclusion

In a number of passages in rabbinic literature various rabbis attempt to prove that the doctrine of the resurrection of the dead is derived from Scripture. As we have seen, their arguments follow the hermeneutical rules laid down by Tannaitic exegetes. In contrast, Jesus' answer to the Sadducees in Mt. 22.31-32, Mk 12.26-27, and Lk. 20.37-38 is not based on any of these rules, and is thus defective from a rabbinic point of view. Though some scholars have mistakenly regarded Jesus' response as typically rabbinic, it is not remarkable that Jesus could use such a defence since the Gospel tradition suggests that he was not skilled in the argumentative style of the Pharisees and Sadducees.

JSNT 15 (1982), pp. 42-50

THE RESURRECTION OF THE DEAD: JESUS AND PHILO

F. Gerald Downing

That God announced himself, according to Scripture, as the God of Abraham, Isaac and Jacob provides Jesus in the Synoptic Gospels with a major argument for the acceptance of a belief in the resurrection of the dead; yet, as Rabbi D.M. Cohn-Sherbok has recently pointed out, there seems to be no argument either of this kind or based on such a text, in any of the later rabbinic records.[1]

Exod. 3.15-16 reads thus (and compare v. 6):

ויאמר עוד אלהים אל־משה כה־תאמר אל־
בני ישראל יהוה אלהי אבתיכם אלהי אברהם אלהי
יצחק ואלהי יעקב שלחני אליכם זה־שמי לעלם וזה
זכרי לדר: דר לך ואספת את־זקני ישראל ואמרת
אלהם יהוה אלהי אבתיכם נראה אלי אלהי אברהם

Jesus' argument in Mk 12.24-27 runs like this (but I shall suggest that vv. 25-26a interrupt the flow):

24. ἔφη αὐτοῖς ὁ Ἰησοῦς, οὐ διὰ τοῦτο πλανᾶσθε μὴ εἰ-
δότες τὰς γραφὰς μηδὲ τὴν δύναμιν τοῦ θεοῦ

25. (ὅταν γὰρ ἐκ νεκρῶν ἀναστῶσιν, οὔτε γαμοῦσιν οὔτε
γαμίζονται, ἀλλ' εἰσὶν ὡς ἄγγελοι ἐν τοῖς οὐρανοῖς.

26. περὶ δὲ τῶν νεκρῶν ὅτι ἐγείρονται,) οὐκ ἀνέγνωτε ἐν τῇ
βίβλῳ Μωϋσέως ἐπὶ τοῦ Βάτου πῶς εἶπεν αὐτῷ ὁ Θεὸς
λέγων, 'εγω ὁ θεὸς Αβρααμ καὶ θεὸς Ισαακ καὶ θεὸς
Ιακωβ

27. οὐκ ἔστιν Θεὸς νεκρῶν ἀλλὰ ζώντων. πολὺ πλανᾶσθε.

---

1. 'Jesus' Defence of the Resurrection of the Dead', *JSNT* 11 (1981), pp. 64-73.

Now there is a passage in Philo which seems to afford some parallels. In his *Abr.* (X-XI) 50-55 he writes as follows of the three patriarchs. (I reproduce only the immediately relevant lines:)

50.　καὶ πάντας φιλοθέους ὁμοῦ καὶ θεοφιλεῖς, ἀγαπήσαντας τὸν ἀληθῆ θεὸν καὶ ἀνταγαπηθέντας πρὸς αὐτοῦ, ὃς ἠξίωσε, καθάπερ δηλοῦσιν οἱ χρησμοί, διὰ τὰς ὑπερβολὰς τῶν ἀρετῶν αἷς συνεβίουν κοινωνῆσαι τῆς προσρήσεως αὐτοῖς.

51.　τὸ γὰρ ἴδιον ὄνομα τοῖς ἐκείνων ἐναρμοσάμενος ἥνωσε, τὴν ἐκ τῶν τριῶν σύνθετον κλῆσιν ἐπιφημίσας ἑαυτῷ. "τοῦτο γάρ μου" φησίν "ὄνομά ἐστιν αἰώνιον, θεὸς Ἀβρααμ καὶ θεὸς Ἰσαακ καὶ θεὸς Ἰακωβ"—ἀντὶ τοῦ καθάπαξ τὸ πρός τι· καὶ μήποτ' εἰκότως· ὀνόματος γὰρ ὁ θεὸς οὐ δεῖται, μὴ δεόμενος δ' ὅμως ἐχαρίζετο τῷ γένει τῶν ἀνθρώπων κλῆσιν οἰκείαν, ἵν' ἔχοντες καταφυγὴν πρὸς ἱκεσίας καὶ λιτὰς μὴ ἀμοιρῶσιν ἐλπίδος χρηστῆς.

Philo concludes the argument with these words:

54b.　ἵνα καὶ τὸ αἰώνιον ὄνομα τὸ δηλούμενον ἐν τοῖς χρησμοῖς ἐπὶ τριῶν μὴ ἐπ' ἀνθρώπων μᾶλλον ἢ τῶν εἰρημένων δυνάμεων λέγηται.

55.　ἀνθρώπων μὲν γὰρ φθαρτὴ φύσις, ἄφθαρτος δ' ἡ τῶν ἀρετῶν· εὐλογώτερον δὲ ἐπιφημίζεσθαι τὸ ἀίδιον ἀφθάρτοις πρὸ Θνητῶν, ἐπεὶ συγγενὲς μὲν ἀιδιότητος ἀφθαρσία, ἐχθρὸν δὲ θάνατος.[2]

2.　In the Loeb text of F.H. Colson, *Philo*, VI (LCL, 289; London: Heinemann; Cambridge, MA: Harvard University Press, 1966 [1935]), pp. 28, 30, 32. I include a slightly amended translation of the most significant lines quoted:

50.　All alike are God-lovers and God-beloved, and their affection for the true God was returned by him, who deigned, as his utterances show... to make them partners in the title he took.

51.　For he integrally joined his name with theirs: by combining the three of theirs, producing a mode of address for himself. 'For this', he said, 'is my eternal name: the God of Abraham, the God of Isaac and the God of Jacob', (using a relative form, 'God of...', rather than 'God' absolute). And surely that is natural. God indeed needs no name: yet although he did not need it, he still of his grace and kindness gave mankind a name suited

At the very least we have here a similar collocation of Exod. 3.(6 and) 15-16, together with questions about the relations between God and man, the immortal and the mortal. But I would like to suggest that this passage in Philo may throw rather more light on the Markan pericope.

It is quite clear, both from what is quoted above, and from the remainder of the passage, that Philo takes the 'relative' ('God of... ') very seriously: seriously enough to be embarrassed by it: for, as he says, it seems to link far too closely the mortal with the eternal. And yet he still feels bound to admit that such relatedness seems to be implied, before going on to re-introduce one of his standard allegories as a way out of the difficulty he senses.

In fact he refers to Exod. 3.6 and 15-16 on at least three other occasions,[3] and in each it is as clear that he sees the phrase as amounting to the nearest that is possible to a characterization of God (though God is essentially un-nameable) whereby God creates and maintains the possibility of relatedness to himself. As Philo reads it, this is quite other than merely a case of Moses identifying the God of whom he speaks as the God whom Abraham, Isaac and Jacob worshipped. Much more, this is God *himself* linking *himself* with them, so far as to characterize himself in terms of these friends, and making that the basis on which he will relate to others, offering them an at least analogous relationship (see again the end of section 51).

> to us, so that men might be able to take refuge in prayer and supplication and not be deprived of comforting hopes.
>
> 54b.   ... so the eternal name revealed in his words is meant to indicate the three said virtues rather than actual men.
>
> 55.   For the nature of man is perishable, but that of virtue is imperishable. And it is more reasonable that what is eternal should be predicated of the imperishable than of the mortal, since imperishableness is akin to eternity, while death is at enmity with it.

For comparison I include the LXX of Exod. 3.15-16:

> καὶ εἶπεν ὁ θεὸς πάλιν πρὸς Μωϋσῆν οὕτως ἐρεῖς τοῖς υἱοῖς Ἰσραηλ Κύριος ὁ θεὸς τῶν πατέρων ὑμῶν, θεὸς Αβρααμ καὶ θεὸς Ισαακ καὶ θεὸς Ιακωβ, ἀπέσταλκέν με πρὸς ὑμᾶς· τοῦτο μού ἐστιν ὄνομα αἰώνιον καὶ μνημόσυνον γενεῶν γενεαῖς· ἐλθὼν οὖν συνάγαγε τὴν γερουσίαν τῶν υἱῶν Ἰσραηλ καὶ ἐρεῖς πρὸς αὐτούς Κύριος ὁ θεὸς τῶν πατέρων ὑμῶν ὦπταί μοι, θεὸς Αβρααμ καὶ θεὸς Ισαακ καὶ θεὸς Ιακωβ.

3.   In the *Migr. Abr.* 125, *Mut. Nom.* 12-13, and *Vit. Mos.* 1.75-76.

As has just been noted, Philo then takes steps to dull the impact of this (apparently obvious) reading of the passage. First he says:

52.   ταῦτα μὲν οὖν ἐπ᾽ ἀνδρῶν ὁσίων εἰρῆσθαι δοκεῖ, μηνύματα δ᾽ ἐστὶ φύσεως ἀδηλοτέρας καὶ πολὺ βελτίονος τῆς ἐν αἰσθητοῖς.

Then, as so often, he drops the 'also' (μὲν... δέ) and concludes:

54.   προσηκόντως οὖν καὶ τὴν τῶν τριῶν λόγῳ μὲν ἀνδρῶν ἔργῳ δ᾽ ὡς εἶπον ἀρετῶν οἰκειότητα συνῆψε, φύσεως, μαθήσεως, ἀσκήσεως... [4]

For (in the words already quoted above from sections 54-55), 'so the eternal name revealed in his words is meant to indicate the three said virtues rather than actual men... it is more reasonable that what is eternal should be predicated of the imperishable... ' Similarly, in the other three passages referred to above, there is a stress on the otherness of God, the weakness or fallibility of men, and a preference for understanding the patriarchs as types of virtues; yet clearly in the second and third of them an admission that *God* seems to be talking of relating *himself* to mortal man.

A platonist such as Philo could resolve the tension created by such a reading of the 'literal' sense of the Bush passage in Exodus by allegorizing the mortal men as eternal virtues. A non-platonist Jew of that age 'naturally' reading the passage in this conventional way would have no such easy escape.

How could the living God *characterize himself* in terms of three corpses (however faithful these men have been in their lifetime)? And how could such a characterization of himself provide (as the passage in Exodus suggests) a valid means of approach to him for those alive in later years? The only resolution available would be to assume (contrary to appearances) that God's relatedness both was and continued to be with Abraham, Isaac and Jacob—as living men. And then such a resolution could only entail the further conclusion that such a living

---

4.   Colson, *Philo*, VI, p. 30:

52.   These words do indeed appear to apply to men of holy life, but they are also statements about an order of things which is not so apparent...'

54.   '...very properly, then, Moses thus associated these three together, nominally men, but really, as I have said, virtues: the taught (Abraham), the spontaneous (Isaac) and the practical (Jacob)...'

relatedness with God was what God meant to offer to all, as he made himself 'the God of...' each and all who responded to him in these terms. (It might even suggest that relatedness to God constitutes a life that death cannot disrupt.)

If it were accepted that such an understanding of Exod. 3.(6 and) 15-16 was general wherever it was that the Markan pericope originated, it would clearly provide an illuminating 'background' for this latter passage.

Certainly the emphasis in Mark lies heavily on it being God who speaks (as in Philo); this is clarified by Matthew (as one might then expect) but missed (or deliberately softened) by Luke.

Mk 12.25-26a (no marriage, but as the angels) thus reads like an intrusion, interrupting the continuity between 'you have not known the Scriptures, nor the power of God' (v. 24) and then the necessary scriptural passage (v. 26b the 'Bush') together with the reference to the relevant aspect of the quality of God's power: the impossibility of supposing it to be linked with the nothingness of the dead (v. 27).

The issues understood to lie in the passage are then precisely those presupposed by Philo, though the conclusion is, of course, as we have seen, different.

As in many of the controversy stories, Jesus' reply by-passes the details of the query, and is addressed to what seems to underlie. Nonetheless this answer does also deal in effect with the Sadducees' mocking tale of the widow to seven brothers (Mk 12.18-23). The life that is ensured when God accepts you into relationship with himself is such that questions of heirs and the perpetuation of your name become irrelevant.

Mark or his community insert v. 25 ('no marriage but as the angels') from stock apocalyptic speculation, with v. 26a to pick up the original thread again, as is acknowledged by quite a few of the commentators.

Would the acceptance of my main case (that Philo's treatment of Exod. 3.6 and 15-16 shows there to have been in circulation the sort of reading of the passage presupposed by the Markan passage 12.24-27) also entail removing Mark's pericope from the early Palestinian Christian communities, and, *a fortiori*, from any list of Jesus' sayings? There seems to me no pressing case for either exclusion, unless a doctrinaire division is made between Hellenistic and Palestinian Judaism. (And there are many other parallels between Philo's exegesis elsewhere and those parts of the apparently Palestinian tradition preserved in later collections.)

If I may permit myself any use of a 'criterion of dissimilarity', I note that in contrast with 1 Corinthians 15, there is the quite striking omission from the Markan pericope of any reference to Jesus' resurrection: this pericope does not resemble post-Easter resurrection talk as we find it elsewhere. On the other hand, and more generally, the assertion of a resurrection life in terms of relatedness to God does fit in a more widely evidenced contemporary 'field of discourse'. Paul in Romans 8 and 1 Corinthians 15 bases his hope of resurrection on the relation with himself that he believes God has inaugurated; and, again, it is a resurrection understood in a 'non-physical' way. As it happens, Philo, too, can write along not dissimilar lines elsewhere (even though in the above passage he avoids the issue, preferring the allegory of virtues, as we have seen). It is often remarked of Philo that he talks of 'immortality' rather than of 'resurrection' as such; yet such 'immortality' is not based on any supposed eternity of mind or soul, but is conditional on a positive relationship with God; at least this is so in one extended passage, in the *Fug.* (X-XI) 55-59:

55.   φοιτήσας οὖν παρὰ γυναῖκα σοφήν, ᾗ σκέψις ὄνομα, τοῦ ζητεῖν ἀπηλλάγην· ἐδίδαξε γάρ με, ὅτι καὶ ζῶντες ἔνιοι τεθνήκασι καὶ τεθνηκότες ζῶσι. τοὺς μέν γε φαύλους ἄχρι γήρως ὑστάτου παρατείνοντας νεκροὺς ἔλεγεν εἶναι τὸν μετ' ἀρετῆς βίον ἀφῃρημένους, τοὺς δὲ ἀστείους, κἂν τῆς πρὸς σῶμα κοινωνίας διαζευχθῶσι, ζῆν εἰσαεί, ἀθανάτου μοίρας ἐπιλαχόντας.

56.   XI. ἐπιστοῦτο μέντοι καὶ χρησμοῖς τὸν ἑαυτῆς λόγον, ἑνὶ μὲν τοιῷδε· "οἱ προσκείμενοι κυρίῳ τῷ θεῷ, ζῆτε πάντες ἐν τῇ σήμερον"· τοὺς γὰρ πρόσφυγας καὶ ἱκέτας τοῦ θεοῦ μόνους ζῶντας οἶδε, νεκροὺς δὲ τοὺς ἄλλους· ἐκείνοις δ', ὡς ἔοικε, καὶ ἀφθαρσίαν μαρτυρεῖ διὰ τοῦ προσθεῖναι "ζῆτε ἐν τῇ σήμερον".

57.   σήμερον δ' ἐστὶν ὁ ἀπέρατος καὶ ἀδιεξίτητος αἰών·...

58.   ἑτέρῳ δ' ἐπιστοῦτο τοιῷδε χρησμῷ· "ἰδοὺ δέδωκα πρὸ προσώπου σου τὴν ζωὴν καὶ τὸν θάνατον, τὸ ἀγαθὸν καὶ τὸ κακόν"—οὐκοῦν, ὦ πάνσοφε, τὸ μὲν ἀγαθὸν καὶ ἡ ἀρετή ἐστιν ἡ ζωή, τὸ δὲ κακὸν καὶ ἡ κακία ὁ θάνατος· καὶ ἐν ἑτέροις· "αὕτη ἡ ζωή σου καὶ ἡ μακρότης τῶν ἡμερῶν, ἀγαπᾶν κύριον τὸν θεόν σου". ὅρος ἀθανάτου βίου κάλλιστος οὗτος, ἔρωτι καὶ φιλίᾳ θεοῦ ἀσάρκῳ καὶ ἀσωμάτῳ κατεσχῆσθαι.

59.   οὕτως οἱ μὲν ἱερεῖς Ναδὰβ καὶ ᾿Αβιούδ, ἵνα ζήσωσιν,
ἀποθνήσκουσιν θνητῆς ζωῆς ἄφθαρτον ἀντικαταλ-
λαττόμενοι βίον καὶ ἀπὸ τοῦ γενομένου πρὸς τὸ
ἀγένητον μετανιστάμενοι· ἐφ᾿ ὧν τὰ σύμβολα τῆς
ἀφθαρσίας ᾄδεται, ὅτι ἐτελεύτησαν ἐνώπιον κυρίου,
τουτέστιν ἔζησαν· νεκρὸν γὰρ οὐ θέμις εἰς ὄψιν ἐλθεῖν
τοῦ θεοῦ. καὶ πάλιν "τοῦτό ἐστιν ὃ εἶπε κύριος· ᾿εν τοῖς
ἐγγίζουσί μοι ἁγιασθήσομαι,᾿" "νεκροὶ δ᾿," ὡς καὶ ἐν
ὕμνοις λέγεται, "οὐκ αἰνέσουσι κύριον"· ζώντων γὰρ
τὸ ἔργον.

The 'no corpse', 'no flesh or body' may be compared with Paul's
'flesh and blood cannot inherit the kingdom of God' (1 Cor. 15.50) as
well as with Mk 12.27. Such independent variants on a similar theme
suggest a widely pervasive common field of discourse.[5]

Whether the common reading that I suggest underlies both Mark and
Philo could, despite Rabbi Cohn-Sherbok's reservations, be fitted into
any of the later-defined rabbinic hermeneutical schemes remains for me
as uncertain. The grammatical point must have been as obvious in
Hebrew as in Greek (Philo uses the technical term πρός τι only in
passing: his stress, as has been said, is on God's act of relating himself to
men—or to virtues). That God here and in a number of other passages
identifies *himself* as 'the God of...' might well be held to constitute a

---

5.   The translation is as follows:

55b.   '...good people, even if cut off from partnership with the body, live for
        ever, and are granted immortality

56.   (which is confirmed by the holy oracle)...' "Ye that did cleave unto the
       Lord your God are alive all of you to this day"... 'to those who have taken
       refuge in God he evidently ascribes immortality by adding, "Ye are alive
       today".

57.   Now "today" is the limitless age that never comes to an end...'

58b.   'Again, elsewhere, "This is the life and length of days, to love the Lord thy
        God". This is a most noble definition of deathless life, to be possessed by
        a love of God and a friendship for God, with which flesh and blood have
        no concern...'

59.   '...a corpse may not come into God's presence. This is what the Lord
mid   has said, "I will be sanctified in them that draw nigh to me", "but dead
       men", as we hear in the psalms, "shall not praise the Lord"...'
       Compare e.g. D.S. Russell, *The Method and Message of Jewish
       Apocalyptic* (London: SCM Press; Philadelphia: Westminster Press,
       1964), ch. 14, and especially p. 372.

'peculiarity' of theirs, and thus demand some distinctive explanation, so falling into the third of Hillel's categories.[6]

Whatever is made of these concluding points, I hope my main contention stands: at least one Jewish near-contemporary of Jesus found himself bound by an interpretation of Exod. 3.6 and 15-16 which took the words to mean that God had related himself so closely to mortal men as to raise awkward and inescapable questions about mortality as such.[7]

6.   Cohn-Sherbok, 'Jesus' Defence', p. 67.
7.   I have not found any reference to Philo, *Abr.* 50-55 in commentaries *in loc.* either on Mark or the parallels in Matthew and Luke, up to and including I.H. Marshall on the latter. E. Meyer, *The Gospel of St Matthew* (trans. W. Stewart; Edinburgh: T. & T. Clark, 1884) understands the logic of the passage in this way: 'seeing that God calls himself the God of the Patriarchs, and as he cannot sustain *such* a relationship with the dead... but only towards the living, it follows the deceased patriarchs must be living' (p. 90). He cites John Chrysostom with approval on this point (though not on the latter's emphasizing the present tense of the Exodus passage); and, as in other matters, Chrysostom could have been aware of this kind of reading which I suggest is presupposed by Philo. But given similar ways of understanding God and scripture, Chrysostom could as easily have come to the same conclusion independently. I note three other passages that seem relevant: *4 Macc.* 7.18-19: 'But as men with their whole heart make righteousness their first thought, these alone are able to master the weakness of the flesh, believing that unto God they die not, as our patriarchs, Abraham and Isaac and Jacob die not, but they live unto God'; with which compare 16.25 (in R.H. Charles, *Apocrypha and Pseudepigrapha of the Old Testament*, II [Oxford: Clarendon Press, 1913]) and Josephus, *Ant.* 11.169 has Nehemiah say,

ἄνδρες Ἰουδαῖοι, τὸν μὲν θεὸν ἴστε μνήμῃ τῶν πατέρων Ἀβράμου καὶ Ἰσάκου καὶ Ἰσακώβου παραμένοντα.

The former two passages clearly see the three patriarchs as symbols of life beyond physical death; the latter (like Philo) seems to see the Exod. 3 passage as inaugurating a very close relationship between God and the patriarchs (μνήμῃ... παραμέγοντα seems to demand something like 'lives with the memory of' rather than Marcus' [LCL] 'cherishes the memory of'). Josephus, of course, does not tell us what effect if any this 'living with the memory of them' by God has on the patriarchs themselves. It still seems to convey an intense commitment from God's side, that could well raise the question as it appears in Mk 12.

Just one remaining puzzle I must admit remains with me: if Philo is so willing in *De fuga et Inventione* to talk of good men being related to God, why does he seem so reluctant to when a similar opportunity offers in *De Abrahamo*? The answer could be that he just is inconsistent; and/or that in the latter, the patriarchs as symbols of virtues were his main theme; and/or that there was a difference in his mind between our love for God and our goodness gaining us immortality, on the one hand, and the incredibility of God relating *himself* to us in our mortal or immortal finitude, on the other. But I don't think this apparent inconsistency affects the tenor of the passage from *De Abrahamo* whose import I have tried to display.

JSNT 23 (1985), pp. 43-58

RESURRECTION AND HERMENEUTICS:
ON EXODUS 3.6 IN MARK 12.26

J. Gerald Janzen

It has become a commonplace in New Testament scholarship to take Jesus' quotation of Exod. 3.6 in Mk 12.26 as an example of ancient 'grammatical' exegetical method. In 1959 F. Dreyfus proposed an alternate ancient interpretive practice as a frame of reference for understanding Jesus' use of this text. Although two or three scholars subsequently have adopted Dreyfus's proposal, the common view cannot be said to have been dislodged. In this paper, I will address this issue from an angle which to my knowledge has not been attempted. In my reading of the Markan pericope, both the Sadducees' 'test case' and Jesus' response to them appear to concern not only the specific issue of resurrection but also the general question of hermeneutics, in such a way as to suggest that there is an intrinsic relation between the specific and the general question. One might pose the relation, preliminarily, in the form of these queries: Is there such a thing as a legitimate resurrectionist textual hermeneutics? And, conversely, is the question of resurrection a question of existential hermeneutics? And is the disagreement between Jesus and the Sadducees therefore doubly hermeneutical?

I

The Sadducees, who are said not to believe in resurrection, are portrayed as coming to Jesus with a story and a question designed to expose the absurdity of the idea of resurrection. A certain woman, they say, had seven husbands under the provisions of the Levirate law and then died. In the resurrection, whose wife will she be? First (v. 25) Jesus characterizes post-resurrection existence in a manner designed to empty their question of its point. Then he addresses the issue of the possibility of resurrection:

> As for the dead being raised, have you not read in the book of Moses, in the passage about the bush, how God said to him, 'I am the God of Abraham, and the God of Isaac, and the God of Jacob?' He is not God of the dead, but of the living (Mk 12.26-27).

However they may differ on other points of interpretation, commentators generally are agreed that the relevance of the quotation from Exod. 3.6 rests upon a sort of grammatical exegesis common in Jesus' day. This sort of exegesis, it is noted, was employed also on other scriptural texts in attempts to establish resurrection or some other kind of immortality. Moreover, in a number of instances the scriptural texts so interpreted concerned the ancestors.[1] In the instance of Mk 12.26, it is generally held, Jesus is to be taken as trading on the implications of the present tense, in the sentence 'I *am* the God of...' The argument which Jesus draws from the quotation supposedly goes something like this: The one who appeared to Moses at the bush is not God of the dead, but of the living. But at the bush that One claimed to *be* (and not only to *have* been) the God of Ancestors. But then, that must mean God still has business with the ancestors, though they have died: they must in some sense still live, or rest in hope of life through resurrection.

In 1959 Dreyfus offered a different interpretation of the manner in which Exod. 3.6 functions in the pericope. As in the consensus view, he draws upon aspects of Old Testament exegesis current in Jesus' day. But

---

1. Reference to this mode of exegesis, and to scriptural texts so interpreted with reference to resurrection, may be found in a number of the standard commentaries. I will cite here only two typical sources: G.F. Moore, *Judaism in the First Four Centuries of the Christian Era*, II (Cambridge, MA: Harvard University Press, 1958), pp. 377-83; and H.J. Cadbury, *The Peril of Modernizing Jesus* (New York: Macmillan, 1937), pp. 58-63. See also E.E. Ellis, 'Jesus, the Sadducees and Qumran', *NTS* 10 (1963–64), pp. 274-79. Interestingly, D.M. Cohn-Sherbok has now argued that Jesus' argument in Mk 12.26 does *not* embody typically rabbinic modes of exegesis. Following a detailed comparison of the Tannaitic rules for exegesis with the argument taken to be implicit in 12.26-27, Cohn-Sherbok concludes that that argument 'is not based on any of these rules, and is thus defective from a rabbinic point of view'. He does not find this surprising since, in his view, 'the Gospel tradition suggests that [Jesus] was not skilled in the argumentative style of the Pharisees and Sadducees'. See his 'Jesus' Defence of the Resurrection of the Dead', *JSNT* 11 (1981), pp. 64-73. For a yet more recent approach to the question, see F.G. Downing, 'The Resurrection of the Dead: Jesus and Philo', *JSNT* 15 (1982), pp. 42-50.

he does so by drawing upon a different exegetical treatment of the ancestors, and thereby he introduces new data into the exegesis of the Markan pericope. Specifically, he investigates the use of the formula 'the God of Abraham and the God of Isaac and the God of Jacob' in the Bible and in the era of Jesus.[2] His argument and results may be summarized as follows.

The 'three-ancestor formula' is used in such a way as to show that the interpretive focus falls, not on the relation of the ancestors to God, but on the relation of God to the ancestors. In quoting this formula, the ancient writers seek not so much to say something about the ancestors as to say something about God. For the formula characteristically is used in contexts which speak of, or which invoke, God as protector and saviour. The point of the use of the three-ancestor formula, then, is by way of appeal to those founding and paradigmatic instances in which God was seen to act protectively and savingly. Moreover, such divine acts and attitudes toward the ancestors were embedded in and manifested God's covenant relation to them, a relation of covenant promise. And this covenant relation pertained not only to the ancestors themselves. For already in the time of the ancestors it was extended promissorily by God to their descendants. When, then, later generations employed the three-ancestor formula in prayers and narratives, thereby they may be said to have situated themselves within the frame of reference of that covenant and to have claimed God's faithfulness to it through fresh acts of protection and salvation in their own time and particular circumstances of need.

Such a general ancient exegetical use of the three-ancestor formula, I suggest, rests upon a hermeneutical assumption. That assumption is the identification of some kind of analogy between the situations of the ancestors and those of the later exegetes. But such a hermeneutical assumption seems to have been made not only by these later exegetes; it seems to be operative already for the narrator in Exodus 3. For it is implicit in the scene at the burning bush that some kind of analogy exists between the ancestral situations and the situation of the generation of Moses. I shall comment more fully on the nature of this analogy, below. Meanwhile, we may note that the use of the three-ancestor formula in Exodus and then by later generations may be said to constitute a three-term analogical vector: the ancestors in their generations; the

2.   F. Dreyfus, 'L'argument scriptuaire de Jésus en faveur de la résurrection des morts (Marc XII, vv. 26-27)', *RB* 66 (1959), pp. 213-24.

generation of the Exodus; and later generations in their respective and various situations.

When Jesus responds to the Sadducees on the question of resurrection, then, his use of the three-fold formula exemplifies both its use in the community of his own time and its function in its original context at the bush. To be sure, and as modern commentators have been at pains to point out, the application of this text to the question of the individual's own resurrection from the dead takes the text into areas of concern beyond the immediate purview of the narrative of the burning bush. It needs to be noted, however, that already at the bush the ancestors were referred to in the context of a plight which in significant respects was dissimilar to the plight from which God had delivered the ancestors. Already within Exodus 3, then, the hermeneutical connection between the ancestors and the generation of the Exodus contains elements of continuity and discontinuity or, as Paul Ricoeur might say, elements of tradition and interpretation.[3] Jesus' application of the formula of Exod. 3.6 to the issue of death and resurrection may then be identified as a further extension of meaning (involving elements of continuity and discontinuity, of traditioning and interpretation) along an analogical vector already set in motion by Exod. 3.6.[4]

It is to be observed that both the common view and the alternative proposed by Dreyfus employ the same approach to the question of the use of Exod. 3.6 in Mk 12.26. For both positions begin with an examination of exegetical procedures current in the time of Jesus, and then seek to identify in Mk 12.26 an instance of one such exegetical procedure. Such an approach, of course, is sound so far as it goes. The results of these two applications of the same approach are divergent in at least two ways. Not only do they understand Mk 12.26 to exemplify different exegetical procedures, but they come to different assessments of the cogency of the procedure in question. For the common view characteristically issues in a verdict that the appeal to Exod. 3.6 in support of

3.   P. Ricoeur, *Hermeneutics and the Human Sciences: Essays on Language, Action, and Interpretation* (Cambridge: Cambridge University Press, 1981).

4.   Dreyfus himself acknowledges that 'Certes, le texte de l'*Exode* ne contient pas en toutes lettres la foi en la résurrection des morts'. He goes on to say, however, 'Mais en l'invoquant, Jésus indique comment ce dogma se rattache en profondeur à l'aspect central de la révélation de l'Ancien Testament, l'Alliance, et comment le salut promis par Dieu au Patriarches et à leur descendance en vertu de l'Alliance, contient implicitement la doctrine de la résurrection' ('L'argument', p. 224).

resurrection ignores and violates the meaning of that text in its original context in Exodus.[5] In Dreyfus's view, on the other hand, Jesus' use of Exod. 3.6 not only respects but depends upon the meaning of that text in its original context.

Curiously, neither the common view nor that of Dreyfus respects the immediate context in which Exod. 3.6 is used—the Markan pericope itself. In my view this is an odd and serious oversight. To appreciate fully how the three-term formula bears upon the question of resurrection, we must consider it as a response specifically to the story by means of which the Sadducees pose their question to Jesus. For it is in the specific details of the Sadducees' story, and in response to that story (not simply the Sadducees' general position on resurrection) that we find the exegetical and hemeneutical clue to Exod. 3.6 as a scriptural warrant for belief in resurrection. In approaching the issue this way, we shall discover that the issue of resurrection and the issue of hermeneutics are two dimensions of one existential concern.

II

The Sadducees are portrayed as introducing their story with a loose and paraphrastic summary of the Levirate law as given in Deut. 25.5ff., and also with a more precise use of the language of Gen. 38.8. The latter language, of course, occurs within the context of that ancestral episode—the Tamar-Judah incident—which exemplifies the practice codified in the Levirate law.

Now, given the nature of the story which the Sadducees relate, against the background of the Levirate law, the allusion to the Tamar-Judah episode of Genesis 38 raises some interesting issues: In splicing the two scriptural quotations into one sentence, are the Sadducees portrayed as intentionally drawing on both passages? (In that case, the expression 'Moses wrote for us' would encompass also the Tamar-Judah episode, and 'Moses', as assumed author of the Pentateuch, thereby would be taken as writing a narrative with the force of exemplary or case law.) Or are the Sadducees portrayed as intending to quote Moses the Torah-

---

5.   A common assessment of this exegetical method is fairly sampled in the following comments: 'Such arguments are doubtless convincing only to those who are willing to accept them' (H.J. Cadbury, *Peril*); and 'The argument is one of high-handed Jewish exegesis' (K. Stendahl, 'Matthew', in M. Black and H.H. Rowley [eds.], *Peake's Commentary on the Bible* [London: Nelson, 1962], p. 791).

giver of Deuteronomy, but inadvertently falling into the language of Gen. 38.8? In either case, as we shall see, there is a dramatic irony in their allusion to the Tamar-Judah episode. For in drawing the language of Genesis 38 into their citation of Scripture, they (deliberately or inadvertently) summon to the hearer's peripheral awareness a scriptural context wider than is strictly needed to introduce their story.[6] The irony lies in the fact that this wider context will provide the means for subverting their story and their theological position insofar as they would seek to ground that position in Scripture. For the wider, ancestral context will provide the basis for Jesus' response.

The preceding suggestion may be thought over-subtle. What is unambiguous is the fact that the Sadducees play on two meanings of the verb 'raise up' and its noun cognate 'raising up/resurrection'. Combined with the above-mentioned citations from Deut. 25.5ff. and Gen. 38.8, this play on words will become the key to a proper appreciation of Jesus' response. But first we must note how it conveys to us the nature of the Sadducees' objection to resurrection.

The way in which they play on these words suggests that their objection operates on two levels. (1) On one level the objection turns on simple arithmetic. In this life the woman was able to have seven husbands because she had them serially—they were a gift, so to speak, made possible by the power of death. But if there is such a thing as resurrection, such a post-mortem power will present her with an embarrassment of riches: seven husbands all at once! Yet, the law being what it is, presumably she cannot have seven husbands at the same time. So, whose wife shall she be? (2) But, as so often is the case in debates on issues such as these, the presented objection, for all its explicitness, masks a deeper and more serious objection.[7] This deeper objection is conveyed implicitly through the story itself, at the point where the story

6. In place of the words from Gen. 38.8 (...καὶ ἐξαναστήσῃ σπέρμα τῷ ἀδελφῷ αὐτοῦ), they could as well have continued to quote from Deut. 25.7 (...ἀναστῆσαι τὸ ὄνομα τοῦ ἀδελφοῦ αὐτοῦ).

7. In his commentary on the Matthean version of Jesus and the Sadducees, Pierre Bonnard draws attention to a modern presented objection: '... un peu comme si, aujourd'hui, on demandait en quel lieu tous les ressuscités pourront être logés (*L'Evangile selon Saint Matthieu* [Paris: Delachaux & Niestlé, 1963], p. 324). For one reasoned response to the hypothetical objection Bonnard cites, see the Ingersoll Lecture of William James, reprinted together with his *The Will to Believe* (New York: Dover, 1956).

turns on the word-play in the verb 'raise up'. (The irony will consist in the way in which the Sadducees, in attempting to debunk resurrection, are shown drawing the very analogy upon which Jesus' argument for resurrection will turn.) In a form of argument from lesser to greater (in this instance, from easier to harder), the Sadducees raise this implicit and more serious objection: If God by the very means divinely provided in the Torah—the Levirate law—cannot or will not raise up children to a dead man (not even after an ideal number of opportunities), on what basis is one entitled to hope that God either will or can raise up that dead man Himself—something for which the Mosaic Torah makes no provision at all? If we identify this deeper objection in this way, we see that it has two facets, one having to do with scriptural warrant and one having to do with divine will and power. That is, the issue is at once hermeneutical and theological. That our two-faceted identification of this deeper objection is correct, is suggested by the two-fold emphasis in Jesus' opening words of response: 'Is not this why you are wrong, that you know neither the *Scriptures* nor the *power of God*?' (Mk 12.24).

We should pause to observe that, in the context of the Gospel narrative as a whole, the Sadducees are part of a group who are presented in such a way as to serve as a foil for the presentation of Jesus' teaching. This should not lead us to overlook the force of their deeper objection, in either of its two facets. In respect to the question of scriptural warrant, one may wonder if they heard Jesus' citation of Exod. 3.6 as an instance of grammatical exegesis, and if they rejected it, the way they rejected other such exegeses in support of resurrection, on the grounds of violation of context.[8] In respect to the theological aspect of the issue, they have to be credited with raising a problem which in one form or another dogs that form of religious existence presented within or based upon the biblical tradition. The problem is this: What credit can one give to the postulates of faith or the claims of revelation, in the face of the unceasing contradictions in human experience of those postulates and those claims? People do die with no one to perpetuate their names—in spite of the provisions of the Levirate law. And while such experience, though lamentable enough, is not theologically problematic for some religious perspectives, it is problematic theologically for a perspective which

8. See the presentation of a discussion between Rabbi Gamaliel (II) and the Sadducees, in Moore, *Judaism*, II, p. 382. To each of Gamaliel's quotations of Scripture in support of God's bringing the dead to life, the Sadducees reply that a simpler exegesis of the text is more likely.

grounds itself in the traditions of the ancestors and the generation of the Exodus.[9] It is to the Sadducees' credit, and it is very much in the spirit of a biblical faith which dares to expostulate with God, that they will not merely blink away such contradictions or pretend that they do not exist, but instead insist on intruding them into the midst of pious hope and conviction. Yet, says Jesus, they err in two ways: they know neither the Scriptures nor the power of God.

If Jesus' response functions in part to articulate two facets of the Sadducees' deeper objection, it serves also to introduce the two continuing parts of Jesus' response, in v. 25 and in vv. 26-27. Just as the Sadducees' story operated subtly, and at more than one level, the first part of Jesus' response, in v. 25, must be taken at more than one level. At one level it addresses the Sadducees' explicit and presented objection, turning on whose wife the woman will be. In effect, Jesus says that in heaven their question will not arise, for '...when they rise from the dead, they neither marry nor are given in marriage, but are like angels in heaven'.

At another level, this answer addresses, albeit obliquely, one aspect of their deeper objection, the one having to do with how beliefs and convictions are scripturally warranted. Commentators observe that the Sadducees' error lies in the supposition that the relation between historical existence and resurrection existence is one of simple continuity, such that the conditions and characteristics of the former control those of the latter. For the Sadducees' question to carry force, one must assume that the conventions and conditions of historical Jewish existence (including, in part, rules pertaining to monogamy) continue unrevised to characterize risen existence. Only on the basis of such a simple and unqualified continuity between the two realms can the arithmetical objection arise. Jesus counters by contending (through concrete imagery which answers to the concreteness of their story) that the relation between historical and risen existence is complex, involving elements both of continuity and of discontinuity. One may assume some continuity, some internal and intrinsic connection and identity between the risen life and the historical life which preceded it. In some sense the risen person must be said to be the same person who historically lived and died. But the conditions of the risen life—its modalities—are such as to display aspects of

9. A contemporary, post-holocaust, post-Hiroshima form of the problem is given in Dilys Laing's poem 'Final Verdict'; see *The Collected Poems of Dilys Laing* (Cleveland: Case Western University Press, 1967).

discontinuity. This means, however, that the conditions obtaining in historical existence, while suggestive or adumbrative of the other, cannot entirely control or determine our envisagement of the other. Such an objection as the Sadducees explicitly raise, therefore, has the critical value of challenging overly detailed envisagements which are literalistic extrapolations made from the details of historical existence. But the Sadducees err in the dogmatic assurance with which they challenge the possibility of resurrection as such, a dogmatism which, in respect to the story through which the challenge is stated, displays an equally literalistic mentality on their part.

At this point we are enabled to see how one's hermeneutics of existence and one's hermeneutics of scriptural texts converge on the question of resurrection. For the logic of Jesus' response to the Sadducees' explicit objection to resurrection also bears upon the question of their knowledge of Scripture. 'Knowing the Scriptures' is not just a matter of *what* one reads, it is equally a matter of *how* one reads. In this respect, v. 25 may now be appreciated for the way in which it prepares the hearer or reader hermeneutically for how Exod. 3.6 is to be taken as bearing upon the question of resurrection. For the hermeneutics of existence implied in v. 25 is a hermeneutics which embraces both continuity and discontinuity, both tradition and interpretation: neither unrelieved and unchanging perdurance nor absolutely discontinuous novelty, but identity continuing through transformation. To 'know the Scriptures' by means of such a hermeneutics, is to affirm the historical meaning of a text. But such a knowledge of the Scriptures will not suppose that the historical meaning of the text exhaustively controls or predetermines one's appreciation of its meaning in later and different contexts and connections. A 'hermeneutics of resurrection' will issue in an exegesis which seeks to discern a recognizable and identifiable continuity between earlier and later meanings, a continuity standing at the centre in each instance, so that later meanings are faithful to and perpetuate the original spirit, while the earlier meaning persists in, informs, and is the life of those later meanings which in other respects will be discontinuous. Such a hermeneutics, we may suggest, is implicit already in the three-term vector which we have identified as connecting the ancestral experience, the experience of the Exodus generation as addressed through Moses in Exod. 3.6, and later generations who called on the God of the burning bush and of the ancestors to succour them in their various plights. It is with such hermeneutical overtones, then, that the first part of Jesus' developed response, in v. 25, prepares us for what is said in vv. 26-27.[10]

In what way, then, does Jesus' use of the text from the burning bush demonstrate and exemplify a knowledge of the Scriptures and of the power of God? The point can be put simply and pregnantly: The Sadducees have told Jesus a story of sterility persisting through much conjugal effort and futile hope, ending in death. By using the formulaic sentence from the burning bush, Jesus responds to their story much more pointedly and fittingly than even Dreyfus's investigation has allowed us to appreciate. Jesus is not just invoking in a general way the tradition of God's protection and power; he is countering *their* story with a reminder of the *ancestors'* story. That story too is one of sterility—or rather, it is three successive stories, indeed four if we include the Tamar-Judah episode. In these stories, sterility persists in the face of divine promise and repeated promise, through much conjugal effort and delayed hope, but giving way finally to Isaac, Jacob and Esau, Joseph and Benjamin, and (in Genesis 38) Perez and Zerah. The three sets of ancestors (not to mention Tamar) all offer us a story which begins similarly to that of the Sadducees, but the development and outcome of which undercuts the story through which the Sadducees have conveyed their deeper objection.[11]

One finds oneself, then, presented with two stories turning on the problem of generativity, that of the Sadducees and that of the ancestral tradition. The question now is: Which story has the better claim to ground one's reading of reality? I suggest that one here finds oneself at a point where existential hermeneutics and textual hermeneutics converge and become one. But in that case, the Sadducees are on the horns of a dilemma, in which they cannot achieve coherence of existential and textual hermeneutics and still prefer their story to the one adduced by Jesus. On the one hand they appeal to the traditions of their community as a basis for their denial of resurrection. But the tradition to which they

10. Another way to state the burden of this paragraph is to say that the pericope concerning Jesus and the Sadducees, when attended to exegetically, conduces to the view that the idea of resurrection is not only a topic for, but a frame of reference for, biblical hermeneutics. In such a view, one's experience of the quickening power of a literary text is already an analogy and an adumbration, within historical existence, of existence in the mode of resurrection. See further W.J. Ong, '*Maranatha*: Death and Life in the Text of the Book', *JAAR* 45 (1977), pp. 419-49, especially his last paragraph on p. 445.

11. One may note that, in this way of reading the pericope, far from presupposing on grammatical grounds that the ancestors are contemporaneous, Jesus' citation presupposes their successiveness.

appeal, insofar as it narratively follows the era of the ancestors, thereby presupposes and attests the validity of the ancestral story. Without the story of ancestral sterility overcome through divine action, there would be no descendants to go down to Egypt, no generation in bondage, and no Moses to hear Yahweh's call at the burning bush, let alone any Moses to receive at Sinai such laws as eventually came to include Levirate provision for offspring in the case of a fruitless marriage.

It could be observed, on behalf of the Sadducees, that the very rise of the Levirate law implicitly constitutes a critique of the ancestral story. To be sure, that law signals a realistic recognition of evil and disappointment, and provides a caution against simplistic appropriations of the ancestral stories with their generative outcomes. Yet even the Levirate law itself does not function merely as such a realistic recognition and caution. One may read that law, in the context of the concrete context occasioning its rise, as yet another expression of the variegated resourcefulness by which the God of the ancestors makes good on the divine promises implicit in the old stories of sterility ending in generativity. Retrospectively, from the standpoint of the New Testament, one may even hazard the suggestion that the Levirate law itself contains a promissory overtone, insofar as it provides for the overcoming of the impasse of death through the action of a kin redeemer.

At this point, it will be helpful to attend more closely to the nature of the plight of the ancestors, within the context of the Genesis narrative as a whole. The plight of the ancestors is first signaled at the point where the first ancestral pair is mentioned, in Gen. 11.30: 'Now Sarai was barren; she had no child'. From a narrative point of view, this statement launches the ancestral story by the way in which it negates the primal blessing announced in Gen. 1.28 and implicit in Genesis 2–3. It is in the tension between the statement of sterility in 11.30 and God's promise of generativity in 12.1-3 that the ancestral narratives make their way.

But the negative side of this tension, 11.30, connects also backward to the genealogical summaries of ch. 11. One of the things which the genealogy in 11.10-26 does (like the one in ch. 5) is to indicate that, whatever the calamity of the garden may signify in respect to mortality as a comprehensive sentence upon human kind, mortality is in some sense qualified or momentarily stayed through the residual powers of life which express themselves in human generativity and the succession of generations. To be a human being in the terms of Genesis 2–3 is to know within oneself two realities, two powers, the power of death and the power of life. The power of death is connected with the passage of time in such a way as to give to human existence the character of a being unto death; it is

> time, strength, tone, light, life, and love—
> And even substance lapsing unsubstantial;
> The universal cataract of death
> That spends to nothingness—and unresisted...

So viewed, death is not merely a terminus, but an aegis under whose hermeneutics one may read historical existence as a living death. Yet after all, death's aegis, if real, is not absolute. The cataract

> ...spends to nothingness—and unresisted,
> Save by some strange resistance in itself,
> Not just a swerving, but a throwing back
> As if regret were in it and were sacred.[12]

It is as such a sacred resistance that we may interpret the generative theme interwoven with the generation-after-generation rehearsal of the fact of death, in Genesis 5 and 11. So long as human couples continue to display generative powers, they are not wholly under the aegis of death.

But if that is the case, then the statement in Gen. 11.30—'Now Sarai was barren; she had no child'—signifies that Sarai and Abram do not possess the saving qualification of their own forebears. They are the end of their line. They are dead while they live, like a tree which, standing among other trees, is dry and leafless. This is implicit in the case of the first ancestral couple, and it becomes explicit on the lips of Sarah's granddaughter-in-law Rachel. As Robert Alter has observed,[13] Rachel's

---

12. R. Frost, 'West Running Brook', in *Complete Poems of Robert Frost* (New York: Holt, Rinehart and Winston, 1964), p. 329. The poem deals generally with themes of time, death and value, arising in connection with the modern notion of entropy. In likening the central image of the 'throwing back' of the wavelet of water as an 'Annunciation', Frost's poem at another point suggestively connects the notion of entropy to the biblical thematics of sterility and generativity.

13. R. Alter, *The Art of Biblical Narrative* (New York: Basic Books, 1981), p. 187. Though Alter's translation is precise, his interpretation of what Rachel means by these words still stops short of the starkness of her cry. For he takes her in this cry as 'someone who claimed to be on the point of death unless immediately given what... she wanted'. Rachel's cry is not a rhetorically calculated nor a hysterically overwrought and exaggerated warning. It is a realistic, if no doubt emotionally charged, assessment of her case, analogous to that of the eunuch who says 'Behold, I am a dry tree' (Isa. 56.3).

plea to Jacob should be translated, 'Give me sons; if not, I am dead'. In a narrative and existential context where life and the power of generativity are virtual synonyms, Rachel sees in Jacob the hermeneutical key to her own situation: If he is not able to give her children, that is an indication (especially in view of Leah's reproductive success) that she has in her no power to give life, her womb is not alive, she is generatively dead. But this means that, for her and in her, the reign of death is virtually absolute, qualified only by the 'throwing back', as a sacred regret, of her power of complaint and petition. She is not a fountain of living waters (Cant. 4.15); she is rather like the earth ever thirsty for water, and her barren womb is the analog of Sheol (Prov. 30.16).

We may discern a similar reading of the ancestral stories—where sterility is seen as a form of death-in-life—in two New Testament passages, Romans 4 and Hebrews 11. These two passages are of particular interest, in the context of our 'internal' reading of the Markan pericope as compared with the 'comparative' approach reflected both in the common view and in that of Dreyfus. We may recall that they seek to identify the exegetical method implicit in the quotation of Exod. 3.6 at Mk 12.26, by reference to similar exegetical method exemplified in one or another contemporary form. To this point, the 'internal' approach of the present paper appears only in contrast, methodologically, to these previous approaches. But our remarks on the two above-mentioned passages will establish that the exegetical method which we identify within the pericope is exemplified also elsewhere in respect to the ancestral story.

In Romans 4 (which ends on the theme of resurrection, the event which for Paul displays the righteousness, i.e., the faithfulness and moral integrity, of God), Paul observes of Abraham that

> He did not weaken in faith when he considered his own body which was as good as dead because he was about a hundred years old, or when he considered the barrenness [νέκρωσις] of Sarah's womb (4.19 RSV).

Sarah's womb is dead, as the word νέκρωσις indicates. But Abraham is said to have believed in the God 'who gives life to the dead, and calls into existence the things that do not exist'. Therefore 'he did not weaken in faith when he considered his own body'. The realism of Abraham as presented in this sentence stands in vivid contrast to the realism of the Sadducees. In full view of this couple's generative deadness (including his own body which was 'already dead'), Abraham believed in God's promise, taking that promise and not his own body as the hermeneutical key to his existence. Though it was the birth of Isaac which materially restored generative life to this couple, such life already invaded their existence in the form of the promise which they received and in accordance with which they lived.

The writer of the Letter to the Hebrews draws the same connection between sterility and death, generativity and resurrection.

> By faith Sarah herself received power to conceive, when she was past the age...Therefore from one man, and him dead... (11.11-12).

This time Sarah is simply said (perhaps with an eye to Gen. 18.11-12) to be 'past the age'. Again, as in Romans 4, this interpretation of the ancestors in terms of sterility viewed as death, followed by the gift of generativity, is set in a context which goes on to speak of resurrection (11.13-16; cf. v. 19). The point to be emphasized is that, in both Romans 4 and Hebrews 11, resurrection is associated with the ancestors, not in terms of their own physical demise and subsequent death, and in terms of the power of God in bringing life from their death through the offspring given to them. *Nevertheless*, their story is read as scriptural backing for the New Testament witness to resurrection of the individual following death. Thus, these two New Testament passages display the same sort of hermeneutical appropriation of the ancestral story as we are proposing to identify in Mk 12.26, an appropriation in which the meaning of the original text is applied to a different sort of crisis and whereby the old and new contexts are joined in the modes of both continuity and discontinuity.

To return to the ancestral plight itself, we may reiterate its character in terms of sterility viewed as a form of death, from which God's deliverance comes through the gift of generativity. Let us now compare this recurrent plight with that of the generation of the Exodus. In the latter instance, the problem is hardly one of sterility! When the Priestly writer in Exod. 1.7 states that in Egypt 'the descendants of Israel were fruitful and increased greatly; they multiplied and grew exceedingly strong, so that the land was filled with them', this summary in the words of Genesis 1 only makes explicit what the concluding chapters of Genesis lead the reader to anticipate and what the non-Priestly narrative in Exod. 1.8 and following presupposes. Now, the new Egyptian policy announced after 1.8 is directed precisely against the generativity of the Hebrews (1.16, 22). As a result of the official decree of the Pharaoh, each male child now comes into a world in which a human sentence of death hangs over his head. In this sense, one may say that the male children are 'as good as dead'. But insofar as the success of this policy will transform the Hebrew community into an exclusively female group available for slave service and concubinage, so that the Hebrews no longer enjoy the power of generativity as a people, this policy means that the community itself is as good as dead. In the community's cries which bring ch. 2 to a close, one hears overtones of anticipatory mourning on its own behalf.

But at this very point God—who earlier had 'remembered' Rachel and 'heard' her and 'opened her womb' (Gen. 30.22)—heard their groaning and remembered the divine covenant with the ancestors (Exod. 2.24). Shortly after (or contemporaneously), at the burning bush we overhear the call of Moses to deliver the Hebrews from Egypt, under the aegis of one who says 'I am the God of Abraham and the God of Isaac and the God of Jacob'. Once again the hermeneutical relation is one of continuity and discontinuity. On the one hand, the specific plight is quite different: biological sterility in the context of geographic opportunity in the one case, and political oppression and murder in the context of biological blessing in the other. On the other hand, these two forms of human plight are modal variants of one generic threat, the threat of death.

To return, finally, to the use of Exod. 3.6 as a response to the Sadducees' objection to the possibility of resurrection: The issue at the heart of their story—the problem of sterility and death—is now seen to be the issue which is addressed by appeal directly to the identical ancestral and the analogous Exodus themes through the quotation of one sentence uttered by God at the bush. If Jesus applies these themes to a novel issue—the question of the individual's possible *post mortem* destiny—this is to give yet one more modulation to those hermeneutical modulations of the ancestral theme already achieved in the context of the Egyptian oppression. (If there were space, one might also identify further such modulations of the ancestral/Exodus vector, in the exilic prophecies of Second Isaiah. There the themes of sterility and generativity are applied to the exilic situation, and the ancestral stories are interpreted as offering hope in this extremity.)

Such a use of Exod. 3.6 at Mk 12.26, it seems to me, displays the deepest sensitivity to the context in which Exod. 3.6 originally occurs and has its meaning.[14] The alternative is to stand before the prospect of

---

14. Compare the general topic addressed by S.L. Edgar, 'Respect for Context in Quotations from the Old Testament', *NTS* 9 (1962–63), pp. 55-62; and see the response by R.T. Mead, 'A Dissenting Opinion about Respect for Context in Old

death, not only as a power operative in one's historical existence, but as the terminus of that existence, and from that position to call to mind the divine address in Exod. 3.6, and then to decide that, for once, this text and what it connotes has nothing hopeful to say. To decline Jesus' interpretation is to decide there is nothing in what Exod. 3.6 connotes which could not be quenched and extinguished by the Sadducees' counterstory. So to decide is to confess that this *locus classicus* of biblically-derived existence, having burned continuously through so many and various other trials, finally found a context within which it burned and was consumed. That would be the end, or at any rate that would establish the limits of the relevance, of Yahwism. It would give an altogether different, and limiting, sense to Jesus' concluding words that the God of the burning bush 'is not God of the dead, but of the living'.[15]

Testament Quotations', *NTS* 10 (1963–64), pp. 279-89. It would be interesting to re-examine the texts discussed in these two papers, from the point of view of the hermeneutics sponsored in this paper.

15. In the Gospel of Mark, resurrection is referred to explicitly at 8.31, 9.10, 9.31, 10.34, 14.28; but in these passages little or nothing is said other than to refer to that event in anticipation. Only in two places in Mark is resurrection contextualized, and therefore explored hermeneutically, in terms of Old Testament thematics. These passages are 12.18-27 and 16.1-8. I hope to publish elsewhere, soon, a study of the latter pericope, in which I argue that 16.1-8 displays literary features of a well-developed biblical type-scene, described as 'the encounter with the future betrothed at a well' by Alter, *The Art of Biblical Narrative*, ch. 3 (see p. 51). Such an analysis enables the recognition that in both 12.18-27 and 16.1-8 resurrection is presented in terms of the same Old Testament thematics of sterility and death overcome by new life and generativity.

JSNT 14 (1982), pp. 88-112

JESUS *BEN DAVID*: REFLECTIONS ON THE *DAVIDSSOHNFRAGE*

Bruce Chilton

A consideration of Jesus' designation as David's son might reasonably be expected to begin with Mt. 22.41-46, Mk 12.35-37, Lk. 20.41-44, where Jesus is portrayed by the Synoptic Evangelists as himself query- ing the scribal (so Mark and Luke [cf. v. 39]) or Pharisaic (so Matthew) notion of the messiah *ben David*. The relevance of the passage for Jesus' understanding of 'David's son' is admittedly oblique, because the saying juxtaposes the phrase to 'messiah', and can therefore only be read as evidence of Jesus' understanding of what *ben David* means after one has appreciated the deliberate tension which is posited with *masiah*. Such an appreciation has not yet been achieved, at least not as a matter of consensus. The saying may be taken to mean that Jesus in some sense is not the messiah, on the understanding that the saying identifies him as David's son and then distances *ben David* from *masiah*.[1] On the

---

1.   In the present paper, conventional designations for early Jewish and rabbinic *theologoumena* are used without an attempt to distinguish between the characteristic usages of various circles. For a relatively recent history of discussion, cf. G. Schneider, 'Die Davidssohnfrage (Mk 12.35-37)', *Bib* 53 (1972), pp. 65-90. Arguments in the direction of the present possibility are offered by A. Suhl, *Die Funktion der alttestamentlichen Zitate und Anspielungen im Markusevangelium* (Gütersloh: Gerd Mohn, 1965), pp. 93, 94; J.A. Fitzmyer, 'The Son of David Tradition and Mt. 22.41- 46 and Parallels', in *Essays on the Semitic Background of the New Testament* (London: Geoffrey Chapman, 1971), pp. 113-26; E. Lövestamm, 'Jésus Fils de David chez les Synoptiques', *ST* 28 (1974), pp. 97-109 (translated by L.-M. Dewailly). Further examples of the approaches here mentioned are available from Schneider's article, although it must be noted that the opposite reading to the present possibility, or a variant of it, has been greatly preferred during the history of discussion. Consequently, this alternative—which is here defended—has not been adequately explored. Fitzmyer simply finds it 'inexplicable' (p. 123) that Jesus would have

understanding that the identification is rather, primarily, with the messiah, the saying denies Jesus' relationship to David,[2] or offers the rather nice distinction that the messiah is not the messiah merely on the basis of such a relationship.[3] All of these possibilities have been argued, both critically and logically, but, in the absence of knowing from which term one should proceed in reading the saying, and what precise associations were evoked by each, no single exegesis seems entirely convincing when compared with the others. Nonetheless, this passage is the only pericope in the New Testament in which Jesus is presented as speaking of David's son, and so it demands the close attention of those who wish to understand why he came to be addressed and known as *ben David*.

Together with the ambiguity of the saying, the understandable doubts as to its authenticity have been another cause of the critical reserve shown towards the passage. These doubts have centred on the use of three christological titles in the passage (David's son, messiah and lord) and on the Septuagintal text-form of the citation from Psalm 110.[4] Neither of these observations, however, can be said to settle the question of the provenience of the saying. The Septuagint, or—to speak more accurately—a tradition of Greek Bible translation which is all but identical to what we call the Septuagint (including its variant readings), is the preferred Old Testament version in the Gospel according to Mark;[5] Mark or a predecessor may well have accommodated much of the tradition handed on to him to the wording of Scripture he considered usual. The former observation, for example as made by Ferdinand Hahn,[6] is in

---

attempted to refute the Davidic descent of the messiah, while Suhl and Lövestamm do not pursue the logic of their observations, but instead replace 'David's son' with other christological categories.

2. Cf. R. Bultmann, *Die Geschichte der synoptischen Tradition* (Göttingen: Vandenhoeck & Ruprecht, 5th edn, 1961), pp. 145-46; C. Burger, *Jesus als Davidssohn: Eine traditionsgeschichtliche Untersuchung* (FRLANT, 98; Göttingen: Vandenhoeck & Ruprecht, 1970), pp. 52-59, 64-70, and Schneider, 'Die Davidssohnfrage', especially p. 65 n. 1.

3. Cf. V. Taylor, *The Names of Jesus* (London: Macmillan, 1953), p. 24; *The Gospel according to St Mark* (London: Macmillan, 1952), pp. 490-93.

4. Cf. F. Hahn, *Christologische Hoheitstitel: Ihre Geschichte im frühen Christentum* (Göttingen: Vandenhoeck & Ruprecht, 1963), pp. 113-15; R. Pesch, *Das Markusevangelium*, II (HTKNT; Freiburg: Herder, 1977), p. 254.

5. Cf. A. Suhl, *Funktion*. In any case, as Pesch shows (*Markusevangelium*), the agreement with the LXX is not perfect.

6. Cf. n. 4.

fact the more telling, but even this is not conclusive. 'Son of David', 'messiah' and 'lord' may indeed be read in the light of the New Testament designation of Jesus under all three categories, employed as christological titles. On this reading, the passage can only have originated after this identification had been achieved, presumably as a consequence of faith in the resurrection. But each of the terms is used in a somewhat unusual way when the passage is placed in the context of their normal usage elsewhere in the New Testament. Indeed, the very supposition, encouraged by Matthew, Luke and Paul, that *ben David* is a category of physical descent which imputes to Jesus a theologically significant lineage is what causes our puzzlement when we read this passage. Even the use of 'messiah' is unusual here, for it appears in a saying of Jesus (cf. Mt. 23.10; 24.5, 23; Mk 13.21; Lk. 24.26, 46, all of which pose special problems of interpretation). And while 'lord' is used of Jesus in the New Testament, its range of meaning is, of course, such that it need not imply that he is identified with κύριος as a translation of אדני. This is certainly not the case in the *Davidssohnfrage*, nor is there any hint that David's address of the messiah as his lord corresponds to a title of Jesus. In fact, the citation of Psalm 110 presupposes a critical distance between 'the lord' (God) and 'my lord' (the messiah) which is not maintained elsewhere in the New Testament (cf. particularly Mk 5.19, 20) when Jesus' identity is in view. One might generally argue that Jesus and God are closely identified when the former is called 'lord', but he is not so designated in the present case. On reflection, then, the so-called christological titles in the passage do not correspond very well to what we, on the basis of ordinary New Testament usage, might expect the early Church to have said about the identity of Jesus.

Conceptually, the passage also does not suit the tendencies of the Synoptic redaction. On one reading, Jesus here denies that he is the messiah, so that the saying gives the lie to Mark's messianic secret, a motif taken up at least partially (whether or not from Mark) by Matthew and Luke. If, on the other hand, Bultmann is correct, and Jesus here denies the Davidic descent of the messiah (and his own descent from David), then the saying explicitly contradicts the Matthean and Lukan genealogies, and does not correspond to any theme which is emphasized by Mark. The redaction critic is left, in passages such as the present one, to speak in conceptual terms, since—apart from the biblical citation—the language in which they are conveyed is not patient of the distinction between redaction and tradition. In the present case, apart from the quotation from Psalm 110, the passage consists only of various and editorially characteristic descriptions of the crowd's reaction (Mt. 22.46; Mk 12.37c; cf. Lk. 20.45, where a positive response of the sort we read of in Mark seems to be presupposed), and Jesus' question itself. As has already been indicated, the question is directed (again, by narrative means) to various groups of opponents in the Gospels. Matthew or a predecessor—as is consistent with his habit of presentation—has a dialectical exchange between Jesus and the Pharisees where Mark and Luke have a straight question from Jesus.[7] The actual wording of Jesus' question, which is practically speaking no more than an introduction to the biblical citation, is so simple that it would be problematic to speak of a distinction in linguistic terms between redaction and tradition.[8]

A linguistic distinction which would help us to decide between the Hellenistic and Palestinian provenience of the tradition is also impossible here.[9] Tradition criticism, so far as it can be conducted at all in respect of this passage, must also proceed on a conceptual basis, and here too one runs across anomalies on either reading of the passage. Bultmann argued that the passage reflected the denial of Jesus' Davidic ancestry in a limited circle of the early Church,[10] but this hypothetical circle would have contradicted, or at least would not have agreed with, the theology of Mt. 1.6, 17, 20, Lk. 1.27, 32, 3.31, Rom. 1.3, 2 Tim. 2.8, Rev. 5.5, 22.16. Indeed, the circle's ideology would be so out of keeping with so

7. Cf. G. Bornkamm, G. Barth, H.J. Held, *Überlieferung und Auslegung im Matthäusevangelium* (WMANT, 1; Neukirchen: Neukirchener Verlag, 1960), particularly H.J. Held's study; P. Bonnard, *L'évangile selon Matthieu* (CNT, 1; Neuchatel: Delachaux & Niestlé, 2nd edn, 1970), p. 330.

8. Cf. B.D. Chilton, *God in Strength: Jesus' Announcement of the Kingdom* (SNTUM, 1; Freistadt: Plöchl, 1979). This earlier study formally distinguishes between the use of redaction criticism to discover the characteristic motives of the Evangelists and its employment as a preliminary step in tradition criticism (cf., e.g., p. 67), although one would not perhaps receive this impression from the review of C. Tuckett in *Scripture Bulletin* 11 (1980), p. 36.

9. For the generally problematic nature of such a distinction in absolute terms, cf. I.H. Marshall, 'Palestinian and Hellenistic Christianity: Some Critical Comments', *NTS* 19 (1972–73), pp. 271-87. I use the terms only relatively to characterize the distance of traditions from the thought world of Jesus (so far as that can be defined). Cf. D.M. Hay, *Glory at the Right Hand: Psalm 110 in Early Christianity* (SBLMS, 18; New York: Abingdon Press, 1973), pp. 110-11.

10. Bultmann, *Geschichte*, pp. 145-46. Cf. Schneider, 'Die Davidssohnhfrage', pp. 66-67.

many strata of the New Testament that, in the absence of positive evidence for its existence, the hypothesis itself seems problematic. Suhl agrees with Bultmann that the Davidic descent of the messiah is here denied, and that the provenience of the passage is post-Easter. On his view, however, Jesus' claim to be the messiah is being defended against the charge that he is not a descendant of David, and Wrede also believed that the passage was handed on to support the claim in the face of such challenges.[11] Again, however, we are required by this reconstruction to postulate groups, theologies and even apologetic circumstances within early Christianity for which we have no evidence other than a rather suppositious reading of our passage. Wrede's well-known assertion that Jesus himself did not claim to be the messiah would at least provide the basis on which to associate the saying with a recognized historical figure, although it imputes an attitude to him which makes his crucifixion on Roman authority difficult to understand, and in fact Wrede himself did use the *Davidssohnfrage* to support his general theory. Taylor's view of the passage, as criticizing the identification between the messiah and a human genealogy, may also be taken to reflect Jesus' attitude (as Taylor himself was inclined to do), but Schneider held that this stance represented a Hellenistic Jewish argument against a Pharisaic understanding of the messiah.[12] None of the three distinctive readings of the passage (as a rejection of one of the terms or an attempt to distance the two), which reflect the logical possibilities which we sketched in the opening paragraph, requires the *Davidssohnfrage* to be taken as authentic or as secondary any more than it requires the rejection of the other two possibilities. Certain scholars have been inclined to argue on analogy from common law that our texts are innocent until proven guilty, that is, that one is to assume the historicity of the Gospels until one is faced with compelling evidence to the contrary.[13] Such a rubric could be applied in instances such as the present case, but there are certain obvious difficulties. Although analogies are, by nature, not to be applied strictly, the present example characterizes the Evangelists and their predecessors as 'innocent' in some sense when they report historically (within our understanding of history) and as guilty in some sense when they express their own faith

11. A. Suhl, 'Der Davidssohn im Matthäus-Evangelium', *ZNW* 59 (1968), pp. 57-81, 57-59.

12. Schneider, 'Die Davidssohnhfrage', pp. 84-85.

13. Cf. S.C. Goetz and C.L. Blomberg, 'The Burden of Proof', *JSNT* 11 (1981), pp. 39-63.

more than they do historical data. The analogy not only permits, but requires the association between theological expression and guilt, since otherwise the 'burden of proof' cannot be placed on the argument that a given passage in the New Testament is not historical, but theological. Far too little is known of the values of the Evangelists and their predecessors for such an argument to be tenable. The authenticity of our passage seems as open a question as its meaning.

Recent studies of the phrase 'son of David' in early and rabbinic Judaism as well as in the Gospel tradition have offered a fresh appreciation of the significance of the phrase, and these results could be applied to our passage, provided we found them acceptable. In an article in the *Harvard Theological Review*, Dennis Duling examines the evidence and the case for the argument that *ben David* was used in early Judaism as a reference to Solomon and his wonder-working and exorcistic power.[14] The general exaltation of Solomon's wisdom in our period is well known and need not be discussed here. More specifically, Psalm 91, used according to rabbinic tradition to exorcize demons, is associated with a mention of Solomon in a text from Cave 11 at Qumran.[15] We may have here an indication that this particular son of David was associated with the exorcistic use of a particular psalm of David. Similarly, David in the *LAB* 60.3 promises that one of his descendants, perhaps Solomon, will rule over the demons,[16] and in Josephus's *Ant.* 8.2, 5 Solomon is said to have composed forms of exorcisms.[17] Further, in the same passage Josephus reports that a Jew named Eleazar 'speaking Solomon's name' performed an exorcism in the presence of Vespasian. Solomon was, of course, a son of David, and he is identified as such in

14. D.C. Duling, 'Solomon, Exorcism, and the Son of David', *HTR* 68 (1975), pp. 235-52. Cf. S. Giverson, 'Solomon und die Dämonen', in M. Krause (ed.), *Essays on the Nag Hammadi Texts in Honour of Alexander Böhlig* (NHS, 3; Leiden: Brill, 1972), pp. 16-21. As P.R. Davies has pointed out to me, in 11QPS^a Dav Comp David himself is said to have composed songs 'for making music over the stricken'; cf. J.A. Sanders, *The Psalm Scroll of Qumran Cave 11* (DJD, 4; Oxford: Clarendon Press, 1965), p. 92.

15. Duling, 'Solomon, Exorcism', p. 239.

16. Duling, 'Solomon, Exorcism', pp. 240-41; K. Berger, 'Die königlichen Messiastraditionen des Neuen Testaments', *NTS* 20 (1973–74), pp. 1-44, 6 n. 23 and cf. 'Zum traditionsgeschichtlichen Hintergrund christologischer Hoheitstitel', *NTS* 17 (1970–71), pp. 391-425.

17. Duling, 'Solomon, Exorcism', p. 241.

Aramaic incantation bowls from a later period.[18] Loren Fisher claimed,
on the basis of research on the incantation bowls, that 'David's son'
could be used as a designation for a healer in the New Testament period,
but Duling disputes this thesis, observing that the phrase is not used in
the bowls as an address, which is how it appears in the New Testament,
but only as an additional identification.[19] Duling is bound to admit,
however, that Solomon is addressed as David's son in the *Testament of
Solomon*.[20] The complex composition history of the *Testament,* however,
makes Duling understandably cautious in evaluating its readings.
Solomon is addressed as 'Solomon, David's son' in his divine commission
(1.7), and in the cry of an old workman who asks Solomon to cure his
son we have 'King Solomon, David's son' (20.1). Duling calls attention
to the indubitably Christian readings in the *Testament*, and suggests that
these addresses are 'not "titular" in the NT sense'.[21]

The latter point is, at first sight, telling, in that Jesus' is simply appealed
to as 'David's son' in some Gospel healing stories (Mt. 9.27 [cf. the *v.l.*
which appends κύριε]; 20.30 [cf. the *v.l.* κύριε and 'Ιησοῦ]; Mk
10.48 [cf. the *v.l.* κύριε and 'Ιησοῦ]; Lk. 18.39 [cf. the *v.l.* 'Ιησοῦ]).
Nonetheless, it is at least noteworthy that some manuscripts supplement
the address 'David's son' in these passages with an additional identification (viz. 'lord', 'Jesus'). Indeed, when we look at the pattern of the
use of the address as a whole in the Gospels, it becomes doubtful that
the so-called 'titular' use of 'David's son' is normative in the context of
healing. In Mk 10.47, Jesus is called 'David's son, Jesus' by Bartimaeus,
and only then in v. 48 simply 'David's son' (although here, as noted,
'lord' and 'Jesus' appear as variant readings). Similarly, the Lukan
parallel has the blind man call out 'Jesus, son of David' first of all (18.38),
and then simply—but not in all manuscripts (cf. the *v.l.* 'Ιησοῦ)—
'David's son' in v. 39. The allegedly titular usages only occur within the
context of healing in the Gospel according to Matthew, and even then
not consistently. The uses at 9.27 and 20.30 are supplemented in some
manuscripts, and 20.31 in any case appends 'lord' (cf. Nestle–Aland [p.
26] on the position of the term). The pattern in respect of Mt. 20.30, 31

18. Duling, 'Solomon, Exorcism', pp. 245-47.
19. L.R. Fisher, 'Can This Be the Son of David?', in F.T. Trotter (ed.), *Jesus and
the Historian: Written in Honour of Ernest Cadman Colwell* (Philadelphia:
Westminster Press, 1968), pp. 82-97; Duling, 'Solomon, Exorcism', p. 247.
20. Duling, 'Solomon, Exorcism', p. 249.
21. Duling, 'Solomon, Exorcism', pp. 242-43.

is therefore reversed when compared to the parallels, Mk 10.47, 48 and Lk. 18.38, 39, in that the less qualified usage of the address appears first. As is well known, the Matthean portrayal of two blind men in this scene appears to be secondary in comparison to the Markan and Lukan accounts,[22] and Duling himself in a later article recognizes that Matthew was led by the diversity of the traditions before him to synthesize a new picture of the son of David.[23] In Duling's view, the innovative aspect in Matthew is the 'therapeutic', and this argument is confirmed by the pattern of presentation in Mt. 20.30, 31, and by 9.27, the doublet of 20.30, 31. Moreover, at 15.22 Matthew has the address in the mouth of the Canaanite woman (with κύριος), while Mark at 7.26 reports the Syro-Phonecian woman's request only indirectly. Above all, at 12.23, Matthew—in a unique summary passage—in respect of exorcistic healing (following a formula citation) has the crowds ask, 'Can this be *the* son of David?'. The titular usage (that is, the consciously titular, articular usage) of 'David's son' in the context of healing appears to be a Matthean invention (whether at the level of tradition or redaction).

For Matthew, the grounds for the usage of the title, however, do not appear to be therapeutic. In 12.23, Matthew only has the crowds ask whether Jesus is the son of David after Jesus has been identified as David's son (1.1) in an emphatically genealogical way (cf. 1.6, 17). The prominence of this aspect within the first Gospel is unmistakable, in that the first address of a person as 'David's son' is here directed, not to Jesus, but to Joseph (1.20). The theological cash value of Jesus' descent comes to open expression at Mt. 21.9, where Jesus is hailed by the *crowds* (cf. 12.23) at the entry into Jerusalem as *the* son of David (cf. Mk 11.10 and Lk. 19.38). This is the climax of Matthew's presentation of Jesus as *ben David*; the therapeutic application in 12.23 is important, but only preparatory, to the messianic application in 21.9.[24] It would

22. Cf. J.M. Gibbs, 'Purpose and Pattern in Matthew's Use of the Title "Son of David"', *NTS* 10 (1963–64), pp. 446-64, 453-57.

23. D.C. Duling, 'The Therapeutic Son of David: An Element in Matthew's Christological Apologetic', *NTS* 24 (1977–78), pp. 392-410.

24. For the Matthean emphasis on Jesus' messianic status, cf. Gibbs, 'Purpose and Pattern', esp. pp. 449, 463, 464, and Suhl, 'Der Davidssohn'. For translations and editions of the *Psalms of Solomon*, which are crucial in this context, cf. G.B. Gray, 'The Psalms of Solomon', in R.H. Charles (ed.), *The Apocrypha and Pseudepigrapha of the Old Testament in English* (Oxford: Clarendon Press, 1913), pp. 631-52; R. Kittel, 'Die Psalmen Salomos', in E. Kautzsch (ed.), *Die Apokryphen und Pseudepigraphen des Alten Testaments*, II (Darmstadt: Wissenschaftliche Buch-

seem that for Matthew, as in the seventeenth chapter of the *Psalms of Solomon* (cf. vv. 4 [5], 21 [23]) the promised king who was to restore Israel was 'David's son' (*not* 'the son of David' as in Kautzsch, Charles and Hølm-Nielsen; cf. the editions of Fritzsche, Ryle–James and von Gebhardt). Since Jesus was, as is explicitly presupposed in the first Gospel, the messiah (1.1), and since his descent was held to accord with the conventional expectation of the king as 'David's son' (cf. vv. 6, 17), it was quite natural for Matthew to style Jesus as 'the son of David', and to do so most openly in an explicitly messianic context (21.9). As compared to the *Psalms*, however, the Matthean title is innovative, and is an almost inevitable consequence of the identification of a particular son of David as the messiah. Duling fails to observe this development, and therefore claims that the usage in the *Psalms* is titular.[25] This is an embarrassment to him, since he argues that the title is a late-comer to the New Testament, and is at least partially based on the application to Jesus of promises to David in view of the resurrection (Rom. 1.3-4 is for Duling the 'earliest point of entry of the promise tradition into early Christianity').[26] In fact, however, a distinction between the non-titular address 'David's son' and the articular title 'the son of David' is

gesellschaft, 1962); S. Hølm-Nielson, *Die Psalmen Salomos*, in W.G. Kümmel, *Jüdische Schriften aus helllenistisch-römischer Zeit. IV. Poetische Schriften* (2 vols.; Gütersloh: Gerd Mohn, 1977); O.F. Fritzsche, *Libri Apocryphi Veteris Testamenti Graeci: Recensuit et cum commentario critico edidit* (Leipzig: Brockhaus, 1871); H.E. Ryle and M.R. James, ΨΑΛΜΟΙ ΣΟΛΟΜΩΝΤΟΣ: *Psalms of the Pharisees, Commonly Called The Psalms of Solomon* (Cambridge: Cambridge University Press, 1891). The last mentioned work is perhaps the source of the ascription of the *Psalms* to 'Pharisees', but this ascription is suppositious. 'Pharisees', whatever the precise meaning of the term, seems to designate a religious movement primarily within the educated group which might generally be called scribal; cf. J.W. Bowker, *Jesus and the Pharisees* (Cambridge: Cambridge University Press, 1973). The *Psalms* appear to reflect the theology of a learned, that is, scribal group in the area of Jerusalem which attempted to come to terms with both Roman hegemony and priestly control of the Temple; cf. the literature in J.H. Charlesworth, *The Pseudepigrapha and Modern Research* (SBLSCS; Missoula, MT: Scholars Press, 1976), pp. 197-202. The situation in respect of the provenience of the *Psalms* cannot be clarified when they are treated in isolation; cf. V. Schüpphaus, *Die Psalmen Salomos: Ein Zeugnis jerusalemer Theologie und Frömmigkeit in der Mitte des vorchristlichen Jahrhunderts* (ALGHJ, 7; Leiden: Brill, 1977).

25. D.C. Duling, 'The Promises to David and their Entrance into Christianity— Nailing Down a Likely Hypothesis', *NTS* 20 (1973–74), pp. 55-77, 68.

26. Duling, 'The Promises to David', pp. 55, 77.

preserved in Matthew's incomplete synthesis, with the titular usage reflecting Christian expression of the *theologoumenon* in the *Psalms of Solomon* and the non-titular usage appearing normally in therapeutic contexts. (The articular usage in 12.23 is, as discussed, clearly messianic in content and obviously secondary in provenience.) Even the non-articular usages of 'David's son' without further qualification in the context of healing are, as comparison with Mark, Luke, and the variant readings in Matthew shows, unusual, and Mt. 20.31 betrays the awareness that 'David's son' alone was not an appropriate address in this context. The address is taken with the Synoptic tradition as a whole as one naturally to be joined with the name ('Jesus') or some other designation ('lord') of the healer. The position is, in other words, as it is in the *Testament of Solomon*, so that Duling's objection that the address in the *Testament* is 'not "titular" in the NT sense' is to be set aside, since not even the therapeutic usages in the Gospels appear to be so.

His cautions in respect of the date of the *Testament*, and the Christian recensional activity which evidently lies behind the extant manuscripts,[27] are far more to the point. Both observations have long been accepted (cf. McCown's still masterful introduction, for example), and Berger's statement that the *Testament* corresponds to the general 'Sprach- und Vorstellungswelt' of the New Testament exorcism stories[28] might be taken to indicate the late provenience of the *Testament* rather than its 'überlieferungsgeschichtliche Wert' (so Berger[29]). On the other hand, it is held to instance, for example, Jewish demonology in the pre-Talmudic period,[30] and so to reflect early Judaism (at least at the most primitive level of the document). Moreover, Berger cites a series of passages in which Solomon is identified as David's son in the *Testament*,[31] and on the whole these cannot be described as limited to the context, conceptualization or wording of New Testament identifications of Jesus as

27. Duling, 'Solomon, Exorcism', pp. 242-43.

28. C.C. McCown, *The Testament of Solomon* (UNT, 9; Leipzig: Hinrich, 1922); F.C. Conybeare, 'The Testament of Solomon', *JQR* 11 (1898–99), pp. 1-45; Berger, 'Die königlichen Messiastraditionen', pp. 6-7.

29. Berger, 'Die königlichen Messiastraditionen', p. 6.

30. Cf. McCown, *The Testament of Solomon*, p. 3; K. Kohler, 'Demonology', in I. Singer (ed.), *The Jewish Encyclopedia* (New York: Funk and Wagnalls, 1903), pp. 514-20; C.C. McCown, 'The Christian Tradition as to the Magical Wisdom of Solomon', *JPOS* 2.1 (1922), pp. 1-24; K. Preisendanz, 'Ein Wiener Papyrusfragment zum Testamentum Salomonis', *Eos* 48 (1956), pp. 161-67.

31. Berger, 'Die königlichen Messiastraditionen', p. 7 n. 31.

David's son.[32] The occurrence is neither purely imitative of the New Testament, nor even so consistently presented as to suggest that they are part of a redactional tendency which came to expression after the traditional material in the *Testament* had been collected. The editor of a Christian recension would scarcely have wished to present Solomon as David's son, as if he was such in the proper sense, and the omission of usages in several manuscripts would tend to support this judgment. Yet Solomon's Davidic sonship is taken as something self-evident in the *Testament*; the sorts of justification—in biblical terms, for example—which one would expect to find in a polemical innovation designed by Jewish tradents or editors to refute Christian claims about Jesus are absent.[33] Indeed, Solomon's physical descent from David is nowhere stressed in the document (cf. the variant readings discussed in n. 32), even though much of the Jewish *Toledoth Jesu* movement during its period of formation was preoccupied with the development of legends aimed at discrediting the New Testament genealogies and Jesus'

32. The usages fall into definite categories. The initial occurrence, in Solomon's account of his commission through an angel, has Solomon addressed as Σολομῶν υἱὸς Δαυείδ (1.7). Because this is his divinely commissioned identity, Solomon can say to a demon, μὴ κρύψῃς ἀπ' ἐμοῦ ῥῆμα, ὅτι ἐγώ εἰμι Σολομῶν υἱὸς Δαυείδ (5.10). Then, Solomon can be addressed as David's son (20.1: βασιλεῦ Σολομῶν υἱὸς Δαυείδ) in a plea for healing. Recension B—to use McCown's terminology— has Solomon apply the designation in a definitely genealogical way (26.9: ἐγὼ οὖν Σολομῶν υἱὸς Δαυείδ υἱοῦ Ἰεσσαί), and this may be taken to support the case made out below for the genealogical background of the application of the address to Jesus. In Recension C, the address also appears in a commission (Prologue I), in an address (12.1—but in the mouth of the demon Paltiel Tzamal: Σολομῶν, υἱὲ Δαυείδ) and in a self-designation (13.12). In MS D, the genealogical aspect of the phrase is again intimated, but in a way which may betray the influence of the New Testament (1.1: ὁ Σολομῶν υἱὸς Δαυείδ ἐγένετο ἐκ τῆς τοῦ Οὐρίου γυναικός, cf. Mt. 1.6). But the oddity of this narrative usage within the pattern established by the other occurrences, and the peculiarity of MS D within the textual tradition of the *Testament of Solomon* should warn us away from using this passage to characterize that tradition generally. MS E has the purely descriptive statement that Solomon was the υἱὸς τοῦ προφήτου Δαυείδ τοῦ βασιλέως (1.1; cf. 2.1) and MS L simply calls him υἱὸς Δαυείδ at 1.1; these narrative usages would not appear to betray the influence of the New Testament (cf. McCown's 'Conspectus Titulorum' in *The Testament of Solomon*, pp. 98-99.

33. Cf. P.R. Davies and B.D. Chilton, 'The Aqedah: A Revised Tradition History', *CBQ* 40 (1978), pp. 514-46; B.D. Chilton, 'Isaac and the Second Night: A Consideration', *Bib* 61 (1980), pp. 78-88.

legitimacy.[34] Although the task of evaluating the *Testament* from a redaction-critical and tradition-critical point of view has not yet even been undertaken (although McCown's edition would provide an excellent basis for this project), Duling's readiness to dismiss the identification of Solomon in the *Testament* as David's son as a possible precedent for or analogy with New Testament usage appears to be premature. The best explanation available at the moment for the distribution and context of the identification is that Solomon, precisely in connection with his wonderful knowledge (including his exorcistic skill), was identified as David's son at an early stage in the development of the *Testament*. The diversity of the usage within the *Testament* suggests that it is not imitative of the New Testament and not the idiom of a single stream of tradition or redaction; given the evidence of Josephus and Qumran Cave 11, the possibility that 'David's son' was known as an identification and address of Solomon in the context of exorcism cannot be excluded.

That 'David's son' was used of Solomon in the context of his healing knowledge might help to explain what has hitherto seemed to be the anomalous distribution of the phrase as used in respect of Jesus in the Gospels. It has been pointed out repeatedly[35] that Jesus is normally called David's son when healing is in view. Indeed, except for the *Davidssohnfrage*, this is always the case in Mark and Luke; in Matthew— as we have seen—a messianic meaning is developed from the genealogical content of Jesus' identification as *ben David* (cf. 1.1, 20; 21.9, 15; cf. 12.23), but it is all the more striking against this background that most of the usages in Matthew also appear as pleas for healing (9.27; 15.22; 20.30, 31). For Duling to argue that Matthew in particular has developed an emphasis on the therapeutic ministry of David's son is decidedly odd, and betrays a reflex tendency to ascribe theologically significant ideas to redactors rather than tradents. Matthew may indeed have framed 12.23 in its present form, the only articular usage of the phrase in a healing context in the Gospels, because such a titular application made good sense against the background of the therapeutic,

34. Cf. J. Maier, *Jesus von Nazareth in der talmudischer Überlieferung* (Ertäge der Forschung, 82; Darmstadt: Wissenschaftliche Buchgesellschaft, 1978).

35. Cf. E. Lohmeyer, *Gottesknecht und Davidssohn* (FRLANT, 43; Göttingen: Vandenhoeck & Ruprecht, 2nd edn, 1953), p. 76: Gibbs, 'Purpose and Pattern', p. 448; Suhl, 'Der Davidssohn', p. 73; Burger, *Jesus als Davidssohn*, pp. 15, 79; Lövestamm, 'Jésus Fils de David', p. 98; C.S. Johnson, 'Mark 10.46-52: Blind Bartimaeus', *CBQ* 40 (1978), pp. 191-204.

promise (see below) and descent traditions of Jesus *ben David*. But
Matthew construed none of these traditions himself; his construction is
the (properly speaking) titular formulation of traditional motives, fundamentally in the interests of a genealogical christology. Manifestly,
Matthew is not responsible for the therapeutic context of the phrase in
Mark and Luke, where such a placement is even more predominant.
There is, in short, no redaction-critical explanation for the distribution of
the phrase in the Gospels. The 'promises of David' motif—to use
Duling's characterization[36]—features Jesus' connection to David in
respect of his triumphant resurrection. The prominence of Rom. 1.3 in
recent discussion has perhaps diverted Duling from emphasizing Rev.
3.7, 5.5, 22.16, in which the heavenly triumph of Jesus comes to
expression precisely with reference to David. Notably, none of these
usages refers to Jesus' descent from David (although the latter two may
imply it), as in Rom. 1.3 and 2 Tim. 2.8. The last two passages indeed
link Jesus' Davidic descent and his resurrection, but the κατὰ σάρκα in
Rom. 1.3 (cf. 9.3, 5; 1 Cor. 1.26; 10.18; 2 Cor. 5.16; 10.2, 3 and κατὰ
πνεῦμα in v. 4) must at least be taken to suggest that the combination
of the two was not completely natural but something of an innovation.[37]
This, in turn, would appear to indicate that Paul or a predecessor combined a Davidic descent motif with a resurrection motif such as we find
in the Revelation. In the Gospel according to Luke, we also see the
descent (1.27) and triumph (1.32, 69) motives mixed together,[38] and we
might well attribute Matthew's synthesis of various traditions which
associate Jesus and David to a similar tendency. But none of the applications to Jesus' resurrection actually use the phrase 'David's son', nor
do the genealogical or descent applications in Luke, Romans and
2 Timothy. The same is true of the objection to Jesus' descent expressed
in Jn 7.42, where, as in Paul and deutero-Paul, the language of 'seed' is
used.[39] Matthew, of course, speaks of Jesus as 'David's son' in the same
sense as he is 'Abraham's son' (1.1), and he develops the titular usage in
order to develop a theology of messianic descent, but even in the first

36. Duling, 'The Promises to David', pp. 55-77.
37. Cf. O. Michel, *Der Brief an die Römer* (KEK; Göttingen: Vandenhoeck &
Ruprecht, 1966), pp. 38-39.
38. Cf. H. Schürmann, *Das Lukasevangelium*. I. *Kommentar zu Kap. 1. 1-9, 50*
(HTKNT, 3.1; Freiburg: Herder, 1969), pp. 42, 47-48, 86-87.
39. Cf. M. Wilcox, 'The Promise of the "Seed" in the New Testament and the
Targumim', *JSNT* 5 (1979), pp. 2-20.

Gospel Jesus is only addressed as David's son in the context of a plea for healing. That is, the connection between Jesus and David in respect of Jesus' descent and in respect of his resurrection are established in the New Testament, but not in the context of healing and without the address of Jesus as David's son. Precisely the last two points, among the most prominent features of New Testament *ben David* usage, are accounted for on the supposition that 'David's son' was the address applied to Jesus at the level of tradition when he was to heal or exorcize in a manner reminiscent of Solomon.

The great difficulty in postulating an analogy between the 'David's son' usage of the *Testament of Solomon* and that of the New Testament, apart from that of chronology, is that it is one thing to call Solomon 'son of David' and quite another to apply the phrase to someone simply in view of his reputation as a healer. In the former case, the usage is a solemn affirmation of a well known fact; in the latter, it is an innovative claim. What Fisher, Berger, Lövestamm and Duling have not so far given us is a clear indication that a healer other than Solomon was known as 'David's son' in our period. In the absence of such evidence, the supposition that Jesus is addressed as such in the Synoptic tradition simply because he is a healer of repute is untenable. On the other hand, given that the Davidic descent of Jesus was public knowledge, whether accurate or not, the application of the address to him in the context of healing would be far more understandable. The Davidic descent of Jesus was recognized from before the time of Paul (cf. Rom. 1.3) and was, presumably, the conviction which spawned the Matthean and Lukan genealogies. Mk 3.33-35, it is true, offers a view of familial bonds as relativized by God's will, and conceivably has been passed on to guard the community against the formation of a dominical Caliphate,[40] but the descent of Jesus is simply not an issue here. To offer the qualification that Jesus is addressed as David's son because he was known as a descendant of David who was also, as Solomon was, a skilled healer, is therefore a refinement on recent discussion which the development of the New Testament tradition as we understand will bear out. Moreover, although it has not been noted in recent discussion, in the *Testament of Solomon* descent is invoked by the use of the phrase 'David's son' in order to identify the status and authority of Solomon.[41]

40. Cf. R. Pesch, *Das Markusevangelium*. I. *Einleitung und Kommentar zu Kap. 1.1–8.26* (HTKNT, 2.1; Freiburg: Herder, 1976), pp. 222-25.

41. Cf. n. 32 and E.L. Abel, 'The Genealogies of Jesus O XPICTOC', *NTS* 20

If the address was used of Jesus for the reasons suggested, the obvious question remains, did he know of or encourage the usage? A direct answer to this question is not to be found, but one can at least maintain that certain sayings of Jesus are patient of the understanding that he did so. In the controversy over his disciples plucking grain on the sabbath, Jesus offers a direct comparison between himself and David (Mt. 12.3, 4; Mk 2.25, 26; Lk. 6.3, 4), a comparison on which his argument is dependent.[42] Because the analogy between his and his disciples' situation and that of David and his company is so weak,[43] the logic of Jesus' case relies on the implicit connection between David and himself. What is startling about this is not only that Jesus is portrayed in the saying as of equal standing with David, but that the propriety of such a comparison is taken for granted. Although a degree of idealization has no doubt been introduced during the transmission of this pericope, Rudolf Pesch has presented sound arguments for the case that it is based 'auf konkreter Überlieferung aus dem Leben Jesu',[44] and to these general considerations we may add that the present Davidic imagery does not seem to be a part of the growing application of Davidic language in respect of Jesus' resurrection in the early Church, nor—of course—in respect of his genealogy (or, more generally, his descent). Perhaps even more striking, however, is the reference made to Solomon in dominical sayings. The aphoristic saying about the lilies and Solomon (Mt. 6.28-29; Lk. 12.27) is hardly probative of the connection, if any, between Jesus and Solomon, but it does put the latter in a remarkably unexalted position, although I have not seen the fact noted in the commentaries, as compared to what we find in the *Testament of Solomon* and Rabbinica.[45] This apparently revised estimate of Solomon's status is, of course, as nothing when compared to Jesus' direct claim to be greater than Solomon (Mt. 12.42; Lk. 11.31). The precise comparison he makes, in

(1973–74), pp. 203-10; J. Chopineau, 'Un notarikon en Matthieu 1/1', *ETR* 53 (1978), pp. 269-70.

42. Pesch, *Das Markusevangelium*, p. 182.

43. Cf. D. Cohn-Sherbok, 'An Analysis of Jesus' Arguments Concerning the Plucking of Grain on the Sabbath', *JSNT* 2 (1979), pp. 31-41. Cohn-Sherbok's work does not take adequate account of the possible anachronism involved in applying the criteria of Mishnah to the pre-rabbinic documents of early Judaism such as the New Testament.

44. Pesch, *Das Markusevangelium*, p. 183.

45. Cf. Str-B, I, p. 438; M. Aberbach and L. Smolar, 'Jeroboam and Solomon: Rabbinic Interpretations', *JQR* 59 (1968), pp. 118-32.

fact, is between Solomon's wisdom, which the queen came to hear, and the 'more' (πλεῖον—n.b. the use of the neuter) which Jesus offers, but is refused. As Howard Marshall puts it in his commentary, 'it is the wisdom spoken by Solomon which is being contrasted with that uttered by Jesus'.[46] By this period, of course, quite aside from the argument being discussed in the present paper, Solomon's wisdom included his healing and exorcistic craft, so that this saying coheres well with the understanding that the address 'David's son' was used of Jesus because he was considered to be of Davidic descent and to be possessed of powers comparable with Solomon's.

In the particular application which 'David's son' had as an address of Jesus, then, his descent and his ability to heal were both in view. We cannot cite an instance in which both are maintained of a contemporary rabbi by means of the address, but neither claim would be unusual in contemporary rabbinic circles. Geza Vermes has already cited the evidence, much of which is already to be found in George Foot Moore's classic study, for the traditions of rabbis as 'charismatic miracle workers', and—although this phrase (particularly with the adjective 'charismatic') exaggerates the position—the fact is that certain rabbis, notably Ḥanina ben Dosa, were noted for the healing, efficacy of their prayers.[47] Moreover, Jacob Neusner has proved that Davidic descent—generally independent of any messianic claim—is ascribed in Rabbinica to Hillel, Judah the Prince, Ḥiyya and Huna.[48] That a Jewish teacher of Jesus'

---

46. I.H. Marshall, *The Gospel of Luke: A Commentary on the Greek Text* (Exeter: Paternoster Press, 1978), p. 486.

47. G. Vermes, *Jesus the Jew: A Historian's Reading of the Gospels* (London: Collins, 1973), pp. 72-78; G.F. Moore, *Judaism in the First Four Centuries of the Christian Era*, I (Cambridge, MA: Harvard University Press, 1946), pp. 377-78.

48. J. Neusner, *A History of the Jews in Babylonia*, I (SPB, 9; Leiden: Brill, 1965), pp. 35-36, 101-104, 175-76; cf. II (SPB, 11, 1966), pp. 225-26 (for the later development of messianic associations in an essentially rabbinic application of the claim, II, p. 56 and V (SPB, 15, 1970), pp. 95-96. Cf. Moore, *Judaism in the First Four Centuries*, p. 329. The passages concerned deserve special treatment, which would go well beyond the scope of the present paper. Cf. G. Kuhn, 'Die Geschlechtsregister Jesu bei Lucas und Matthäus, nach ihrer Herkunft untersucht', *ZNW* 22 (1923), pp. 206-28; E. Lohse, 'Der König aus Davids Geschlecht, Bemerkungen zur messianischen Erwartung der Synagoge', in O. Betz, M. Hengel, P. Schmidt (eds.), *Abraham unser Vater: Juden und Christen im Gespräch über die Bibel. Festschrift für Otto Michel* (AGSU, 5; Leiden: Brill, 1963), pp. 337-45; E. Lohse, 'υἱὸς Δαυίδ', *TWNT*, VIII, pp. 482-92; M.D. Johnson, *The Purpose of the Biblical Genealogies*

period should be called *ben David*, and that this address should have associations with the wisdom of Solomon when that rabbi was possessed of healing powers, is therefore plausible, and, while a certain development of contemporary categories is posited, this assertion does not require the extra-historical—but unfortunately fashionable—claim that Jesus 'transcended' or 'transformed' Judaism.[49] In short, such an understanding of the address 'David's son' as applied to Jesus makes common sense history.

A considerable question, however, obviously remains. In calling attention to the rabbinic and exorcistic associations of the address, we have left the messianic association entirely out of account. There is no doubt that such an association was current in the first century, especially in the environs of Jerusalem.[50] The evidence includes not merely the *Psalms of Solomon* 17, which has already been discussed, but the Qumran scrolls and the Shemoneh Esreh.[51] Mowinkel documented the Davidic orientation of rabbinic messianology overall,[52] and the evidence, which has been cited many times, need not be repeated here: that the *mesiaḥ ben David* was anticipated in Jerusalem to restore the dominion to Israel is recognized. Indeed, the fourteenth benediction in both recensions of the Shemoneh Esreh associates the prayer for the restoration of Jerusalem with a mention of David, although only the Babylonian recension contains a prayer for the צמח דוד (in the fifteenth benediction).[53] Within the

with *Special Reference to the Setting of the Genealogies of Jesus* (SNTSMS, 8; Cambridge: Cambridge University Press, 1969); R.R. Wilson, *Genealogy and History in the Biblical World* (Yale Near Eastern Researches, 7; London: Yale University Press, 1977).

49. Cf. J. Riches, *Jesus and the Transformation of Judaism* (London: Darton, Longman and Todd, 1980). The incisive attack on the modern view of Judaism as legalistic offered by E.P. Sanders, *Paul and Palestinian Judaism: A Comparison of Patterns of Religion* (London: SCM Press, 1977) will need to be considered by all serious students of Jesus' life as well as those who are concerned with Paul.

50. Cf. Burger, *Jesus als Davidssohn*, p. 24; W. Wifall, 'Son of Man—A Pre-Davidic Social Class?', *CBQ* 37 (1975), pp. 331-40.

51. Cf. Burger, *Jesus als Davidssohn*, p. 24.

52. S. Mowinkel, *He That Cometh* (trans. G.W. Anderson; Oxford: Basil Blackwell, 1956), pp. 270 n. 2, 286 n. 1 (cf. n. 2), 291, 292 n. 3, 305-306 (although many of the examples are from Strack-Billerbeck). Cf. Moore, *Judaism in the First Four Centuries*, II, p. 329.

53. Cf. D.W. Staerck, *Altjüdische liturgische Gebete ausgewählt und mit Einleitungen* (Kleine Texte für theologische und philologische Vorlesungen und Übungen; Bonn: Marcus & Weber, 1910), pp. 13, 18.

New Testament, however, although the resurrection/promise motif of Romans, 2 Timothy and the Revelation might be said to be consistent with the messianic *ben David* teaching of contemporary Judaism, only Matthew—apparently, as we have seen, at the level of redaction—represents Jesus as the messiah because he is *ben David* and can be addressed as such (Lk. 1.27, 32 are consistent with the connection between the messiah and David's son, but the address is not used, and these verses in any case probably stem from the reflective stage of New Testament tradition which produced the resurrection/promise motif).[54] Even including the resurrection/promise motif (and the Lukan material), which could have arisen, apart from messianic *ben David* associations, on the basis of Jesus' Davidic descent alone, the simple fact is that the earliest traditions do not substantiate Jesus' messianic status with reference to his Davidic descent, whatever the *Psalms of Solomon* and Rabbinica might lead us to expect.

Within the Synoptic tradition, of course, the earliest material is notoriously circumspect about identifying Jesus as messiah in any sense, despite the fact that 'messiah' could be used quite flexibly within early Judaism.[55] Although the Gospel according to Mark is written on the assumption the reader knows Jesus as Christ (1.1; 9.41), prior to the *Davidssohnfrage* only the confession at Caesarea Philippi explicitly justifies the identification (8.29), and even then Jesus' response can scarcely be styled a complete acceptance of 'messiah' as a description of his status (8.30-33). The position is not qualitatively different in respect of Matthew and Luke. 'Christ' is used editorially (and, in Lk. 2.11, angelically) in both Gospels before the *Davidssohnfrage*, but Caesarea Philippi is the nearest Jesus comes in any of the Synoptics explicitly to accepting a messianic characterization of his mission before his entry into Jerusalem. Yet in the blind men (Mt. 20.30) or Bartimaeus (Mk 10.46) or blind man (Lk. 18.35) pericope, that is, immediately prior to the entry in Matthew and Mark and shortly beforehand in Luke, Jesus is portrayed as countermanding the attempt of the crowd to repress his being addressed with the cry 'David's son' (Mt. 20.31-32; Mk 10.48-49; Lk. 18.39-40) and as confirming the identification by healing the man or men of blindness (Mt. 20.34; Mk 10.52; Lk. 18.42-43a). The therapeutic associations of the address are therefore openly

54. Cf. Schürmann, *Das Lukasevangelium*, p. 40.
55. Cf. M. de Jonge, 'The Use of the Word "Anointed" in the Time of Jesus', *NovT* 8 (1966), pp. 132-48.

embraced here, and the entry complex, with its evident reference to Zech. 9.9, has unmistakably messianic implications. Matthew (21.9, 15) presents the innovative acclamation 'the son of David' in order to express both the therapeutic and (more especially) the messianic side of Jesus' mission, and he formed the title from the non-titular address and the designation, 'David's son'. Mark, as is well known, here reads 'blessed be the coming kingdom of our father David' (11.9, cf. the Shemeneh Esreh), and Luke merely refers to 'he who comes, the king' (19.38; cf. Jn 12.13). Except at the level of Matthew's redactional synthesis, the question of Jesus' messianic identity is not solved by means of the *ben David theologoumenon*. Within the literary context of the Synoptic tradition, the paradox of an emphatic *ben David* christology and an elusive *mesiah* christology is the setting of the *Davidssohnfrage*. Whatever difficulties it may give us, there seems little doubt but that, within this context, the question is rhetorical. Jesus presupposes his identification as David's son, and denies that this is a messianic claim. Given the literary structure of the Gospels as they stand, and our understanding of the development of the Synoptic tradition before it was fixed literarily, there is no evidence to commend the opposite solution, viz. that Jesus claimed to be messiah but denied or qualified the importance of Davidic descent.

The apparent anomaly here is that, after this point, Jesus does confess to the famous charge of the high priest(s) (Mt. 26.63; Mk 14.61; Lk. 22.67) with the result that he is delivered to Pilate and condemned to die. The Evangelists preserve a traditional 'David's son' motif and a traditional 'christ' motif in Jesus' words, but—except for Matthew—the two sorts of tradition are not mixed together, and at precisely the point where the traditions might have coalesced—in the *Davidssohnfrage*—they are emphatically distinguished. This distinction, and the *Davidssohnfrage* itself, does not correspond to the theological interests of the Evangelists; indeed, the Matthean redaction proceeds in the opposite direction. The association between Jesus' Davidic descent and his identification as messiah, moreover, seems to be a secure feature of early Church tradition (cf. Rom. 1.3; 2 Tim. 2.8; Rev. 22.16 cf. v. 21 [*v.l.*]), so that it is problematic to assign the *Davidssohnfrage* to the secondary development of Jesus' message.

The best explanation for the *Davidssohnfrage*, in other words, is that Jesus said pretty much what is attributed to him, and that he intended to deflect the growing suspicion that he claimed to be messiah. His Davidic descent, his willingness to be called David's son in the context of healing, his comparison of himself with David and Solomon, his entry into Jerusalem must all have contributed to this suspicion, which was finally confirmed as a result of Jesus' direct (so Mk 14.62) or indirect (so Mt. 26.64; Lk. 22.67-69) answer to the question whether he was christ. His admission was sufficient to substantiate the charge against him in the eyes of the authorities (Mt. 26.65-66; Mk 14.63-64; Lk. 22.71), and therefore to warrant his condemnation to Pilate. The much disputed question of the nature of this charge ('blasphemy', according to Mt. 16.65; Mk 14.64) is only problematic when one tries to place all of the emphasis on this messianic admission (or non-contestation) rather than on the context of the initial question.[56] Jesus is not simply asked whether he is messiah, a claim which would not have been punishable by itself,[57] but whether he claims messianic authority as one who according to some[58] asserted he would replace the Temple (Mt. 26.59-61; Mk 14.55-59) and who, as was commonly known, had on one occasion occupied it (Mt. 21.12-13; Mk 11.15-17; Lk. 19.45-46). Matthew (21.15-16) records the formal complaint to Jesus by high priests and scribes that the title 'the son of David' is being used of Jesus (as a healer, cf. v. 14) in the Temple, and although this notice—especially in its reference to the titular form of acclamation—is coloured by Matthew's synthetic christology, the issue he points to is a real one. If Jesus claims to act with Davidic or Solomonic authority in the Temple, he is more than a nuisance to the Temple authorities; he poses a direct challenge to them. For the messiah son of David was expected, in the hope of Jews living near Jerusalem,[59] to establish his rule from the Temple. By his occupation, therefore, and perhaps already by his festal entry into the city,[60] Jesus had crossed a Rubicon. His Davidic descent and his reputation as a healer had

56. Cf. J.C. O'Neill, 'The Charge of Blasphemy at Jesus' Trial before the Sanhedrin', in E. Bammel (ed.), *The Trial of Jesus: Cambridge Studies in honour of C.F.D. Moule* (SBT, 13; Naperville: Allenson, 1970), pp. 72-77.

57. *Pace* W.L. Lane, *The Gospel according to Mark* (London: Marshall, Morgan and Scott, 1974), p. 536; cf. Str-B, I, pp. 1008-1009.

58. That they were false witnesses (as in Matthew and Luke) is hardly an objective judgment, and might in any case apply to their motivation rather than to their testimony. Cf. Lane, *Mark*, pp. 533-35.

59. Cf. the section on מקדשא and on משיחא in B.D. Chilton, *The Glory of Israel: The Theology and Provenience of the Isaiah Targum* (JSOTSup, 23; Sheffield: JSOT Press, 1982).

60. Cf. Lane, *Mark*, pp. 393-94.

amounted to a potential claim to messianic status if they were expressed
in the context of Jerusalem expectation, and now he had not only entered
Jerusalem, but had made a claim to reform the Temple cult. The danger,
from the point of view of the Temple authorities, was not one of a merely
messianic pretension or of a merely cultic reform movement,[61] but of a
claim to be the Davidic messiah, which threatened their own power and
the normal exercise of Israel's worship. In the *Davidssohnfrage*, in the
very heat of the Temple controversy, Jesus successfully managed to
disentangle Davidic claims from messianic pretensions (and therefore,
implicitly, from a cultic reform movement) by undermining the scribal
expectation of a messiah son of David with an exegetical argument.
Later, he would taunt his custodians with a reminiscence of his
successful self-defense, Why did you not seize me in the Temple
(Mt. 26.55b; Mk 14.49; Lk. 22.53)?

Mark and Luke, immediately after their accounts of the Temple occupation, explain the delay in the prosecution by the high priests and
scribes with reference to Jesus' popular support (11.18; 19.47-48).
Whatever their motivation, Jesus' opponents did seek to formulate a
charge against him, based on his admission to the question of his identity
and his acknowledged activity in the Temple. The messianic dimension
of his attempt to reform the cult had earlier been obscured by Jesus,
because he had rejected the scribal expectation of the Davidic messiah.
In the end, however, this was only effective as a delaying tactic. The
scribes and high priests, given their messianic expectations, could hardly
see Jesus except as a Davidic messianic pretender, and therefore could
not see his preaching and actions other than as a direct challenge to the
integrity of the Temple they administered. The *Davidssohnfrage* had
given Jesus time, but the question remained: did he claim as messiah to
reform the Temple? During this period, others had disputed the rightful
place for commercial activity in relation to the cult, and the battle
between Caiaphas and the other members of the Sanhedrin may have
been the occasion of the *stasis* mentioned by Mark (15.7) and Luke
(23.19). Jesus was also involved, and that involvement by itself could
have caused no legitimate concern.[62] But as one addressed as *ben*

61. Cf. V. Eppstein, 'The Historicity of the Gospel account of the Cleansing of
the Temple', *ZNW* 55 (1964), pp. 42-58, for the controversy over Temple trading
during this period as reflected in Rabbinica.

62. As Eppstein shows, the reform of Caiaphas in respect of Temple trading
caused considerable opposition. He apparently attempted to bring the commercial

David, did he occupy the Temple as a messianic pretender?

An affirmative answer to this question also had obvious political implications, and here again the precise application of the *ben David* address to Jesus was crucial. Although Davidic descent could be claimed by rabbis without a necessarily political pretension,[63] and Jesus, on the basis of the Davidic descent ascribed to him, could well have found himself addressed as David's son in an essentially therapeutic sense, the claim of such descent could easily have another application. As part of his attempt to legitimate his rule within the terms of reference of early Judaism, Herod—although an Idumean—had claimed Davidic descent through Babylonian Jewry.[64] Jacob Neusner argues that a group of rabbis called the *bene Bathyra* in our sources are to be seen as named after the city called Bathyra.[65] Bathyra was given as a tax-free gift by Herod to an emigrant from Babylon named Zamaris, and even enjoyed privileged status under Herod's successors. The new town was militarily important to Herod, and the noted *bene Bathyra*—who disputed with Hillel, another Babylonian who claimed Davidic descent[66]—could be relied on to support him in another sense. As well as supporting Herod's regime, and therefore perhaps his claim to Davidic descent, their prominent place in the Temple administration made them a power to be reckoned with in Jerusalem and beyond as chief partisans of the Herodian settlement.[67] Precisely in the context of controversy concerning the Temple, and after the triumphal entry, the Herodians in the Markan (12.13) and Matthean (22.16) accounts ask their deliberately embarrassing question about paying taxes to Caesar. The Herodians are frequently described in the commentaries as merely political partisans for the Herods,[68] but their question here is not just a party political one, and in

activity formerly cited on the Mount of Olives into his own sphere of influence, but the resistence was such that he did not succeed.

63. Cf. n. 47.

64. Neusner, *A History of the Jews*, I, p. 35.

65. Neusner, *A History of the Jews*, I, pp. 38-41.

66. Neusner, *A History of the Jews*, I, p. 40 n. 1. The chronological difficulty of such a dispute mentioned by Neusner does not emerge if one accepts that it occurred during the period of Hillel's prominence, and not at the beginning of his career.

67. Neusner, *A History of the Jews*, I, pp. 43-49. One would not expect rabbinic sources to acknowledge Bathyran support for Herod's Davidic claims, but it is clear that Herod expected and received such support from his Jewish clients, cf. Josephus, *Ant.* 14.1.3 §9.

68. Cf. H.W. Hoehner, *Herod Antipas* (SNTSMS, 28; Cambridge: Cambridge

Mk 3.6 they resolve to destroy Jesus after a series of healings which were controversial in halakhic terms (1.40–3.5). Their motivation, then, is both political and legal, and the Temple is their especial sphere of interest and influence; in all of these features, the New Testament Herodians correspond to the rabbinic *bene Bathyra*, the former designation being a more pejorative, perhaps explanatory, description of what the latter already implies. Moreover, it is at least notable (although by itself it does not establish the argument) that in Mk 3.6 the resolve of the Herodians is mentioned after, albeit not immediately after, Jesus' appeal to the precedent of David for permitting his disciples to pluck grain on the sabbath (2.25-26).

Mark's portrayal of the early resolve of the Herodians to destroy Jesus may be anachronistic, but Jesus' claim of Davidic descent may have brought him to the attention of the *bene Bathyra* even in Galilee, in that they enjoyed excellent communications with many Jewish communities.[69] Jesus' direct appeal to the example of David to justify irregular sabbath practice would have brought him into open conflict with the halakhah of most teachers in his time, and would have compounded the annoyance of those to whom the David descent he claimed was also suspect. When Jesus accepted the 'David's son' address, entered Jerusalem, occupied the Temple and disputed the authority of the Temple authorities, the *bene Bathyra* understood his Davidic programme to be messianically motivated and diametrically opposed to their own, and they sought to entrap him in open sedition—for them the logical consequence of his position—with their question about the payment of tax to Caesar.

The failure of this line of attack was only temporary, in that it raised the possibility in real political terms of impeaching Jesus to Caesar's deputy if a suitable charge could be found and substantiated. The *Davidssohnfrage*, as suggested, represents the attempt of Jesus to deflect the charge that his pretensions about the Temple were messianic by challenging the scribal teaching of the messiah *ben David*. At that stage, the only hope of the authorities was to interrogate Jesus directly,

University Press, 1972), pp. 331-42. Hoehner's inclination to identify the Herodians with the Boethusians suffers from the inability of this supposition to account for references to the Herodians outside of a Temple context. Cf. also Mk 8.15 (with the variant 'Herodians' for 'Herod', and the parallelism to 'Pharisees'); Pesch, *Das Markusevangelium*, p. 195.

    69. Neusner, *A History of the Jews*, I, pp. 41-43.

and in fact this expedient proved effective: Jesus confessed that his stance in Jerusalem derived not only from an understanding of halakhah, but from his conviction that he was God's anointed, and that in a sense which could be construed to be politically seditious (as in the event it was by Pilate). Behind the designation of Jesus as David's son there lie a claim of descent, cries for healing, a view of the Temple, and a possibly political pretension. The *Davidssohnfrage* represents Jesus' attempt to clarify his own view of the meaning of the address and to ward off prosecution on the basis of the scribal expectation of a *ben David*. In the end, however, the conviction that he did claim to be God's messiah, no matter what he said about his being David's son, prevailed, and Jesus himself could not deny the suspicion. 'Messiah' and 'David's son' were too inextricably linked in the Jerusalem theology of his day for Jesus successfully to disentangle them; even Luke and (more especially) Matthew fell under the sway of the equation which had been part of the case against their lord.

LINGUISTIC AND STYLISTIC ASPECTS OF JESUS' TEACHING

JSNT 28 (1986), pp. 63-80

THE NEGLECTED ROLE OF SEMANTICS IN THE
SEARCH FOR THE ARAMAIC WORDS OF JESUS

L.D. Hurst

Some years ago the eminent scholar Chaim Rabin[1] produced a valuable essay which attempted to clarify the difficulties involved in determining whether small divergences of the LXX from the MT reflect an alternate *Vorlage* or problems in the translation process. Rabin felt that the answer lay in the second option, and in order to prove his case he surveyed some of the complexities involved in translating *any* text, ancient or modern. Some of the issues he raises are of relevance to the search for the alleged Aramaic substratum of words of Jesus in the Gospels, and in this study we shall attempt to survey how these principles are affecting, and will continue to affect, that embattled arena.

1. *Polysemy*

Linguists often point out that within any community, no matter how small, there is a 'language world' composed of many different sublanguages. This 'world' is usually comprised of the difference between 'high' and 'low' language, written and spoken language, direct and polite language, etc. Between the source and receptor languages in translation the 'worlds' will differ sufficiently to make a perfect 'fit' or synonymity impossible. Hence *choice* is involved in translation, 'and choice is the essence of style—allowing for alternative but not equivalent ways of expression, subject to varying degrees of regulation by social forces such as fashion'.[2] The element of choice is central to the translation

---

1.   C. Rabin, 'The Translation Process and the Character of the Septuagint', *Textus* 6 (1968), p. 1.
2.   Rabin, 'Translation Process', p. 2.

process, in which, using the language of communication theory, the translator is both receiver and sender at the same time.[3] Translation involves that which has a fairly 'predictable relation'[4] between the structures of encoding (original writing) and recoding (the translated writing), although the two fields of experience never perfectly overlap. Experiences which are determined by natural and social circumstances (e.g. animals, plants, marriage customs, etc.) will differ and may at times have no accurate counterpart.[5] Also, Rabin points out, many cultures exhibit diglossia, in which two languages existing side by side in a culture have 'different uses apportioned to them [and] each may be equipped to deal only with the subjects involved in those uses'.[6] This may have been the situation in Palestine with respect to the use of Aramaic and Greek.

Rabin discusses the claim of modern linguists that the symbols which a language uses to represent reality are more or less arbitrary, 'and are not necessarily correlated to any structure that reality may possess'.[7] The task of the translator is thus largely intuitive; he instinctively prizes loose from the original system the language of the text before him and imposes the structure of his receptor language upon it, a process which will represent the original string of words, different as their position may have been from the new string. Since words are polysemic, the word which he chooses will represent *only one meaning of the original word by only one of its own meanings*. Which meanings will operate is almost impossible to predict; they are conditioned by the translator's previous experience with the chosen word.[8] B. Siertsema has compared the situation to 'a net and the dry sand it is spread out on; one language puts the net this way and includes within one of its meshes a piece of sand that in another language, which puts its net that way, falls partly or wholly within an adjoining mesh'.[9] Siertsema presents the following examples in the table below:[10]

3.   Rabin, 'Translation Process', p. 3.
4.   Rabin, 'Translation Process', p. 4.
5.   C. Naish and G. Story, 'The Lord is My Goat-Hunter', *BT* 14 (1963), p. 91.
6.   Rabin, 'Translation Process', p. 5. Cf. also P.C. Clark, 'Are They Really Bilingual?', *BT* 23 (1972), pp. 436-38, for examples from Spanish ghettos in New York City.
7.   Rabin, 'Translation Process', p. 6. Cf. also B. Siertsema, 'Language and World View (Semantics for Theologians)', *BT* 20 (1969), pp. 5-8.
8.   Rabin, 'Translation Process', p. 7.
9.   Siertsema, 'Language', p. 9.
10.   Siertsema, 'Language', p. 9.

Parts of reality outside language	English arrangement	Dutch arrangement
seat in a park	seat	
		bank
money exchange establishment		
	bank	
margin of a river		
		oever
margin of the sea	shore	
flesh on the body	flesh	
		vleeṣ
cooked 'flesh'		
	meat	
food as opposed to drink, etc.		eten, spijze

The recognition that words are polysemic brings one to the central issue with regard to detecting translation Greek in the New Testament. One of the underlying assumptions of biblical study this century has been the idea that words have only one basic meaning which is more or less immutable and can be directly and painlessly discerned in whatever context they appear. It is, for instance, the *modus operandi* of many of the articles appearing in Kittel's *Theological Dictionary of the New Testament* (as James Barr has demonstrated).[11] Barr became convinced, in examining biblical words used for such concepts as 'time', 'being' or 'word', that much of biblical study this century has been conducted in almost complete ignorance of the current contributions of the science of linguistics, and has, in fact, been going in the opposite direction. In his study of the word *dabar*, for instance, O. Procksch used etymological arguments to maintain that the term has a basic meaning of 'the hinterground of

---

11. Cf., e.g., J. Barr, *The Semantics of Biblical Language* (Oxford: Oxford University Press, 1961), *passim*; *Biblical Words for Time* (London: SCM Press, 1962); 'Hypostatization of Linguistic Phenomena in Modern Theological Interpretation', *JSS* 7 (1962), pp. 85-94; 'Semantics and Biblical Theology—A Contribution to the Discussion', *VTS* 22 (1972), pp. 11-19; and K.A. Tånberg, 'Linguistics and Theology: An Attempt to Analyze and Evaluate James Barr's Argumentation in *The Semantics of Biblical Language* and *Biblical Words for Time*', *BT* 24 (1973), pp. 301ff.

being',[12] and that that item thus betrays something basic to the 'Hebrew mind'. This meaning of the word in Hebrew, furthermore, is said to be at odds with the corresponding term in another language, such as Greek, in which the term *logos* reveals a distinctively 'Greek' way of looking at reality.[13] This has become familiar territory and we need not explore it here at length.

The science of linguistics indicates that language does not work in the way that these authors envisaged. Aside from minor peculiarities, all languages are essentially the same, and their symbols are primarily arbitrary and unrelated to reality. Thus, because a Hebrew used certain language to speak of something does not necessarily require that he was *referring* to that thing. Similarly, when today one uses the word 'foot', he may not be referring at all to what that four-lettered word normally brings to mind, precisely because the context in which he uses it may give it a new meaning (e.g. 'the foot of a mountain'). A person from a different culture may refer to the same thing as the 'buttocks' of the mountain, as do the Yoruba tribe of Nigeria. Neither term necessarily says anything about the way a particular people conceives of the mountain in reality.[14] The so-called 'three-tiered universe' of the Hebrews may come under this heading. The divide between sense and referent is well illustrated by a remark of William Temple, who, while listening to an obscure paper being read at a learned society, was asked if he knew what the speaker was saying. 'Yes', he replied, 'but I do not know what he is saying it about'.[15]

Words and phrases are thus polysemic, that is, they have many different meanings which expand or contract with time. This process of change is easily illustrated by examples from the English language. The modern word 'furniture', for example, formerly had a broader semantic range than it does today in common speech, meaning any kind of equipment. In the seventeenth century it needed to be qualified by a modifier, such as 'household furniture' or 'a young woman's furniture', and, depending upon the modifier, the term could mean widely different

---

12. Cf. *The Theological Dictionary of the New Testament* (Grand Rapids: Eerdmans, 1964–74), IV, pp. 91-100.

13. Cf. T. Boman, *Hebrew Thought Compared with Greek* (London: SCM Press, 1960).

14. Siertsema, 'Language', p. 3.

15. Quoted in G.B. Caird, 'The Glory of God in the Fourth Gospel', *NTS* 15 (1968), p. 265.

things. In time one of its many meanings won out, and today we need not qualify it; everyone understands us to mean the appointments of a house. But if an uninitiated modern were to encounter a seventeenth-century English work and find the phrase 'a young woman's furniture', while he would know what the author was saying, he might certainly be wrong on what he was saying it about.

2. *Attempted Retranslation*

We now come to the relevance of polysemy to the translation process, with particular reference to the attempted retranslation process. In any translation three things may happen when a word or phrase is to be translated into another language:

(1) A word will be chosen which is true to the source text, but inappropriate in the receptor language, resulting in incomprehension (i.e. 'overtranslating', as in 'the buttocks of the mountain').

(2) A word chosen from the receptor language will import its own original meaning into the context of the source language, so that the translated document will mean something new (e.g. 'the Lord is my goat-hunter').

(3) The original language will be so powerful that the word in the receptor language will take on all of the meanings of the word it is translating. Rabin calls this tendency 'semantic tolerance', a process in which the context absorbs any deviation from a correct linking in a translation:

> The force of the context is such that even some degree of deviation from the meanings with which the reader or listener is familiar will not spoil the sense; on the contrary, if it is noticed at all, it may add spice to an otherwise routine context, or open new insights—a matter sufficiently known from literature... in particular, it creates a possibility for solving the question of words to which the receptor language has no previous equivalent.[16]

The degree of 'semantic tolerance' is, of course, greater in a text displaying a high degree of 'verbal linkage', and lesser in a freer translation. Since the LXX is a 'formal equivalence' translation with a predominance of verbal linkage, it repeatedly absorbs the semantic deviation of classical Greek terms and pours its own meaning into them.

---

16. Rabin, 'Translation Process', pp. 9-10.

This in turn leads to the occurrence of semantic 'twists'. The history of the Hebrew word *kabod* illustrates this phenomenon well. Originally it meant 'worth', 'weight' or 'dignity'. In Babylon, however, Ezekiel had visions by the river Chebar, and amidst the heavenly train he saw a blinding figure on the throne (1.44ff.). 'Such', he concluded, 'was the appearance of the likeness of the *kabod* of the Lord'. At this point the term *kabod* still had had its common meaning of 'worth', 'dignity', etc.; but from the moment that the prophet used it in that particular context, *kabod* became associated with a vision of heavenly radiance, and *kabod* began then to mean 'radiance'.[17]

This semantic twist is reflected in the translation Greek of the LXX, for there too δόξα, its profane nuances overpowered by the Hebrew, came to mean 'heavenly, blinding radiance' almost overnight. This twist was so decisive that when one reads the New Testament nativity story, he finds that 'there were shepherds in the field, and the glory (δόξα) of the Lord shone round about them' (Lk. 2.9; cf. Acts 22.11; 2 Cor. 3.7–4.6, etc.). Using a model suggested by G.B. Caird,[18] this is an example of the 'Humpty Dumpty' phenomenon, a situation in which a word is 'forced to work overtime and is paid extra'. Thus, from meaning something very subjective ('opinion' or 'reputation'), δόξα came to mean the objective splendour of divine light.

It is fortunate that a recognition of these factors has, over the past twenty years, begun to influence the way in which scholars approach the issue of attempted retranslation of the Greek of the Gospels into Aramaic. The work of Joseph Fitzmyer,[19] J.A. Emerton,[20] and

---

17. Cf. G.B. Caird, *The Language and Imagery of the Bible* (London: Gerald Duckworth, 1980), pp. 28-30, 76, and 'The New Testament Conception of Doxa' (unpublished D.Phil. thesis, Merton College, Oxford, 1942). Cf. also L.H. Brockington, 'The Septuagintal Background to the New Testament Use of δόξα', in D.E. Nineham (ed.), *Studies in the Gospels* (Oxford: Basil Blackwell, 1955), pp. 1-8. On the subject of δόξα in extra-biblical Greek, cf. also N. Turner, 'Jewish and Christian Influence on New Testament Vocabulary', *NovT* 16 (1974), p. 158.

18. Cf. Caird, *The Language and Imagery of the Bible*, pp. 38-39, referring to Lewis Carroll, *Alice's Adventures in Wonderland and Through the Looking Glass* (London: Oxford University Press, 1971), pp. 190-91.

19. Cf., e.g., J. Fitzmyer, 'The Languages of Palestine in the First Century AD', *CBQ* 32 (1970), pp. 501-31, and 'Methodology in the Study of the Aramaic Substratum of the New Testament', in *Jésus aux origines de la Christologie* (BETL, 40; Gembloux: Duculot, 1975), pp. 73-102.

20. Cf., e.g., J.A. Emerton, 'The Problem of Vernacular Hebrew in the First

B.D. Chilton,[21] among others, has stressed the importance of a study of the language of the targums nearest to the time of Jesus in dealing with the question, and the impact of this research is now beginning to be felt. The articles of Emerton especially have underscored the complexities involved in Aramaic source detection, and his research presupposes a sophisticated understanding of the semantic interplay of words and their meanings.

The problems are many, but an impression of the dangers involved in attempted retranslation may be gained by extending the discussion of δόξα in Ezekiel. Let us assume hypothetically that our only extant copies of Ezekiel were the Greek of the LXX, and that our only examples of Hebrew writings were copies of the Old Testament books which were either written *before* the time of Ezekiel, or which had no contact with the Ezekiel tradition. From the general features of our Greek copies of Ezekiel we would probably assume that it is translation Greek rather than an original Greek composition (it has a high degree of parataxis, asyndeton, etc.), and thus far we are on safe ground. But if a reconstruction of the underlying Hebrew is attempted, what might happen at Ezek. 1.28? Looking at the context in which the term δόξα is found, and knowing of its subsequent usage in the New Testament, we would probably decide that it means 'brightness', 'light' or 'radiance'. Which Hebrew word will be chosen to underlie it? Perhaps *'or*, or a related term; certainly not *kabod*, which we 'know' means 'worth', 'dignity', 'weight', etc. Thus, unaware of the broadened semantic field of *kabod* and its shift of meaning *at that particular time*, we would commit a blunder. Thirty years ago, however, we would have been within our rights, and we might even have detected an assonance of the word *'or* with another word in the passage, thus receiving the plaudits of the scholarly community (following the publication of our findings as *A Hebrew Approach to the Book of Ezekiel*) for the brilliance of our reconstruction. But we would still be wrong.

Recent study into the Aramaic language close to the time of Jesus has

Century AD, and the Language of Jesus', *JTS* 24 (1973), pp. 8-13; and 'The Aramaic Background of Mark X.45', *JTS* 11 (1960), pp. 334-35.

21. Cf., e.g., B.D. Chilton, *The Glory of Israel: The Theology and Provenience of the Isaiah Targum* (JSOTSup, 23; Sheffield: JSOT Press, 1983); *A Galilean Rabbi and His Bible: Jesus' Use of the Interpreted Scripture of His Time* (Wilmington: Glazier, 1984); and 'Targumic Transmission and Dominical Tradition', in R.T. France and D. Wenham (eds.), *Gospel Perspectives*, I (Sheffield: JSOT Press, 1980).

been attempting to avoid such mistakes. The frequent assumption of the older studies was that Aramaic words have a 'principal' or 'basic' meaning which is fixed, and that there is only one Aramaic word, or at the most two, in question to underlie each Greek word which is analyzed. Fitzmyer in particular has done much to show how for decades it was felt that this kind of certainty could be had from sources which were hundreds of years older than the documents in question. According to Burney,[22] 'though it is unfortunate that we do not possess any contemporary evidence for the Galilean Aramaic of the first century AD, it is unlikely that the dialect underwent any substantial change during the four or five centuries following'. Burney, of course, is now quite dated, but in one of the more recent works to be published on the topic of the Aramaic substratum of the gospels, F. Zimmermann's *The Aramaic Origin of the Four Gospels* (New York: Ktav, 1979), the 'older' methodology remains substantially intact. Texts hundreds of years older than the Gospels are used as the authority for the Aramaic, and the work of Emerton, Fitzmyer and others upon texts closer to the time of the Gospels is ignored.

One of the positive effects of the work of these Targumic specialists is our new awareness that a static condition is not the rule in languages during long periods. Over centuries it is inevitable that in any language meanings of words will undergo some change as semantic fields expand or contract. We are beginning to sense that we are not in a position to speculate as to how much or how little change a language or dialect underwent over a period of four or five centuries without first having an adequate sampling of texts which are distributed throughout the entire period. It may even be that we do not at present have enough examples of the semantic interplay of first-century Palestinian Aramaic terms in order to make positive declarations as to which term underlies a given Greek term. This is worth considering when recalling the following comments of Aramaists of a former generation:

1.   'In a surprising number of cases we can translate our reconstructed Greek text back literally into Aramaic without the slightest difficulty or doubt'.[23]

---

22. Rabin, 'Translation Process', p. 7. Cf. his note 26 for an excellent example of this.

23. A.T. Olmstead, 'Could an Aramaic Gospel be Written?', *JNES* 1 (1942), p. 74.

2. 'Every Greek term has its corresponding Aramaic idiom, which it reproduces'.[24]
3. 'The Greek renderings are so literal that the expert reader can see not merely the idiom, but the precise words'.[25]

The first statement, that of Olmstead, speaks of the case of translating Greek back into Aramaic. But behind this ease stands the assumption that the same Aramaic word will always be translated by the same Greek word, regardless of context, and this is almost precisely what Torrey says in the second statement. This attitude now seems quite dated, primarily because it goes against the principles outlined above; but it is also becoming increasingly obvious that it goes against the findings of LXX lexicography. That δόξα represents some forty-three other Hebrew roots besides *kabod* in the LXX should serve as a sufficient warning. In this light the third statement, also by Torrey, seems especially shocking. If one could not have reproduced accurately the Hebrew underlying a high linkage text such as the LXX, how much more hopeless would it be to expect an accurate reproduction in a text (the Gospels) in which, as Rabin puts it, 'the distance between their language and the syntax and semantic structure of the assumed Semitic source is a great deal wider than in the LXX'.[26] This must be seen as a devastating blow to those who express great confidence in the retranslation process. Yet, even if one *could* find Aramaic idioms in the language Jesus spoke which correspond rather directly to the Greek, there is no guarantee in any given instance of a saying in the Gospels that there is any direct relationship. As Chilton has said, albeit in another context, ' "literal agreement" is still the battle cry of those who argue literary dependence, but the latter is not a necessary inference from the former'.[27]

The work of Olmstead, Torrey and Burney has, of course, been largely overthrown, but occasionally the same assumptions are found to operate beneath the work of more careful scholars, such as Matthew Black.[28] In the third edition of *An Aramaic Approach to the Gospels*

24. C.C. Torrey, *Our Translated Gospels* (London: Hodder & Stoughton, 1936), p. liv.
25. Torrey, *Translated Gospels*, p. lix.
26. Rabin. 'Translation Process', p. 26.
27. Chilton, 'Targumic Transmission and Dominical Tradition', p. 32.
28. Fitzmyer, 'Methodology', pp. 77-78, claims that Black, while criticizing Wellhausen, Dalman, Torrey and others for depending upon late texts, himself 'depends largely on what others have said'. 'All too frequently', he continues, 'he

and Acts, for instance, one is told that *'abed* is the equivalent of ποιῶν, while *'abd* = δοῦλος (Jn 8.34);[29] *q^{e}lal* = ἐλαττοῦσθαι, while *k^{e}lal* = πεπλήρωται (Jn 3.29-30);[30] *m^{e}rabbya* = μεγαλύνει (Lk. 1.46);[31] and *q^{e}dhasha* = 'a ring' (Mt. 7.6).[32] Black seldom mentions more than one Aramaic term as a possibility, largely because the sampling of texts is too small to supply a second option.

As suggested above, a fruitful way of advancing this discussion will be the application of the insights, as they come in, of the emerging discipline of LXX lexicography. Black's assertion that, because it makes a striking assonance, the simple, one-to-one equivalent in Aramaic of δοῦλος is *'abd*, should not be seen as more than a guess at this point. R.A. Kraft points out that in the LXX

> the rendering of such a common term as the Hebrew *'eved* ('servant') varies with various sections…In the Pentateuch, *pais* predominates while *therapon* and *oiketes* also occur in significant quantity (*doulos* is almost lacking); the original translator of Job may have used *therapon* exclusively, while in Proverbs (see also Sirach), *oiketes* is preferred; *doulos* tends to

[Black] cites would-be Aramaic expressions, culling them from others without sufficient scrutiny so that his book, especially in its third edition, remains a compilation of proposals about Aramaisms in the Gospels and Acts that are good, bad, and indifferent.'

29. M. Black, *An Aramaic Approach to the Gospels and Acts* (Oxford: Clarendon Press, 3rd edn, 1967), p. 171.

30. Black, *Aramaic Approach*, p. 147.

31. Black, *Aramaic Approach*, p. 151.

32. Black, *Aramaic Approach*, pp. 200ff. This is a famous example of an alleged mistranslation of Aramaic in the Gospels, in which *q^{e}dhasha*, 'a ring', has been misread as *qudhsha*, 'holy', thus making the original read:

> Give not a (precious) ring to dogs
> and cast not your pearls before swine.

Apart from the suggestion's perennial attractiveness, as with all conjectural mistranslation, it is necessarily founded upon lexicographical guesswork which involves not one but *two* terms in Aramaic which appears to amount to double jeopardy. As Fitzmyer, 'Methodology', p. 95, points out, 11QtgJob 38.8 confirms the contemporary usage of *q^{e}dhasha* in a parallel construction ('and they gave him [Job], each one a lamb and a ring of gold'). While in *this* case Black's suggestion has been vindicated, it is precisely such confirmation of his (and others') assumptions which is needed, and which to date has been wanting.

predominate in Samuel–Kings (but special problems exist here), Psalms, Ezekiel, and the minor prophets (and is standard for 'Aquila'). An adequate historical explanation for such a situation is worth seeking... [33]

The 'adequate historical explanation' is probably the polysemy of each of the Greek terms involved, and that at some point (unknown to us) the semantic range of the respective Greek word overlapped at a certain point with one of the meanings of *'eved* which had been stressed in the translator's particular experience. (Just how much the opposite could have happened in the case of the Gospels—i.e. one Greek term translating other Aramaic terms, now lost to us, which meant 'servant'—is also worth considering.) 'Only at a very high degree of sophistication will a translator arrive at the choice of the word because it represents something of the gamut of meaning of the source word in its native structure', says Rabin.[34]

Returning to the hypothetical example above, if one were to encounter a 'modernized' version of an old English work, and in it was contained the sentence 'the knight was without his equipment', an inquisitive mind might set out to guess what the original work had said. But in order to do so we would need a sufficient acquaintance with the history of the English language which would enable us to know most of the possible variables of overlapping semantic ranges at that particular time. We would need to know the semantic history of the term 'furniture', for one, as well as any other terms (which may in other contexts have a widely disparate meaning) whose ranges overlapped *at that particular point*. The difficulty is this: it requires that the 'reconstructor' has at his disposal enough old English texts contemporary with the document in question to give him an adequate sampling of the same words in different contexts. Linguists observe that a language of normal development and structure contains about 100,000 words, while the number of words an average person has in active use is about 24,000.[35] This number may be broken down into such groups as 'registers' and 'styles'. J.F.A. Sawyer's important monograph *Semantics in Biblical*

33. R.A. Kraft, 'Translation Technique and Jewish Greek Idiom: Some Examples and Prospects', paper presented at the International Organization for Septuagint and Cognate Studies, on 19 December 1968, abstracted in *IOSC Bulletin* 2 (October, 1969), pp. 6-7.

34. Rabin, 'Translation Process', p. 7.

35. Rabin, 'Translation Process', p. 12.

Research[36] explores the nature of such groupings. A 'register', he observes, is 'the variety of language proper to a particular situation',[37] such as 'language adopted by people addressing their god'.[38] In order to be able to make such groupings of that many words, therefore, we will need a considerable number of texts, as well as years of immersion in those texts.

As observed above, one of the more important results of recent research into Aramaic close to the time of Jesus is the knowledge that we still know little of the language spoken by Jesus.[39] It may be appropriately represented in only a few documents known to us, and even these have not yet been thoroughly studied. Sawyer has shown the importance of having a thorough semantic knowledge of a language *before* one begins to translate it; hence 'semantic analysis should be monolingual', that is, the language should be studied *from within*:[40]

> Instead of defining a word L in terms of another language, it can be defined as associated with A, B, C (in the same language), opposed to D, influenced semantically by G because of frequent collocation with it in idiom I, and so on. This is the most reliable method, and must precede translation, not follow it.[41]

If this be true of translation, how much more will it be true of *retranslation*? Yet, with our currently meagre supply of Palestinian Aramaic texts from the first century, from where is this detailed internal knowledge to come? It may even be questionable whether today Aramaists may be termed 'experts' of the Aramaic used by Jesus, any more than medieval physicians, with their limited understanding of the human body, would *by today's standards* be considered 'experts' of the human body. Fitzmyer and Emerton stress that our few surviving fragments of the

36. J.F.A. Sawyer, *Semantics in Biblical Research* (SBT, 24; London: SCM Press, 1972), p. 116.

37. Sawyer, *Semantics*, p. 17.

38. Sawyer, *Semantics*, p. 18.

39. Black understates the problem somewhat when he says that 'our knowledge of Palestinian Aramaic is still far from complete' (*Aramaic Approach*, p. 133). For a helpful survey of more recent opinion on the development of the Aramaic language, cf., e.g., A.D. York, 'The Dating of Targumic Literature', *JSJ* 5 (1974), pp. 49ff.; M. Sokoloff, 'The Current State of Research on Galilean Aramaic', *JNES* 37 (1978), p. 161; and the various other works cited in Chilton's 'Targumic Transmission'.

40. Sawyer, *Semantics*, p. 116.

41. Sawyer, *Semantics*, pp. 31-32.

mother tongue of Jesus (e.g. the Genesis Apocryphon) are the tip of the Aramaic language iceberg. The publication by Fitzmyer and Harrington, *A Manual of Palestinian Aramaic Texts* (Rome: Biblical Institute Press, 1978), reduces the difficulty in only a partial way. At present our texts give us at most only a few contexts in which a given term occurs. Olmstead once claimed triumphantly that rarely in our retranslation do we have more than two Aramaic terms with which to concern ourselves.[42] This was meant to stress the ease of the retranslator's task; now it is seen as an indication of its difficulty. As with the biblical idea of 'glory', a term may receive a new twist of meaning almost overnight, or have one particular nuance which is singular to a particular geographical area,[43] or even to a particular sub-language within that geographical area. The following complications make the problem even more critical: (1) the sub-languages of any given two languages will never entirely overlap; (2) the sub-language in which Jesus' words were originally given and the sub-language in which they have come to us are not identical (Jesus' words were spoken language, while the Gospels are written language); (3) it may be impossible to know how freely a term or phrase has been rendered; and (4) we have no guarantee that a translator has not rendered a text freely for the sake of a greater decodability, and then *artificially* reintroduced features of the original language for the sake of authentic flavour (as Luke may have done). Obviously, the situation is more complex than Torrey, Burney or others could have foreseen. Yet, according to Vincent Taylor, 'in these matters we are dependent on a small band of Aramaic experts, and other students of the New Testament naturally hesitate to express opinions'.[44] What Taylor means is that in his day few people questioned an Aramaist when he said that in context A stands a certain Aramaic word, and therefore in context B we may reasonably assume that the same Aramaic word is involved. That this process involves the erroneous view that there is a principal or basic meaning for both terms (which may be counted upon

42. Olmstead, 'Aramaic Gospel', p. 74.

43. Emerton, 'Vernacular Hebrew in the First Century AD', p. 13, following W. Chomsky and J.M. Grintz, discusses an amusing example from *b. Ned.* 66b of a Babylonian Jew and his Palestinian wife who apparently speak different dialects of Aramaic. He tells her to break some lamps on the 'head', presumably meaning the top of the door, and she immediately leaves and breaks them on the head of a local rabbi!

44. V. Taylor, 'The Semitic Background of the Gospel', in *The Gospel According to St Mark* (London: Macmillan, 1952), p. 56.

to agree in translation) needs to be said over and over by the new specialists until it filters down to the general level of the New Testament academic. Also, while the point should not be overstressed,[45] the inability of many of the specialists to agree on the 'basic meaning' of many of the Aramaic words, or on which Greek term 'regularly' translates a particular Aramaic idiom, contributes to the healthier caution of the more recent work.

D.F. Payne makes a valuable remark which helps to point the way forward.

> Modern linguistic science might suggest another method of approach to the vocabulary of the NT, namely the study of 'semantic fields'. This approach has been pioneered for OT Hebrew by T. Donald, in an article where he examined the implications of the various Hebrew words associated with folly in the Wisdom literature of the OT, assessing in particular the overtones of culpability carried by the differing terms. It is conceivable that comparisons of semantic fields in Hebrew or Aramaic with their counterparts in Greek would throw some light on Luke's use of vocabulary. *But a great deal of basic research would need to be done before any effective comparative work became possible.*[46]

Yet Payne also raises a disturbing point. Certain words, he says, may have been *avoided* in a source for reasons unknown to us. Luke, for instance, may have avoided certain terms because of associations with Qumranic thought. Thus 'the "poor" of Jerusalem, so much a matter of concern to Paul, are nowhere in Acts described as πτωχοί—*the obvious word for them, one would have thought'.*[47] The term ἐπίσκοπος is also avoided by Luke, which, along with πτωχοί, is thought by Fitzmyer to have had similar semantic fields to the terms *'bywnym* and *mbqr* at Qumran.[48]

Among the many things which may transpire in translation which are relevant to this discussion, one of the most crucial is the phenomenon

---

45. Fitzmyer is probably correct to stress that the inability of Aramaists to agree can become an excuse for fleeing from the problems. 'Will Aramaists—or any other group of human beings—ever be unanimous? Perhaps, however, a more rigorous methodology and approach will eliminate some of the disagreement.'

46. D.F. Payne, 'Semitisms in the Book of Acts', in W.W. Gasque and R.P. Martin (eds.), *Apostolic History and the Gospel* (Exeter: Paternoster Press, 1970), p. 150 (italics mine). His reference is to T. Donald, 'The Semantic Field of "Folly" in Proverbs, Job, Psalms and Ecclesiastes', *VT* 13 (1963), pp. 285-92.

47. Payne, 'Semitisms', p. 148 (italics mine).

48. Payne, 'Semitisms', p. 148.

called 'semantic tolerance', in which a Greek term is given a new nuance by the force of its highly linked context. With the complex interchange of Greek and Semitic languages in the first century, certain Greek words may have picked up a particular Semitic meaning in a context which is now lost to us, that is, in a famous statement by a Jew, a well-known joke or pun, a political edict, or any of the other facets of Semitic life which were significant enough to have been rendered into Greek for those in Palestine who were given to that language. This may be a product of either actual or virtual translation.[49] The *opposite* phenomenon, however, is equally possible: the word or idiom chosen for the receptor language may import its *own* meaning into the original context. The chances of this happening, of course, are directly related to the degree of 'formal equivalence'. If there has been a 'change of attitude' between the LXX and New Testament, with a greater distance resulting between source and receptor text, this means that in the case of the New Testament the context may not be sufficiently Hebraic for the Greek term to be 'Humpty Dumptied' and 'paid extra'; hence there will be a degree of semantic distortion which will further hinder an accurate reconstruction of the original Aramaic.

E.A. Nida and C.R. Taber have championed an approach to translation which is of relevance here. Numerous translators assert that in order 'to preserve the context of the message the form must be changed':[50]

> Translating is not a technique for producing strings of supposedly corresponding words. Rather, it consists in reproducing the closest natural equivalent, first in meaning and secondly in style.[51]

49. Much more work needs to be done with the fact that most of the New Testament writers were probably bi- or tri-lingual speakers, which means that the use of words with overlapping semantic ranges in the two languages may mean the introduction of a Greek word into a context which would not normally be expected, and which might give the appearance of a 'mistranslation'. Cf. L.A. Jakobivits and W.E. Lambert, 'Semantic Satiation among Bilinguals', *Journal of Experimental Psychology* 62 (1961), pp. 576-82.

50. E.A. Nida and C.R. Taber, *The Theory and Practice of Translation* (Leiden: Brill, 1969), p. 5. Also cf. K.R. Crim, '"Your Neck is like the Tower of David" (The Meaning of a Simile in the Song of Solomon)', *BT* 22 (1971), p. 71: 'Because every language has its own distinctive nature, any translation involves more, not less, of these changes than a dynamic equivalence translation'.

51. E.A. Nida, 'Translation and Word Frequency', *BT* 10 (1959), p. 107.

Nida agrees with Barr that meaning does not lie chiefly in vocabulary, but in larger units which he calls 'kernels'.[52] The 'kernel' is the basic unit, or thought being expressed, which is then 'transformed' into the 'surface structure' (or the way we speak).[53] This phenomenon, under whatever name it is called (often it has been put under the more general term 'dynamic equivalence'), is hardly unique to modern translation practice, as Martin Luther's *Open Letter on Translating* demonstrates.[54] Modern translation theory is more concerned with describing the way languages have always worked than with discovering new ways of doing things. Some of the New Testament writers, as part of what Rabin calls 'the change of attitude', may have departed from the old word-for-word technique of the LXX and translated in a manner more akin to what Nida terms the 'kernel' method.[55]

52. Cf. Nida and Taber, *The Theory and Practice of Translation, passim*, and E.A. Nida, 'Linguistics and Translators', *BT* 23 (1972), pp. 228-29.

53. This approach to translation has come under some attack during recent years from transformational linguists themselves. Cf., e.g., M. Masterman, 'Bible Translating by Kernel', in *The Times Literary Supplement* 3,551 (19 March 1970), pp. 299-301. For Masterman the Nida approach 'brutalizes the capacity of the pupil to understand the Bible as it really is. For in the name of science, the pupil-translator (through a whole series of exercises) is trained to substitute short, concrete, colloquial English sentences called "kernels" for the subtle combination of syntactic, semantic, and referential "cues" actually given by the original text, in the original language; and he is taught to treat these kernels as the ultimate ingredients of biblical fact'. It should be noted, however, that Masterman seems to regard as self-evident what is 'biblical fact'. D. Filbeck, 'The Passive, an Unpleasant Experience', *BT* 23 (1972), p. 331 n. 1, claims that 'current transformational theory has abandoned the concept of kernels and derived structures. The theory now states that all that is semantically relevant to the interpretation of a sentence must be contained in a base of underlying structure. Transformational rules, therefore, function as a road map mapping base structures (and sometimes filtering ungrammatical structures out) into surface structure, or the way we speak.' Aside from these and several other detractors, however, Nida's approach has been universally applauded.

54. According to Luther, 'the task of the translator is not that of reproducing in one language words exactly equivalent to the words of another language, but of reproducing in vigorous vernacular idiom the meaning originally expressed... ultimately, the sense itself in the original must determine whether the rendering in translation will be literal or relatively free...' (from *Luther's Works*, XXXV [Philadelphia: Fortress Press, 1969], p. 207; cf. also pp. 213-14). Cf. also W. Schwarz, *Principles and Problems of Biblical Translation* (Cambridge: Cambridge University Press, 1955), for a helpful survey of the history of biblical translation from the LXX to Luther.

55. Rabin, 'Translation Process', p. 19, demonstrates that Greek society 'did not

An example of 'kernel' method is the TEV's rendering of the Greek of 2 Cor. 8.3, ὅτι κατὰ δύναμιν μαρτυρῶ καὶ παρὰ δύναμιν as 'I assure you, they gave us as much as they could, and even more than they could'. The extent of this kind of freeness in the New Testament with Aramaic sources may be an issue for future debate, and this is precisely one area on which attention should continue to focus. Failure to do so can only result from the unfortunate adherence to the artificial but stubborn distinction between translation and literary activity, or perhaps from an *a priori* exclusion of 'kernel'-type translation as 'too modern' or 'impossibly free' for a sacred text. It is often forgotten that the spirit and purpose of the early church was probably closer to that of the United Bible Society than to that of committees which produce wooden-literal translation such as the 1901 *American Standard Version*. Chilton[56] has observed that it was probably *because* the early church regarded the sayings of Jesus as on the same level as those of Moses and the prophets that they felt a certain freedom to 'play' with the wording, a point which those today who claim to have the highest view of the canonical text have been unwilling to grant. Chilton's intensive study of the Isaiah targum has led him to detect in the Gospels similar exegetical techniques to those used by the meturgeman in dealing with the Old Testament text, and while there are differences between this approach and Nida's dynamic equivalence strategy, *both* stress a departure from the word substitution idea in dealing with the sayings of Jesus. In support of Chilton's point it may be observed that between Matthew and Luke it is often the latter who is said to preserve the more 'faithful', Palestinian form of a saying of Jesus,[57] notwithstanding the traditional belief of the

go in for translation, but for independent rewriting of information'. In this regard the LXX is an anomaly, with its remarkable 'flat, bald surface', its 'failure to shape a telling sentence which may strike the ear and linger in the memory' (p. 22), and 'the occasional appearance of literal translations which make no sense in Greek' (p. 23). When we come to Josephus's *Jewish Wars*, however, Rabin claims that 'an entirely different standard of translation can be observed' (p. 26). While this may be the result of acquaintance with high Roman translation standards, 'the same does not apply to the NT'. His conclusion is that 'if part of the Gospels are translated from Aramaic (or from some type of Hebrew), the distance between their language and the syntax and semantic structure of the assumed Semitic source is a great deal wider than in the LXX, and that in spite of the extensive use of LXX allusions. There evidently had been a change in attitude, towards a greater insistence on acceptability'.

56. Chilton, 'Targumic Transmission', p. 39.

57. Cf., e.g., E.E. Ellis, *The Gospel of Luke* (NCB; London: Oliphants, 1966),

church that he was a Gentile. But it may be that it was precisely that he *was* a Gentile, that is, an 'outsider', that he felt *less* free to tamper with the sayings tradition, whereas Matthew, in accord with his familiarity with Jewish targumic practices, assumed that what had been done to the Tanach was equally fitting for the tradition of Jesus' teaching.

If there is evidence of targumic or dynamic equivalence techniques in the Gospels, it would be worse than useless to attempt a reconstruction of one Aramaic term out of a given Greek term. This would be equivalent to focusing on the word 'gave' in the TEV's version of 2 Cor. 8.3 and speculating on which Greek word underlies it in Paul's original.[58]

A recognition of such factors suggests that a skepticism to older approaches used in reconstructing the language of Jesus is a healthy trend among more recent studies. It should not be taken as a purely negative force, for its caution provides the necessary safeguard against misinterpreting fresh evidence as it comes in, evidence which may bring us ever closer to the *Vorlage* underlying our Greek Gospels.

p. 3, who comes out strongly for the use of Semitic sources as the explanation of many of the Semitisms, citing Grobel, Manson and Winter in support. The view of H.F.D. Sparks ('The Semitisms of St Luke's Gospel', *JTS* 44 [1943], pp. 129ff., and 'The Semitisms of the Acts', *JTS* NS 1 [1950], pp. 16ff.) that Luke has deliberately 'Septuagintalized' his Greek is possible in some instances, but has not won general assent as an explanation of the more 'Palestinian' flavour of many of the sayings of Jesus when compared with the sayings recorded by Matthew.

58. Or cf. Chilton, 'Targumic Transmission', p. 37, who notes that in *Targum Onqelos* Exod. 24.10 is rendered 'and they saw the *glory* of the God of Israel'. 'Glory', of course, is not present in the Hebrew, but if we only had the targum, would we not be tempted to speculate on the 'underlying' Hebrew term?

JSNT 40 (1990), pp. 33-41

THE ARAMAIC DIMENSION IN Q WITH NOTES ON LUKE 17.22 AND MATTHEW 24.26 (LUKE 17.23)

Matthew Black†

In his comprehensive and detailed study, *The Formation of Q*,[1] John Kloppenborg, after concluding that Q was originally a documentary and not an orally transmitted Gospel source, goes on to consider whether 'it was originally composed in Aramaic and only then translated into Greek' (p. 51). He thereupon offers a critique of the case for an Aramaic Q, from (1) external evidence, which he finds only in the well-known testimony of Papias about a 'Hebrew' Gospel (understood as an Aramaic Gospel); and (2) from 'internal evidence' (translation mistakes and translation variants pointing to an allegedly Aramaic *Vorlage*), evidence which I had presented in my *An Aramaic Approach to the Gospels and Acts*.[2] He concludes that 'there is no convincing proof of a literary formulation in Aramaic' behind Q (p. 59), and then proceeds, in a section entitled 'Q as a Greek Compilation', to support his own main thesis of a purely Greek Q by illustrations of 'non-translation Greek' in Q to which I had also drawn attention.

On his external evidence Kloppenborg concludes that 'Papias' testimony...is of no probative worth in the quest for an Aramaic Q. His claims are apologetically motivated, and they refer to the canonical Gospels, not to their sources' (p. 54). That this complicated issue is not so easily disposed of I have argued in a recent article; Papias may well be referring to a 'Hebrew', that is, Aramaic Chreiae (Sayings, etc.) collection of which Q is the Greek equivalent and for which it is the main source.[3]

1. *Trajectories in Ancient Wisdom Collections* (Studies in Antiquity and Christianity; Philadelphia: Fortress Press, 1987).
2. Oxford: Clarendon Press, 3rd edn, 1967.
3. 'The Use of Rhetorical Terminology in Papias on Mark and Matthew', *JSNT* 37 (1989), pp. 31-41.

The main purpose of this paper is not only to reopen the question of 'internal evidence' for 'Semitisms/Aramaisms' and 'translation Greek' in Q, but also to draw attention to the possible relevance for this problem of other, also mainly patristic, external evidence, namely the so-called 'free sayings' of Jesus or 'free-saying tradition', especially in the Apostolic Fathers, but also in the Agrapha or 'unknown Sayings of Jesus', some twenty-one of which have been claimed to be 'perfectly compatible with the Synoptic tradition, and whose authenticity admits of serious consideration'.[4]

In his comprehensive survey of the Synoptic tradition in the Apostolic Fathers Helmut Koester suggested that at *1 Clem.* 13.2 'Perhaps the author is drawing on some written Lord's-sayings collection which we no longer know, but which may be older than our Gospels'.[5] Similarly, in related studies, J.M. Robinson refers to 'one collection of sayings that occurs in free variation frequently enough in the early Church to suggest it must have been some common catechetical cluster'.[6] In other words, Q was not the only Greek sayings-collection in circulation in the second century or earlier.

A feature noted by Koester in sayings citing or alluding to the Old Testament at *1 Clem.* 7.7 and 15.2, with Synoptic parallels at Mt. 12.41, Mk 7.6 and Mt. 15.8, is that *1 Clement* here too is drawing on different, if related, traditions of the Old Testament text of the saying.[7] Moreover *1 Clem.* 7.7 is also more closely related to rabbinical traditions than

---

4.   J. Jeremias, *Unknown Sayings of Jesus* (London: SPCK, 1964), pp. 42-43. The title 'Unknown Sayings of Jesus' is a modern invention; Agrapha is more accurate—these sayings were 'uncanonical', since they did not appear in the 'written' Gospels. See A. Resch, *Agrapha: Aussercanonische Evangelienfragmente* (TU, 15.3-4; Leipzig: Hinrichs, 1906; repr. Darmstadt: Buchgesellschaft, 1967), p. 1. Resch's collection of material, which included the 'free sayings' of the Apostolic Fathers, 'is still the standard work on the subject today' (Jeremias, *Unknown Sayings*, pp. 4-5). See also additional Resch material in TU, 10.1-3 (1893–97), 15 (1906).

5.   *Synoptische Überlieferung bei den apostolischen Vätern* (TU, 65; Berlin: Akademie, 1957), p. 16 and cf. p. 23 E.

6.   J.M. Robinson and H. Koester, *Trajectories through Early Christianity* (Philadelphia: Fortress Press, 1971), p. 43. While commenting on the (limited) range of Robinson's 'trajectory', Kloppenborg has only a passing reference to the free-sayings tradition in Koester's *Synoptische Überlieferung* and its possible relevance to the Aramaic problem (Kloppenborg, *Formation*, pp. 30-31 and p. 55 n. 47).

7.   *Synoptische Überlieferung*, pp. 21-22.

Mt. 12.41,[8] a feature found elsewhere in the patristic tradition (e.g. the Golden Rule is more frequently cited in its negative form as in rabbinical sources).[9] An exegetically significant use of the Old Testament is found in the frequently quoted saying at Mt. 5.27-28 where the *Didasc.* = *Apost. Const.* reads: 'Whoever shall look on the wife of his neighbour (τοῦ πλησίον) to covet her, has already committed adultery with her in his heart'.[10] Was this addition freely inserted to present the Seventh Commandment (Exod. 20.14) in terms of v. 17 (the 'coveting' of a neighbour's wife, like a neighbour's house or a neighbour's maid-servant), but in a sharpened form, so that even the covetous look at a married woman was itself tantamount to the act of adultery? Or, if we assume that the Old Testament 'addition', giving a text γυναῖκα [τοῦ πλησίον] πρὸς τὸ ἐπιθυμῆσαι αὐτήν, is original, was the omission of τοῦ πλησίον a redactor's attempt to sharpen the dominical saying still further by making the text mean 'Whoever looks *at any woman to lust after her...*', interpreting the verb in LXX Exod. 20.17 οὐκ ἐπιθυμήσεις (and at Mt. 5.28) in its more familiar Greek sense? In further support of the 'free addition', it may be argued that 'adultery' in Jewish law was always an offence against *a married woman*; to make the lustful look on any woman 'adultery' implies a less restricted definition. Whoever is responsible for the text of Matthew may well have had rabbinical parallels in mind.[11]

So far as the Agrapha, strictly speaking, are concerned, Jeremias has drawn attention to such striking Semitic features as antithetic *parallelismus membrorum*, typically Palestinian in style and 'so

8. Koester, *Synoptische Überlieferung*, pp. 21-22.

9. See Resch, *Agrapha* (TU, 15.3-4), pp. 61, 174.

10. Patristic material in Resch, *Agrapha* (TU, 10.1), pp. 86-87 (where there is a variant 'the wife of another' for 'of his neighbour'). Resch frequently notes 'translation variants' from his 'Hebrew Gospel'. A Resch-conjectured 'mistranslation' at Mt. 11.12 is more convincingly explained from Aramaic. See additional note in my article, 'Use of Rhetorical Terminology', pp. 38-39. Ignatius, *Eph.* 4.2 (Koester, *Synoptische Überlieferung*, p. 42) reads 'the tree is shown (φανερόν) by its fruit' for Mt. 12.33b (Q 'is known', γινώσκεται), and could contain an Aramaic translation variant from *yedia'*, supported by Dan. 3.18 *yedia'*, LXX φανερόν, Theod. γνωστόν. Cf. T.W. Manson, *Studies in the Gospels and Epistles* (Cambridge: Cambridge University Press, 1962), pp. 79-80; Black, *Aramaic Approach*, pp. 188, 190.

11. See C.G. Montefiore (ed.), *Rabbinical Literature and Gospel Teachings* (New York: Ktav, 1970), pp. 41-42.

characteristic of Jesus', in two of his selected passages (pp. 62, 99). The long and important Papyrus fragment *P. Oxy.* 840, written in a Synoptic-type Greek, contains numerous Semitisms, identified, in some cases, as 'Aramaisms'.[12]

In the section entitled 'Internal Evidence' (pp. 54-59), Kloppenborg pays me the compliment of singling out for detailed scrutiny evidence which I had adduced 'which might bespeak an Aramaic original' (p. 56). He concludes that I have convincingly demonstrated the presence of Semitisms in Q, but, in the alleged absence of a demonstrative proof in the '(mis)translation Greek' hypothesis (phenomena explicable in other ways), 'we are obliged to conclude that while parts of Q betray a semitizing Greek style, and possibly an origin in an Aramaic-speaking milieu, there is no convincing proof of a literary formulation in Aramaic' (p. 59). Finally it is stated, 'Q was composed originally in Greek. Of course, it must be conceded... that the style of Q is not literary *Koine*. And no one would seriously dispute that Q was formulated in proximity to a semitic-speaking area, under the influence of the semitizing Greek of the LXX, *and in part, from orally transmitted sayings which had their origin in Aramaic-speaking circles'* (p. 64, italics mine).

With this conclusion I am largely in entire agreement. Kloppenborg cites (with approval) my own view but only in an abbreviated form: the complete quotation reads (omissions by Kloppenborg in square brackets): '... it is doubtful if we are justified in describing Q, without qualification, as a translation of Aramaic. [Certainly it seems clear that the most the Aramaic element can *prove* is an Aramaic origin, not always translation of an Aramaic original, and], *it is the Greek literary factor which has had the final word with the shaping of the Q tradition.* [The evidence from the Gospels themselves for the existence of an Aramaic document is necessarily speculative'] (*Aramaic Approach*, p. 191).

It was not my intention, however, to rule out altogether the possibility of a 'literary formulation [of Q] in Aramaic'; and I have found no reason to change my mind that 'It seems to me to be reasonably certain that over large tracts of Q[A] [passages where identity of language is high] we have to do with a translated tradition' (*Aramaic Approach*, p. 188). What I sought to do was to indicate those *parts* of Q which were originally composed in Aramaic; I would now add, parts transmitted *either* orally *or* in written form, and that this was the Aramaic *Vorlage*

---

12. Listed by him in *Coniectanea Neotestamentica XI in honorem A. Fridrichsen* (Lund: Gleerup, 1947), pp. 97-99.

of Q. We may not be able to prove that there was an Aramaic Chreiae collection identical with parts of Q, but we cannot, as Kloppenborg does, reject the hypothesis altogether.

Where I differ fundamentally from Kloppenborg is in his characterization of the linguistic phenomena to which I drew attention as generally 'Semitisms'. This, of course, they all are,[13] but he has failed to recognize the tell-tale presence among them of distinctive 'Aramaisms' which point to sayings originally influenced by or actually composed in Aramaic. Among these I would class as test cases, pointing to an Aramaic origin for other 'Semitisms', especially in sayings attributed to Jesus, Lk. 6.23, 11.4, 41 pars. This need not exclude the influence of the LXX or of 'semitizing Greek' generally in the work of the Greek translators of the Q tradition.

Lk. 6.23/Mt. 5.12 σκιρτήσατε/ἀγαλλιᾶσθε. The root *dwṣ* occurs once only in biblical Hebrew, at Job 41.14 (22) where the meaning is uncertain although the verb is clearly related to the common Aramaic/ Syriac *dwṣ*, either 'leap' (e.g. for joy) or 'rejoice'. Kloppenborg considers that 'redactional modification of the Greek text by either Luke or Matthew is the more parsimonious solution' (p. 56). *Parallelismus verborum* in both Gospels, however, demands the meaning 'rejoice'; to suggest that this was redactionally modified by Luke to become 'leap' is straining credibility. (The views of Schulz and Schürmann to which Kloppenborg refers are no more convincing.) The Aramaic conjecture offers a credible and straightforward explanation.

Luke 11.4 τὰς ἁμαρτίας for Mt. 6.12 τὰ ὀφειλήματα, lit. 'debts'. The latter is a distinctive Aramaism (cf. Syr. *ḥub*), nowhere attested in

---

13. A Hebrew equivalent of QMt. 5.3 οἱ πτωχοὶ τῷ πνεύματι—Lk. 6.20 οἱ πτωχοί—has been found at 1QM 14.7, '*aniyye* (*not* '*anawey*) *ruah*, lit. 'the humbled/ afflicted in spirit', not 'the humble in spirit'. (The text has been correctly read by Yadin; in '*nwy, yodh* attached to *nun* has been misread as a *waw*.) The Semitic word is primarily a sociological term; the parallel phrase at Isa. 66.2, etc., is 'the crushed in spirit'. It seems to me more than probable that it is this (Aramaic) expression which lies behind the Matthaean translation-Greek πτωχοὶ τῷ πνεύματι; Luke simplifies by eliminating the Semitism, but lays himself open to the charge of 'ebionitism'. If this is correct, the interpretation of Mt. 5.3 proposed seems to rule out altogether or to relegate the 'religious' or 'spiritual' understanding of the First Beatitude to a subsidiary role; and it links Mt. 5.3 (and 4) with Isa. 61.1-2 RSV ('...the Lord has anointed me) to bring good tidings to the afflicted ('*aniyyim* for MT '*anawim*)'. Cf. W.D. Davies and D.C. Alison, *Matthew 1–7* (ICC; Edinburgh: T. & T. Clark, 1988), pp. 442-43.

biblical Hebrew usage; it was evidently only in Aramaic that 'sin' was conceived in terms of 'debt'.[14] It is an archaism still familiar in many Scottish (and no doubt other) church services. Kloppenborg argues that, since it appears in liturgical material which has a life of its own apart from its function within a document, it is unwise to attach too much significance to it. It could be said, however, that Luke's ἁμαρτία would be more intelligible to a Greek-speaking audience (p. 57 n. 58). A more economical solution is that it is a pure Aramaism, translating literally a word of Jesus.

Wellhausen's brilliant conjecture that Mt. 23.26 καθάρισον and Lk. 11.41 τὰ ἐνόντα δότε ἐλεημοσύνην go back to *dakkau* ('cleanse') and *zakkau* ('give alms') is, according to Kloppenborg, in view of Luke's interest in almsgiving, 'best regarded as a Lucan reformulation and explication of a Q saying which is perhaps best represented by Matthew' (p. 58). Wellhausen's objection to a similar explanation by Dalman still stands: 'give alms' for 'cleanse' is 'naturally complete nonsense'. Moreover, Kloppenborg's statement that 'זכי can mean *both* "to purify" and "to give alms" and hence דכי is not needed to explain Matthew's meaning' is philologically more than doubtful.[15] It is possible, as Wellhausen suggested, that the two words were orthographically identical, and they both come from the same root, but *zakke* 'to make pure' *is used always in a moral and never in a physical sense.* The view that 'the currency of the word זכי in Palestinian Aramaic seems precarious' is surprising in view of G. Dalman's full attestation of the verb meaning 'to give alms' in Jewish Palestinian Aramaic, mostly from the Palestinian Talmud.[16]

---

14. An (inconclusive) case for Hebrew has been made by Resch, *Agrapha* (TU, 10.1), p. 104.

15. *Lev. R.* 34.7 supporting this claim is cited as 'The poor man says to his neighbor: Give me alms (זכי בי) or give me charity (דכי בי), by which he means, become pure through me (זכי נרמך בי)'. The Soncino version reads the text as: A poor man would say to his neighbour: 'Give me alms' (*zakki bi*) or 'give me charity' (*rakki bi*) by which he means 'benefit yourself through me'. In this last clause Slotki is rendering *zakki garmak bi*, from which Kloppenborg ('become pure through me') gets the meaning 'cleanse' for *zakki*! The clause in fact is the Aramaic equivalent of *hiṣṭaddēq* (*ṣdq* hithp.) lit. 'assert your righteousness through me' (cf. Sir. 7.5 RSV), and so 'acquire merit through me', 'benefit yourself through me'. Hebrew *zākâ* 'be clear, pure', like Aramaic *zeka'* 'always in a moral sense' (BDB) is a synonym of *ṣdq*; 'cleanse' is *d/zakki*.

16. A complete list in *Die Worte Jesu* (Leipzig: Hinrichs, 1898), p. 71, omitted

It is not possible virtually to turn a Nelson eye on such evidence, since we have to do with linguistic phenomena in sayings attributed to Jesus in Q, where the hypothesis that they bespeak an Aramaic original is the most likely explanation; Jesus taught, as he spoke, in the indigenous language of his homeland. And such Semitic phenomena supply a not unimportant criterion of authenticity.

The Day of the Son of Man (Lk. 17.22)

Luke 17.22 contains a notoriously difficult *crux interpretum*, the enigmatic μίαν τῶν ἡμερῶν τοῦ υἱοῦ τοῦ ἀνθρώπου. The expression 'the days of the Son of Man' is found only in Luke in the New Testament, here and at v. 26 only; what precisely is meant by 'one of the days of the Son of Man' has been widely debated; Fitzmyer lists a number of ingenious interpretations, including alleged Semitisms.[17] Joachim Jeremias has noted that the expression μία τῶν ἡμερῶν occurs four times in Luke only (5.17; 8.22; 17.22; 20.1).[18]

In my *Aramaic Approach* (p. 105), in listing the uses of εἷς = *had* as an indefinite pronoun, I noted instances with a following genitive (= partitive *min*), meaning simply 'a certain so and so': thus Dan. 7.16, '(I came near) to a certain bystander' ('*al ḥad min qaʿamayya*, LXX πρὸς ἕνα τῶν ἐστώτων). I would suggest now that, from an exegetical point of view, Lk. 17.22 is an important example of this Semitism, most probably an Aramaism.[19] I would render, recognizing this Semitic idiom, '(The days are coming when you will desire to see) *a certain Day of* (or *for*, objective gen.) *the Son of Man*', that is, a Day still unknown (the pronominal adjective is indefinite), but, nevertheless, the Son of Man on his day, coming 'like a flash of lightning' from the heavens above. We have a similar expression when we refer to some event that is to happen 'one day'; the 'certain Day' at Lk. 17.22 is the Day of the sudden and unexpected Advent of the Son of Man.

from Eng. edn, pp. 86-88; briefly attested in Eng. edn, p. 63 (cf. *Worte Jesu*, p. 50).

17. *The Gospel according to Luke*, II (AB, 28A; New York: Doubleday, 1985), pp. 1168-69.

18. *Die Sprache des Lukasevangeliums: Redaktion und Tradition im Nicht-Markusstoff des dritten Evangeliums* (Göttingen: Vandenhoeck & Ruprecht, 1980), p. 267.

19. A Syriac parallel is cited from Bar Hebraeus by Gesenius, *Thesaurus*, p. 62: *beḥad men yaumata*, 'on one of the days', i.e. 'on a certain day'.

'Lo! he is in the inner rooms' (QMt. 24.26; cf. Lk. 17.23)

Though QLk. is generally a more reliable guide to the original sayings of Jesus than QMt., the fuller form here in QMt., with its balanced contrast, ἰδοὺ ἐν τῇ ἐρήμῳ... ἰδοὺ ἐν τοῖς ταμείοις, and its background in Jewish tradition[20] could point to QMt. here preserving the more original form of the saying. Besides, Lk. 17.23 looks suspiciously like a variant version of Mk 13.21.

A conjecture—which does not seem to have been made before— would support the hypothesis of the superiority of QMt. to the Lukan parallel. There are two closely related Aramaic nouns, (1) *'idron* (Heb. *ḥeder*) 'inner chamber', e.g. *Targ. Gen.* 43.30, the 'inner chamber' (LXX ταμιεῖον) into which Joseph retired to weep after seeing Benjamin; (2) *'edra*, either a Greek borrowing from ἕδρα, 'seat', 'session' or 'council chamber', or (more probably) Aramaic *'idar*, *'idra*, 'threshing floor', 'area', and then a synonym of *si'ta* (Syr. *si'ta*), 'assembly', 'congregation', but also the rotunda of the Sanhedrin and hence the Sanhedrin itself. Thus *Targ. Prov.* 27.22, 'If you chastise a fool with stripes in the Assembly (*sita*), in your Sanhedrin (*be'idrak*, LXX ἐν μέσῳ συνεδρίου) his folly will not depart from him'.

Is it possible that a Greek translator mistook *be'idrayya*, ἐν ταῖς/τοῖς/ἕδραις/συνεδρίοις, for *be'idronayya*, and rendered by ἐν τοῖς ταμείοις? We then obtain the contrasting ἐν τῇ ἐρήμῳ, *bemadbara*, with ἐν τοῖς συνεδρίοις *be'idrayya* (with a characteristic assonance): 'If they tell you, Lo, he is in the wilderness, do not go out; or if they say, Lo, he is in the Assemblies/Sanhedrin, do not believe it'.

---

20. See now J. Gnilka, *Das Matthäusevangelium* (HTKNT, 2.2; Freiburg: Herder, 1988), p. 325.

JSNT 23 (1985), pp. 23-33

THE SON OF MAN:
'A MAN IN MY POSITION' OR 'SOMEONE'?

Richard Bauckham

A Critique of Barnabas Lindars's Proposal

Professor Barnabas Lindars's new book, *Jesus, Son of Man*,[1] is a work
of major importance for the 'Son of Man' debate, and deserves the
closest consideration. Its importance lies as much in its discussion of the
extension and development of Son of Man sayings in Q and the four
Gospels as in its novel proposal on the meaning of Jesus' use of the
phrase, but my comments here are largely concerned with the latter.
Lindars stands within the general trend of Son of Man scholarship pio-
neered (in its recent phase) by Geza Vermes and pursued also by
Maurice Casey, which takes as the clue to Jesus' usage the examples of
bar nash and *bar nasha* as a form of self-reference in later Jewish
Aramaic. But, like Casey, he rejects Vermes's claim that there are
examples in which *bar nasha* is an idiomatic form of exclusive self-reference (a periphrasis for 'I'), and agrees with Casey that all the examples
in which *bar nasha* functions as a self-reference are examples of the
generic use, in which self-reference is possible because the speaker is
included among those to whom *bar nasha* refers. But whereas Casey
recognized only a properly generic use (*bar nasha* = 'mankind', 'each
and every man'), Lindars claims that there are examples of 'the
idiomatic use of the generic article, in which the speaker refers to a class
of persons, with whom he identifies himself' (*bar nasha* = 'a man in my
position'). 'It is this idiom... which provides the best guidance to the use
of Son of Man in the sayings of Jesus'.[2] He proceeds to use this idiom as

1. (London: SPCK; Grand Rapids: Eerdmans, 1983).
2. Lindars, *Jesus, Son of Man*, p. 24.

criterion of dominical authenticity: only Son of Man sayings which use the phrase as this kind of self-reference can be considered authentic. On this basis, Lindars identifies (in ch. 3) six Son of Man sayings from Mark and Q as authentic, and (in ch. 4) adds three passion predictions: a total of nine authentic Son of Man sayings which can be plausibly interpreted according to the 'idiomatic generic' use of *bar nasha*.

This brilliantly argued case unfortunately, it seems to me, fails at two points: in the use of rabbinic examples to establish the idiom, and in the application of the idiom to sayings of Jesus. On the first point, it should first be noticed that Lindars discusses only four passages in which *bar nash(a)* is a self-reference, and considers two of these examples of the alleged 'idiomatic generic' use. These four passages are the four adduced in Vermes's abbreviated discussion in *Jesus the Jew*.[3] Lindars does not discuss the other five passages included in Vermes's more extended, original discussion.[4] This is unfortunate. The known cases of *bar nash(a)* as a self-reference are so few that any attempt to determine their exact nuance should take all of them into consideration. It is especially unfortunate for Lindars's own case, since two or three of the passages he does not discuss would fit the idiom he is attempting to establish as well as or even better than the two passages which are his actual evidence for it.

His discussion of these two passages (*y. Ber.* 3b; *y. Šeb.* 38d, with parallels) does not convince me that they are not examples of the properly generic use (*bar nasha* = 'mankind'). In the first, Simeon ben Yohai is, of course, only *interested* in requesting two mouths for those who are going to use one to recite the Torah, and really only interested in requesting two mouths for himself, since it is he who wants to do this, but possession of one or two mouths is a feature of *human nature* and so his prayer has to be that God would create mankind, human nature as such, with two mouths. Lindars's argument, that *bar nasha* refers to a class of men of which Simeon is in fact the only member, though in principle there might be others, seems rather contrived. Any statement about one person which *could* in principle also be true of other similar

---

3.   G. Vermes, *Jesus the Jew* (London: Collins; Philadelphia: Fortress Press, 2nd edn, 1976), pp. 164-67.

4.   G. Vermes, 'The Use of בר נש/נשא in Jewish Aramaic', in *Post-Biblical Jewish Studies* (SPB, 8: Leiden: Brill, 1975), pp. 147-65 (reprinted from M. Black, *An Aramaic Approach to the Gospels and Acts* [Oxford: Clarendon Press, 3rd edn, 1967], pp. 310-28).

people, if there were such people, would by this argument become 'generic'.

In the second example (*y. Šeb.* 38d) I see even less reason to prefer Lindars's interpretation to the properly generic one. To understand the sense of Simeon's conclusion as simply, 'No man perishes without the will of heaven', seems both obvious and wholly appropriate to the context. More to the point would have been a passage not discussed by Lindars (*y. Ber.* 5b: 'The disciple of *bar nasha* is as dear to him as his son'[5]), where one has to concede that the generic sense of *bar nasha* is a qualified generic sense. It applies not to every man, but to every man who has a disciple (i.e. every rabbi). But this is a natural way of using a noun generically, because the qualification is obviously provided by the context (just as it is in 'A man who... ' or 'A good man... '). It does not justify postulating an idiom in which *bar nasha* refers to a limited class of men ('a man in my position') where the limitation is *not* obviously provided by the context.

Even if Lindars's 'idiomatic use of the generic article' were established from the later Jewish evidence, it has to be stretched considerably to accommodate most of the six allegedly authentic sayings discussed in ch. 3. The saying which it fits most easily is the first (Mt. 8.20 = Lk. 9.58), where *bar enasha* could in that case be rendered 'everyone in my position' (this is what the idiomatic generic use ought to mean). But it certainly cannot be said that 'the generic usage is *essential* to the purpose of the saying', as Lindars claims.[6] If 'the Son of Man' were an exclusive self-reference (and Lindars must admit that this is how the Evangelists understood it), it would still be a perfectly adequate reply to the disciple's words in Mt. 8.19 = Lk. 9.57.

In saying 3 (Mt. 12.32 = Lk. 12.10) the case for a generic sense is a good one, but here it is the proper generic sense ('mankind'), and Lindars makes no attempt to argue for the special idiomatic generic sense in which the reference is restricted to a class of men. It should also be noticed that a simple indefinite sense ('a man') would also be an appropriate interpretation, since in this kind of generalizing context ('Everyone who speaks a word against a man') there is no real difference between the generic and indefinite senses.

A good test of whether the alleged idiomatic generic sense can really be detected in the sayings examined in ch. 3 is to try the translation,

---

5. Quoted from Vermes, 'The Use of בר נשא/בר נש', p. 160.
6. Lindars, *Jesus, Son of Man*, p. 30.

'everyone in my position', since the idiom means that what is said of *bar enasha* is said of every man in the class to which the speaker belongs. This translation appears possible in saying 5 (Mt. 9.6 = Mk 2.10-11 = Lk. 5.24), but impossible in sayings 2, 4 and 6, because in these sayings what is said of *bar enasha* actually applies to one man only, even if there *could* in principle be other people to whom it *could* be applied. Thus in saying 2 (Mt. 11.19 = Lk. 7.34) Jesus is not suggesting that his hearers are saying, 'Behold, a glutton and a drunkard...', about a whole class of non-ascetic evangelists. It will not do to claim that 'the generic *bar enasha* raises the matter to the level of a principle',[7] because the statement about *bar enasha* is not made in the *form* of a principle, but in the form of a statement of a specific fact about one man, precisely parallel to the preceding statement about John the Baptist. *Bar enasha* could be made generic only by changing the grammatical structure of the sentence and spoiling the parallelism with the statement about the Baptist. Of course, the statement does not exclude the possibility that there *could* be other people in a similar position (non-ascetic evangelists) who *would* incur the same treatment;[8] but it does not refer to them. As a matter of fact, the translation of *bar enasha* which Lindars himself offers for this saying is not, 'everyone in my position' (or something of that kind), but 'someone else'.[9] This translation makes good sense, but 'someone else' is indefinite, not generic.

The suspicion that 'generic' and 'indefinite' are being misleadingly equated is confirmed in the discussion of saying 4 (Lk. 11.30): 'It is another case of the generic usage... Just as Jonah was a sign to the Ninevites... so there is a man who will be a sign to the present generation.'[10] But this is not a generic usage. 'A man' here is neither 'each and every man' nor 'each and every member of a class of men', but just one man. *Bar enasha*, in that case, would be indefinite ('a man', 'someone'), not generic ('each and every man'). The role of being a sign to the present generation might be one which a number of men *could*, in principle, fulfil, but the saying is a statement about only the one man who does (or will) fulfil it. Again, only a grammatical change (which Lindars suggests, but does not insist on, as the meaning of the

7.   Lindars, *Jesus, Son of Man*, p. 33.
8.   Cf. Lindars, *Jesus, Son of Man*, p. 33.
9.   Lindars, *Jesus, Son of Man*, pp. 33, 174.
10. Lindars, *Jesus, Son of Man*, p. 41.

postulated Aramaic original[11]) could make *bar enasha* generic here: 'so a man *may be* to this generation'.[12] Is it not easier to explain *bar enash(a)* as indefinite?

Lindars makes the same move in the discussion of saying 5, where he offers the translation, 'But that you may know that *a man may have* authority... ',[13] but in the case of saying 6 no such suggestion is made. Lindars's exegesis of saying 6 (Mt. 10.32-33 = Lk. 12.8-9) is attractive and plausible, but it involves no real attempt to make *bar enasha* generic, as distinct from indefinite. Lindars's paraphrase of the first half of the saying is: 'All those who confess me before men will have a man to speak for them (i.e. an advocate) before the judgment seat of God... ' The point is intended to be that Jesus stresses that there will be an advocate, rather than that he himself will be the advocate (though this is implied). But then *bar enasha* means 'someone' (indefinite), not 'each and every man' (generic) or 'each and every member of the class of men that includes me' (idiomatic generic). In this saying, any appeal to the special idiom seems to have become quite redundant. According to Lindars's own exegesis, Jesus is not identifying himself with some class of people (advocates at the last judgment) but referring to himself obliquely as 'someone'. Reconsideration of sayings 2, 4 and 5 suggests that this is also likely to be the idiom there.

Besides the six Son of Man sayings discussed in ch. 3, Lindars believes that three passion predictions, discussed in ch. 4, are authentic because they use the alleged idiomatic generic idiom. The argument of this chapter (too intricate to be discussed here) involves reconstruction and interpretation of the sayings which can really only be justified if the alleged idiom has already been established as characteristic of Jesus' usage. The argument of ch. 4 requires that of ch. 3 for its premise; it cannot come to its aid.

I conclude that this highly ingenious attempt to make Jesus' usage conform to an otherwise attested idiomatic use of *bar nasha* is a failure, though an heroic one. The idiom is not convincingly attested elsewhere, and it cannot explain all of even the small number of sayings of Jesus which Lindars judges authentic. However, as will become apparent, I do not consider Lindars's exegetical work to be wasted.

---

11. Lindars, *Jesus, Son of Man*, p. 42.
12. Cf. Lindars, *Jesus, Son of Man*, p. 172.
13. Lindars, *Jesus, Son of Man*, p. 45; his emphasis.

Where Do we Go from Here?

Recent study of the available Jewish evidence seems to me to lead to the following two conclusions, which must be taken as premises for further discussion of 'Son of Man' in the Gospels: (1) 'Son of Man' was not a recognized title for an apocalyptic figure, and cannot therefore by itself constitute an allusion to Daniel 7.[14] Only Son of Man sayings which otherwise allude to Daniel 7 could have been understood as allusions to the figure in Dan. 7.13 on the lips of Jesus. (2) The later Jewish evidence for the use of *bar nash(a)* as a self-reference seems to be evidence only for the properly generic use, where what is said of *bar nash(a)* is true of all men (unless the context provides an obvious qualification of 'all') and therefore also of the speaker. There is no real support for *bar nash(a)* as an exclusive self-reference equivalent to *hahu gabra* (Vermes),[15] or for Lindars's idiomatic generic use.

These conclusions imply that, if Jesus' use of 'Son of Man' conformed to an accepted usage for which we have evidence, there would seem to be only two possible types of authentic sayings: (1) Authentic Son of Man sayings are those in which allusion to Daniel 7 is explicit apart from the phrase 'Son of Man' itself.[16] (2) Authentic Son of Man sayings are those which conform to the properly generic use (Casey). However, neither of these possibilities is at all satisfactory. The major problem in each case is that such a body of authentic sayings makes it very difficult to account for the later proliferation of Son of Man sayings in the Gospel traditions, particularly in the light of Lindars's very valuable study of the use of 'Son of Man' in Q and the four Gospels. Lindars shows that there was never a Son of Man christology in the

14. For the growing acceptance of this point in recent scholarship, see G. Vermes, 'The Present State of the "Son of Man" Debate', *JJS* 29 (1978), pp. 130-32.

15. J.A. Fitzmyer, 'Another View of the "Son of Man" Debate', *JSNT* 4 (1979), p. 58, seems to admit that Vermes's interpretation applies in one case: the Cairo Geniza fragment of the Palestinian Targum to Gen. 4.14 (see Vermes, 'The Use of בר נש/בר נשא: p. 159). Clearly *bar nash* is here a substitute for 'I', but it may be a substitute introduced precisely in order to give an additional, generic nuance: no *man* (such as Cain) can hide from *God*.

16. Against the thesis of A.J.B. Higgins, *The Son of Man in the Teaching of Jesus* (SNTSMS, 39; Cambridge: Cambridge University Press, 1980), it is important to emphasize that, of the future Son of Man sayings, it is those in which the allusion to Dan. 7.13 is most explicit which have the best chance of authenticity, since the phrase 'Son of Man' *itself* cannot convey the idea of an eschatological judge.

early church: the use of 'Son of Man' was purely a feature of the literary editing of the sayings of Jesus. But in that case there has to have been a sufficient body of authentic Son of Man sayings to establish 'Son of Man' as a characteristic self-designation of Jesus, which could then be extended to other sayings. Lindars also demonstrates that, although in the Gospels 'Son of Man' becomes at least quasi-titular, it is not understood as a true messianic title but as a self-designation of Jesus, which not even the Evangelists (except perhaps Mark) regard as everywhere carrying an allusion to Dan. 7.13. This makes it difficult to regard 'Son of Man' as a title for Jesus which originates purely from exegesis of Dan. 7.13, it seems there must have been some authentic sayings of this type.

Thus the possibility that the original Son of Man sayings (whether authentic or not) were only sayings which allude to Dan. 7.13 is ruled out. But Casey's view, that the only authentic sayings are those in which *bar enash(a)* can carry the properly generic sense, is also problematic. Very few sayings can plausibly be given this sense without becoming incredible (e.g. Mt. 8.20 = Lk. 9.58) or rather banal, and it could be argued that Casey, like Lindars, has extended his list of authentic sayings by including cases where the meaning he accepts is really indefinite, not generic.[17] But the fewer the authentic Son of Man sayings and the more restricted the types of Son of Man sayings which are regarded as authentic, the more difficult it is to account for the existence of inauthentic Son of Man sayings. Three or four authentic sayings in which *bar enash(a)* means 'mankind' are not likely to have given the impression that the term was a characteristic self-designation of Jesus or to have suggested a connection with Dan. 7.13.

A further possibility, however, should be explored: that Jesus used *bar enash* (probably, rather than *bar enasha*) in the indefinite sense ('a man', 'someone'), which is itself a very common usage,[18] but used it as a form of deliberately oblique or ambiguous self-reference. This possibility has been suggested by my criticism of Lindars above, and would in

---

17. E.g. Mt. 11.19 = Lk. 7.34, which M. Casey, *Son of Man: The Interpretation and Influence of Daniel 7* (London: SPCK, 1979), p. 229, calls a 'general statement', on the authority (*ibid.*, p. 240 n. 13) of Colpe and Jeremias, but in fact both these scholars are quite explicit in interpreting it as indefinite, not generic: C. Colpe, *TDNT*, VIII, pp. 431-32 (especially n. 241), and J. Jeremias, *New Testament Theology*, I (ET; London: SCM Press; New York: Charles Scribner's Sons, 1971), pp. 261-62.

18. Cf. Vermes, 'The Use of בר נש/בר נשא', pp. 155-56.

fact preserve as correct a good deal of Lindars's exegesis of the sayings he accepts as authentic.[19] It should be noticed that although this use of *bar enash* is *grammatically* indefinite, meaning 'someone', in practice it can easily and naturally (like 'someone' in English) refer to a definite, though unidentified, person.[20] (Vermes gives an example from *y. Yeb.* 13a: 'I am sending you *bar nash* like myself'.[21]) Thus it could be used as an oblique self-reference, in which the self-reference would normally be exclusive but implicit. Jesus would be referring to an unidentified 'someone', but those who fully understood his meaning would infer that the 'someone' was himself. Since the indefinite use (like 'a man' in English) can have a generic sense in certain contexts (e.g. *y. Ber.* 5c; *y. Ket.* 35a[22]), there will be no need to exclude the generic sense with self-reference in the few cases where it works (notably Mt. 12.32 = Lk. 12.10), but in a much larger number of sayings the plausible meaning is indefinite, referring not to 'everyone' but to 'someone' (Mk 2.10 = Mt. 9.6 = Lk. 5.24; Mk 2.28 = Mt. 12.8 = Lk. 6.5; Mk 8.31 = Lk. 9.22; Mk 9.12; Mk 9.31 = Mt. 17.22 = Lk. 9.44; Mk 10.33 = Mt. 22.18 = Lk. 18.31; Mk 14.21 = Mt. 26.24 = Lk. 22.22; Mk 14.41 = Mt. 26.45; Mt. 8.20 = Lk. 9.58; Mt. 11.19 = Lk. 7.34; Mt. 12.40 = Lk. 11.30; Mt. 26.2; Lk. 12.8-9 [cf. Mk 8.38 = Lk. 9.26]; Lk. 22.48; Jn. 1.51).

This proposal permits the authenticity of a similar range of sayings to those accepted by Casey and Lindars (to determine precisely which sayings are, by this criterion, authentic, would of course require detailed discussion), while allowing them, in some cases, a more natural exegesis, in other cases, a very similar exegesis. It also has other advantages. It would not, in the first place, necessarily exclude the authenticity of some Son of Man sayings which allude to Daniel 7. (The most obvious candidate for authenticity here would be Mk 14.62.) In such sayings, the use of the indefinite 'a man' (*bar enash*) would be neither a title nor unambiguously a self-reference, but a literal echo of Dan. 7.13

---

19. The suggestion has been made with reference to a few sayings (J.Y. Campbell, 'The Origin and Meaning of the Term Son of Man', *JTS* 48 [1947], p. 152, of Mt. 11.19; Colpe, *TDNT*, VIII, pp. 430-33; Jeremias, *New Testament Theology*, pp. 261-62, both of Mk 2.10; Mt. 11.19; Mt. 8.20), but I know of no attempt to see it as Jesus' characteristic usage in a substantial number of sayings.

20. So Campbell, 'Son of Man', pp. 151-52.

21. Vermes, 'The Use of נש בר/נשא בר', p. 156.

22. Quoted in Vermes, 'The Use of נש בר/נשא בר', pp. 158-60.

(*ke-bar enash*). There seems no reason why Jesus should not have exploited the coincidence between his accustomed form of oblique self-reference and the language of Dan. 7.13, so that *bar enash* in a saying alluding to Dan. 7.13 becomes the same kind of veiled hint of his own status as other authentic Son of Man sayings convey. This would not at all imply that *bar enash* has any connection with Dan. 7.13 in sayings which do not themselves allude to Daniel 7.

The indefinite use therefore permits the authenticity of a wide range of types of Son of Man sayings, including some future Son of Man sayings which allude to Daniel 7. This makes the process by which 'Son of Man', understood in Greek translation at quasi-titular,[23] was extended to other sayings, whether freshly created sayings or sayings in which 'Son of Man' was not original, quite readily intelligible. Once 'Son of Man' was understood as quasi-titular, this extension was simply an extension of the same kind of usage as was known in the authentic sayings.

It might appear a disadvantage of the proposal that it cannot appeal to parallels in later Jewish Aramaic.[24] But if Jesus' use of *bar enash* was a form of deliberately ambiguous self-reference, then *ex hypothesi* there do not need to be parallels to it. If Jesus had used a well established form of indirect self-reference, such as *hahu gabra*, the self-reference would have been explicit and easily recognized in most contexts. But if Jesus wished to refer to himself in a way which was not necessarily immediately obvious, so that his hearers had to infer or guess the self-reference, then it is understandable that he should adopt a way of speaking which was not so well recognized an idiom. For such a purpose the use of the indefinite 'a man' or 'someone' is well suited. It is in fact a relatively straightforward development of the natural use of 'a man' with reference to the speaker in contexts which make the reference entirely obvious (e.g. Jn 8.40).

The ambiguity of the self-reference will vary from saying to saying, from cases where the self-reference is obvious in the context (Lk. 22.48), through cases where the self-reference is deliberately unstressed

---

23. The translation of *bar enash* by the definite ὁ υἱὸς τοῦ ἀνθρώπου is sufficiently explained by the translator's wish to avoid the ambiguity of Jesus' own idiom: in his mind ὁ υἱὸς τοῦ ἀνθρώπου was a definite person, Jesus (cf. Casey, *Son of Man*, p. 230).

24. But cf. Paul's use of ἄνθρωπον (as a modest form of self-reference) in 2 Cor. 12.2.

(Mt. 10.32-33 = Lk. 12.8-9, following Lindars's exegesis), to cases where the saying has a somewhat enigmatic or riddling character (Lk. 11.30; the passion predictions), and cases where some hearers might easily assume Jesus' reference to be to a figure other than himself (sayings alluding to Daniel 7). This does not make the proposed usage inconsistent, but rather reveals an habitual form of oblique self-reference which in all cases expresses Jesus' accustomed reticence about his status and authority, for which there is abundant evidence. The point is not that Jesus did not wish his God-given role and authority to be recognized, but that he wanted people to recognize them for themselves. Claims are easy to make and as easily dismissed. By his oblique self-reference Jesus avoided claims, but invited people to think for themselves about the implications of the undeniable facts of his ministry. Then, in the paradoxical situation of the suffering and rejected prophet, he made the only kind of claim which is appropriate to that situation: a reference to future vindication, in which the obliqueness of the self-reference serves to leave the vindication to God who alone can vindicate him.

For the present, three brief illustrations must suffice:

(1) Mk 2.10-11. The reference to 'a man' follows naturally as a response to v. 7, but the point is not that Jesus' healing of the paralytic demonstrates the general principle that men have authority to forgive sins. Jesus neither denies nor asserts that others have such authority, but points to his healing as evidence that at any rate one man, himself, does have it. Thus he claims no more than his deed demonstrates, and the obliqueness of the self-reference serves to make his authority not so much a claim as an inference which his hearers may draw for themselves from what they see.

(2) Lk. 11.30. Here the self-reference is less obvious, more enigmatic, but the implication is similar. To those who see the significance of Jesus and his ministry, he *is* a sign. To those who do not, who cannot recognize the evidence which is before their eyes, there is no point in *claiming* to be a sign. All that can be said is that there is someone who is a sign.

(3) Mt. 26.64 = Mk 14.62 = Lk. 22.67-68. Jesus avoids a direct claim to messiahship which, if his accusers cannot believe it from the evidence they already have (cf. Lk. 22.67), he cannot prove. Although, in the context, the allusion to Dan. 7.13 must amount to a self-reference, the obliqueness makes his status one which he leaves it to God to vindicate.

The allusion to Dan. 7.13 is made not because Jesus prefers the 'title' Son of Man to those offered by the high priest, but because (along with Ps. 110.1) it is appropriate to the thought of eschatological vindication and allows an indefinite third person reference.

JSNT 23 (1985), pp. 35-41

RESPONSE TO RICHARD BAUCKHAM:
THE IDIOMATIC USE OF *BAR ENASHA*

Barnabas Lindars, SSF†

It is pleasing to respond to a colleague who has devoted such careful attention to my *Jesus, Son of Man* and made such generous comments in connection with it. I am also grateful to have the opportunity to try to clarify the idiom which is at the heart of my thesis. This is not easily grasped, and it may be that I have sown the seeds of confusion by using the word generic in an imprecise way. So this must be dealt with first.

1. *The Generic Article*

It is necessary to be clear at the outset that what we are concerned with is the idiomatic use of the definite article in indefinite statements. This usage is described in the *Hebrew Grammar* of Gesenius–Kautzsch §126*q*. In a generic statement what is said is true of every person or thing in that class, and in English either the definite or more often the indefinite article may be used, for example, Shakespeare's 'bearded like the pard' (i.e. like a leopard; all leopards have beards). This usage is also found in Greek, for example, Lk. 6.45, 'the good man'. But in an indefinite statement, where one or an unspecified number of persons or things is singled out, English usually requires the indefinite article (plural 'some'), whereas Hebrew and Aramaic tend to use the definite article, denoting a particular but unspecified member or group of members of the class. This is the generic article. This is virtually mandatory in such phrases as 'to write in a book' (Hebrew: 'the book', i.e., the one needed for the purpose) and 'in a vision of the night' (e.g. Dan. 2.19, Aramaic: בחזוא, 'in the vision'). But it is also used 'to denote a single person or thing (primarily one which is as yet unknown, and therefore not capable of being defined) as being present to the mind under given circumstances'

(Gesenius–Kautzsch). The classic example is Amos 5.19, 'As if a man fled from a lion (the lion, i.e., the particular lion pursuing him at the time) and a (the) bear met him'. In Gen. 14.13 'one who had escaped came' (Hebrew: הפליט = the refugee, i.e., the particular one who came just then). In Ezek. 37.1 the prophet is brought in trance into 'the midst of a valley' (the valley, i.e., the one required for the scene which is to be described). All these are indefinite statements in which the generic article is used, and they are entirely distinct from generic statements applying to a whole class.

2. *Rabbinic Examples with* bar nasha

In New Testament times the forms used are *bar enash* (absolute, used for the indefinite) and *bar enasha* (emphatic, used for the definite). The rabbinic examples use the later spelling *bar nash* and *bar nasha*. In his study of 'The Use of בר נש/נשא in Jewish Aramaic', G. Vermes was concerned to establish the use of the word as a third-person circumlo-cution for the first person. From this point of view the emphatic form suggested an exclusive self-reference. Vermes did not explore the pos-sibility that the form might be better explained as an example of the generic article. In *Jesus, Son of Man* I applied this possibility to the examples given by Vermes in *Jesus the Jew*, and found it to be both convincing and illuminating.

Bauckham has taken me to task for confining attention to the exam-ples in *Jesus the Jew*. This may have been the wrong decision, but it was deliberate, because I was writing for the same kind of audience rather than for the more specialized audience assumed in the original discus-sion. The additional examples, few as they are, do indeed confirm my interpretation. First we may note two examples which do not constitute a self-reference.

(a) The *Palestinian Targum* (*Neofiti*) to Gen. 2.23 reads: 'This time, but not again, woman shall be created out of a (the) man (text: בר נש), as this one has been created out of me'. The idea is reversal of the fruit of sexual union, so that the husband is the child-bearer. The generic article denotes the particular man in a given case.

(b) *y. Kil.* 32b: 'Rabbi was very humble and used to say, I am prepared to do whatever בר נשא tells me'. Though this saying in *Gen. R.* 33.3 (on Gen. 8.1) has בר נש, there is a real difference between 'what-ever anyone tells me' as a general statement and 'whatever the man (i.e.

the particular one who is talking to me) tells me'. It serves as an oblique way of saying 'whatever *you* tell me'. This example is instructive, because it shows the use of the idiom to avoid direct reference to the person in a situation where some delicacy is required.

This can be seen when we turn to the examples where the speaker uses the idiom to refer to himself.

(c) *y. Ber.* 5b: 'When R. Hiyya ben Adda died...R. Levi received his valuables. This was because his teacher used to say, The disciple of בר נשא is as dear to him as his son'. This is not a generic statement, as it is not true of all teacher-pupil relationships, but rather a proverbial way of speaking whereby R. Hiyya indicates his special affection for his disciple. The generic article denotes a particular member of the class of those who have disciples. By singling out one as a typical example, Hiyya can delicately suggest the self-reference which is his real intention.

(d) *y. Ket.* 35a: 'It is related that Rabbi was buried in a single sheet, for he said: It is not as בר נשא goes that he will come again. But the rabbis say: As בר נש goes, so he will come again.' This was elucidated in *Jesus, Son of Man* (p. 21), as a case of the use of a proverb, or proverbial type of statement, to explain one's own intentions, and this may now appear more convincing in the light of the preceding example. The generic article singles out a particular member of the class of those who are 'going', that is, approaching death. Other texts have בר נש, which turn it into a general rule, as in the opinion of the rabbis which follows.

(e) *y. Ber.* 3b (Simeon ben Yohai's wish that *bar nasha* might have two mouths) and (f) *y. Šeb.* 38d (Simeon's comment on the escape of a bird, 'How much less בר נשא) were dealt with in *Jesus, Son of Man*, pp. 21-23, and it is only necessary here to recall that we are concerned with the use of the generic article in indefinite statements, though in both cases there are parallels which move in the opposite direction, making them explicit self-references. In the first case the generic article denotes the particular man who might happen to be on Mount Sinai at the time of the giving of the Torah, and the self-reference is obvious. But Simeon uses the idiom to soften the boldness of the request. In the second case the generic article singles out a particular man who might find himself in the same situation as the birds. Seeing that what is said can be taken to be a general ruling, some texts take it as such (e.g. *Gen. R.* 79.6 [on Gen. 33.18]). But the use of the generic article adds to the comment the sense of discovery, true in every case, no doubt, but true in his own case too.

(g) *Gen. R.* 38.13 (on Gen. 11.28) records a smart exchange between Abraham and one who would entice him to worship an idol. Abraham forces his friend to redefine his suggestion until finally he puts it into the form, 'Let us worship the wind'. Abraham then says, 'Let us rather worship בר נשא who bears the wind (רוח)', and so has the last word. Vermes points out that there is likely to be deliberate ambiguity, as Abraham could mean 'the man who bears the Spirit'. Thus he reaches the *reductio ad absurdum* of the argument, the worship of an idol being modified in such a way that it becomes worship of a Spirit-bearing man. Of course all men bear the Spirit according to Gen. 2.7 (cf. Ezek. 37.9), but the generic article denotes a particular unnamed member of that class. Obviously the reference is to Abraham himself. So what he is saying is virtually 'You may as well worship *me!*'

3. The Sayings of Jesus

It is my contention that such Son of Man sayings as have an Aramaic base used the emphatic form, בר אנשא, and that this is best explained by the idiom of the generic article. The use of this idiom in cases implying either a reference to the speaker or a reference to some other specific person, as in (b) above, is always done for a reason such as the need for delicacy or the irony of the situation. Much of the exegesis in my book on the sayings of Jesus is taken up with the reason in each case. Here I will seek only to clarify the idiom, bearing in mind Bauckham's complaint of confusion at this point.

In the 'foxes' saying (Mt. 8.20 = Lk. 9.58) the class of persons denoted by בר אנשא is indicated by the context (Jesus and prospective disciples). The generic article specifies an individual, but leaves his identity ambiguous. It could be a self-reference (the one, i.e., myself, whom you wish to follow) or it could be the disciple himself (the one who follows me). I regard the idiom as essential to the irony of the saying, which is lost if it is treated as an exclusive self-reference. It should also be noted that, because this type of saying is always done for a reason, it must always have a context, as in the rabbinic examples above. When the context is dropped, the saying automatically becomes an exclusive saying about one person. This is what has happened in *Gos. Thom.* 86.

In the 'glutton' saying (Mt. 11.19 = Lk. 7.34) anyone who comes eating and drinking is contrasted with John the Baptist, who was an ascetic. A group which can embrace both is implied. The generic article specifies one of this class who might come eating and drinking, and the context shows that he is to be identified with Jesus. The 'sign of Jonah' saying (Lk. 11.30) is similar, but here it is a comparison rather than a contrast. Jonah as a sign-figure in his generation is compared with anyone who might be a sign-figure in the present generation. The generic article specifies one such figure, and the context implies that this is Jesus himself.

The 'blasphemy' saying (Mt. 12.32 = Lk. 12.10) is a generic state-ment (indicated by the opening 'everyone who') which requires an indefinite object (a man) in the relative clause, unless a particular object is specified (the Holy Spirit in the parallel). The generic article points to a particular example of such a man, and so allows an oblique reference to Jesus himself. This applies also to the 'authority' saying (Mk 2.10), where Jesus indicates a class who may have authority to forgive sins, but by using the generic article singles out one example which is, of course, himself. Finally the 'advocate' saying (best preserved in Lk. 12.8-9) comprises parallel generic statements as in the 'blasphemy' saying, but the references to the man who is to act in the future can only be indefinite, because it is not a function which applies to everyone, and the identity of such a person is left undisclosed. The generic article indicates a particular example of such a person, who can be identified with Jesus. The change to the first person in Mt. 10.32-33 is comparable to the rabbinic parallels where an exclusive expression is substituted for בר נשא.

To complete the picture a brief word may be said about the passion sayings. Behind both the passion predictions and the betrayal sayings I postulated a common original (אתמסר בר אנשא). Although this is too frag-mentary to show that בר אנשא is the indefinite noun with generic article, so that the case had to be argued on the basis of wider considerations, the 'destiny' saying (Mk 14.21a) and the 'ransom' saying (Mk 10.45) are sufficiently well preserved to illustrate the idiom. They are comparable to the two sayings attributed to Hiyya and Rabbi in (c) and (d) above. It is also worth repeating that the passion prediction has spawned no less than six Son of Man sayings in Mark (8.31; 9.12; 9.31; 10.33; 14.21b; 14.41), nearly all with parallels in Matthew and Luke. It would thus be misleading to suggest that I argue for *only* nine authentic sayings, as if all the rest are therefore to be regarded as 'inauthentic'. Mark in my view has only three inauthentic sayings—2.28 (derived from 2.10), 13.26 and 14.62 (both derived from Danielic interpretation of the 'advocate' saying, already visible in 8.38). The number of inauthentic sayings in Matthew and Luke is rather larger, but similarly should not be overestimated. Of course the presence of the Aramaic idiom does not *prove* authenticity, but adds weight to the *possibility* of authenticity in each case.

Bauckham's proposal correctly sees that we are dealing with indefinite statements, but because he has not grasped the idiom of the generic article he denies the force of the article, and even suggests that anarthrous בר אנשא lies behind the Greek. But this is inconceivable, as בר אנשא is always translated υἱὸς ἀνθρώπου in the few places where we have both Aramaic and Greek versions. Moreover to treat the sayings as indefinite without regard to the idiomatic use of the generic article does not really open up the possibility of enlarging the number of those which may be considered authentic. If the sayings are really indefinite, the בר אנשא must mean 'anyone', and cannot represent 'someone' in the sense of a certain person. Thus in Mk 14.62 Jesus would be saying to the high priest, 'you will see someone or other (*not* a particular person) coming with the clouds of heaven...' Alternatively it would not be an indefinite statement, but would mean 'you will see a man (i.e. a particular person, as in narrative style)'. But if the meaning were indefinite, and at the same time Jesus intended to denote himself, then the generic article would be used. The difficulty is to interpret the saying as basically an indefinite statement. Both the context and the manifest allusion to Dan. 7.13 make this extremely unlikely. It is even more difficult to interpret Jn 1.51 in this way. Unlike the 'advocate' saying these future sayings do not leave open the sort of possibility which it contains that there might be several advocates and accusers, only one of whom is particularized to effect the link with Jesus himself.

Application of the generic article to the problem of the Son of Man seems to me to be the best linguistic solution. At the same time it has proved unexpectedly rich in interpretation in a way that does not apply to any other approach. It always demands a reason, and so opens the way to living situations in the Jesus tradition and glimpses of his way of dealing with them. Perhaps it is appropriate that a follower (in Aramaic 'the follower') of St Francis should point to the *chutzpah* of Jesus.

JSNT 18 (1983), pp. 75-84

MATTHEW 23.39 = LUKE 13.35B AS A CONDITIONAL PROPHECY

Dale C. Allison, Jr

Mt. 23.39 (= Lk. 13.35b: Q) reads as follows: 'For I say to you, you will not see me from now on until you say, "Blessed is he who comes in the name of the Lord"' (cf. Ps. 118[117].26).[1] Whether with reference to Matthew or Luke, to Jesus or Q, interpretations of this verse have generally followed one of two paths. Either it has been construed as a declaration of unqualified judgment, or commentators have thought the verse to hold forth the hope that Israel might one day accept her messiah, Jesus (cf. Rom. 11.25-27). (The two readings agree in assuming that the eschatological redemption is in view.[2]) John Calvin, representing the first alternative, wrote, 'He [Jesus] will not come to them [the Jews] until they cry out in fear—too late—at the sight of his Majesty, "truly He is Son of God"'.[3] T.W. Manson paraphrased to similar effect: 'The time will come when you will be ready to say to me, "Blessed is he that cometh in the name of the Lord"; but then it will be too late'.[4] And J.C. Fenton has affirmed that, according to Mt. 23.39, 'Jesus will not be

---

1. Luke does not have Matthew's 'from now on' (ἀπ' ἄρτι), which must be regarded as redactional (cf. 26.29 and 64). Matthew does not have Luke's 'the time comes when' (ἥξει ὅτε), which may have stood in Q; but there is much uncertainty here. ἥξει ὅτε has weak textual support (D lat sy$^{s\,c}$). Simple ἕως is read by p^{75} B L R sy^P sa 892. ἕως ἄν is found in p^{45} ℵ N Θ f13. N–A^{26} has ἥξει ὅτε in the text but in brackets, indicating doubtful authenticity.

2. For the reasons, see T.W. Manson, *The Sayings of Jesus* (London: SCM Press, 1949), pp. 127-28. Luke, however, may have seen the saying's fulfillment in the triumphal entry; see Lk. 19.38. Matthew, by placing the verse after Jesus' arrival in Jerusalem, excludes this possibility.

3. J. Calvin, *A Harmony of the Gospels Matthew, Mark and Luke*, III (trans. A.W. Morrison; Edinburgh: Saint Andrew, 1972), p. 71.

4. *Sayings*, p. 128.

seen by Jerusalem again before he comes in judgment, and then they will greet him, but with mourning'.[5] But against Calvin, Manson and Fenton, εὐλογεῖν and εὐλογημένος are not words of fear and trembling, nor are they typically voiced by the ignorant, the condemned or those in mourning. In the LXX—including, notably, Ps. 117.26, which is cited in our text—and in the New Testament, εὐλογεῖν and εὐλογημένος (like the Hebrew ברך) are usually expressions of joy, and they consistently have a very positive connotation: 'to praise', 'to extol', 'to bless', 'to greet'.[6] For this reason, it is not easy to envision the words of Ps. 118(117).26 as coming, begrudgingly or otherwise, from the lips of those for whom the messianic advent must mean only destruction. Further, what precedent is there in ancient Jewish or early Christian literature for the notion that the wicked man or the unbeliever will utter a blessing when the Lord or his messiah comes to the earth? When the Son of Man comes on the clouds of heaven with power and great glory, the faithless tribes of the earth will not bless him and God; rather will they weep and wail (Mt. 24.30; Rev. 1.7).[7]

Over against the interpretation just criticized, Mt. 23.39 = Lk. 13.35b can be understood to mean that, when the messiah comes, Jerusalem will know salvation. That is, the recitation of Ps. 118(117).26 will be offered freely and with joy. The messiah will come to his people and they will welcome him and say, 'Blessed is he who comes in the name of the Lord'. This reading, which has some scholarly support,[8] and which is more in accord with the spirit of Psalm 118(117), has against it

---

5. J.C. Fenton, *Saint Matthew* (Middlesex: Penguin, 1963), p. 377. Cf. S. Schulz, *Q: Die Spruchquelle der Evangelisten* (Zürich: Theologischer Verlag, 1972), p. 358.

6. See H. van der Kwaak, 'Die Klage über Jerusalem (Mt. 23.37-39)', *NovT* 8 (1966), pp. 165-66; W. Beyer, 'εὐλογέω κτλ.', *TDNT*, II, pp. 754-65; and J. Scharbert, 'ברך', *TDOT*, II, pp. 279-308.

7. According to E. Schweizer (*The Good News according to Matthew* [Atlanta: John Knox, 1975], p. 445), Mt. 21.9 shows 'that one can rejoice while still in ignorance, without realizing what one is doing'. This, however, hardly applies to Mt. 23.37-39, where the eschatological vindication of Jesus is in view: that event will not leave people in ignorance.

8. F. Godet, *A Commentary on the Gospel of St Luke* (Edinburgh: T. & T. Clark, 5th edn, 1957), II, pp. 131-32; I.H. Marshall, *Commentary on Luke* (NIGTC; Grand Rapids: Eerdmans, 1978), p. 577; and J. Ernst, *Das Evangelium nach Lukas* (RNT; Regensburg: Friedrich Pustet, 1977), p. 434. Schweizer (*Matthew*, p. 445) and D. Hill (*The Gospel of Matthew* [NCB; London: Oliphants, 1975], p. 316) leave the question open.

this: Mt. 23.39 = Lk. 13.35b can hardly be read in isolation, but is bound up with Mt. 23.38 = Lk. 13.35a (see below). However, Mt. 23.38 = Lk. 13.35a is a pronouncement of judgment, and if its sequel, Mt. 23.39 = Lk. 13.35b, is nothing but a straightforward declaration of salvation in the offing, the result is the coupling of discontiguous sentiments. One naturally expects a harsher note to conclude the preceding lines.[9] So if Mt. 23.39 = Lk. 13.35b is simply a promise of salvation, then one is almost compelled to treat it as a secondary—and infelicitous—addition.[10] But this is not an attractive option. Not only should one prefer, if possible, to make sense of a text as it stands, but Mt. 23.39 = Lk. 13.35b is more firmly wedded to its immediate context than has been recognized.

Concerning this last point, Ps. 118(117).26a is the Scripture quoted in Mt. 23.39 and its parallel, and the Old Testament verse is followed by this: 'We bless you from the house (בית/οἴκου) of the Lord' (118[117].26b). Now the prophecy of Mt. 23.39 = Lk. 13.35b is also joined to a statement about the 'house' (οἶκος) of the Lord: 'Behold, your house is forsaken' (Mt. 23.38 = Lk. 13.35a).[11] This is probably not to be put down to coincidence. Psalm 118(117) tells not only of worshippers blessing the one who comes in the name of the Lord (26a), it also speaks of a blessing that comes from the house of the Lord, from the temple (26b). This fact best explains why Q's assertion about the forsaken house—which we take to include Jerusalem and the temple[12]—

9. Cf. van der Kwaak, 'Klage über Jerusalem', p. 615.

10. Cf. R. Bultmann, *The History of the Synoptic Tradition* (New York: Harper & Row, rev. edn, 1963), p. 115.

11. Matthew adds ἔρημος, 'desolate', at least according to most early MSS.

12. Scholars have debated whether the οἶκος of Mt. 23.38 = Lk. 13.35a is the temple or Jerusalem; see, e.g., O.H. Steck, *Israel und das gewaltsame Geschick der Propheten* (WMANT, 23; Neukirchen-Vluyn: Neukirchener, 1967), p. 228 n. 3; D.E. Garland, *The Intention of Matthew 23* (NovTSup, 52; Leiden: Brill, 1979), pp. 198-200; and F.D. Weinert, 'Luke, the Temple, and Jesus' Saying about Jerusalem's Abandoned House (Lk. 13.34-35)', *CBQ* 44 (1982), pp. 75-76. But it is not necessary to distinguish here between temple and city. Jewish 'texts dealing with the Temple always implicitly, and usually explicitly, implicate the city, just as Jerusalem became the quintessence of the land, so also the Temple became the quintessence of Jerusalem'. As far as the ancient literature is concerned, one may speak of 'the interpenetration or the identification of the City and the Temple and the indiscriminate transition from the one to the other'. So W.D. Davies, *The Gospel and the Land* (Berkeley: University of California Press, 1974), pp. 152 and 144, respectively. For texts and discussion see further, pp. 144-45 and 150-54; also L.R. Fisher, 'The Temple Quarter', *JSS* 8 (1963), pp. 34-41.

is accompanied by another which concerns the coming redemption. Mt. 23.38 = Lk. 13.35a implies that Jerusalem and its temple have fallen into sin and hence are headed for disaster; cf. Mk 11.17;13.2; 14.58; and Lk. 23.27-31. It follows that the temple in the capital cannot be, as it is in Ps. 118(117).26, the source of any proper blessing. It likewise follows that those in the temple do not now bless God's spokesman, Jesus, he who will someday come as the messiah. But this means that the words of Ps. 118(117).26, if they be understood (as they are in Mt. 23.39 = Lk. 13.35b) as prophetic,[13] must refer to some time yet ahead. And this is precisely what one finds in our synoptic text: the time for the blessing of the one who comes in the name of the Lord is moved into the future. So it appears that Mt. 23.38-39 = Lk. 13.35 reflects a consistent interpretation of Ps. 118(117).26. 'Your house is forsaken' is the reason why there is presently no fulfillment of the prophetic Psalm, why the exclamation, 'Blessed is he who comes in the name of the Lord', is thought of as outstanding. The lines from Q are accordingly best regarded as a unit, which puts a question mark over any interpretation that requires us to divide them.

There is a third possible interpretation for Mt. 23.39 = Lk. 13.35b, one which, I urge, should be adopted. 'Until you say' (ἕως ἂν εἴπητε or ἕως ἥξει ὅτε[14]) can be understood to signal a conditional sentence.[15] The text then means not, when the messiah comes, his people will bless him, but rather, when his people bless him, the messiah will come. In other words, the date of the redemption is contingent upon Israel's acceptance of the person and work of Jesus. Four considerations bolster this interpretation.

First, belief in the contingency of the time of the final redemption is well-attested in Jewish sources of the second century and later. The following passages are typical: (1) R. Eliezer b. Hyrcanus (ca. 80–120 CE) is purported to have said that *if* Israel does not repent she will not be

---

13. In the early church Ps. 118 was viewed as containing prophecies of the messianic advent; it was an important source of *testimonia*. Note Acts 2.33; 4.11; Mk 11.9-10; 12.10; and 1 Pet. 2.7 and see B. Lindars, *New Testament Apologetic* (London: SCM Press, 1961), pp. 43-44, 111-12, 169-74, 179-80, 184-86. There is also evidence that Ps. 118 was interpreted messianically in Judaism; see E. Werner, ' "Hosanna" in the Gospels', *JBL* 65 (1946), pp. 97-122 and J. Jeremias, *The Eucharistic Words of Jesus* (London: SCM Press, 1966), pp. 256-60.

14. See n. 1 above.

15. Cf. van der Kwaak, 'Klage über Jerusalem', pp. 165-70.

delivered; but *if* she does repent she will be delivered (*b. Sanh.* 97b).[16]
(2) According to R. Simeon b. Yoḥai (ca. 140–160 CE), *if* the nation
would keep only two Sabbaths, the Lord would immediately usher in
salvation (*b. Šab.* 118b). (3) In *b. Sanh.* 98a we read that Ze'iri (middle
Amoraic) declared in the name of R. Ḥanina b. Ḥama (early Amoraic)
that the Son of David will not come until no conceited men remain in
Israel. (4) *Sifre Deut.* §41 (on Deut. 11.13; 97b, Tannaitic) announces
that *if* Israel were to keep the Law, God would therewith send Elijah.
Similar sentiments are expressed in, among other places, *b. B. Bat.* 10a
(R. Judah, ca. 170–200 CE), *b. Sanh.* 97b (R. Samuel b. Nahmani
[middle Amoraic] in the name of R. Jonathan [early Amoraic]), *b. Sanh.*
98a (R. Alexandri, early Amoraic), *b. Yom.* 86b (R. Jonathan, early
Amoraic), and *y. Ta'an.* 63d (R. Joshua b. Levi, early Aromaic). In
addition to the wealth of the relevant rabbinic material, Acts 3.19-21—
which probably contains pre-Lukan tradition—supplies firm evidence
that belief in a contingent eschatology could be found already in the
first century.[17] Moreover, there are a number of places in the
Pseudepigrapha where repentance and the consummation of the age are
held together, and in some of these it seems likely that repentance is
assumed to be a precondition for the coming redemption.[18] Possibilities

16. It should be noted that R. Eliezer's statement occurs in a debate with
R. Joshua, who takes the other side: the redemption will come even before Israel
repents. For discussion of this debate, see L. Landman, 'Introduction', in L. Landman
(ed.), *Messianism in the Talmudic Era* (New York: Ktav, 1979), pp. 19-23 and
E.E. Urbach, 'Redemption and Repentance in Talmudic Judaism', in R.J. Zwi
Werblowsky and C.J. Bleeker (eds.), *Types of Redemption* (Studies in the History of
Religion, 18; Leiden: Brill, 1970), pp. 191-206.

17. For discussion of Acts 3.19-21, see especially R.F. Zehnle, *Peter's Pentecost
Discourse* (SBLMS, 15; Nashville: Abingdon Press, 1971), pp. 45-60, 71-75 and
F. Hahn, 'Das Problem alter christologischer Überlieferungen in der Apostelgeschichte
unter besonderer Berücksichtigung von Act 3, 19-21', in J. Kramer (ed.), *Les Actes
des Apôtres: Traditions, rédaction, théologie* (BETL, 48; Gembloux: J. Duculot;
Leuven: Leuven University Press, 1979), pp. 129-54.

18. We cannot here enter into the problem created by the juxtaposition of apocalyptic determinism and a contingent eschatology in some of the intertestamental literature—except to observe that the undeniable contradiction is not extraordinary but
simply one more instance of those paradoxes or antinomies that run throughout all
religious traditions, including the biblical. Is the conjoining of a *Naherwartung* with
belief in the conditional nature of prophecy any more difficult than the rabbinic statements that hold together divine foreknowledge and human free-will? 'All is foreseen,
but freedom of choice is given' (*m. Ab.* 3.16). One can hardly answer, Yes, especially

include *T. Dan* 6.4 (1st or 2nd cent. BCE?), *T. Sim.* 6.2-7 (1st or 2nd cent. BCE?), *T. Jud.* 23.5 (1st or 2nd cent. BCE?), *Ass. Mos.* 1.18 (2nd cent. BCE, or 1st cent. CE), *2 Bar.* 78.7 (late 1st or early 2nd cent. CE), and *Apoc. Abr.* 29 (2nd cent. CE?).[19] Finally, *4 Ezra* (late 1st, early 2nd cent. CE) rebuts the thought that the Kingdom of God has been delayed on account of the sins of those who dwell on the earth[20] and thereby evidently discounts the claim—presumably made by someone known to the author—that righteousness might hasten the climax of the eschato-logical drama.[21]

Secondly, ἕως can indicate a contingent state in Greek sentences in which the realization of the apodosis is dependent upon the realization of the protasis.[22] In such cases the meaning of ἕως is not simply temporal ('until')[23] but properly conditional (close to 'unless'). Mt. 5.26 =

in view of the 'essential irrationality' of eschatological thinking; see R. Otto, *The Kingdom of God and the Son of Man* (London: Lutterworth, rev. edn, 1943), pp. 59-63. It is also to be observed that several apocalypses combine the ideas of deter-minism and human freedom; contrast, e.g., *1 En.* 41.8; *2 Bar.* 42.7; and *Apoc. Abr.* 22 with *1 En.* 43.2; *2 Bar.* 54.15, 19; 85.7; and *Apoc. Abr.* 26.

19. In *Apoc. Abr.* 29 we have a vision in which righteous men 'hasten' the glory of God's name: 'And then shall righteous men of thy seed be left in the number which is kept secret by me, hastening in the glory of My Name to the place prepared beforehand for them...' (Box). Cf. the σπεύδοντας of 2 Pet. 3.12.

20. 4.39: 'It is perhaps on account of us that the time of threshing is delayed for the righteous—on account of the sins of those who dwell on earth' (RSV). The seer goes on to reject this notion; see 4.40-43.

21. We should also perhaps observe that in the *Testament* (or *Assumption*) *of Moses*, it is the death of Taxo and his sons—a death that is actively sought—which 'forces' the end; see J. Licht, 'Taxo, or the Apocalyptic Doctrine of Vengeance', *JJS* 12 (1961), pp. 95-103 and D.C. Carlson, 'Vengeance and Angelic Mediation in *Testament of Moses* 9 and 10', *JBL* 101 (1982), pp. 85-95. And it is interesting that *Ps. Sol.* 17 places the promise of redemption within a context of moral exhortation and thus seems to assume that national penitence can hasten the divine intervention; cf. S. Mowickel, *He That Cometh* (Oxford: Basil Blackwell, 1956), p. 297.

22. Cf. W.W. Goodwin, *Syntax of the Moods and Tenses of the Greek Verb* (New York: St Martin's, 1965), pp. 235-37.

23. In some instances, of course, ἕως, like the Hebrew and Aramaic עד (with which we shall be concerned below), loses altogether the idea of termination and expresses 'a limit which is not absolute (terminating the preceding action), but only relative, beyond which the action or state described in the principal clause still continues' (E. Kautzsch and A.E. Cowley, *Gesenius' Hebrew Grammar* [Oxford: Clarendon Press, 2nd edn, 1910], p. 503). See, e.g., Gen. 26.13; 49.10; Ps. 112(111).8; Mt. 10.23; Mk 9.1; and 13.19.

Lk. 15.59, Mt. 18.30, Acts 23.12, and 2 Thess. 2.7 are examples from the New Testament.[24] Similarly, the Hebrew or Aramaic עַד—which, presumably, lies behind the ἕως of Mt. 23.39 = Lk. 13.35b if we have to do with a word of Jesus or the Palestinian community (cf. the Syriac: עדמה)—sometimes signifies more than the inevitable passing of a temporal span: it can also be used when an envisioned state is contingent upon some act that may or may not be performed.[25] Illustrations of this are: Gen. 19.22: 'I can do nothing until (עַד; LXX: ἕως) you arrive there'. Gen. 29.8: 'We cannot water the sheep until (עַד; LXX: ἕως) all the flocks are gathered and the stone is rolled away from the mouth of the well'. Deut. 22.2: 'It shall be with you until (עַד; LXX: ἕως ἄν) your brother seeks it' (cf. 11QTemple 64.15). Ezra 4.21: 'Make a decree... that this city not be built again until (עַד) a decree is made by me'. *Ahiqar* 130-31: 'Rest for your soul do not take until (עַד) you have paid back the loan'. Cowley 2, 17: 'Ours you have a right to seize until (עַד) you are indemnitied in full'. 1QS 7.19: 'No member of the Covenant who blatantly takes away a word from all that is commanded shall touch the sacred meal...until (עַד) his deeds are cleansed from all error'. 11QTemple 58.18: 'And he will not go forth until (עַד) he has first gone before the high priest'. *m. Ber.* 7.5: 'The blessing over wine may not be said until (עַד) water be added to it'. *b. Sanh.* 98a: 'The Son of David will not come until (עַד) all judges and officers are gone from Israel'. *Lev. R.* 24.3 (on Lev. 19.2): 'They should not go away from this place until (עַד) they notice a clot of blood on the surface of the water'. *y. Ter.* 46c: 'They shall not see me until (עַד) they have taken a bath'. In most of the texts just cited, 'unless' would be no less adequate a translation than 'until'.

Thirdly, the structure of Mt. 23.39 = Lk. 13.35b argues for the conditional interpretation. There appears to have been a standard way of expressing one's belief as to what condition(s) must be realized before the eschatological redemption could come. Consider the following passages:

b. Sanh. 98a: Ze'iri (middle Amoraic) said in R. Ḥanina's name (late Tannaitic): 'The Son of David will not come until (עַד) there are no conceited men in Israel'.

---

24. Cf. van der Kwaak, 'Klage über Jerusalem', p. 170.
25. For further discussion of עַד, see K. Beyer, *Semitische Syntax im Neuen Testament* (SUNT, 1; Göttingen: Vandenhoeck & Ruprecht, 1962), p. 132 n. 1.

b. Sanh. 98a: R. Ḥama b. Ḥannina (early Amoraic) said: 'The Son of David will not come until (עד) even the pettiest kingdom ceases to hold power over Israel'.

b. Sanh. 98a: R. Simlai (early Amoraic) said in the name of R. Eleazar b. Simeon (late Tannaitic): 'The Son of David will not come until (עד) all judges and officers are gone from Israel'.

b. Sanh. 98a: R. Ḥanina (late Tannaitic) said: 'The Son of David will not come until (עד) a fish is sought for an invalid and cannot be procured'.

b. 'Abod Zar. 5a: R. Jose (ca. 130 CE) said: 'The Son of David will not come until (עד) all the souls destined for bodies are exhausted'.

b. Sanh. 98b: Rab (last half of the second century CE) said: 'The Son of David will not come until (עד) the (Roman) power enfolds Israel for nine months'.

Each of these texts has the same structure, which can be set forth thus:

- (a)   statement about the messianic advent with adverbial particle of negation attached ('The Son of David will not come')
- (b)   conditional particle (עד)
- (c)   condition to be met (in Israel) for fulfillment of the messianic advent (e.g. 'no conceited men in Israel').

Now Mt. 23.39 = Lk. 13.35b can be analyzed as having precisely the same structure:

- (a)   statement about the messianic advent with adverbial particle of negation attached ('You will not see me', 'me' being Jesus, the messiah)
- (b)   conditional particle (ἕως)
- (c)   condition to be met (in Israel) for fulfillment of the messianic advent (those in Jerusalem utter, 'Blessed is he who comes in the name of the Lord', and thereby acknowledge the person and work of Jesus).

It therefore appears that the synoptic verse sets forth, in a traditional fashion, a condition for the great redemption.

Fourthly, we have argued that whereas, on the one hand, Mt. 23.39 =

Lk. 13.35b is not likely to be a statement of utter rejection, on the other hand, an unqualified announcement of salvation does not follow well upon Mt. 23.37-38 = Lk. 13.34-35a (see above). The conditional interpretation commends itself by finding a middle ground that avoids the pitfalls of the other alternatives. The thought of judgment is present because, for now, Israel has not received the messenger of God; she has refused to accept the one sent to her, and therefore the redemption has not come. And yet, despite this element of judgment, the thought of salvation is also present. For Jesus affirms that, if she will, Jerusalem can, in the end, bless in the name of the Lord the one who will come, and her doing so, that is, her repentance, will lead to deliverance.

Even if it does not require a *Sitz im Leben* within Judaism or early church, we cannot be certain that the lament over Jerusalem, Mt. 23.37-39 = Lk. 13.34-35, was spoken by Jesus.[26] But whatever one concludes concerning the genesis of our text, its conclusion, Mt. 23.39 = Lk. 13.35b, was evidently formulated to give expression to the convict that, if Israel would repent, the end would come. The verse should thus be compared with Acts 3.19-21, in which Peter exhorts the people of Jerusalem to repent and turn again, in order that times of refreshing might come from the Lord, that is, that he might send Jesus the messiah. Both the text from Q and the sentence from Peter's sermon make the time of the Kingdom's coming hinge upon the repentance of God's people (cf. also 2 Pet. 3.11-12 and *2 Clem.* 12).

---

26. At least five points can be made in favor of authenticity. (1) The threat against Jerusalem and its holy place has its parallel in Jesus' prediction of the end of the temple (Mk. 13.2 and parallels). (2) Jesus elsewhere spoke of the violent fate that the true prophet must suffer (Lk. 13.31-33; Lk. 6.22 = Mt. 5.11-12; Mt. 23.34-36 = Lk. 11.49-51). (3) The fate of being stoned is perhaps envisioned for the speaker (so J. Jeremias, *New Testament Theology* [New York: Charles Scribner's Sons, 1971], p. 284). (4) There are synoptic passages which, if authentic, show us that Jesus did not think of the time of the eschatological redemption as unalterably fixed; see, e.g., Lk. 13.6-9; 18.1-8; and Mk 13.18. (5) No explicit claim to messiahship is made: the status of the speaker is only indirectly indicated, which is consistent with what we otherwise know of Jesus.

JSNT 38 (1990), pp. 37-66

JESUS' REFUSAL TO PRODUCE A 'SIGN' (MARK 8.11-13)

Jeffrey Gibson

The Pharisees came out and began to dispute with him, seeking from him a sign from heaven, testing him. And he sighed deeply in his spirit and said, 'Why does this generation seek a sign? Amen, I say to you, no sign shall be given to this generation!' And he left them, and getting into the boat again he departed to the other side.

In Mk 8.11-13 Jesus is portrayed as solemnly and adamantly refusing to accede to a demand made of him by the Pharisees. The demand for a σημεῖον, a 'sign',[1] is specifically for a 'token of trustworthiness', a 'means of confirmation' to authenticate Jesus' claims that God stands behind all his words and works.[2] But why does Jesus say 'no' so categorically to this demand? Why, according to Mark, does he not grant what is asked of him?

The critical consensus in this regard is that Jesus refuses the Pharisees' demand because, in Mark's portrayal of things, Jesus feels his ministry is by its very nature self-authenticating, needing no external or additional proof of its validity. To offer such proof would not only be a concession to unbelief, but would make unlikely, if not impossible, the response of radical faith which Jesus demands from all who are confronted by what he says and does.[3]

---

1. Here and throughout this article the English equivalent for σημεῖον is placed in inverted commas to distinguish it as a technical term and to make clear that as such it has a meaning that is different from other senses that σημεῖον bore in the ancient world.

2. On this, see K.H. Rengstorf, 'σημεῖον', *TDNT*, VII, pp. 200-61 esp. pp. 234-36; and especially O. Linton, 'The Demand for a Sign from Heaven (Mk 8.11-12 and par.)', *ST* 19 (1965), pp. 112-29.

3. Among the many commentators who hold this view are E.P. Gould (*A Critical*

Now, there is much to be said for this. After all, according to Mark, it is those who are 'outside', those who have willfully 'blinded' themselves to seeing and recognizing God's activity when it is in their midst, who make the demand.[4] And it is true that later on in his Gospel, within his story of the crucifixion (i.e. in Mk 15.28-32), Mark portrays Jesus as tacitly refusing to use a 'sign' to engender belief in the truth of his mission and ministry even when he could have done so.[5] I wish to argue,

and Exegetical Commentary on the Gospel according to St Mark [ICC; Edinburgh: T. & T. Clark, 1896], p. 145); Alan Menzies (*The Earliest Gospel* [London: Macmillan, 1901], p. 163); H.B. Swete (*The Gospel according to St Mark* [London: Macmillan, 1905], p. 168); A.W.F. Blunt (*The Gospel according to Saint Mark* [Oxford: Clarendon Press, 1929], p. 193); A.E.J. Rawlinson (*St Mark* [London: Methuen, 1931], p. 257); B.H. Branscomb (*The Gospel of Mark* [London: Hodder & Stoughton, 1937], p. 138); C.E.B. Cranfield (*The Gospel according to St Mark* [Cambridge: Cambridge University Press, 1959], pp. 257-58); G. Delling ('Botschaft und Wunder im Wirken Jesu', in H. Ristow and K. Matthiae [eds.], *Der historische Jesus und der kerygmatische Christus* [Berlin: Evangelische Verlagsanstalt, 1960], pp. 389-402); V. Taylor (*The Gospel according to St Mark* [London: Macmillan, 1961], p. 361); K. Rengstorf ('σημεῖον', p. 235); D.E. Nineham (*St Mark* [Baltimore: Pelican, 1963], pp. 210-12); C.F.D. Moule (*The Gospel according to Mark* [Cambridge: Cambridge University Press, 1965], pp. 60-61); K. Tagawa (*Miracles et évangile: La pensée personnelle de l'évangeliste Marc* [Paris: Presses Universitaires de France, 1966], pp. 75-80); E.J. Mally ('The Gospel according to Mark', in R.E. Brown, J.A. Fitzmyer, R.E. Murphy [eds.], *The Jerome Biblical Commentary* [Englewood Cliffs, NJ: Prentice-Hall, 1968], p. 39); E. Schweizer (*The Good News according to Mark* [London: SPCK, 1971], p. 159); R.P. Martin (*Mark: Evangelist and Theologian* [Exeter: Paternoster Press, 1972], pp. 172-74); W.H. Kelber (*The Kingdom in Mark* [Philadelphia: Fortress Press, 1974], p. 61); W.L. Lane (*The Gospel according to Mark* [Grand Rapids: Eerdmans, 1974], pp. 277-78); W. Barclay (*The Gospel of Mark* [Philadelphia: Westminster Press, 1975], pp. 175-76); H. Anderson (*The Gospel of Mark* [London: Oliphants, 1976], p. 91); W. Harrington (*Mark* [Dublin: Veritas, 1979], p. 111); L. Williamson, Jr (*Mark* [Atlanta: John Knox, 1983], p. 143).

4. On the Pharisees as among 'those outside', see J. Coutts, '"Those Outside" (Mark 4.10-12)', *SE*, II (TU, 87; Berlin: Akademie Verlag, 1964), pp. 155-57. On 'blindness', i.e., willful refusal to acknowledge the presence of God, as an identifying characteristic of 'those outside', see Mk 4.12 and E.E. Lemcio, 'External Evidence for the Structure and Function of Mark 4.1-20, 7.13-23, and 8.14-21', *JTS* 29 (1978), p. 335. See also R. Pesch, *Das Markusevangelium*, II (HTKNT, 2.1; Freiburg: Herder, 1977), p. 223 and M. Boucher, *The Mysterious Parable: A Literary Study* (CBQMS, 6; Washington, DC: Catholic Biblical Association, 1977), pp. 60, 84.

5. Cf. Mk 15.27-32.

however, that despite this the supposition is untenable. Something other than a blanket opposition to offering proof of the validity of his ministry and message must account for the Markan Jesus' refusal to comply with the Pharisees' demand. In support of this claim I shall attempt to show that in Mk 2.1-12, the story of the healing of the paralytic, Mark portrays Jesus as actually producing a 'sign' to prove that his proclamation is 'of God' when the truth of that proclamation and its divine origin are questioned.

I

Does Mark's story of the healing of the paralytic present Jesus as producing without compunction an open proof of the validity of his message and ministry? At first glance, the answer might seem to be 'no'. For none of Jesus' actions in Mk 2.1-12 is specifically labeled a 'sign'. Nor does the word σημεῖον appear within those verses. But this is not decisive. The issue is hardly whether Mark has applied a given designation to the actions that he there has Jesus undertake. Rather, it is whether Mark has cast the basic features of those actions—their overall pattern, the circumstances prompting them, the intention behind them—in terms of the features characteristic of the phenomenon of 'signs'.[6]

6. The nature and extent of Mark's redactional and/or compositional contribution to the present form of 2.1-12 is still a matter of debate. Some commentators, such as R. Pesch (*Das Markusevangelium*, I [HTKNT, 2.1; Freiburg: Herder, 1976], pp. 151-62), J. Gnilka (*Das Evangelium nach Markus* (Mk 1–8, 26) [EKKNT, 2.1; Zürich: Neukirchener Verlag, 1978], pp. 95-98), and G.H. Boobyer ('Mark II, 10a and the Interpretation of the Healing of the Paralytic', *HTR* 47 [1954], pp. 115-20) see it as a matter only of Mark slightly modifying, or adding to, the wording of a completely unified pre-Markan story. Others, such as R. Bultmann (*The History of the Synoptic Tradition* [Oxford: Basil Blackwell, 2nd edn, 1968], p. 15) following W. Wrede ('Zur Heilung des Gelähmten (Mc 2,1ff.)', *ZNW* 5 [1904], pp. 454-58), M. Dibelius (*From Tradition to Gospel* [Cambridge and London: James Clarke, 1934], pp. 66-68), Taylor (*Mark*, pp. 191-92), and H. Tödt (*The Son of Man in the Synoptic Tradition* [London: SCM Press, 1963], pp. 118-21) see Mark as having inserted vv. 5b-10, a section of a traditional, originally longer 'saying' (apophthegm), into a traditional healing narrative in which v. 11 originally followed v. 5a, thus giving the material now in Mk 2.1-12 a shape it never had before it came to Mark. Still others, such as Rawlinson (*Mark*, p. 25) and J. Dewey ('The Literary Structure of the Controversy Stories in Mark 2.1–3.6', *JBL* 92 [1973], pp. 394-401), argue that a large portion, if not all, of the story is wholly a Markan composition. That Mk 2.1-12 was in some way shaped by Mark's hand is, however, never doubted.

Is this, then, the case? This depends, of course, on the answer we give to another question, namely, What are the features characteristic of the phenomenon of 'signs'? These are to be uncovered by examining the references to 'signs' in the Hebrew Scriptures and the literature dependent on it.

Characteristics of the 'Signs' Phenomenon[7]
When these background texts[8] are examined with regard to what they reveal concerning the significant features of the phenomenon, five things stand out.

First, a 'sign' is always a public event. Its occurrence is meant to be seen or perceived, as well as publicly acknowledged as having happened.

Secondly, a 'sign' happens—or is anticipated as happening—not accidentally or fortuitously, but on command. It is something that can be sought, promised, worked, or produced.

Thirdly, a 'sign' is sought, promised, worked or produced for one of two reasons: either to certify the truth of a distrusted prophecy, or to establish the validity of a disputed claim that a certain course of action and the person initiating it are 'of God'. The narrative and thematic context of such activity is typically as follows:

1.   A claimant to divine authority or insight into the mind of God engages in an activity, or utters a prophecy or doctrinal statement, that in his eyes bears God's approval.

---

7.   For the substance of the following material I am indebted to the comprehensive discussion of 'signs' carried out by Linton in his article 'The Demand for a Sign' referred to in note 2 above.

8.   References to 'signs', 'tokens of trustworthiness' in biblical literature are many and various. They are mentioned in the Pentateuch (Gen. 4.15; Exod. 3.12; 4.8-9; Num. 14.11, 22; Deut. 13.1-12), the Historical Writings (Judg. 6.17; 1 Sam. 2.4; 10.1; 14.10; 1 Kgs 13.3; 2 Kgs 19.29; 20.8, 9; 2 Chron. 32.24; Neh. 9.10), the Prophets (Isa. 7.10, 14; 37.30; 38.7, 22), and the Wisdom Literature (Pss. 78 [77].43; 105 [104].27; 135 [134].9) of the Old Testament, in the Pseudepigrapha (*4 Ezra* 4.51; 6.11, 20; 7.25; 8.63), in Josephus (*War* 2.13.4 §258; 6.4.6 §258; 6.5.2 §288; *Ant.* 8.11.4 §347; 10.2.1 §28; 20.5.1 §97-99; 20.8.6 §168), in the Dead Sea Scrolls (1Q27 1 cols. 1, 5), in the *Mishnah* (*b. B. Meṣ.* 59b), in the *Babylonian Talmud* (*b. Sanh.* 89b, 98a, 98b), in the *Midrash* (*Exod. R.* 5.13 [on Exod. 4.30]) and in the New Testament (Mk 13.4; 13.22; [16.17, 20]; Mt. 12.39; 16.4; 24.3, 4; Lk. 2.12; 11.16, 29; 21.7; Jn 2.18; 6.30; Acts 4.16; 8.16; 14.3; 1 Cor. 1.22; 2 Thess. 2.9; Rev. 13.13-14).

2.   Observers are struck by the fact that the action or the utter-
     ance is either (a) strange and surprising, or (b) contrary to
     common sense, conventional wisdom or practical considera-
     tions, or, worse, (c) a direct contravention of Mosaic Law.
     Given this, they conclude that the truth of the action or utter-
     ance and its divine origin are not immediately apparent.

3.   The claimant, wishing to secure acceptance of what he has said
     or done, responds to the skepticism with which his action or
     utterances is greeted by proposing (or agreeing to submit to) a
     kind of test. He selects (or accedes to a demand for) some phe-
     nomenon and promises to have it come to pass. He does this
     with the understanding that should the phenomenon occur
     both as and when he says it will, the skepticism surrounding his
     action or utterance will then vanish.

When, for instance, Ahaz doubts Isaiah's prophecy that 'within sixty-five
years Ephraim shall be broken', Isaiah offers to produce a 'sign' (cf. Isa.
7.8ff.). When Isaiah wants to prove to Hezekiah that, contrary to all available evidence, Hezekiah is not to die, Isaiah proposes to work a 'sign',
letting Hezekiah himself choose between two such phenomena, one that
is difficult or one that is 'easier' (LXX κοῦφον) to produce (2 Kgs. 20.1-
10; cf. Isa. 38.1-20). Jonathan and his armor bearer expect to receive a
'sign' to let them know that, as promised, they will receive divine protection when they go up into battle against the Philistines (1 Sam. 14.10,
cf. v. 16). Theudas and other so-called 'Sign Prophets'[9] promise to work
specific 'signs' expressly to substantiate their respective claims that they
were anointed by God and divinely commissioned to the sacred purpose
of delivering the Jewish nation from the yoke of Roman oppression (cf.
Josephus, *War* 2.259, 261-63; *Ant.* 20.97-99, 167-68, 188). A 'sign' is
demanded of Jesus when he claims that divine authority stands behind
his 'cleansing' of the Temple (Jn 2.18, cf. 2.13-18, esp. v. 16), and, later,
when he teaches that he is sent from God (cf. Jn 6.29-30). A 'sign',
therefore, is an event that was thought of as having the power to certify
or confirm something that could otherwise be doubted and dismissed.

The fourth thing that stands out about 'signs' in texts referring to

---

9.   On this as the proper or appropriate designation for Theudas and figures like
him, see P.W. Barnett, 'The Jewish Sign Prophets—AD 40–70—Their Intentions and
Origin', *NTS* 27 (1981), pp. 679-97. The activities and aims of these men are
discussed in more detail below.

them is that the function peculiar to a 'sign'—that is, its ability to prove
the truth of a distrusted utterance or the legitimacy of a claim that a
person and his actions are 'of God'—is grounded in the public experience of a coincidence between a prior prophecy (what is designated as
the 'sign') and a subsequent event (its actual manifestation). For instance,
in the story of Jonathan and his armor bearer (1 Sam. 14.6-15) Jonathan
is initially skeptical of the idea, placed in his mind by God, that if he but
tries, he will be able to conquer a garrison of Philistines on his own. It is
only when the requested authenticating 'sign' actually occurs that he
believes God and engages the Philistines in combat. Indeed, Jonathan
himself admits that if the 'sign' had not come to pass, he would not
have risked the undertaking, which, on purely practical grounds, was
extremely foolhardy (cf. vv. 9-10). Accordingly, a 'sign' does its work
when it is effectuated in exact conformity with its predicted or
previously stipulated 'shape'.

The fifth and last thing that stands out in references to 'signs' is that,
as either promised or manifested, a 'sign' does not need to have a spec-
tacular content in order to stand as a token of trustworthiness. As the
Isaiah/Ahaz story shows, 'signs' whose content is ordinary[10] are offered
or accepted as 'proof' as readily as those which are stupendous or extra-
ordinarily miraculous (e.g. the 'signs' offered by Theudas and the
other 'Sign Prophets').[11] The important thing about a 'sign's' 'shape' is
not whether it is in itself miraculous or ordinary, but whether, once
manifested, it then appears in complete correspondence with its own
terms, whatever they have been stated to be.

Jesus and 'Signs' in Mk 2.1-12
With all of this in mind, let us now turn to Mark's story of the healing of
the paralytic. The story opens with Jesus besieged in a house in
Capernaum by a crowd which is eager to hear his word (Mk 2.1). It
then goes on to narrate the attempt of four men to bring a paralytic to
Jesus so that Jesus might heal him. When the men find that the press of
bodies denies them normal access to Jesus, they go up to the roof of the

10. The 'sign' that Isaiah here offers to Ahaz is that a young woman whom Isaiah
had no reason to know was pregnant, would shortly be found to be so and would give
birth to a boy (on this, see J.L. McKenzie, 'Behold the Virgin', in his *The New
Testament without Illusion* [New York: Crossroad, 1982], pp. 103-13, esp. pp. 105-
106).
11. On the exact 'shape' of these 'signs', see below.

house, break open the part of the ceiling directly above Jesus, and lower the paralytic down to him (Mk 2.3-4). Jesus, the story notes, is impressed with the obvious lengths to which they were willing to go to bring the paralytic into contact with his healing power. But he does not at this point act to fulfill their desires. Instead, he makes a formal statement that the paralytic's sins are forgiven (Mk 2.5). At this point particular members if the crowd, religious authorities whom Mark calls Scribes, having heard Jesus' declaration, realize that Jesus has in effect made a claim to be in possession of, and authorized to use, a power that they believed was reserved to God alone. The claim is all too much for them, and privately they refuse to accept it (Mk 2.6-7). But Jesus becomes aware of what is going on in their minds (Mk 2.8a), and in response to their musings he does two things. First, he openly expresses disappoint-ment with the Scribes for doubting his word and the claim implicit within it (Mk 2.8b). Secondly, he proposes a test whereby the Scribes may see for themselves that their doubt is groundless (Mk 2.9), and then goes ahead and publicly submits himself to it (Mk 2.10-11). The story then ends with a notice that Jesus passes the test successfully (Mk 2.11), and that he is roundly acknowledged as having done so (Mk 2.12).

When the story is set against what I have said regarding 'signs', it is readily apparent that Jesus is there portrayed as offering and producing a 'sign'.

For in the first place, the type of conflict that here prompts Jesus to cure the paralytic is the same as that which, according to the biblical model, would prompt a 'sign' worker to produce a 'sign', namely the rejection of a claim—in this case over both Jesus' possession of author-ity to forgive sins and whether or not his proclamation in v. 5 effectuates what it proclaims—that at a given time, one is speaking or acting on God's behalf with divine approval.

Secondly, the response that Jesus secures from the Scribes by healing the paralytic is identical with that which the biblical model shows us was won by 'sign' workers from their interlocutors when they effectu-ated the 'signs' they had added to their disputed words or deeds. The Scribes accept the truth of the utterance or the implications of the action for which the subsidiary prophecy stands as proof.[12]

---

12. We must take seriously the fact that Mark does not exclude the Scribes from those who marvel at what Jesus does in his healing of the Paralytic. It is, Mark notes at Mk 2.12, specifically 'all' (πάντας) who were present on this occasion who 'were astounded and gave glory to God' (ὥστε ἐξίστασθαι πάντας καὶ δοξάζειν τὸν

Thirdly, the activity that Jesus immediately resorts to after the Scribes' initial rejection of his words, and all they imply, is formally the same as that which Old Testament, Jewish, and Christian 'sign' workers engage in when the truth of their words or deeds is challenged. Like those 'sign' workers, Jesus responds to the gauntlet thrown down against the validity and the import of his statement, not by initiating a discussion or argument, but by offering to make something happen. Given its context, in function this is nothing less than offering a 'sign'.[13]

Finally, and perhaps most importantly, Jesus says that his reason for undertaking the cure of the paralytic is precisely to prove the claim that he has made in Mk 2.5. He explicitly declares at Mk 2.10 that he performs the healing so that those who have expressed doubt over the truth and the import of this claim may 'know that the Son of Man has authority on earth to forgive sins' (ἵνα δὲ εἰδῆτε ὅτι ἐξουσίαν ἔχει ὁ υἱὸς τοῦ ἀνθρώπου ἀφιέναι ἁμαρτίας ἐπὶ τῆς γῆς, v. 10).[14] In other

---

Θεόν). To say, with T.A. Burkill, that in Mk 2.1-12 'The impression produced [by the healing] on the hostile Scribes finds no mention, for they would hardly be included among those who glorify God in verse 12, and we are perhaps meant to take it for granted that they are temporarily put to silence' (*Mysterious Revelation* [Ithaca, NY: Cornell University Press, 1963], p. 127) is to engage in special pleading.

13. See M.D. Hooker, *The Son of Man in Mark* (London: SPCK, 1967), p. 88. In support of this, it is important to note that Mark has cast Jesus' offer to make something happen in such a way as to call to mind the similar offer on the part of Isaiah in the 'sign' story of the healing of Hezekiah in 2 Kgs 20.1-11. According to Mark, Jesus, like Isaiah, points up two courses of action that he is willing to take to meet the skepticism that he has encountered (cf. Mk 2.9 with 2 Kgs 20.9). Also, as does Isaiah, Jesus allows the decision as to which course of action he is to take to be made for him. Finally, note the verbal resemblance between Jesus' question in Mk 2.9, 'Which is easier...' (τί ἐστιν εὐκοπώτερον, κτλ.) and Hezekiah's remark in the LXX of 2 Kgs 20.10, 'It is easy...' (καὶ εἶπεν Ἐζεκίας, κοῦφον, κτλ.).

14. J. Duplacy, following a suggestion first made by D.S. Sharp in *ExpTim* 38 (1927), p. 428, contends that here ἵνα with the subjunctive εἰδῆτε expresses a command and therefore this verse should be translated 'Know that the Son of Man has authority on earth to forgive sins' ('Marc II, 10, note de syntaxe', in *Mélanges A. Robert* [Travaux de l'Institut Catholique de Paris, 4; Paris: Bloud et Gay, 1957], pp. 424-26); see also C.J. Cadoux, 'The Imperatival Use of *hina* in the New Testament', *JTS* 42 (1944), pp. 165-73; H.G. Meecham, 'The Imperatival Use of ἵνα in the New Testament', *JTS* 43 (1942), p. 179; and the summary of the evidence by C.F.D. Moule in his *An Idiom-Book of New Testament Greek* (Cambridge: Cambridge University Press, 2nd edn, 1959), p. 144. If this is the case, then Jesus' intention to prove his authority is all the more pronounced.

words, Jesus himself here identifies his cure of the paralytic as a 'sign'.

Given all of this, I think I am justified in claiming that, despite the absence in Mk 2.1-12 of the word σημεῖον or the explicit labeling of any of Jesus' actions as a 'sign', Mark's story of the healing of a paralytic presents Jesus as validating his actions or utterances by means of a 'sign'. Indeed, to my mind, the story actually makes clear that in Mark's eyes, Jesus was quite ready ordinarily not only to produce 'signs' but to offer to do so when he or others felt they were needed. To argue that it says otherwise[15] is, I think, to refuse to allow both the story and Mark to speak on their own terms.[16]

This being the case, we may then dismiss as wholly untenable the conventional position on the reason why Mark has Jesus refuse to produce a 'sign' at Mk 8.11-13. In light of the evidence of Mk 2.1-12, it does not seem possible to assert that the Markan Jesus held principled reservations against involving himself in any of the activities associated with the phenomenon of 'signs'.[17]

It has, however, frequently been suggested that Mark did not mean 2.10a to be seen as a statement of Jesus to the Scribes. Rather it is a parenthetical remark addressed by the evangelist to the Christian readers of the Gospel to explain the significance of the closing phase of the healing for them (cf. Dibelius, *From Tradition to Gospel*, p. 67; Boobyer, 'Mark II, 10a', pp. 115-20; C.P. Ceroke, 'Is Mk 2, 10 a Saying of Jesus?', *CBQ* 22 (1960), pp. 369-90; Cranfield, *Mark*, p. 100; J. Murphy-O'Connor, 'Péché et communauté dans le Nouveau Testament', *RB* 74 [1967], pp. 181-85; L.S. Hay, 'The Son of Man in Mk 2.10 and 2.28', *JBL* 89 [1970], pp. 71-73; N. Perrin, 'The Christology of Mark: A Study in Methodology', in *A Modern Pilgrimage in New Testament Christology* [Philadelphia: Fortress Press, 1974], pp. 112, 116 n. 24; Lane, *Mark*, p. 98; and R.M. Fowler, *Loaves and Fishes* [SBLDS, 54; Chico, CA: Scholars Press, 1981], pp. 161-62). I do not find this conjecture convincing; it is based primarily on a questionable assumption, namely that the title 'Son of Man' is here a designation of transcendent dignity which Mark would not have Jesus publicly apply to himself so early in his ministry. For trenchant criticisms of this assumption, see Hooker, *The Son of Man in Mark*, pp. 84-85; C. Tuckett, 'The Present Son of Man', *JSNT* 14 (1982), pp. 58-81 and J.D. Kingsbury, *The Christology of Mark* (Philadelphia: Fortress Press, 1983), pp. 83-84.

15. As does, for instance, Anderson, *Mark*, p. 101.

16. 'The stated purpose of the healing was a demonstration that Jesus had the power to forgive sins. There is no escaping the language and intention of the text' (W. Wink, 'Mark 2.1-12', *Int* 38 [1984], p. 61).

17. It should be noted that both Mk 1.21-28 and 3.1-6 also provide evidence for this conclusion. In 1.21-28 Mark presents Jesus as healing a demoniac to demonstrate, in the face of mild skepticism to the contrary (cf. v. 22), that he is in rightful

II

But why, then, if Jesus in Mark is not in principle opposed to the enterprise of producing, or giving in to the demand for, 'signs', does he refuse to engage in this activity when, as Mark recounts, the Pharisees demand that he do so?

The answer lies in focusing attention on the 'sign' that the Pharisees ask for, and assuming that it is of a peculiar type, a type which the Markan Jesus would find offensive. Three observations serve to justify this assumption: in Mk 8.11-13 the 'sign' demanded of Jesus is (1) designated by a specific name; (2) associated with one expected by 'this generation'; and (3) identified as one which is 'given'.

1. *The Name of the 'Sign' Demanded of Jesus*

At Mk 8.11 Mark calls the 'sign' by a specific name. It is, he says, one which is ἀπὸ τοῦ οὐρανοῦ. Now, it is often thought that this phrase means nothing more than 'from God', and therefore what Mark is doing in using it here is making a statement concerning not the content but the 'author' of the 'sign' demanded of Jesus.[18] But this cannot be the case, for the following reasons.

In the first place, Mark had no need to specify who ultimately stood behind the 'sign'. It was of the very nature of 'signs' to be 'from God', otherwise they would never have been taken, as we have seen they were, as evidence of trustworthiness. A phrase meaning 'from God' would here be superfluous and redundant. So if Mark had merely intended that the Pharisees should be seen as content to receive any 'sign' so long as it had God as its author, he would have written only

---

possession of the authority with which he speaks (cf. D. Hill, 'Jesus and Josephus' "Messianic" Prophets', in E. Best and R.McL. Wilson (eds.), *Text and Interpretation: Studies in the New Testament Presented to Matthew Black* [Cambridge: Cambridge University Press, 1979], p. 150). In 3.1-6 Mark has Jesus propose, and then carry out, a healing of a man with a withered hand in order to show that, contrary to the opinion of Pharisees and Herodians (cf. v. 6, v. 2), his actions of 'doing good' and 'saving life' prior to this occasion (i.e. the actions described in 1.16–2.27) are authorized by God even though they sometimes fly in the face of the Mosaic Law.

18. See, for instance, Rengstorf, 'σημεῖον', p. 235, Lane; *Mark*, p. 275 n. 18; F. Hahn, *The Titles of Jesus in Christology* (London: Lutterworth, 1969), p. 378; Gnilka, *Das Evangelium nach Markus*, I, p. 306; J. Swetnam, 'No Sign of Jonah', *Bib* 66 (1985), p. 126.

'...seeking from him a "sign"' (...ζητοῦντες παρ᾽ αὐτοῦ σημεῖον, κτλ.) and not, as he does, 'seeking from him a "sign from heaven"' (ζητοῦντες παρ᾽ αὐτοῦ σημεῖον ἀπὸ τοῦ οὐρανοῦ, κτλ.).[19] In the second place, when Mark does want to designate something as having divine origin, and uses a circumlocution to do so, the phrase he employs is ἐκ τῶν οὐρανῶν (ἐξ οὐρανοῦ), not ἀπὸ τοῦ οὐρανοῦ.[20] Accordingly, Mark's calling the 'sign' demanded of Jesus ἀπὸ τοῦ οὐρανοῦ must have another purpose. And that must be to specify not the source of the 'sign', but its 'shape'.

The phrase is an appelative, and as such it indicates that the 'sign' demanded of Jesus is one of a peculiar type, in a class all of its own, distinct in its content from any or all other 'signs' that the Pharisees might have requested.[21] But in Mark's eyes then, what content did a 'sign' ἀπὸ τοῦ οὐρανοῦ have? Could he have thought it to be, as some have suggested,[22] a celestial portent? οὐρανός does sometimes mean 'sky' in Mark's Gospel (e.g. at 1.10; 4.32; 13.25). But that, according to Mark, the 'sign' demanded of Jesus was a 'sign out of the sky'—as this understanding of οὐρανοῦ would render the phrase—seems unlikely. For in the first place, 'sky' as a meaning of οὐρανός is hardly normal for Mark. In the twelve other instances in his Gospel (excluding Mk 8.11) in which he employs οὐρανός, it does not bear this sense.[23] And in two out of the three instances in which it does mean 'sky' the word is part of an Old Testament quotation.[24] In the second place, in biblical literature the phrase ἀπὸ τοῦ οὐρανοῦ, when used as it is here—with an object—seems to have had a specific, technical meaning. This becomes apparent when we consider the following.

When the LXX uses ἀπὸ τοῦ οὐρανοῦ as Mark does in Mk 8.11—that is, in apposition (9 times out of 12 instances)—it is an appelative for:

19. Cf. Mt. 12.38 where a group of Pharisees (and Scribes) is portrayed in exactly this way and their demand is only διδάσκαλε, θέλομεν ἀπὸ σοῦ σημεῖον ἰδεῖν.

20. Cf. Mk 1.11; 11.30, 31.

21. See H. Traub, 'οὐρανός', *TDNT*, V, p. 509. On ἀπό with the genitive as an appelative, see F. Blass and A. Debrunner, *A Greek Grammar of the New Testament and Other Early Christian Literature* (trans. R.W. Funk; Chicago: University of Chicago Press, 1961), p. 113 §209.

22. E.g. Cranfield, *Mark*, p. 258; G.R. Beasley-Murray, *Jesus and the Kingdom of God* (Exeter: Paternoster Press, 1986), p. 254.

23. Cf. Mk 1.11; 6.41; 7.34; 10.21; 11.25, 26, 30, 31; 12.25; 13.27, 31; 14.62.

24. Mk. 4.32 = Dan. 4.12; Mk 13.25 = Isa. 34.4.

(1)   the rain that God has used to rid the earth of sinful humanity
       (Gen. 8.2);
(2)   the celestial phenomenon which the sun- and moon-worship-
       ping heathen regard as portents of their gods (Jer. 10.2);
(3)   a figure called a 'watcher' (εἴρ) who pronounces and then
       brings doom on King Nebuchadnezzar of Babylon for not
       acknowledging Yahweh as the Supreme God (Dan. 4.10, 20,
       28, Theodotion);
(4)   God's all-powerful word (ὁ παντοδύναμός σου λόγος)
       which, in the form of a 'stern warrior carrying a sharp sword'
       who 'stood and filled all things with death', was unleashed
       against the Egyptian first-born on the first Passover (Wis. 18.15);
(5)   the particular but unspecified phenomenon which Judas
       Maccabaeus and his men knew to have been the decisive factor
       in destroying a Galatian army that set itself against God and his
       power (2 Macc. 8.20);[25]
(6)   the aid which, in the form of a spectacularly armored warrior
       angel, accompanies the Maccabean army and helps to bring
       defeat to Lysias, the commander of Greek forces besieging
       Jerusalem (2 Macc. 11.10);
(7)   the divine intervention that had given victory to a hopelessly
       outnumbered Maccabean army (2 Macc. 15.8).

When in the New Testament the phrase is so used (6 times out of 9
instances, excluding Mk 8.11), it appears as an appelative for:

(1)   the type of fire that Jesus' disciples want God to rain down on
       certain Samaritan villages as punishment for their inhabitants'
       refusal to receive Jesus (Lk. 9.54, cf. vv. 51-56);
(2)   the fiery phenomena that the Lukan Jesus says will be mani-
       fested on the day that the son of Man comes to judge men for
       their iniquities (Lk. 17.29, cf. 11.30);
(3)   the terrors and great signs (σημεῖα!) that will herald the arrival
       of the 'day of retribution' (Lk. 21.11, cf. v. 22);
(4)   an angel which appears to Jesus during his ordeal in
       Gethsemane (Lk. 22.23);

---

25. For the historical event referred to in this verse, see J. Goldstein,
II Maccabees (AB, 41A; Garden City: Doubleday, 1983), pp. 331-34.

(5) the particular appearance of Jesus which, according to Paul, will signal the arrival of the Day of the Lord (2 Thess. 2.17);

(6) the wrath of God, the revelation of which betokens the decisive unveiling of the righteousness of God in judgment against the unrighteousness of men (Rom. 1.18).

In other words, in Greek biblical literature objects which are ἀπὸ τοῦ οὐρανοῦ are (with the exception of Jer. 10.2) apocalyptic phenomena which embody or signal the onset of aid and comfort for God's elect and/or the wrath that God was expected to let loose against his enemies and those who threaten his people.

This being the case, then a 'sign' which was ἀπὸ τοῦ οὐρανοῦ is most likely a phenomenon which embodied 'Salvation'.[26]

2. *The Association of the 'Sign' with 'This Generation'*

In Mk 8.12b—a castigation by Jesus of the Pharisees' demand[27]—Mark has Jesus state that the 'sign' demanded of him is of a certain type. It is one of those 'signs' that 'this generation' expected it would be shown should one claiming to be 'of God' wish to ensure that it ('this generation') would put its trust in him. But in Mark's view of things, what type of 'sign' was this? For this information I turn to Mk 15.28-32:

26. In support of this, it is important to note that in two of the three times in the LXX (the exception being Job 7.9) and in each of the four times in the New Testament where ἀπὸ τοῦ οὐρανοῦ is used adverbially the phrase is *also* linked with events or phenomena embodying some aspect of salvation. In Wis. 16.20 it is recalled that Israel was saved from perishing in the wilderness by bread sent by God ἀπ' οὐρανοῦ (καὶ ἕτοιμον ἄρτον αὐτοῖς ἀπ' οὐρανοῦ ἐπέμψας). According to Sir. 46.17 the phenomenon that destroyed the Philistines and Tyrians besetting Samuel was God's thundering ἀπ' οὐρανοῦ (καὶ ἐβρόντεσεν ἀπ' οὐρανοῦ Κύριος). The author of Hebrews states that the Israelites who were punished for disobedience were those who were being warned ἀπ' οὐρανῶν of the loss of their salvation (οἱ τὸν ἀπ' οὐρανῶν ἀποστρεφόμενοι, Heb. 12.25). It was, according to 1 Pet. 1.12, the phenomenon of the Holy Spirit being sent ἀπ' οὐρανοῦ (ἐν πνεύματι ἁγίῳ ἀποσταλέντι ἀπ' οὐρανοῦ) that stood behind the experience of salvation (σωτηρίας, cf. v. 10) kindled in the readers of the epistle by the words of the early Christian evangelists. In 1 Thess. 4.16 it is the event of Jesus' coming ἀπ' οὐρανοῦ (ὁ Κύριος... καταβήσεται ἀπ' οὐρανοῦ) that heralds the resurrection of the saints. And in Mt. 24.29 the arrival of the Son of Man for judgment is accompanied by stars that fall ἀπὸ τοῦ οὐρανοῦ (καὶ οἱ ἀστέρες πεσοῦνται ἀπὸ τοῦ οὐρανοῦ).

27. On this, see M. Meinertz, 'Dieses Geschlecht im Neuen Testament', *BZ* 1 (1957), pp. 283-89.

And with him they crucified two robbers, one on his right and one on his left. [29] And those who passed by derided him, wagging their heads, and saying, 'Aha! You who would destroy the Temple and build it in three days, [30] save yourself and come down from the cross!' [31] So also the Chief Priests mocked him to one another with the Scribes, saying, 'He saved others; he cannot save himself. [32] Let the Christ, the King of Israel, come down now from the cross, that we may see and believe.' Those who were crucified with him also reviled him.

As even a casual glance at these verses shows, this is a story in which Jesus is asked to prove certain claims he is believed to have made by making something happen. In other words, it is a story in which Jesus is faced with a demand for a 'sign'. Three things need to be noted here:

The first thing is that according to Mark those who demand a 'sign' from Jesus are members of 'this generation'.[28]

Secondly, the claim that Jesus is here called upon to prove by means of a 'sign' is that he is, as he has or is thought to have said, Lord of the Temple,[29] Saviour, and the King of Israel (cf. vv. 29b, 31b, 32a). In other words, the issue in dispute, especially in light of Jesus' present ignoble circumstances, is whether or not he himself is 'of God'.

Thirdly, here the members of 'this generation' not only demand that Jesus make something happen before they accept his claims. They

28. This is sufficiently clear from the fact that Mark has these particular people—passers-by, chief priests, and Scribes—mock Jesus and hurl insults at him. But Mark underscores this point in several other ways. First, he portrays those here demanding a 'sign' specifically in terms of the wicked who in Pss. 22, 109, Wis. 2, and Lam. 2 heap derision on God's elect (on this, see Lane, *Mark*, p. 569; Taylor, *Mark*, pp. 591-92). Secondly, at 15.32 Mark has the mockers contemptuously appeal to Jesus for help in 'seeing' when they obviously have no intention to do so. In this, Mark recalls Jesus' declaration at 4.11-12 that the behavior especially characteristic of 'this generation' is a refusal to engage in the 'seeing' that would lead to belief (on the emphasis in 15.32 on 'seeing' in order to believe as a reference to 4.12, see F.J. Matera, *The Kingship of Jesus* [SBLDS, 66; Chico, CA: Scholars Press, 1982], p. 28). And finally, at 15.29 Mark identifies the mockery engaged in by those who here demand a 'sign' as blasphemy, i.e., willful and perverse rejection of the revelation of God. According to Mark, blaspheming is an identifying mark of 'this generation' (cf. Mk 3.28-30; 7.6-9).

29. This is the implication of the mocking charge '. . . You who would destroy the Temple and rebuild it in three days. . . ' (Mk 15.29b). See D. Senior, *The Passion of Jesus in the Gospel of Mark* (Wilmington, DE: Michael Glazier, 1984), p. 119; F.J. Matera, *Passion Narratives and Gospel Theologies* (Mahwah, NY: Paulist Press), p. 44.

dictate to him what he must make happen before they will 'see and believe' (cf. v. 32). They do not leave it up to him to decide the terms of the 'sign' they will accept from him. This fact is significant. It implies that the particular 'sign' here demanded of Jesus is the *only* type of 'sign' that would be taken by 'this generation' as proof for the truth of the claims that are now under dispute.

There is, then, according to Mark, a strong formal connection between the 'sign' demanded of Jesus by the Chief Priests and others at Jesus' crucifixion and that demanded of Jesus by the Pharisees at Mk 8.11-13. The respective 'signs' are similar, if not identical, in 'shape'. Accordingly, once we determine the 'shape' of the 'sign' demanded of Jesus in Mk 15.28-32, we will also have determined the 'shape' of the 'sign' that Jesus is asked to produce in Mk 8.11-13.

What, then, is this 'sign'? Mark notes that it is Jesus 'saving' himself by 'coming down from his cross' (σῶσον σεαυτὸν καταβὰς ἀπὸ τοῦ σταυροῦ, v. 30; καταβάτω νῦν ἀπὸ τοῦ σταυροῦ, v. 32). In other words, the 'sign' demanded from Jesus is a phenomenon that effects 'deliverance'. But deliverance of whom, and from what? Certainly at the very least it is rescue of an individual from personal tragedy, since the call to 'save yourself' and 'come down from the cross' goes out to a broken man who is embroiled in a life-threatening situation. But it is much more than this. For, in the first place, in Mark's Gospel to 'save oneself' by 'coming down from the cross' represents blatant self-aggrandisement and not simply self-preservation. This is clear from the fact that Mark has had Jesus define 'saving one's self' through a willful rejection of 'cross bearing' as tantamount both to asserting oneself over others at their expense[30] and to the attempt—on the part of both individual and nations—to gain and use worldly power to conquer and dominate their enemies.[31] In the second place, according to Mark, the appeal to Jesus to 'save himself' is addressed to him not just as an individual, but as the supreme Jewish national figure—'the King of Israel' (and therefore, the embodiment of the people of God)—who has been reduced to his present fate (the cross) in this identity by conquerors of

30. Cf. Mk 8.34-38.

31. Cf. Mk 10.42-45. That Mark intended to have these verses seen as a continuation of Jesus' teaching at 8.34-38 on the nature of 'cross bearing' seems abundantly clear if only from the fact that, as with 8.34-38, Mark has prefaced 10.42 with a 'passion prediction' of Jesus and a story of the disciples failing or refusing to understand this prediction (cf. 8.31-33; 10.32-41).

Israel.[32] So, according to Mark, the deliverance attested to by the 'sign' of Jesus 'coming down from the cross' is the deliverance, through conquest and not suffering-service, of Israel from national oppression.[33]

In light of this it is clear that according to Mark the type of 'sign' that 'this generation' typically sought and desired was a phenomenon that was associated with (and indeed intimated) Israel's liberation from, and conquest of, its enemies. Accordingly, the 'sign' demanded of Jesus at Mk 8.11-13 must also be a phenomenon of this sort, since it, too, is labeled as a 'sign' sought by 'this generation'.[34]

3. *The 'Sign' as One which is to be 'Given'*

In Mk 8.12c Mark has Jesus define the 'sign' demanded of him as one which is to be 'given' (δοθήσεται). Significantly, this is a signal characteristic of the 'signs' which, according to Jesus in Mk 13.22, will be offered by certain 'sign' workers to the inhabitants of Jerusalem and Judea during a time of grave national crisis (cf. Mk 13.14ff.). These 'signs' are also ones that are to be 'given' (δώσουσιν σημεῖα κτλ.).[35] It seems clear, then, because of this, that in Mark's eyes the type of 'sign' that is demanded of Jesus at Mk 8.11 is cut from the same cloth as those which the 'sign' workers of Mk 13.22 are wont to produce.

32. Cf. Mk 15.24-25.

33. Cf. Matera, *Passion Narratives*, p. 44; Senior, *Passion of Jesus*, pp. 119-21; J. Blackwell, *The Passion as Story: The Plot of Mark* (Philadelphia: Fortress Press, 1986), pp. 72-73.

34.   It should be pointed out that in the New Testament this connection between 'this generation' and 'signs' of this type is not Mark's alone. Paul also knows it to be the case, as is apparent from 1 Cor. 1.22 where he attributed the rejection of a crucified Christ by Jews who are among 'the foolish' and 'those who are perishing' (Pauline equivalents for 'this generation') to a desire for 'signs' (σημεῖα). The author of the Gospel of John makes reference to it when he has Jesus complain that belief does not arise in his contemporaries unless they 'see signs and wonders' (ἐὰν μὴ σημεῖα καὶ τέρατα ἴδητε, οὐ μὴ πιστεύσητε, Jn 4.48). On this, see R.E. Brown, *The Gospel according to John I–XII* (AB, 29; Garden City: Doubleday, 1966), pp. 195-96. On the meaning of the terms σημεῖα καὶ τέρατα, see below.

35.   D Θ §13 the Diatessaron a (Origen) Victor of Antioch and certain other witnesses describe these σημεῖα as those which will be 'shown' or 'performed' (ποιέω), rather than 'given' (δίδωμι). On δώσουσιν σημεῖα, κτλ. rather than ποιήσουσιν σημεῖα, κτλ. as the preferred reading for Mk 13.22, see C.H. Turner, 'Western Readings in the Second Half of St Mark's Gospel', *JTS* (1928), pp. 9-10; Taylor, *Mark*, p. 516; B.M. Metzger, *A Textual Commentary on the Greek New Testament* (New York: UBS, 1971), p. 112.

But what type of 'sign' are they? How does Mark envision their content? He lets us know this in three ways:

(a) by giving specific information concerning the identity of the men who work these 'signs',

(b) by calling these 'signs' σημεῖα καὶ τέρατα and,

(c) by noting the effect that these 'signs' might have upon those who see them.

a. *The identity of the 'sign' workers of Mk 13.22.* Mark, through Jesus, characterizes the men who produce the 'signs' referred to in Mk 13.22 in three different ways. The first way is as 'false christs' (ψευδόχριστοι, 13.22). Now, for Mark, Jesus is the Christ (cf. Mk 1.1), and since Mark takes great pains to show that Jesus' identity *as* the Christ is grounded in suffering and service, and stands solidly against triumphalism, chauvinism, and domineering imperialism (cf. esp. Mk 8.27-37; 9.31-37; 10.32-45), then Mark's designation through Jesus of the 'sign' workers of Mk 13.22 as 'false christs' means one thing. They are Messianic pretenders who hold that their identity as Messiah brings engagement in violence, conquest, and war.[36]

They are also referred to as 'false prophets' (ψευδοπροφῆται, 13.22). For Mark, a prophet is primarily one who calls Israel to become the people that God would have them be.[37] Accordingly, a 'False Prophet' is someone who leads Israel towards national behavior that is the antithesis of what God has ordained for her. Now, in Mark's Gospel Jesus is, among other things, a prophet.[38] And it is as a prophet that he warns Israel against taking its status as the chosen people as a pretext or justification for becoming involved in any form of exclusivistic nationalism.[39] He calls Israel to see that its national identity as the People of God

36. See Lane, *Mark*, p. 473; G.R. Beasley-Murray, *A Commentary on Mark Thirteen* (London: Macmillan, 1957), p. 83.

37. Cf. Mk 1.2-8, where John the Baptizer, who is, according to Mark, the embodiment of the prophet Elijah, does precisely this.

38. He is not only called this by others at Mk 6.15 and 8.28, but, according to Mark, he refers to himself as such at 6.4. Moreover, Mark underscores the idea of Jesus as prophet by portraying Jesus as following in the footsteps of John the Baptizer. The idea of Jesus as prophet is also possibly intimated in Mark's designation of Jesus as ὁ ἐρχόμενος (on this, see Hahn, *Titles*, p. 380).

39. This is the import of such stories as the Calling of Levi (Mk 2.13-17) and the Healing of the Syro-Phoenician Woman's Daughter (Mk 7.24-30) as well as of Jesus' teaching on the tradition of the elders (Mk 7.1-23).

is bound up with being a servant to, and not a lord of, other nations.[40] By implication then, for Mark, 'false prophets' are men who advocate for Israel behavior that is despotic in character and is set upon achieving worldly domination.

Finally, the 'sign' workers of Mk 3.22 are identified by Mark as identical with the 'many' spoken of in Mk 13.5-6.[41] Now, according to Mark, the 'many "come in my name"' (ἐλεύσονται ἐπὶ τῷ ὀνόματί μου), and 'proclaim "I am"' (λέγοντες ὅτι ἐγώ εἰμι). What do these actions signify? Many scholars have taken the view that since, on the one hand, the phrase 'to come in my name' generally means 'appealing to me as their authority', 'claiming to be sent by me'[42] and in this case probably 'usurping my identity',[43] and, on the other hand, that the personal pronoun in this phrase (μου) can only refer to the speaker, Jesus (cf. 13.3),[44] this action signifies the laying of a claim on the part of people within the Christian community to be speaking to other Christians on Jesus' behalf[45] or even to be Jesus himself returned from on high.[46] But this cannot be the case. In the first place, there is nothing

40. This is most apparent in Jesus' teaching to the Twelve (i.e. the New Israel) in Mk 9.33-36 and 10.42-45. But it is also the special import of Jesus' prophetic-symbolic act of 'cleansing' the Temple (11.15-19, cf. esp. v. 17). On this, see Hill, 'Jesus and Josephus' "Messianic" Prophets', p. 150; G.W. Buchanan, 'Mark II, 15-19: Brigands in the Temple', *HUCA* 30 (1959), pp. 169-77; C. Roth, 'The Cleansing of the Temple and Zechariah 14.21', *NovT* 4 (1960), pp. 174-81; W.W. Waty, 'Jesus and the Temple—Cleansing or Cursing?', *ExpTim* 93 (1981–82), pp. 235-39.

41. This is clear from the fact that Mark describes both groups in identical terms. They both 'lead astray' (cf. Mk 13.22; cf. vv. 5, 6).

42. Cf. H. Bientenhard, 'ὄνομα', *TDNT*, V, p. 271; Cranfield, *Mark*, p. 359.

43. Cranfield, *Mark*, p. 359; W. Heitmuller, *Im Namen Jesu* (Göttingen: Vandenhoeck & Ruprecht, 1903), p. 63; Beasley-Murray, *Mark Thirteen*, pp. 32-33; M. Hooker, 'Trial and Tribulation in Mark XIII', *BJRL* 64 (1982), p. 85.

44. Cf. E. Klostermann, *Das Markusevangelium* (HNT, 3; Tübingen: Mohr [Siebeck], 1950), p. 133.

45. Cf. J.V. Bartlet, *St Mark* (New York and Oxford: Oxford University Press, 1922), p. 352; C.H. Turner, *The Gospel according to St Mark* (London: SPCK, 1928), p. 63; W. Grundmann, *Das Evangelium nach Markus* (THKNT, 2; Berlin: Evangelische Verlagsanstalt, 1965), p. 263; T.J. Weeden, *Mark—Traditions in Conflict* (Philadelphia: Fortress Press, 1971), pp. 88-89; W.H. Kelber, *The Kingdom in Mark: A New Time and a New Place* (Philadelphia: Fortress Press, 1974), p. 115.

46. This is, at least at first glance, a plausible position to take in this regard since the pronoun μου must refer to the speaker of the phrase ἐπὶ τῷ ὀνόματί μου, who is in this case Jesus (cf. Mk 13.5). But whether or not it is actually the case turns on

in the text that would indicate that Mark intended the audience of the 'many' to be seen as the Christian community.[47] Certainly, Christians will hear them (cf. v. 5), but that seems to be only by accident. For in 13.5-7, the people that the 'many' target and win over with their proclamations are specifically distinguished from the disciples and other followers of Jesus: they have never been privy, as the disciples and other followers of Jesus have (cf. v. 5), to Jesus' warnings about the ill effects of the proclamation of the 'many'.[48] Secondly, in 13.5-7 Mark, through Jesus, designates the 'many' who 'come in my name' as originating outside of the circle of Jesus' followers. He does this by having Jesus speak of the 'many' in the third and not the second person. Had Mark wanted the 'many' to be seen as Christians, he would have had Jesus say something like 'many of you will come in my name...'[49] And finally, the referent of the phrase ὀνόματί μου cannot be the name 'Jesus'. For a number of reasons, it must be a title that Jesus alone has the right to bear, namely the title 'messiah'.[50] (1) One cannot construe the phrase 'coming in my name' as a claim either to stand in for 'Jesus' (i.e. the man from Nazareth) or to be him without rendering that sentence in which it appears contradictory. As W. Weiffenbach long ago observed, 'He who legitimizes himself through the *onoma* of Jesus cannot at the same time claim the same ὄνομα'.[51] (2) If Mark meant the

knowing what persona it is in which here Mark has Jesus speaking. Is it as the carpenter from Nazareth, the son of Mary, or is it more officially as God's anointed? On this, see below.

47. Contra J. Wellhausen, *Das Evangelium Marci* (Berlin: George Reimer, 1909), p. 101; W. Manson, 'EGO EIMI of the Messianic Presence in the New Testament', *JTS* 48 (1947), p. 139, and all of the authors cited above in note 45.

48. Indeed, this is why they are seduced by the 'many'. See Hooker, 'Trial and Tribulation', p. 85.

49. Cf. E. Best, *Mark: The Gospel as Story* (Edinburgh: T. & T. Clark, 1982), p. 48; Beasley-Murray, *Mark Thirteen*, p. 31; Hooker, 'Trial and Tribulation', p. 85. In line with this, we should also note that there is no independent evidence (Acts 20.29 and 1 Jn 2.18 notwithstanding) of the existence of such Christians in the Early Church.

50. Gould, *Mark*, p. 243; Swete, *Mark*, p. 298; Cranfield, *Mark*, p. 395; Beasley-Murray, *Jesus and the Kingdom of God*, p. 325; J. Schniewind, *Das Evangelium nach Markus* (NTD, 1; Göttingen: Vandenhoeck & Ruprecht, 1944), p. 167; R. Pesch, *Naherwartungen: Tradition und Redaktion in Mk 13* (Düsseldorf: Patmos, 1968), p. 111.

51. W. Weiffenbach, *Der Wiederkunftsgedanke Jesu nach den Synoptikern kritisch untersucht und dargestellt* (Leipzig: Breitkopf und Härtel, 1873), p. 169.

'many' to be seen as claiming to be standing in for Jesus or to be him, it is difficult to see why at v. 6 he did not write simply πολλοὶ ἐλεύσονται.[52] (3) Matthew understood the claim made by the 'many' in Mk 13.6 to be a claim to be the messiah (cf. Mt. 24.5). (4) Most importantly elsewhere in Mark's Gospel, when the phrase 'in (on) my name' appears on the lips of Jesus, the 'name' referred to is not the personal name 'Jesus' but the title *Christos*.[53] The phrase 'coming in my name', then, in this context means claiming to be God's Anointed, his Deliverer,[54] attempting to rival Jesus for recognition as the figure empowered by God to bring salvation to Israel.[55]

Since, as D. Daube has shown,[56] the phrase ἐγώ εἰμι was associated in Mark's time primarily with Yahweh's presence, especially as that presence was made known during the time of the Exodus, to proclaim 'I am' is therefore tantamount to announcing the dawning of the time in which Israel would be liberated from her enemies. So according to Mark, the 'sign' workers of Mk 13.22 are to be seen as men who not only claim to be elected by God to be his instrument in bringing about his deliverance, but who also announce that the time of deliverance is now at hand.[57]

Now it should be pointed out that these characteristics are exactly those of the so-called 'Sign-Prophets'—Theudas, the unnamed *Goetes*, the 'Egyptian'—who were active in Judea in the years immediately

52. Cf. Klostermann, *Markusevangelium*, p. 133; Beasley-Murray, *Mark Thirteen*, p. 32.

53. Cf. Mk 9.37, 39, 40.

54. Blunt, *Mark*, p. 239; Hooker, 'Trial and Tribulation', p. 85; Beasley-Murray, *Jesus and the Kingdom of God*, p. 325.

55. Gould, *Mark*, p. 243; Swete, *Mark*, p. 243; Branscomb, *Mark*, p. 235; Rawlinson, *St Mark*, p. 184; Blunt, *Mark*, p. 239; Klostermann, *Markusevangelium*, p. 133; Beasley-Murray, *Mark Thirteen*, p. 31; *idem, Jesus and the Kingdom of God*, p. 325; Cranfield, *Mark*, p. 395; Lane, *Mark*, pp. 454-57; M.J. Lagrange, *Evangile selon Saint Marc* (Paris: Gabalda, 1929), p. 336; H. Conzelmann, 'Geschichte und Eschaton nach Mc xiii', *ZNW* 50 (1959), p. 218; S.E. Johnson, *The Gospel according to St Mark* (BNTC; London: A. & C. Black, 1960), p. 213; C.S. Mann, *Mark* (AB, 27; Garden City, NY: Doubleday, 1986), p. 524.

56. 'The "I Am" of the Messianic Presence', in *The New Testament and Rabbinic Judaism* (London: Athlone, 1956), pp. 325-29.

57. Cf. Klostermann, *Markusevangelium*, p. 136; Beasley-Murray, *Jesus and the Kingdom of God*, pp. 325-26; Pesch, *Naherwartungen*, pp. 110-11. Notably, this is exactly how Luke understands this phrase. He renders it not as a statement of identity or a claim to dignity, but as the specific announcement ὁ καιρὸς ἤγγικεν (Lk. 21.8).

preceding the outbreak of the Jewish Revolt against Rome[58] and who were known to both Mark and his readers. They, too, claimed that they were expressly sent by God to fulfill a divine plan of liberation and worldly exaltation of Israel which involved the violent overthrow of Israel's enemies,[59] and, announcing that the time of salvation had arrived, they gathered followers and encouraged them to rise up against their oppressors.[60] So not only is there a correspondence in Mark's Gospel between the 'sign' workers of Mk 13.22 and the historical 'Sign-Prophets' mentioned in Josephus and other sources,[61] there is a

58. Theudas appeared during the procuratorship of Cuspius Fadus (44–48 CE), the 'Egyptian' and a group of *Goetes* when Antonius Felix was procurator (52–60 CE), and an unnamed *Goes* when Porcius Festus ruled (60–62 CE).

59. The claim of Theudas in this regard is inherent in his declaring himself to be προφητής (*Ant.* 20.5.1 §97), that is, one like Moses (cf. R. Meyer, 'προφητής', *TDNT*, VI, pp. 812-28, esp. p. 826; J. Jeremias, 'Μωϋσῆς', *TDNT*, IV, pp. 848-73, esp. p. 862) and Joshua *redivivus* (cf. *Ant.* 20.5.1 §97), and in that, as Gamaliel is recorded as noting in Acts 5.36, he 'gave himself out to be somebody' (λέγων εἶναί τινα ἑαυτόν), that is, God's instrument for salvation (on this, see O. Betz, 'Miracles in the Writings of Josephus', in L.H. Feldman and G. Hata [eds.], *Josephus, Judaism, and Christianity* [Detroit: Wayne State University Press, 1987], pp. 212-35, esp. p. 229). It also stands behind the fact that Cuspius Fadus felt constrained to send his troops against Theudas when Theudas's claim became known. In the case of the 'Egyptian', this is clear from the fact that he, too, used the title ὁ προφητής and presented himself as a new Joshua (*Ant.* 20.8.6 §169-170) and that he proclaimed himself destined not only to overthrow the Roman garrison in Jerusalem but to be τοῦ δήμου τυράννειν (the King of the People, *War* 2.13.5 §262). It also is implied by the fact that the Roman governor of Judea arrested him as a rebel against Rome (*War* 2.13.5 §262). The claim to this commission on the part of the *Goetes* active during Felix's procuratorship is implied by the fact that they presented themselves as capable of securing the blessings that Moses had from God for Israel (cf. *Ant.* 20.8.6. §167-168; *Ant.* 2.15.4 §327) and in that, as Josephus reports things, they declared their activities to be 'in accord with God's plan of Salvation' (κατὰ τὴν τοῦ θεοῦ προνοίαν γινόμενα). It is also implied by the fact that Felix regarded their posturing and promises as tantamount to encouraging revolt (*War* 2.13.5 §261). In the case of the unnamed *Goes*, this is clear from the fact that he declared that he was capable of bringing to Israel 'salvation' (σωτηρίας) and 'rest from troubles' (παῦλαν κακῶν, 20.8.10 §188). On all of this, see Hill, 'Jesus and Josephus' "Messianic Prophets"', pp. 147-48; Jeremias, 'Μωϋσῆς', p. 862; Betz, 'Miracles', pp. 226-31.

60. Cf. *Ant.* 20.5.1 §97-99; 20.8.6 §167-168, 169; 20.8.10 §188; *War* 2.13.4 §258-259; 2.13.5 §261; 6.5.2 §284-286.

61. Besides the passages from Josephus and Acts that I have already noted, ref-

correspondence so exact that it cannot be anything but intentionally drawn. Accordingly, in describing and characterizing the 'sign' workers of Mk 13.22 in the particular ways he does, Mark was clearly identifying them with Theudas and his ilk.

Given this, it is extremely important to note that the 'signs' offered by these 'Sign-Prophets' were phenomena copying the substance of one or another of the events of the time of the Exodus and Conquest which were instrumental in securing freedom from subjugation and dominance for the people of God. The 'sign' that Theudas offered on his own behalf—and which, notably, was intended to grant safe passage for any who would march into Jerusalem against the Romans—was a re-enactment of Moses' division of the Reed Sea and/or Joshua's division of the Jordan.[62] The 'signs' offered by the unnamed *Goetes* active during the procuratorship of Antonius Felix were embodiments of the plagues which foreshadowed and brought about the liberation of God's people from their Egyptian bondage or re-runs of the events wrought by Moses when he confronted Pharaoh's court magicians that indicated the eventual subjugation of Pharaoh to God.[63] The 'signs' promised by the *Goes* who was active during Porcius Festus's procuratorship were to intimate the relief from slavery that the Israelites experienced when Yahweh vanquished Pharaoh.[64] And the 'sign' that the 'Egyptian' sought to work— a 'sign' which, he thought, would in its manifestation specifically serve to overthrow the Roman garrison in Jerusalem—was the act of judgment performed by Joshua against Jericho.[65]

---

erences to the Judean 'Sign-Prophets' can also be found in Acts 21.38; Eusebius, *History of the Church* 2.21; *b. Sanh.* 67a, and possibly Mt. 24.11-12, 24-26.

62. Cf. Meyer, 'προφητής', p. 826; Jeremias, 'Μωϋσῆς', p. 862; Barnett, 'Jewish Sign Prophets', p. 681; Betz, 'Miracles', p. 228.

63. According to Josephus, the first of these 'signs' were 'signs of freedom' (σημεῖα ἐλευθερίας). Notably, this is a term which Josephus employs in his Exodus narrative for the plagues that foreshadowed the coming 'liberation' of God's people (cf. *Ant.* 2.15.4 §327, τὸ... τὴν ἐλευθερίαν αὐτοῖς σημεῖον). The second of these were 'wonders and signs' (τέρατα καὶ σημεῖα) which were to 'accord with God's plan' (κατὰ τὴν τοῦ Θεοῦ προνοίαν γινόμενα). This is a term which Josephus specifically applied to the σημεῖα wrought by Moses when he confronted Pharaoh's court magicians (cf. *Ant.* 2.13.3 §286). On this, see Rengstorf, 'σημεῖον', p. 225.

64. On this, see Barnett, 'Jewish Sign Prophets', p. 685.

65. He promised that upon his command (ὡς κελεύσαντος αὐτοῦ) the walls of Jerusalem would collapse (*Ant.* 20.8.6 §169). On the correspondence in the mind of

The ultimate effect, then, of Mark's characterization of the 'sign' workers referred to in Mk 13.22 as 'false christs', 'false prophets' and identical with the 'many' of Mk 13.6 is not only to identify these 'sign' workers with the historical 'Sign-Prophets' mentioned in Josephus and other sources. It is to specify the type of 'sign' that, according to Mark, these 'sign' workers were wont to offer. Since Mark intended the 'sign' workers of Mk 13.22 to be seen as identical with the likes of Theudas, the 'Egyptian', and the *Goetes*, then he also meant the 'signs' that the former group are said to offer to be taken as identical in type with those proffered by the latter. They, too, are 'signs of salvation', 'signs of freedom', phenomena betokening Israel's impending deliverance from national oppression.

b. *The name given to the 'signs' of Mk 13.22.* Through Jesus, Mark calls these 'signs' σημεῖα καὶ τέρατα (13.22). This phrase is sometimes found in ancient literature with the sense of 'miracle',[66] so Mark's calling the 'signs' offered by the 'sign' workers of Mk 13.22 by this name could be an indication more of character than of content. However, S.V. McCasland has demonstrated that in the LXX the phrase σημεῖα καὶ τέρατα was a *terminus technicus* for the 'mighty deeds', the acts of deliverance which God gave to Israel through to Moses, Aaron, and Joshua in connection with the Exodus and Conquest.[67] As McCasland notes:

> Miraculous deeds are found in other places [in the Old Testament], such as Judges and Kings, especially in the careers of Elijah and Elisha, but these events are never referred as signs and wonders in the characteristic passages in which the idiom occurs. It is evident that although the Hebrews believed in the continuous activity of God as the sovereign of history, who manifested his personal interest and power in all the great experiences of the Hebrew people, it was his intention to deliver them from Egypt and lead them into Canaan which became the unique revelation of Yahweh's true character. The story was normative for the idea of God as far as signs and wonders were concerned.[68]

the 'Egyptian' between Jerusalem and Jericho, see Barnett, 'Jewish Sign Prophets', p. 683; Betz, 'Miracles', p. 229.

66. Cf. Rengstorf, 'σημεῖον', pp. 206-207; M. Whittaker, '"Signs and Wonders": The Pagan Background', *SE* 5 (1965), pp. 155-58.

67. 'Signs and Wonders', *JBL* 76 (1957), pp. 149-52.

68. 'Signs and Wonders', p. 150.

Now this is certainly the sense the phrase bears in Mk 13.22. For, in the first place, as McCasland also notes,[69] 'the mighty deeds by which God liberated Israel from Egypt' is the primary meaning which the phrase had in the New Testament as well, particularly in its writings or sections of writings that, like Mark 13, are apocalyptic in nature or tone. Secondly, Mark is careful always to use only the word δύναμις, when he wants to designate a deed or an event a 'miracle'.[70] Thirdly, there is a specific allusion in Mk 13.22 to Deut. 13.2-3 ('If a prophet arises among you... and gives to you a sign or a wonder, and if the sign or the wonder comes to pass, and if he says, "Let us go after other gods," which you have not known, "and let us serve them", you shall not listen to the words of that prophet... for the Lord is testing you... ') where the expression 'sign or wonder' (σημεῖον ἢ τέρας) is a direct reference to the God's wonders in the days of Moses.[71]

So we may conclude that in calling the 'signs' of the 'sign' workers of Mk 13.22 σημεῖα καὶ τέρατα, Mark was identifying these 'signs' specifically with the liberating works carried out by God during the Exodus.

c. *The effect of seeing the 'signs' of Mk 13.22.* According to Mark, the 'signs' referred to in 13.22 are of a type that, once seen, threaten to 'lead astray' (πρὸς τὸ ἀποπλανᾶν) the people of Jerusalem and Judea,[72] even though these people have witnessed the appearance of the 'abomination of desolation standing where he ought not' (cf. v. 14). Now, for Mark, the abomination is an act of sacrilege so appalling that tribulation is certain to follow in its wake.[73] Its appearance signals two things: first, that the destruction of the Temple and its environs is both inevitable and near;[74] and, secondly, that for the people of God flight from Jerusalem and Judea is both imperative for survival as well as

69. 'Signs and Wonders', p. 151; see Rengstorf, 'σημεῖον', p. 241.

70. Cf. V.K. Robbins, 'Dynameis and Semeia in Mark', *BR* 18 (1973), pp. 5-20, esp. pp. 17-20.

71. Cf. Rengstorf, 'σημεῖον', p. 221. That Mark is alluding in Mk 13.22 to Deut. 13.1-3, see Swete, *Mark*, p. 310; Beasley-Murray, *Mark Thirteen*, pp. 83-84; Lane, *Mark*, p. 473.

72. Cf. Mk 13.14-21.

73. On this see *Mark*, pp. 466-72.

74. Cf. Lane, *Mark*, p. 466; D. Daube, 'The Abomination of Desolation', in *The New Testament and Rabbinic Judaism*, pp. 418-37; B. Rigaux, 'ΒΔΕΛΥΓΜΑ ΤΗΣ ΕΠΗΜΩΣΕΩΣ (Mc 13, 14; Mt 24, 15)', *Bib* 40 (1959), pp. 675-83.

divinely mandated.[75] So in Mark's eyes, then, to be 'led astray' means to be made to think that all of this is not the case.

Accordingly, 'signs' that threaten to 'lead astray' are those which tempt one to believe, despite clear evidence and divine warnings to the contrary, that for the Temple and the people of Jerusalem and Judea, deliverance, not destruction, was at hand.

But what kind of 'signs' would serve to convince a people whose survival and faithfulness depends upon fleeing their circumstances, that flight is not only unnecessary, but actually a form of unbelief? What, if anything, was the 'shape' of these signs?

To answer this we turn to Josephus, specifically his description in Book 6 of *The Jewish War* of an event in the last stages of the revolt of the Jews against Rome which in substance is an exact parallel (if not the actual historical referent) of that envisioned in Mk 13.22.[76] The event occurred when Titus's soldiers breached the Temple Gates and began to mount the attack which ended in their setting fire to the Holy of Holies. Josephus tells us that just prior to this, the Jews of Jerusalem, ignoring clear and repeated warnings from God that the city was doomed and would be destroyed by the encroaching Roman forces (cf. *War* 6.288-315), and oblivious to an abominating sacrilege committed in their midst by one of their number (cf. 6.201-19), had gathered in the inner sanctuary of Herod's Temple. There, they thought, they would be safe and could continue their rebellion undaunted, for they had convinced themselves that the Temple was still impregnable and the inner courts inviolable. So the breach of the gates sounded the death knell to Jewish hopes for the success of the revolt. It was the final and unmistakable signal that Jerusalem had met its end, and it made flight from the city imperative for those who wished to escape the Roman sword. Yet despite this, one man (whom, notably, Josephus labels a ψευδοπροφήτης, 6.285) was still able to induce 'thousands',[77] who were on the verge of

75. Cf. Mk 13.14a-19. On this, see Daube, 'Abomination', pp. 422-23; Beasley-Murray, *Mark Thirteen*, pp. 57-58.

76. That Mark is here referring to this event is, of course, denied by the scholars cited in notes 45 and 47 above. Notably, however, the truth of my argument here does not rest upon Mark having the event recorded by Josephus in view at Mk 13.22, though in my mind he does.

77. Josephus gives the total number as 6000, including the women, children, and the elderly who had accompanied the last remnants of the Jewish army into the Temple.

fleeing the Sanctuary and saving themselves, not only to stay their ground, but to go out into the outer courts of the Temple to face the army that was waiting there to cut them down (6.284). He did this, Josephus notes, by promising to effectuate specific 'signs', namely 'signs of salvation' (σημεῖα τῆς σωτηρίας, 6.285). Now, the expression 'signs of salvation' is another one of Josephus's equivalents for the actions of God during the Exodus which decimated the enemies of his people and led to the liberation of Israel from national subjugation.[78] It is clear, then, that the type of 'sign' that could and would serve to forestall and make light of necessary flight—the type of 'sign' which Mark, through Jesus, says the 'sign' workers of Mk 13.22 were wont to offer—was that which, in content, embodied 'the mighty hand' and 'the outstretched arm' of Yahweh and recapitulated one of the 'great and terrible deeds' which God wrought on Israel's behalf at the time of the Exodus.

From all of this, it is abundantly clear that according to Mark 'signs' that are 'given' are 'signs' that embody and betoken the deliverance from bondage that Israel experienced at the Exodus. And since, as we have seen above, the 'sign' demanded of Jesus at Mk 8.11 is designated in the following verse as one such 'sign', then it, too, in Mark's view, is a phenomenon of this sort.

Conclusions

The facts, then, that the 'sign' demanded of Jesus in 8.11 is designated by Mark as ἀπὸ τοῦ οὐρανοῦ, is associated with one expected by 'this generation', and is specified as one which is 'given', justify my assumption that this 'sign' is of a peculiar type. From all that is implied by these facts, it is clear that according to Mark the 'sign' is a phenomenon whose content is apocalyptic in tone, triumphalistic in character, and the embodiment of one of the 'mighty deeds of deliverance' that God had worked on Israel's behalf in rescuing it from slavery.

III

In drawing this conclusion, it is important to note that in Mark's time these particular 'signs' seem to have been perceived in a particular way. They were viewed as a 'means of confirmation' accrediting as 'of God'

---

78. Cf. Rengstorf, 'σημεῖον', pp. 223-25; Barnett, 'Jewish Sign Prophets', p. 686; Betz, 'Miracles', p. 227.

those in whose behalf they were to be worked; it appears that they were also thought of as something that, once manifested, would prompt a rerun of the saving action God undertook on Israel's behalf during the period of the Exodus and Conquest. That this was indeed the case is the implication of the following facts.

First, that the 'Sign Prophet' Theudas was certain that after his 'sign' was effected he could walk, as he planned, into Jerusalem unmolested by the Roman forces stationed there despite his knowledge of the fact that these forces would certainly take his 'sign' as a challenge to their authority and act accordingly (on this, see Josephus, *Ant.* 20.97-99).

Secondly, that Theudas could gather followers who were willing to accompany him to the banks of the Jordan (where, as we have seen above, his 'sign' was to be manifested) despite the known risk that in response to doing so, Roman troops would be sent out against them (cf. Josephus, *Ant.* 20.99).

Thirdly, that the 'Egyptian' could claim that immediately upon actuating his 'sign', the Roman garrison stationed in Jerusalem would be overcome and he would be set up as Ruler of Israel (cf. *Ant.* 20.169; *War* 2.261; Acts 21.38).

Fourthly, that the mere promise from the 'Egyptian' of his 'sign' roused 'thousands' to go on a march from the wilderness into Judea in spite of the knowledge that the Roman authorities there would, viewing such a march as a prelude to rebellion, take repressive action against it (cf. *Ant.* 20.169; *War* 2.261).

Fifthly, that anti-Roman sentiment stiffened among the Jews after the Roman procurator Felix prevented the Egyptian and his forces from getting near Jerusalem (cf. *Ant.* 20.169).

Finally, that, as already noted, a great multitude of Jews, who during the death throes of the Judean revolt against Rome had been promised 'signs of salvation', were willing to rush into the outer courts of the Temple where these 'signs' were to be seen, even though they knew the soldiers of Titus, having breached the Temple's defences, were waiting there to cut them down (cf. *War* 6.284-86).

In any case, Mark certainly shared this view. This is clear from the fact that, as we have seen, in his portrayal of the 'sign' workers of 13.22, Mark notes that the offering of such 'signs' would give confidence to those both working and seeing them that, despite overwhelming evidence to the contrary, they would be saved from the imminent and certain destruction that was about to befall them.

Once we realize this—that for Mark 'signs' of the type which Jesus is asked by the Pharisees to produce were, given their content, 'levers' by which the hand of God could be activated, indeed, even forced, into bringing about the destruction of Israel's enemies[79]—then the reason why Jesus is portrayed at Mk 8.11-13 as refusing to accede to a demand for such a 'sign' becomes clear. Mark has Jesus refuse this demand because for Jesus to do otherwise would be nothing less than to advocate, initiate, and engage in triumphalism—a type of activity that, according to Mark, was forbidden to Jesus if he wished to remain faithful to the exigencies of his divine commission.[80]

In support of this contention, I offer three considerations. The first is Mark's designation of the Pharisees' demand as something which causes Jesus to experience πειρασμός (8.11).[81] Elsewhere in Mark's Gospel, when Jesus is portrayed as subjected to πειρασμός, he is always faced with an open choice between obedience to or abandonment of the constraint laid upon him by God to fulfill his role as Messiah by eschewing violence and triumphalism.[82] Is it not, then, unlikely that Mark would also designate the Pharisees' demand for a 'sign' as something in which Jesus encounters πειρασμός unless he saw it as embodying the sort of challenge that, given my conclusion regarding the nature of the demand, I have argued it contains?

The second consideration arises from what is implied by the manner in which Jesus, according to Mark, refuses to comply with the Pharisees' demand. Jesus' refusal is couched within the phrase εἰ δοθήσεται τῇ γενεᾷ ταύτῃ σημεῖον (lit., 'if a sign shall be given to this generation'). This phrase is a literal rendering of an adapted form of a peculiar Hebraic oath of self-imprecation: May I die (or some great evil befall me) if such-and-such is done.[83] This oath not only said 'no' forcefully to a

79. Cf. Barnett, 'Jewish Sign Prophets', p. 688; Betz, 'Miracles', pp. 227-31.

80. This is especially clear in Mk 8.27–9.1 (cf. e.g. J.L. Mays, 'An Exposition of Mk 8.27–9.1', *Int* 30 [1976], pp. 174-78), but it is a theme which permeates Mark's Gospel.

81. Mk 8.11. The participle πειράζοντες should, I think, be taken as an editorial comment concerning what the Pharisees' demand does to Jesus rather than an unveiling of the Pharisees' intentions in making the demand. On this, see C.G. Montefiore, *The Synoptic Gospels*, I (London: Macmillan, 1927), p. 174.

82. Cf. R.P. Martin, *Mark: Evangelist and Theologian* (Exeter: Paternoster Press; Grand Rapids: Zondervan, 1972), pp. 168-69. Mk 10.2 may seem at first glance to be an exception to this. I hope to show elsewhere that this is not the case.

83. Cf. F.C. Burkitt, 'Mark 8.12 and *ei* in Hellenistic Greek', *JTS* 28 (1926–27),

suggested course of action, but made plain how imperative was the need to avoid it.[84] That Jesus uses this particular asseveration to refuse the demand implies that its challenge cuts him to the quick and represents a powerful threat to his integrity. Since, as we have seen, a call to produce a 'sign' is in itself not objectionable to Jesus, would not the demand in Mk 8.11 have to be interpreted along the lines I have set out to do exactly this?

Finally, there is the consideration that, according to Mark, when the Pharisees' demand for a 'sign' is first made, it prompts Jesus to 'sigh (or groan) deeply' (ἀναστενάξας τῷ πνεύματι αὐτοῦ, 8.12a). As I have shown elsewhere,[85] in the ancient world, to give vent to this out-burst was to express dismay at finding oneself in a situation which might prove one's readiness to obey a given divine decree either foolish or wanting. Accordingly, Jesus' 'sighing deeply' in response to the demand indicates that the demand is meant to be seen as challenging Jesus' faith-fulness. But how could the demand do this unless inherent within it was the invitation that I have argued must be seen there?

It would seem, then, that the reason the Markan Jesus refuses to pro-duce a 'sign' when the Pharisees demand one of him is not because he is, according to Mark, opposed to the enterprise of producing 'signs'. Rather, given Mark's assumptions concerning the type of 'sign' demanded in this instance and what this 'sign' would activate once manifested, it is because in producing such a 'sign' Jesus would involve himself in the sort of triumphalistic, imperious activities that throughout Mark's Gospel he condemns and sets himself against.

pp. 274-76; R.E. Edwards, *The Sign of Jonah* (SBT, 18; London: SCM Press, 1971), p. 75; Lane, *Mark*, p. 276. On the Hebrew oath, see K. Kautzsch (ed.), *Gesenius' Hebrew Grammar* (Oxford: Clarendon Press, 2nd edn, 1910), p. 471 and G.W. Buchanan, 'Some Vow and Oath Formulas in the New Testament', *HTR* 58 (1965), pp. 319-26, esp. pp. 324-25.

84. Cf. Edwards, *Sign of Jonah*, p. 75; Taylor, *Mark*, pp. 362-63; Lane, *Mark*, p. 278; Buchanan, 'Some Vow and Oath Formulas', pp. 324-25.

85. J.B. Gibson, 'Mk 8.12a. Why Does Jesus "Sigh Deeply"?', *Technical Papers for the Bible Translator* 38 (1987), pp. 122-25.

INDEXES

INDEX OF REFERENCES

OLD TESTAMENT

Genesis		Exodus		22.10-12	136
1.27	99	1.7	189	22.14	136
1.28	186	1.8	189	24.7-8	71
2–3	186	1.16	189	34.21	104
2	155	1.22	189	35.5	104
2.7	259	2	190		
2.24	99	2.24	190	Leviticus	
3	143	3	174, 178,	6.1-5	55
4.15	274		179	12.1-8	38
5	186, 187	3.6	159-63,	12.4	38
8.1	257		167, 169,	15.16-24	38
8.2	282		171, 174,	15.31	38
9.6	110		176, 177,	19	116
11	186, 187		179, 180,	19.2	268
11.10-26	186		184, 188,	19.12	114, 116,
11.28	259		190, 191		140, 141
11.30	186, 187	3.12	274	19.18	89
12.1-3	64, 186	3.15-16		24.17	110
14.13	257	(LXX)	169	24.22	110
17.17	64	3.15-16	167, 169,	25.36-38	34
18.10-14	64		171, 174	27.30	97
18.11-12	189	4.8-9	274		
19.22	268	4.30	274	Numbers	
21.8	64	11.3	161	5.5-7	55
26.13	267	12.3-4	18	9.2	133
29.8	268	12.21	18	14.11	274
30.22	190	15.1	165	14.22	274
33.18	258	15.7	65	15.38-41	87
38	180, 181,	20.7	140, 141	18.28	164
	185	20.14	239	19	38
38.8	180, 181	20.17	239	28.2	133
49.10	267	20.17 (LXX)	239	28.9-10	133
		21.12	110	28.9	137
		22.10-13	115	28.10	134

30.3	114	19.29	274	*Song of Songs*	
		20.1-11	278	4.15	188
Deuteronomy		20.1-10	275		
6.5	89	20.8	274	*Isaiah*	
6.13	115	20.9	274, 278	2.1-5	57
10.20	115	20.10 (LXX)	278	5.24	65
11.9	165			6.1-3	74
11.13	266	*2 Chronicles*		6.1-2	74
13.1-12	274	32.24	274	7.8	275
13.2-3	294			7.10	274
14.22-23	97	*Ezra*		7.14	274
16.3	164	4.21	268	16.7	13
18.15	63			34.4	281
18.18	63	*Nehemiah*		37.30	274
22.2	268	9.10	274	38.1-20	275
22.22	154	10.32	104	38.7	274
23.21	114	13.15-22	104	38.22	274
24.1-4	99, 111, 114			47.14	65
24.1	111, 112,	*Job*		51.1-2	63, 64
	154	7.9 (LXX)	283	56.2	104
24.4	111	21.18	65	56.3	187
25.5	180, 181	41.14	241	56.6-8	57
25.7	181			60.3	57
32.39	165	*Psalms*		61	74
		1.4	65	61.1-2 (RSV)	241
Judges		22	284	61.1	74
6.17	274	35.5	65	61.2	74
		56.14	114	66.2	241
1 Samuel		77.43 (LXX)	274		
2.4	274	78.43	274	*Jeremiah*	
10.1	274	91	197	10.2	282, 283
14.6-15	276	104.27 (LXX)	274	17.13	65
14.9-10	276	105.27	274	17.21-27	104
14.10	274, 275	109	284	29.5	65
14.16	275	110	193-95	31.31-34	70, 71
21	93	110.1	255	41.15-16	65
21.1-6	92, 105, 134	111.8 (LXX)	267		
		112.8	267	*Lamentations*	
2 Samuel		117 (LXX)	263, 264	2	284
7.12	63	117.26 (LXX)	262-65		
		118	263, 264	*Ezekiel*	
1 Kings		118.26	262-65	1.44	224
2.45	161	134.9 (LXX)	274	37.1	257
13.3	274	135.9	274	37.5-6	68
				37.9	259
2 Kings		*Proverbs*		37.12-14	68
4.8	161	30.16	188		
4.29	164				

Daniel
2.19   256
2.35   65
3.18   239
3.18 (LXX)   239
4.12   281
7   250, 253, 254
7.13   250-55, 261
7.16   243
7.16 (LXX)   243

Hosea
2.23   68
6.6   91, 95, 96, 99
13.3   65

Amos
5.19   257

Obadiah
18   65

Micah
6.8   97, 99

Habakkuk
3.14   65

Zephaniah
2.2   65

Zechariah
8.4   164
9.9   210

Malachi
3.19   65
4.1   65

Wisdom of Solomon
2   284
16.20   283
18.15   282

Ecclesiasticus
7.5 (RSV)   242
23.9-11   142
46.17   283

2 Maccabees
2.22   119
8.20   282
11.10   282
15.8   282
15.9   90

NEW TESTAMENT

Matthew
1-2   28
1.1   199, 200, 203, 204
1.6   195, 199, 200, 202
1.7   200
1.17   195, 199
1.20   195, 199, 203
2   19
2.15   121
2.23   15, 18
3   63
3.8   64
3.9   63, 64
3.10   65, 79
3.12   65
3.15   120, 121
4.12-17   18
4.12-16   18
4.13   18
5   102, 109, 116, 119
5.3-12   74
5.3   74, 241
5.4   74, 241
5.5   74
5.6   74
5.11-12   270
5.12   115, 241
5.17-48   106
5.17-19   70, 106, 117, 118, 122
5.17-18   69
5.17   90, 118-21, 124, 125, 127, 128
5.18-19   122, 124-26, 128
5.18   119, 122-25
5.19   119, 122, 125
5.20   59, 125
5.21-48   107, 122, 127
5.21   108, 122
5.23-26   78
5.27-28   239
5.28   239
5.31-32   111, 113
5.31   111
5.32   112
5.33-37   142, 145
5.33-34   142
5.33   108, 114
5.34-36   114
5.34   116, 142
5.37   114, 115
5.43   98
5.46-47   59
6.7   59
6.12   241
6.28-29   206
7.6   228
7.12   90, 96, 97
7.13-14   78, 80
7.15-20   80
7.21-23   80
7.24-27   80
8.11   56

8.19	247	12.8	106, 127,	21.9	199, 200,
8.20	247, 251,		252		203, 210
	252, 259	12.12	94, 105	21.11	15
8.21	55	12.23	199, 201,	21.12-13	211
8.22	69, 70		203	21.14	211
9.6	95, 248, 252	12.25-26	94	21.15-16	211
9.9-13	35, 55	12.27	94	21.15	203, 210
9.11-13	30	12.28	29, 94	21.31	53
9.13	96, 99	12.32	247, 252,	21.32	54
9.14-17	55		260	21.43	25
9.20	87	12.33	239	22.1-10	58, 80
9.27	198, 199,	12.38-42	77	22.16	213
	203	12.38	281	22.18	252
9.37-38	79	12.39	274	22.24	63
10.6	30, 82	12.40	252	22.31-32	157, 158,
10.7-16	79	12.41-42	54		166
10.15	80	12.41	238, 239	22.31	158
10.23	267	12.42	206	22.32	158
10.32-33	72, 73, 80,	12.46-50	19	22.34-40	88
	249, 254,	12.47	19	22.41-46	192
	260	12.49-50	19	23.2-3	102
10.34-36	19	13.24-30	81	23.3	59
10.37	70	13.47-50	81	23.8	19
11.2-6	29	13.48	121	23.10	194
11.5-6	74	13.53-58	19	23.23	97, 99
11.5	32, 74	15.1-20	99	23.26	242
11.7-18	63	15.8	238	23.32	121
11.12	239	15.11	102	23.34-36	270
11.13	118, 121	15.22	199, 203	23.37-39	263, 270
11.16-19	35, 78	15.24	30, 82	23.37-38	270
11.18-19	54	16.4	274	23.38-39	265
11.18	54	16.65	211	23.38	264, 265
11.19	35, 248,	17.22	252	23.39	262-65,
	251, 252,	17.24-27	87		268-70
	259	18.10-14	31	24.3	274
11.20-24	54	18.15-17	59	24.4	274
11.20-23	80	18.30	268	24.5	194, 290
11.25	31	19.3-12	99, 111	24.11-12	292
11.28	32	19.7	111	24.23	194
12	96	19.8	112	24.24-26	292
12.1-8	131, 134	19.9	112	24.29	283
12.3-4	92	19.16-22	100	24.30	263
12.3	206	20.30	198, 199,	24.34-35	124
12.4	206		203	24.35	123
12.5-6	105, 137	20.31	198, 199,	25.40	19
12.5	133		201, 203	26.2	252
12.7	95, 99	20.34	209	26.24	252
				26.28	71

26.29	56, 262	2.6-7	277
26.45	252	2.7	254
26.55	212	2.8	277
26.59-61	211	2.9	149, 277, 278
26.63-64	143		
26.63	210	2.1-3.6	16
26.64	211, 254, 262	2.10-11	248, 254, 277
26.65-66	211	2.10	252, 260, 278, 279
26.71	15		
28.10	19	2.11	13, 277
28.19-20	25	2.12	277, 278
28.19	59	2.13-17	35, 55, 77, 287
		2.14	52
Mark		2.15-17	52
1	15, 18, 26	2.15	56
1.1-9	14	2.16-17	30
1.1-3	14	2.16	17, 30
1.1	209, 287	2.17	30
1.2-8	287	2.18-22	55
1.4	15	2.19	56, 149
1.9	14-16, 18	2.21-22	71
1.10	281	2.23-28	131, 133, 134, 153
1.11	281		
1.13	16	2.24	17, 153
1.14-15	18	2.25-26	92, 105, 149, 214
1.15	67		
1.16–2.27	280	2.25	206
1.16-20	16	2.26	13, 206
1.19–8.14	16	2.27	91, 94, 106
1.21-38	16	2.28	106, 252, 260
1.21-28	279		
1.22	279	3	17, 18, 27
1.24	15	3.1-6	279, 280
1.39-45	16	3.2	280
1.40–3.5	214	3.4	94
1.40-45	77, 78	3.5	149
2–3	24	3.6	17, 214, 280
2	27	3.13-19	17
2.1–3.6	24, 149-51, 153	3.14	18
2.1-12	13, 273, 278, 279	3.20-35	17, 19, 20
		3.20-21	17, 24
2.1	13, 14, 16, 276	3.20	13, 17
		3.21	17, 19
2.3-4	277	3.22-30	20
2.5	277, 278	3.22	17, 288

3.28-30	284
3.31-35	17, 19, 20, 24
3.33-35	205
3.35	25
4	149, 152
4.1	16
4.10	18, 152
4.11-12	284
4.12	284
4.32	281
4.36	16
5.1	17
5.19	13, 194
5.20	194
5.38	13
6	17
6.1-6	17-20
6.1	16
6.4	16, 287
6.7-13	79
6.7	18
6.12	79
6.14	15
6.15	287
6.24	15
6.25	15
6.41	281
7	100
7.1-23	99, 104, 153, 287
7.1	17
7.6-9	39, 284
7.6	238
7.7-13	103
7.15	102, 103, 126
7.17	13
7.19	70, 102
7.24-30	287
7.26	199
7.30	13
7.34	281
8.2–10.52	150
8.2-26	150
8.3	13
8.5	19

8.11-13	271, 279,	10.2-11	111		166, 177,
	280, 285,	10.2	17, 148, 298		183, 185
	286, 298	10.5	111, 112	12.26	158, 167,
8.11-12	271	10.6	112		171, 176,
8.11	17, 280-82,	10.9	112		177, 179,
	286, 296,	10.17-22	100		188-90
	298, 299	10.21	281	12.27	158, 167,
8.12	143, 283,	10.32-45	287		171, 173
	286, 299	10.32-41	285	12.28-34	88
8.15	214	10.32	18	12.35-37	192
8.26	13	10.33	252, 260	12.37	195
8.27–9.13	150	10.34	191	12.42	150
8.27-9.1	298	10.42-45	285, 288	13	294
8.27-37	287	10.42	285	13.1-2	24
8.28	15, 287	10.45	260	13.1	18
8.29	209	10.46-52	150	13.2	265, 270
8.30-33	209	10.46	16, 209	13.3	288
8.31-33	285	10.47	14-16, 198,	13.4	274
8.31	191, 252,		199	13.5-7	289
	260	10.48-49	209	13.5-6	288
8.34–9.1	150	10.48	198, 199	13.5	288, 289
8.34-38	285	10.52	209	13.6	288, 290
8.34-37	148	11.1-11	16	13.14-21	294
8.38	72, 252, 260	11.1	18	13.14-19	295
9	16	11.9-10	265	13.14	286, 294
9.1	19, 267	11.9	210	13.18	270
9.10	191	11.10	199	13.19	267
9.11	17	11.11	18	13.21	194, 244
9.12	252, 260	11.15-19	288	13.22	274, 286-
9.14–10.45	150	11.17	13, 265, 288		88, 290-97
9.28	13	11.18	212	13.25	281
9.31-37	287	11.25	281	13.26	260
9.31	191, 252,	11.26	281	13.27	281
	260	11.30	281	13.31	281
9.33-36	288	11.31	281	14	153
9.35	18	12	153, 174	14.3-9	150
9.37	290	12.10	265	14.10	18
9.39	290	12.13	213	14.13	18
9.40	290	12.18-27	191	14.17	18
9.41	209	12.18-23	171	14.20	18
9.42	31	12.24-27	167, 171	14.21	252, 260
9.43-47	78, 148	12.24	167, 171,	14.24	71, 72
10	16, 112,		182	14.25	56, 143
	149, 153	12.25-26	171	14.28	191
10.1-12	148-50,	12.25	167, 171,	14.41	252, 260
	153, 154		176, 183-	14.43	18
10.1	16		85, 281	14.49	212
10.2-12	99	12.26-27	157, 158,	14.55-59	211

14.58	24, 265	4.16-20	18
14.61	210	4.16	18, 87
14.62	211, 252,	4.18	32
	254, 260,	4.34	15
	261, 281	5.17	243
14.63-64	211	5.24	248, 252
14.64	211	5.27-32	35, 55
14.67	15	5.30-32	30
15.7	212	5.32	30, 52
15.24-25	286	5.33-39	55
15.28-32	272, 283,	6.1-5	131, 134
	285	6.3-4	92
15.29	284	6.3	206
15.30	284	6.4	206
15.31	284	6.5	106, 252
15.32	284, 285	6.9	94
15.43	14	6.20	32, 74, 241
16.1-8	191	6.21	74
16.6	14, 15	6.22	270
16.17	274	6.23	241
16.20	274	6.45	256
		7.22-23	74
Luke		7.22	32, 74
1–2	28	7.31-35	78
1.26–2.51	28	7.34	35, 248,
1.27	195, 204,		251, 252,
	209		259
1.32	195, 204,	8	21
	209	8.4-21	19, 20
1.46	228	8.19-21	20
1.69	204	8.20-21	20
2	20	8.22	243
2.9	224	8.28-29	20
2.11	209	9.22	252
2.12	274	9.26	252
2.22-23	38	9.44	252
2.35	19	9.51-54	282
2.39	38	9.54	282
2.41-52	19	9.57	247
2.49	19	9.58	247, 251,
3–24	28		252, 259
3	63	9.59-60	55
3.8	63, 64	9.60	69, 70
3.9	64, 65, 79	10.1-16	79
3.17	65	10.13-15	54
3.18	118	10.25-28	88
3.31	195	11.4	241
4.16-30	18	11.14-22	20

11.16	274		
11.27-28	20		
11.28	101		
11.29-32	77		
11.29	274		
11.30	248, 252,		
	254, 260,		
	282		
11.31	206		
11.32	54		
11.41	241, 242		
11.42	97		
11.49-51	270		
12.8-9	72, 73, 75,		
	249, 252,		
	254, 260		
12.10	247, 252,		
	260		
12.27	206		
12.51-53	19		
13.1-5	54, 77		
13.6-9	79, 270		
13.14	105		
13.16	105		
13.24	78		
13.31-33	270		
13.34-35	270		
13.35	262-65,		
	268-70		
14.1-6	95		
14.5	105		
14.15-24	58, 80		
14.26	20, 70		
15.1-32	36		
15.1-2	30, 36		
15.4	36		
15.6	36		
15.7	30, 31, 36,		
	52		
15.9	36		
15.10	31, 36, 52		
15.18	36		
15.32	36		
15.59	268		
16.16-17	117		
16.16	70, 90, 117,		
	123, 124		

16.17	70, 117,	24.19	15	3–12	23
	122, 124	24.26	194	3–11	22
16.18	112, 124	24.44	90	3.6	15
17.22	243	24.46	194	3.19-21	266, 270
17.23	244			3.19-20	67
17.26	243	*John*		4.10	15
17.29	282	1.35-42	63	4.11	265
18.1-8	270	1.45	15, 90	4.16	274
18.2	16	1.51	252, 261	5.34	23
18.9-14	30, 37	2.1-5	25	5.36	291
18.18-23	100	2.12-13	25	6.13-14	24
18.31	252	2.12	25	6.14	15
18.35	209	2.13-18	275	8.16	274
18.37	15, 16	2.13	18	9.26	76
18.38	198, 199	2.16	275	9.42	67
18.39-40	209	2.18	274, 275	10.38	15
18.39	198, 199	3.29-30	228	10.45	23
18.42-43	209	4.22-24	25	11.2-3	23
19.1-10	30, 52, 78	4.44	25	11.2	23
19.1-9	51, 77	4.48	286	11.17	67
19.38	199, 210,	5.1	18	11.19-21	24
	262	6.4	25	12–21	25
19.45-46	211	6.29-30	275	12	24
19.47-48	212	6.30	274	12.17	21, 23
20.1	243	6.60-71	25	13–14	24
20.37-38	157, 158,	7.2-5	25	13.15	90
	166	7.5	25	14.3	274
20.37	158	7.10	18, 25	15	21-23
20.38	158	7.42	204	15.1	22
20.41-44	192	7.49	37	15.2	22
20.45	195	8.34	228	15.5	22
21.7	274	8.40	253	15.6	23
21.8	290	10.22	18	17.2	87
21.11	282	11.1	14	19.1-7	63
21.22	282	11.55	25	20.29	289
21.33	123	12.13	210	21.18	21, 22
22.19	56	18.5	15	21.38	292, 297
22.20	71	18.7	15	22.8	15
22.22	252	19.19	15	22.11	224
22.23	282	19.25-27	25, 28	23.6-9	23
22.48	252, 253	19.38	14	23.6	41
22.53	212	20.17	25	23.12	268
22.67-69	211			23.23	90
22.67-68	254	*Acts*		24.5	15
22.67	210, 254	1.14	21, 22	24.14	90
22.71	211	1.22	118	26.9	15
23.19	212	2.22	15		
23.27-31	265	2.33	265		

Romans
1.3-4   200
1.3   195, 204,
               205, 210
1.9   144
1.13   81
1.18   283
3.21   90
4   188, 189
4.17   64
9.1-3   144
9.3   204
9.5   204
10.4   104
11.13-14   81
11.25-27   67, 81, 262
11.26   81
12.14   146
4.19 (RSV)   188

1 Corinthians
1.22   274, 286
1.26   204
7.25   145
9.5   23
10.18   204
11.25   71, 72
12.1   81
15   172
15.7   21
15.20-23   81
15.31   144
15.50   173

2 Corinthians
1.17-20   141
1.18   144
1.23   144
2.17   144
3.7–4.6   224
4.2   144

5.16   204
8.3   235, 236
10.2   204
10.3   204
10.4   204
11.10-11   144
11.31   144
12.2   253
12.19   144

Galatians
1.14   41
1.18-19   21
1.18   26
1.19   23
1.20   144
2.1-10   57, 66, 67
2.4   59
2.9   21
2.11-13   24
2.12   22
2.15   49, 59
2.16   67

Philippians
1.8   144
1.29   67
3.6   41

Colossians
2.5   67

1 Thessalonians
2.5   144
2.10   144
4.13-18   81
4.13   81
4.16   283

2 Thessalonians
2.7   268

2.9   274
2.17   283

2 Timothy
2.8   195, 204,
               210

Hebrews
5.20-26   55
11   188, 189
11.11-12   189
11.13-16   189
11.19   189
12.25   283

James
5.12   141, 142,
               145-47

1 Peter
1.10   283
1.12   283
2.7   265

2 Peter
3.11-12   270
3.12   267

1 John
2.18   289

Revelation
1.7   263
3.7   204
5.5   195, 204
13.13-14   274
22.16   195, 204,
               210
22.21   210

PSEUDEPIGRAPHA

1 Enoch
41.8   267
43.2   267
83–90   34

2 Enoch
49.1-2   142, 143

2 Baruch
42.7   267
54.15   267
54.19   267

78.7	267		26	267		T. Iss.	
85.7	267		29	267		5.2	89
						7.6	89
4 Ezra			Apoc. Mos.				
4.39 (RSV)	267		18.1–20.2	143		T. Jud.	
4.40-43	267					23.5	267
4.51	274		Ass. Mos.				
6.11	274		1.18	267		T. Sim.	
6.20	274					6.2-7	267
7.25	274		LAB				
8.63	274		23.4	64		T. Sol.	
14	63		60.3	197		1.1	202
						1.7	198, 202
4 Maccabbees			Pss. Sol.			2.1	202
7.18-19	174		17	200, 267		5.10	202
16.25	174		17.4	200		12.1	202
18.10	90		17.5	200		13.12	202
			17.21	200		20.1	198, 202
Ahiqar			17.23	200		26.9	202
130-31	268						
			T. Dan.				
Apoc. Abr.			5.3	89			
22	267		6.4	267			

QUMRAN

11QTemple			1QS			1QpHab	
58.18	268		1.3	116		2.3-4	67
64.15	268		1.9-10	116			
			2.4-9	116		CD	
11QtgJob			5.13-14	63		6.19	67
38.8	228		7.19	268		8.21	67
						11.13-17	105
1Q27			1QSa			15.1-2	142
1 col. 1	274		1.1-3	58		15.5-11	67
1 col. 5	274		1.1-2	68		20.12	67

| 1QM | | | | | | | |
| 14.7 | 241 | | | | | | |

INDEX OF AUTHORS

Abel, E.L. 205
Aberbach, M. 206
Abrahams, I. 33, 109, 158
Allen, W.C. 96
Allison, D.C. 73, 241
Alter, R. 187, 191
Anderson, B.W. 84
Anderson, H. 91, 92, 94, 95, 99, 100,
    102, 272, 279
Aulén, G. 39, 42-45

Bacon, B.W. 85, 100
Bahnsen, G.L. 83, 85, 103, 107, 119,
    120, 124, 128
Baltensweiler, H. 113
Banks, R. 85-89, 91-93, 98-100, 102,
    103, 110-12, 114, 116, 118-21,
    124, 126, 127, 134, 152
Barclay, W. 272
Barnett, P.W. 275, 292, 293, 296, 298
Barr, J. 221
Barr, O.S. 94
Barrett, C.K. 73
Barth, G. 87, 90, 95-97, 103, 108, 109,
    115, 118, 125, 195
Bartlet, J.V. 288
Bauernfeind, O. 144
Beare, F.W. 65, 92-94
Beasley-Murray, G.R. 281, 287-90,
    294, 295
Beernaert, S.J. 150
Behm, J. 112
Berger, K. 84, 90, 97, 119, 197, 201,
    205
Bertram, G. 91, 110
Best, E. 289
Betz, O. 291-93, 296, 298
Beyer, K. 268
Beyer, W. 263

Bietenhard, H. 116, 288
Black, M. 16, 109, 227, 228, 230, 237,
    239, 240, 243
Blackwell, J. 286
Blass, F. 281
Blomberg, C.L. 196
Blunt, A.W.F. 272, 290
Boman, T. 222
Bonnard, P. 110, 119, 124, 181, 195
Bonsirven, J. 113
Boobyer, G.H. 273, 279
Bornkamm, G. 89, 195
Boucher, M. 272
Bousset, W. 32
Bowker, J.W. 200
Branscomb, B.H. 85, 87, 90, 94, 95, 97,
    102, 113, 119, 131, 272, 290
Braun, H. 39, 86, 95, 107
Brockington, L.H. 224
Brown, R.E. 286
Buchanan, G.W. 288, 299
Bultmann, R. 51, 56, 85, 107, 193-96,
    264, 273
Burchard, C. 89, 120
Burger, C. 193, 203, 208
Burkill, T.A. 278
Burkitt, F.C. 298

Cadbury, H.J. 30, 177, 180
Cadoux, C.J. 278
Caird, G.B. 157, 222, 224
Calvin, J. 262, 263
Campbell, J.Y. 252
Carlson, D.C. 267
Carlston, C. 95, 98, 103, 107, 125
Carroll, L. 224
Carson, D.A. 104, 106
Casey, M. 245, 251-53
Charles, R.H. 174

Charlesworth, J.H. 142, 200
Childs, B.S. 119
Chilton, B.D. 195, 202, 211, 225, 227,
  230, 235, 236
Chomsky, W. 231
Chopineau, J. 206
Clark, P.C. 220
Cohn-Sherbok, D.M. 174, 177, 206
Cohon, S. 131, 132, 134
Colpe, C. 106, 251, 252
Colson, F.H. 168, 170
Conybeare, F.C. 201
Conzelmann, H. 118, 290
Coutts, J. 272
Cowley, A.E. 267
Cranfield, C.E.B. 89, 93, 94, 100, 104,
  124, 272, 281, 288-90
Creed, J.M. 19
Crim, K.R. 233

Dalman, G. 109, 119, 242, 243
Daube, D. 64, 109, 119, 132, 133, 135,
  137, 151, 294, 295
Dautzenberg, G. 140-45, 147
Davids, P.H. 146
Davies, P.R. 197, 202
Davies, W.D. 69, 71, 76, 81, 85, 88, 97,
  99, 103, 104, 107, 109, 114, 116,
  120, 123, 127, 133, 241, 264
Debrunner, A. 281
Delitzsch, F. 111
Delling, G. 272
Derrett, J.D.M. 99
Descamps, A. 107, 108, 118-20
Dewey, J. 150, 273
Dibelius, M. 107, 146, 273, 279
Dickens, C. 43, 44, 46
Doeve, J.W. 132, 134, 157-59, 163,
  164
Donald, T. 232
Downing, F.G. 177
Dreyfus, F. 176-80, 188
Driver, S.R. 112
Duling, D. 197-201, 204, 205
Dunn, J.D.G. 125, 126, 146
Duplacy, J. 278
Dupont, J. 107, 115, 116, 120

Edgar, S.L. 190
Edwards, R.E. 299
Ellis, E.E. 177, 235
Emerton, J.A. 224-26, 230, 231
Eppstein, V. 212
Ernst, J. 263
Esser, H.-H. 96

Fairbairn, P. 108, 124
Farmer, W.R. 53
Fee, G.D. 14
Fenton, J.C. 157, 262, 263
Feuillet, A. 90, 120
Fichtner, J. 116
Fiedler, P. 29, 30, 52
Filbeck, D. 234
Fils, F. 92
Filson, F.V. 120
Finkelstein, L. 33, 38
Fisher, L.R. 198, 205, 264
Fitzmyer, J.A. 112, 113, 152, 192, 224,
  226-28, 230-32, 243, 250
Fletcher, J. 83
Foerster, W. 116
Fowler, R.M. 279
France, R.T. 93
Frankemölle, H. 74
Friedlander, G. 110, 114
Fritzsche, O.F. 200
Frost, R. 187
Fuller, R.H. 89
Furnish, V.P. 89, 90, 116

Gager, J.G. 81
Garland, D.E. 264
Gaston, L. 81
Gerhardsson, B. 105
Gibbs, J.M. 199, 203
Gibson, J.B. 299
Giverson, S. 197
Gnilka, J. 244, 273, 280
Godet, F. 106, 263
Goetz, S.C. 196
Goldstein, J. 282
Gooch, P. 145
Goodwin, W.W. 267
Goppelt, L. 93
Gould, E.P. 271, 289, 290

Gray, G.B. 199
Greeven, H. 146
Grimm, W. 74
Grintz, J.M. 231
Grundemann, W. 288
Grundmann, W. 118, 119, 123
Guelich, R. 74, 107-109, 111, 113,
　　121, 123, 125, 143, 144
Gutbrod, W. 85, 87, 101, 116, 124

Hahn, F. 67, 71, 79, 193, 266, 280, 287
Hamerton-Kelly, R.G. 107, 118, 123,
　　125
Harnack, A. 85
Harrington, W. 231, 272
Harvey, A.E. 69
Hasler, V. 99, 115, 116
Hay, D.M. 195
Hay, L.S. 279
Heitmuller, W. 288
Held, H.J. 195
Hendriksen, W. 108
Hengel, M. 79
Henry, C.F.H. 83, 85, 100, 107, 117,
　　120
Higgins, A.J.B. 250
Hill, D. 89, 96, 104, 109, 113, 114,
　　123, 263, 280, 291
Hølm-Nielson, S. 200
Hoehner, H.W. 213, 214
Honeyman, A.M. 123
Hooker, M. 106, 278, 279, 288-90
Houlden, J.L. 91
Hubaut, M. 87
Hultgren, A.J. 30, 32, 35, 92

Isaakson, A. 113

Jakobivits, L.A. 233
James, M.R. 200
James, W. 181
Jeremias, J. 29, 31, 32, 34, 37, 41-43,
　　45, 47, 52, 53, 55, 56, 58, 63, 102,
　　107, 110, 120, 238, 240, 243,
　　251, 252, 265, 270, 291, 292
Jervell, J. 104
Jocz, J. 120
Johnson, C.S. 203
Johnson, M.D. 207

Johnson, S.E. 93, 290
Jonge, M. de 209

Kaiser, W.C. Jr 97, 103
Käsemann, E. 104, 106
Kautzsch, E. 267
Keil, C.F. 111
Kelber, W.H. 272, 288
Kilpatrick, G.D. 13
Kingsbury, J.D. 279
Kittel, G. 108, 221
Kittel, R. 199
Klausner, J. 32
Kloppenborg, J. 237, 238, 240-42
Klostermann, E. 288, 290
Koester, H. 238, 239
Kohler, K. 201
Kraft, R.A. 228, 229
Kuhn, G. 207
Kümmel, W.G. 64, 85, 102-104, 118,
　　120, 122
Kutsch, E. 114
Kwaak, H. van der 263-65, 268

Lafontaine, S.J. 150
Lagrange, M.-J. 108, 120, 124, 290
Laing, D. 183
Lambert, W.E. 233
Lambrecht, J. 103
Landman, L. 266
Lane, W.L. 92-94, 100, 103, 106, 112,
　　211, 272, 280, 284, 287, 290,
　　294, 299
Lemcio, E.E. 272
Lenski, R.C.H. 120, 123
Licht, J. 267
Lincoln, A.T. 125
Lindars, B. 245-52, 254, 256-58, 265
Linton, O. 116, 271
Ljungman, H. 119, 120
Lohmeyer, E. 90, 109, 120, 203
Lohse, E. 92, 94, 104, 107, 207
Lövestamm, E. 192, 205
Luther, M. 234
Luz, U. 140, 142, 143

M'Neile, A.H. 98, 102, 106, 110, 116,
　　123
MacKintosh, R. 87, 88, 95, 124

Maier, J. 203
Malina, B. 112
Mally, E.J. 272
Mann, C.S. 151, 290
Manson, T.W. 88, 108, 114, 120, 239,
    262, 263
Manson, W. 289
Marshall, I.H. 89, 92, 93, 95, 101, 106,
    116, 118, 123, 174, 195, 207, 263
Martin, R.P. 272, 298
Masterman, M. 234
Matera, F.J. 284, 286
Mays, J.L. 96, 298
McArthur, H.K. 85, 86
McCowan, C.C. 201-203
McKenzie, J.L. 276
Mead, R.T. 190
Meecham, H.G. 278
Meier, J.P. 86, 97, 100, 107-109, 111,
    113-15, 118-21, 123-25
Meinertz, M. 283
Menzies, A. 272
Metzger, B.M. 286
Meye, R.P. 73
Meyer, B.F. 108, 120, 121, 127
Meyer, E. 174
Meyer, R. 291, 292
Michel, O. 116, 204
Mielziner, M. 137
Moffatt, J. 89
Montefiore, C.G. 86, 102, 110, 114,
    116, 239, 298
Moo, D.J. 69
Moore, G.F. 78, 134, 177, 182, 207,
    208
Moule, C.F.D. 100, 110, 272, 278
Mowinckel, S. 208, 267
Murphy-O'Connor, J. 279
Murray, J. 107, 115, 116

Naish, C. 220
Neirynck, F. 92
Neusner, J. 40, 41, 207, 213, 214
Nida, E.A. 233-35
Nineham, D.E. 95, 105, 131, 165
Nixon, R. 88, 120
Nolan, A. 32, 43
Noth, M. 115

O'Neill, J.C. 211
Olmstead, A.T. 226, 227, 231
Ong, W.J. 185
Otto, R. 267

Payne, D.F. 232
Percy, E. 86, 103, 107-109
Perrin, N. 31, 36, 48-51, 55-57, 279
Pesch, R. 32, 71, 73, 92-94, 103, 106,
    193, 205, 206, 214, 272, 273,
    289, 290
Pittenger, N. 83
Plummer, A. 96, 102, 110, 124
Polag, A. 27
Preisendanz, K. 201
Procksch, O. 221, 222
Pusey, K. 64

Quesnell, Q. 103

Rabin, C. 142, 219, 223, 226, 227, 229,
    234, 235
Rawlinson, A.E.J. 272, 273, 290
Rengstorf, K.H. 271, 272, 280, 292-94,
    296
Resch, A. 238, 239, 242
Reuss, J. 19
Richardson, P. 145
Riches, J. 50, 208
Ricoeur, P. 178, 179
Ridderbos, H. 85, 98, 100, 107, 108,
    113, 120, 127
Rigaux, B. 294
Rivkin, E. 41
Robbins, V.K. 294
Robinson, J.M. 238
Rordorf, W. 83, 94, 95, 104-106, 131,
    135
Roth, C. 288
Russell, D.S. 173
Ryle, H.E. 200

Sand, A. 107, 119, 123
Sanders, E.P. 34, 61-64, 66-70, 75-82,
    142, 208
Sanders, J.A. 197
Sawyer, J.F.A. 229, 230
Schäfer, P. 127

Scharbert, J. 263
Schiffmann, L. 49, 64
Schlatter, A. 63, 120
Schmahl, G. 111
Schnackenburg, R. 89, 90, 107, 120
Schneider, G. 192, 193, 195, 196
Schneider, J. 114
Schniewind, J. 120, 289
Schoeps, H.J. 93, 99
Schrenk, G. 121, 124, 125
Schulz, S. 103, 107, 116, 118, 120, 123, 263
Schüpphaus, V. 200
Schürer, E. 41, 46
Schürmann, H. 72, 74, 93, 95, 106, 125, 204, 209
Schwarz, G. 65
Schwarz, W. 234
Schweizer, E. 107, 108, 120, 123, 165, 263, 272
Seitz, O.J.F. 116
Senior, D. 284, 286
Sharp, D.S. 278
Siertsema, B. 220, 222
Sloyan, G. 107, 124
Smith, D. 64
Smith, M. 46, 47, 109, 116
Smolar, L. 206
Sokoloff, M. 230
Sparks, H.F.D. 236
Spicq, C. 91, 107, 116
Staerck, D.W. 208
Steck, O.H. 264
Stein, R.H. 142-44
Stendhal, K. 81, 180
Stern, M. 46
Stonehouse, N.B. 85, 99, 102, 115, 116
Story, G. 220
Strack, H. 164
Strecker, G. 90, 97, 119, 140, 142, 143
Suggs, M.J. 108
Suhl, A. 192, 193, 196, 203
Swete, H.B. 94, 272, 289, 294
Swetnam, J. 280

Taber, C.R. 233, 234
Tagawa, K. 272

Tånberg, K.A. 221
Taylor, V. 91, 92, 94, 100, 101, 103, 157, 193, 196, 231, 272, 284, 286
Thomas, K.J. 99, 100, 102
Tödt, H. 273
Torrey, C.C. 227
Traub, H. 281
Trilling, W. 90, 99, 109, 119, 120, 124
Tuckett, C. 195, 279
Turner, C.H. 13, 286, 288
Turner, N. 224

Urbach, E.E. 90, 266

Vaux, R. de 106
Vermes, G. 68-70, 207, 245-47, 250-52, 257
Verweijs, P.G. 86, 92, 103, 108, 126
Vögtle, A. 72

Wacholder, B.Z. 69
Waty, W.W. 288
Weeden, T.J. 288
Weiffenbach, W. 289
Weinert, F.D. 264
Wellhausen, J. 289
Wenham, D. 103, 111, 124, 145
Werner, E. 265
Westerholm, S. 33, 39, 55, 128
Whittaker, M. 293, 294
Wifall, W. 208
Wilcox, M. 204
Wilder, A.N. 102, 120
Williamson, L. Jr 272
Wilson, R.R. 208
Windisch, H. 85, 110
Wink, W. 279
Wolff, H.W. 96
Wrede, W. 196, 273
Wrege, H.-T. 122, 123

York, A.D. 230

Zahn, T. 119, 120
Zehnle, R.F. 266
Zerwick, M. 89
Zimmermann, F. 226